External Intervention and the Politics of State Formation
China, Indonesia, and Thailand, 1893–1952

This book explores ways in which foreign intervention and external rivalries can affect the institutionalisation of governance in weak states. When sufficiently competitive, foreign rivalries in a weak state can actually foster the political centralisation, territoriality, and autonomy associated with state sovereignty. This counterintuitive finding comes from studying the collective effects of foreign contestation over weak states as informed by changes in the expected opportunity cost of intervention for outside actors. When interveners associate high opportunity costs with intervention, they bolster sovereign statehood as a next best alternative to their worst fear – domination of that polity by adversaries. Sovereign statehood develops if foreign actors concurrently and consistently behave this way toward a weak state. This book evaluates that argument against three "least-likely" cases – China, Indonesia, and Thailand between the late nineteenth and mid twentieth centuries.

Ja Ian Chong is Assistant Professor of Political Science at the National University of Singapore. He received his PhD in politics from Princeton University in 2008 and was a 2008–2009 Research Associate with the Princeton-Harvard China and the World Program. His research has received support from the Chiang Ching-kuo International Foundation for Scholarly Exchange, the Woodrow Wilson Society of Fellows, the Bradley Foundation, the Social Science Research Council, the Princeton Institute of International and Regional Studies, and the Princeton East Asian Studies Program. He has worked in the International Security Program at the Center for Strategic and International Studies in Washington, DC, as well as the Institute of Defence and Strategic Studies and the East Asian Institute in Singapore. He has previously taught at the Hong Kong University of Science and Technology. His work has appeared in *Twentieth-Century China* and *Security Studies*.

To my parents, Chong Tjee Teng and Yuan Chien,
and my wife, Grace.

External Intervention and the Politics of State Formation

China, Indonesia, and Thailand, 1893–1952

JA IAN CHONG
National University of Singapore

CAMBRIDGE
UNIVERSITY PRESS

32 Avenue of the Americas, New York NY 10013-2473, USA

Cambridge University Press is part of the University of Cambridge.

It furthers the University's mission by disseminating knowledge in the pursuit of education, learning, and research at the highest international levels of excellence.

www.cambridge.org
Information on this title: www.cambridge.org/9781107013759

© Ja Ian Chong 2012

This publication is in copyright. Subject to statutory exception and to the provisions of relevant collective licensing agreements, no reproduction of any part may take place without the written permission of Cambridge University Press.

First published 2012
Reprinted 2013

A catalog record for this publication is available from the British Library.

Library of Congress Cataloging in Publication data
Chong, Ja Ian.
External intervention and the politics of state formation : China, Indonesia, and Thailand, 1893–1952 / Ja Ian Chong.
    pages   cm
Includes bibliographical references and index.
ISBN 978-1-107-01375-9
1. State, The – Case studies.   2. Political development – Case studies.   3. China – Politics and government – 20th century.   4. Indonesia – Politics and government – 20th century.   5. Thailand – Politics and government – 20th century.   I. Title.
JC273.C585   2012
320.95–dc23   2012001014

ISBN 978-1-107-01375-9 Hardback

Cambridge University Press has no responsibility for the persistence or accuracy of URLs for external or third-party Internet Web sites referred to in this publication, and does not guarantee that any content on such Web sites is, or will remain, accurate or appropriate.

Contents

List of Abbreviations		*page* vii
Acknowledgements		ix
1	Moulding the Institutions of Governance: Theories of State Formation and the Contingency of Sovereignty in Fragile Polities	1
2	Imposing States: Foreign Rivalries, Local Collaboration, and State Form in Peripheral Polities	27
3	Feudalising the Chinese Polity, 1893–1922: Assessing the Adequacy of Alternative Takes on State Reorganisation	46
4	External Influence and China's Feudalisation, 1893–1922: Opportunity Costs and Patterns of Foreign Intervention	75
5	The Evolution of Foreign Involvement in China, 1923–1952: Rising Opportunity Costs and Convergent Approaches to Intervention	112
6	How Intervention Remade the Chinese State, 1923–1952: Foreign Sponsorship and the Building of Sovereign China	151
7	Creating Indonesia, 1893–1952: Major Power Rivalry and the Making of Sovereign Statehood	173
8	Siam Stands Apart, 1893–1952: External Intervention and Rise of a Sovereign Thai State	200
9	Domesticating International Relations, Externalising Comparative Politics: Foreign Intervention and the State in World Politics	224
Appendix: Questions for Focused, Structured Comparisons		237
References		239
Index		279

Abbreviations

AH	Academia Historica, Taipei
AS	Institute of Modern History Archives, Academia Sinica, Taipei
CCP	Chinese Communist Party
FHAC	First Historical Archives of China, Beijing
KMT	Kuomintang (Guomindang); Chinese Nationalist Party
KMTPA	Party Archives, Kuomintang Party History Committee, Taipei
PKI	Partai Komunis Indonesia; Indonesian Communist Party
PNI	Partai Nasional Indonesia; Indonesian National Party
PRCFMA	PRC Foreign Ministry Archives, Beijing
SHAC	Second Historical Archives of China, Nanjing

Note: I use Hanyu Pinyin transliteration for Chinese except for names and terms where other transliteration methods are more popular. Examples include Chiang Kai-shek, Chiang Ching-kuo, H.H. Kung, Hong Kong, Kaohsiung, Kuomintang, Sun Yat-sen, T.V. Soong, and Taipei.

Acknowledgements

A project of this scale incurs many debts of gratitude that are impossible to repay. I am grateful to my teachers, Thomas J. Christensen, G. John Ikenberry, Lynn T. White III, and William C. Wohlforth, for their patient mentorship, encouragement, support, and much-needed criticism. This was especially important in my graduate school environment. My intellectual development and this book owe much to their generosity and assistance. I am grateful to Chou Chih-P'ing, Steven Chung, Martin Collcutt, Benjamin Elman, Sheldon Garon, David Leheny, Susan Naquin, and Willard Peterson for welcoming me into East Asian Studies at Princeton University. As a political scientist who draws heavily from history and the humanities, the advice and experience of cross fertilisation I received at the EAS Department was especially inspiring. Special thanks must go out to Yü Ying-Shih, who took the time to guide me over particularly trying historical material. I am also grateful to the anonymous reviewers of this book and the more preliminary articles from which this volume draws.

I appreciate the invaluable help I received from so many. They include Lewis Bateman, Mark Beissinger, Janice Bially Mattern, Timothy Brook, Joshua Busby, Allen Carlson, Miguel Centeno, Chen Jian, Chen Qianping, Pei-yi Chu, Ping-Tzu Chu, Bridget Coggins, Cui Zhiqing, Wolfgang Danspeckgruber, Christopher N. Darnton, Patrick Deneen, Nicola DiCosmo, Ding Decheng, Thomas Dolan, Prasenjit Duara, Andrew S. Erickson, M. Taylor Fravel, Robert Gilpin, Scott Gregory, Todd H. Hall, Wenkai He, Yinan He, Peter Holquist, Huang Zhenping, Victoria Tin-bor Hui, Serene Hung, Alastair Iain Johnston, David Kang, Scott Kastner, Stanley Katz, Andrew B. Kennedy, Robert Keohane, Jonathan Kirshner, Koh Khee Heong, Charles Kupchan, Lai Yuyun, James Z. Lee, Seung-joon Lee, Wah Guan Lim, Liu Xiaofeng, Xiaobo Lu, Lorenz Luthi, Stephen Macedo, Michael Mastanduno, Levi McLaughlin, Kathleen McNamara, James Millward, Erik Mobrand, Andrew Moravscik, Terry Nardin, Daniel Nexon, Ong Chang Woei, John Owen, Philip Pettit, Peter Purdue, Qi Xuemin, Eri Saikawa, Wayne Soon, Hendrik Spruyt, Brent Strathman, Robert Sutter, Stephen Teiser, Peter Trubowitz, Nancy Bernkopf Tucker, Wang Gungwu, Wang Xiaoyun, Yuan-Kang Wang, Brantly Womack,

x   *Acknowledgements*

Thomas Wright, Wu Liwei, Xiao Wu, Xin Xu, Dali Yang, David Yang, Yang Lijun, Rur-bin Yang, Min Ye, Feng Zhang, and Zheng Yongnian. They graciously provided important comments, advice, and other forms of professional assistance – sometimes on several occasions. I am grateful to the late Charles Tilly for sharing his thoughts on this project at its inception. All mistakes and inadequacies in the work are solely my own.

My graduate student colleagues played a critical role in aiding me along the process in countless ways. These comrades include Asli Bali, Pamela Bromley, Barbara Buckinx, Arudra Burra, Ian Chapman, Eric Dinmore, Chunmei Du, Paul Eason, Maren Ehlers, Yulia Frumer, Katie Gallagher, Matteo Giglioli, Hu Jun, April Hughes, Esther P. Klein, Li Yaqin, Jennifer Lieb, Hsueh-Yi Lin, John Lombardini, Bryan Lowe, Mao Sheng, Quinton Mayne, Christopher Mayo, Mark Meulenbeld, Rachel Beatty Reidl, Prerna Singh, Brigid Vance, Ian Ward, James Wilson, Lanjun Xu, Ye Minlei, Evan Young, Ya Zuo, and so many others. I was fortunate to have so many fellow travellers to run ideas against and help bring good cheer to what otherwise could be an isolating process. Fellows at the Princeton-Harvard China and the World Program as well as participants of the China and the World Workshop, East Asian Studies Colloquium, Cracked Pot, Woodrow Wilson Fellows Seminar, and the international relations seminar at Princeton were also key resources for me.

This project would not have been possible without the generosity of the Bradley Foundation, Chiang Ching-kuo Foundation for International Scholarly Exchange, Hong Kong Research Grants Council, Institute for Qualitative Research Methods, Princeton East Asian Studies Programme, Princeton-Harvard China and the World Program, Princeton Institute for International and Regional Studies, Princeton University Graduate School, Social Science Research Council, and Woodrow Wilson Circle of Fellows. I am also grateful for library support from Martin Heijdra at the Gest East Asian Library at Princeton University; Geographic Information System assistance from Tsering Wangyal Shawa and Isaac Low; and administrative aid from Rita Alpaugh, Richard Chafey, Hue Kim Su, Danette Rivera, and Timothy Waldron. Archivists at the Academia Historica, Academia Sinica Institute of Modern History, First Historical Archives of China, Kuomintang Party History Committee, and Second Historical Archives of China provided valuable advice on the use of their materials. Thanks also go to *Security Studies*, Ohio State University Press, the Taylor and Francis Group, and *Twentieth-Century China* for giving me permission to use material from articles I published with them.

I owe my family special appreciation for their unwavering support during this very extended process. To my parents, Chong Tjee Teng and Yuan Chien, my wife, Grace, as well as Nathan and Ethan, thank you all for being there and bearing with me. I am also grateful to my uncle, Chong Chi Tat, for all his help and guidance. It is indeed my good fortune to have such understanding people around me. To anyone I inadvertently missed – thank you.

CHAPTER I

Moulding the Institutions of Governance

Theories of State Formation and the Contingency of Sovereignty in Fragile Polities

Why and how did polities outside the modern European states system come to organise themselves along the lines of the sovereign state by the mid twentieth century? After all, alternative state forms – such as colonial states, feudal states, and suzerain-vassal arrangements – were well-established in the global periphery going into the nineteenth and twentieth centuries.[1] Take Northeast and Southeast Asia. China had centuries of history as a continental empire. Parts of what is today Indonesia had been subject to colonial domination by various European powers since the sixteenth century.[2] Siam was suzerain over vassals such as Cambodia to the east, Vientiane and Luang Prabang to the northeast, and sultanates on the Malay Peninsula to the south since the eighteenth century.[3] State form in these instances did not have the strong emphasis on the high levels of political centralisation, territorial exclusivity, and external autonomy characteristic of the sovereign state.

At the same time, the experiences of imperialism, colonisation, and collaboration during World War II, the Cold War, and the War on Terror suggest that external agents may have tremendous influence over how governance and political authority develop. Moreover, events in Malaya and South Vietnam after World War II, as well as more recent examples in Iraq, Afghanistan, Libya, and Egypt, indicate that foreign intervention may demonstrate significant variation in how it can shape institutions of rule. Developments in these polities indicate that outside intervention into domestic politics may be responsible for everything from sovereign statehood to political fragmentation and subjugation.

However, the relationship between external intervention and state formation is one that both international relations and comparative politics scholarship underemphasise empirically and theoretically. This opens questions about how external actors can affect the direction and timing of shifts in state form, especially in fragile polities where institutions of governance may be less stable

---

[1] Tønnesson and Antlöv, 1996.
[2] Before European domination, several indigenous kingdoms divided the archipelago. Ricklefs, 1993, 3–147.
[3] Wyatt, 1984, 8, 36, 88, 126, 143–74.

and more malleable. Such issues may prove particularly significant given that foreign involvement in the development of institutions and governance in weak states appears to be an enduring phenomenon in world politics.

To address these tensions, I propose an explanation for state formation in weak polities that endogenises the role of foreign involvement. Such an approach allows for a systematic consideration of the interactions amongst local political groups, domestic institutions, external actors, and international systemic pressures. I contend that the institutional nature of governance and political authority in a weak state results from the collective effects of external competition over access. Conditioning such collective effects are the expectations each intervening government holds about the opportunity costs of interceding into the domestic politics of the locale in question. Shifts in the organisation of rule in fragile states come about from the machinations of outside actors trying to forward their interests under changing international systemic constraints.

Specifically, sovereign statehood develops in a weak polity when foreign actors uniformly expect high costs to intervention and settle on a next best alternative to their worst fear, domination of that state by a rival. Attempts at outside intervention thus move from the sponsorship of local proxies and collaborators to the abetment of a nationalist group that seems most able to guarantee equal access to all outside actors. Absent such considerations, foreign actors seek indigenous partners that can secure complete access denial or regulate access to a fragile polity instead. Depending on the configuration of foreign intervention efforts, the targeted state may turn into a vassal state, fracture, become a colonial state, or cease to exist. Simply, I argue that differing patterns of outside intervention in domestic politics, given variations in expected costs amongst intervening actors, foster the development of alternative state forms in weak polities.

At the heart of my argument is the view that intervening actors tend to seek full denial of access by external rivals through direct control of a targeted weak state. These same actors may, however, settle for less complete levels of access denial and more indirect forms of control if the opportunity costs of attaining their maximal goals seem too high to feasibly undertake. This position sees relative gains over access to peripheral areas to be of primary concern to intervening powers, but higher expected costs of intervention can force these actors to focus on absolute gains.[4] Such views guide an external power's approach toward competing and intervening in a weak polity.

Expected intervention costs are the gains that leaders of a would-be intervening power anticipate to acquire from interceding into the politics of a targeted polity less the opportunities they anticipate to forgo from engaging in such action. Such expectations are effectively understandings about the opportunity costs of intervention. These assessments rest on an understanding of the material

---

[4] The logic that an actor can experience varying levels of acuteness over relative gains concerns parallels arguments put forward by Robert Powell and Joseph Grieco. Grieco, 1988a, 485–507, 1988b, 600–24, 1990, 27–50; Powell, 1991, 1303–20.

Moulding the Institutions of Governance

benefits of access to markets and resources, but are also susceptible to the influences of ideology, miscalculation, and misunderstanding.[5] After all, if no problems with information and knowledge exist, actors can realise optimal net gains without the trouble of jostling with each other on the ground. My analysis will look empirically at how leaders have weighed their available options. Developing theoretical explanations of the psychological, ideational, and other origins of such expectations may provide fruitful lines for enquiry, but lies beyond my current focus.

Expected costs need not closely track material reality and can diverge substantially from objective measures of cost. Government leaders, for example, may value symbolic or normative goals over material ones. I ascertain the expected costs of intervention for a particular government from relevant policy debates, discussions, and statements about intervening in a target polity before such action occurs. Specifically, I empirically highlight where intervention into a particular polity stood within the range of priorities policymakers faced. I acknowledge that such views may vary from exogenously derived measures of material cost, but evaluating how, and to what degree, actual and expected intervention costs differ are beyond this project's scope.

Local actors feature less prominently in my argument even though they clearly populate the localities where intervention takes place. The apparent absence of local agency comes from the fact that weak polities tend to contain many more-or-less evenly matched domestic rivals. Winning foreign assistance becomes a means to quickly become competitive vis-à-vis local adversaries. Since domestic actors usually outnumber foreign interveners, acquiring foreign help in these highly contentious environments usually means abiding by terms set by outside interveners lest the latter shift support to local opponents who are more cooperative. This commitment problem erodes the effects of local agency on state formation even if domestic groups are politically active, and may last until one local actor can dominate a polity enough to play interveners against each other.

The second-image reversed approach I advance augments an underdeveloped area of extant arguments on state formation.[6] Apart from drawing on the early modern European as well as, to some extent, African and Latin American experiences, attempts to understand state creation tend to view change agents as largely domestic.[7] Arguments that consider international politics generally see such dynamics as background structural conditions or one-off, exogenous shocks.[8] Theories that explore the role external actors play in shaping state

---

[5] For more about perceptions and the understanding of costs and policy, see Christensen, 1996; Friedberg, 1988; Khong, 1992; Kupchan, 1994; Wohlforth, 1993.

[6] A second-image reversed approach uses international system-level variables to explain domestic political phenomena. Gourevitch, 1978.

[7] Acemoglu, Johnson, and Robinson, 2001; Centeno, 2002; Herbst, 2000; Jackson, 1990; Philpott, 2001; Tilly, 1990.

[8] Ertman, 1997; Skocpol, 1979; Spruyt, 1994; Strayer, 1970; Tilly, 1990.

4 *External Intervention and the Politics of State Formation*

characteristics tend to concentrate on the entry and exit of various polities from the international system.[9] Analyses that insufficiently account for intervention risk overlooking a critical element of state formation in fragile polities that may speak to externally led attempts to bolster stability and instil order in places like Afghanistan and Iraq today.

SOVEREIGN STATEHOOD IN HISTORICAL PERSPECTIVE

Sovereign statehood represents a departure from preexisting political arrangements in most parts of the world during the mid twentieth century. For much of the nineteenth and early twentieth centuries, many polities in the global periphery existed as colonies, vassal states, and feudalised states to list a few examples. This is despite the fact that some of these places may have hosted states with sovereign attributes earlier in their histories.[10] Nonsovereign approaches to arranging the state over the past century and a half or so have institutional characteristics distinct from the sovereign state.

Colonial states may exclude outside actors from intervening within their spatial boundaries and centralise domestic governance, but are subordinate to an outside authority. Feudalised states may be free from higher external sources of authority, but they did not experience much centralisation of governance internally. Even if a vassal state was politically centralised, it was subject to an external suzerain that reserved the right to shape political, economic, and social developments. Empires and suzerain states tend not to recognise the limits imposed by territorial boundaries even if they are politically centralised and independent of any other political authority.

Simply, the simultaneous possession of high degrees of political centralisation, territorial exclusivity, and external autonomy that typifies the sovereign state is vastly different from other state forms. In fact, the institution of the sovereign state was, for the most part, relatively rare outside much of Europe before the end of World War II.[11] Nevertheless, most of the world enthusiastically embraced the transplantation of sovereign statehood shortly after World War II, and was often ready to spill blood to do so.

Amongst common understandings about the institutional and organisational changes behind the export of sovereign statehood from Europe during the mid twentieth century are those that stress nationalism and self-determination. Specifically, as nationalist and self-determination beliefs took hold amongst both colonisers and the colonised, this brought a convergence of efforts to create sovereign states where they did not exist. Such forces saw revolution and decolonisation from Africa to Asia and the Americas.

Nationalist movements agitating for sovereign state creation were, however, highly active across much of the non-European world since the late nineteenth

---

[9] Fazal, 2004; Krasner, 1999, 2001.
[10] Hui, 2005.
[11] Huang, 1993; Tilly, 1990, 192–227; Wong, 1997.

Moulding the Institutions of Governance

century if not earlier. Chinese nationalists were active since the last decade of the nineteenth century, well before the overthrow of the Manchu regime in 1911. Likewise, Filipino nationalists helped bring about the end of Spanish colonial control in 1898. In fact, Filipinos had revolted against Spanish rule thirty-four times by 1872.[12] Filipino nationalist armies were even able to stall American colonial designs for almost a decade and a half after the end of Spanish rule.

Proto-nationalists under Diponegoro were similarly able to fight the Dutch to a standstill in the Java War during the 1820s.[13] Yet, from the Philippines to Indonesia and China, sovereign statehood did not emerge until the mid-twentieth century. In contrast, Siam was well on its way toward sovereign statehood by the early twentieth century despite not having a coherent nationalist movement until the 1910s. Moreover, international support for national self-determination enjoyed prominence since the early twentieth century as an enduring legacy of the Versailles Conference.

Even as those arguing for the self-determination of peoples gained the upper hand in intellectual and diplomatic circles after World War I, substantive change in many areas under foreign domination was often slow and limited. Forceful domestic and external calls for the establishment of sovereign statehood in India aside, the subcontinent stayed a British colony until 1947. On top of running governmental institutions such as the Customs Service, external powers likewise maintained spheres of influence, special economic and political privileges, extra-territorial rights, and colonies in China. Despite promises of self-determination and independence, Burma, the East Indies, Malaya, the Philippines, and areas of Africa remained under their respective colonial yokes through World War II. Even post–World War II de-colonisation in most places occurred over several decades, extending into the 1960s and 1970s for much of Asia and Africa – and arguably into the 1990s in parts of Eastern and Central Europe and Central Asia.[14]

The lag between the rise of nationalism and self-determination and the establishment of national states suggests that these dynamics alone were unable to establish sovereign statehood. Likewise, explanations highlighting the importance of nationalism and self-determination norms are at pains to show why the institutionalisation of sovereign statehood can sometimes occur prior to, or in the absence of, these factors. This phenomenon is especially evident when thinking about areas like Singapore, Malaysia, or Thailand, where sovereign statehood did not result directly from protracted struggles against foreign overlordship. Accounts about nationalist mobilisation and the spread of sovereignty-supporting norms may therefore be underestimating the influence of other dynamics.

---

[12] Schoonover, 2003, 84.
[13] Ali, 1994, 247–338; Ricklefs, 1993, 111–18; SarDesai, 1997, 93–95; Williams, 1976, 97–98.
[14] Beissinger and Young, 2002.

Some nationalist accounts of sovereign state creation underscore the critical importance of long-standing indigenous identity and cultural traditions. However, if such forces are fundamental to nationalist movements, then it is curious that most nationalist groups explicitly shunned reversion to more traditional institutional approaches to organising the state, be it an empire, suzerain, vassal, or feudalised state. Instead, nationalists largely adhered to an approach to organising the state that approximated a nineteenth and early-twentieth-century European ideal, and often saw traditionalists as enemies of progress.[15] Unless they are self-contradictory, incoherent, or both, it is not easy to see how culture and identity can be simultaneously sticky and pliable whenever convenient. Moreover, established identity and traditions are not a prerequisite for sovereignty – Tatars, Tamils, and Xhosa being examples of such groups that do not have an attendant sovereign state.

This discussion does not aim to suggest anything uniquely twentieth-century, contemporary, or European about sovereign statehood as an institutional form. Polities approximating the sovereign state existed in Warring States China (475 BC–221 BC) and showed signs of emerging in parts of precolonial Africa.[16] It is also possible to locate the roots of the sovereign state in Europe's mediaeval past, well before the supposed modern heyday of sovereignty.[17] In Europe, alternatives to the sovereign state such as empires, city leagues, and even chartered trading companies controlling vast territory lasted into the nineteenth and twentieth centuries.[18] The pervasiveness of European-inspired sovereign state-making projects in the periphery during the mid twentieth century is a phenomenon worth rethinking since sovereignty-supporting conditions long existed in many of these areas.

Given the large theoretical and empirical questions that popular perspectives about the most recent wave of sovereign state creation leave open, rethinking the dynamics surrounding this process remains important to academic and policy-related studies. To better appreciate how an essentially foreign institutional form came to take root in fragile polities at a specific historical moment, it may be necessary to reconsider the dynamics behind sovereign state creation in such instances. To do so, I focus on the processes of state formation in China, Indonesia, and Thailand from the late nineteenth century until the mid twentieth. These are "least likely" cases with different, but individually well-established, accounts of sovereign state formation that run counter to my hypothesis.

---

[15] In the Chinese case, those in support of nationalist causes tended to treat those calling for a reinstitution of the empire – such as Gu Hongming, Kang Youwei, Zhang Xun, and former members of the Qing Court – as outcasts and opponents. Nationalist groups even viewed moderates like Liang Qichao, who supported a constitutional monarchy, with disdain.

[16] Hui, 2005; Kiser and Cai, 2003; Young, 1994.

[17] Anderson, 1974a, 1974b; Strayer, 1970.

[18] Adams, 2005; Doyle, 1986; Spruyt, 1994; Watson, 1992.

EAST ASIA AND THE CONTINGENCY OF SOVEREIGN STATEHOOD IN THE PERIPHERY

There is nothing necessary about the establishment of sovereign statehood amongst peripheral polities across East Asia. Sovereign states are simply one institutional option for organising governance. As late as the 1930s, it was not even clear that sovereign statehood would be the fate for most polities in both Northeast and Southeast Asia. Moreover, sovereign statehood does not guarantee wealth or power, as the unhappy recent histories of many postcolonial African and Asian states readily show.[19] It does not even necessarily ensure security for the life and property of those living under its control. How this approach to organising the institutions of state came to dominate East Asia and elsewhere, and why this development took place at a particular historical juncture warrants further examination.

The conditions just mentioned make examining the polities of East Asia highly informative for attempts to understand the processes of state formation in weak states more widely. Sovereign statehood developed during the mid twentieth century for most fragile polities around the global periphery, replacing various forms of the state that previously existed in these areas. These included indigenous, traditional approaches to organising governance and political authority as well as foreign colonial arrangements. Like so many regions in the world, East Asia felt the force of nationalist mobilisation, external intrusion into domestic politics, and the consequences of major power competition between the end of the nineteenth century and the middle of the twentieth. In this regard, state formation experiences in East Asia between the late nineteenth and mid twentieth centuries may be broadly representative of dynamics at work in weak polities elsewhere.

Apart from its wider theoretical relevance, a study of sovereign state creation has particular salience for East Asia. This is one region where issues of sovereignty remain contentious. Unlike Europe and North America, disputes over borders, the integrity of singular, centralised polities, and the ability of a polity to exercise agency internationally continue to be likely sources of unrest and armed conflict. These include differences over the political status of Takeshima/Dokdo, the Diaoyutai/Senkaku Islands, Taiwan, the South China Sea, Ambalat, and Preah Vihear amongst many others. In this sense, the dynamics of sovereignty and consequences of state formation continue to have real and direct consequences for international politics in the region. Ironically, conceptions of state form – the structure of a state's internal politics and external relations – that inform these issues come most recently from "Western" traditions of politics and governance that societies in East Asia tried to resist over the past two centuries.

What many see as European notions of the sovereign state are so deeply internalised that alternative, indigenous approaches to organising the state

---

[19] Centeno, 2002; Herbst, 2000; Jackson, 1990; Kohli, 2004.

8 *External Intervention and the Politics of State Formation*

such as the suzerain-vassal system no longer feature prominently in the politics of East Asia, except rhetorically.[20] It seems that institutional approaches to organising the state in East Asia represent a reversal of the old Chinese adage, "*zhongxue wei ti, xixue wei yong*".[21] Rather, "Western" learning now provides the fundamentals for state organisation, and "Eastern" learning the mere instruments of everyday politics.[22] Such features are apparent in the polities that form the empirical focus of this study – China, Indonesia, and Thailand.

One of the distinguishing features of Chinese politics from the mid nineteenth century on is an embrace of modernist notions of sovereignty. Nowhere is this more apparent than when considering Chinese attempts to organise relations with the outside world. From discussions about China's role in the world to relations with foreign powers and the duties of government, matters of sovereignty appear to play a key role in major Chinese political debates between the Self-Strengthening Movement of the mid 1800s and the founding of the People's Republic. In fact, popular accounts often see the clamour for "sovereignty" as central to the popularity of the Chinese nationalist and communist movements that saw the rise of the contemporary Chinese state.[23] Today, sovereignty issues remain central to Chinese politics – if contention over jurisdiction by international organisations, Taiwan's political status, and territorial boundaries are any indication.[24]

Nonetheless, as the most recent formula for drawing borders and forming political relationships, sovereign statehood is a fresh feature of modern Chinese politics that draws heavily from foreign influences.[25] This is despite the fact that discussions of sovereignty share close associations with treatments of nationalism, identity, and modernity in contemporary China.[26] Until the early twentieth century, ideas of nonintervention, self-determination, and external juridical equality that help define modern notions of sovereignty had yet to definitively take root in Chinese politics. Even more striking is the fact that, except in retrospect, it was not entirely clear that China was heading down the path towards sovereign statehood. As late as the 1930s, communist internationalism, acceptance of foreign supremacy, and even anarchism remained potential substitutes to sovereign statehood.

Questions about modern conceptions of sovereignty are just as important for politics in present-day Indonesia. From the Moluccas and Irian Jaya to Aceh and Timor, the national government based in Jakarta expended much blood and treasure to hold the archipelago together. The ability of the Indonesian

---

[20] Acharya, 2004; Kang, 2004, 2005a, 2005b.

[21] The term means "Chinese learning for the fundamentals, Western learning for the instrumentals".

[22] This reformulation of the old line reads, "*Xixue wei ti, Zhongxue wei yong*". I take this reformulation from Ray Huang's argument about contemporary Chinese historiography. Huang, 1998.

[23] Johnson, 1962, 1969; Perry, 1980.

[24] Carlson, 2005; Fravel, 2005.

[25] On older approximations of sovereign statehood in China, see Hui, 2005.

[26] Leifer, 2000a, 1–125, 273–325, 361–401; Zheng, 1999.

Moulding the Institutions of Governance

government to maintain centralised political control and territorial exclusivity over a vast area affects the security of vital sea-lanes of communication such as the Malacca and Sunda Straits, as well as energy-rich areas like the Natunas and Aceh. A breakdown of the sovereign Indonesian state may cause significant disruptions to trade and energy supplies across East Asia, potentially causing economic, political, and social unrest.

For all of its present concerns over sovereignty, many observers attribute a pan-archipelagic movement that agitated for centralised political control, territorial exclusivity, and external autonomy against Dutch colonial rule for creating what is now Indonesia. This is despite the fact that a centralised system of governance covering the Netherlands Indies only emerged late into Dutch rule. Moreover, Dutch, British, and even Japanese control over the East Indies rested on cooperation between disparate local elite groups and the intervening external power. Such arrangements for political division, collaboration, and rule had precedents extending to early-seventeenth-century Dutch colonialism in the East Indies.

In contrast, Siam avoided formal colonisation and never experienced the sorts of external domination prevalent in the former Dutch East Indies and China. Between the late seventeenth and mid nineteenth centuries, the Siamese monarchy based in Bangkok even held suzerainty over Cambodia, parts of current-day Laos, and sultanates on the Malay Peninsula. Thailand even displayed the high degrees of territorial exclusivity, external autonomy, and political centralisation typical of a sovereign state arguably by around the turn of the twentieth century.

Siam clearly did not experience the same anti-imperialist, nationalist struggles prevalent elsewhere. Thai nationalism is in many respects an outgrowth, rather than a cause, of successful sovereign state-making. Popular accounts see the Siamese government's ability to manoeuvre foreign powers against each other and compromise where necessary as key to its early adoption and sustenance of sovereign statehood. Nonetheless, Siam renounced claims over most former vassals – with the notable exception of the former Malay kingdom of Pattani in the south, now part of a centralised Thai state. Such conditions raise questions about how Thailand accepted reduced territorial jurisdiction for a clearer demarcation of physical boundaries and a deeper penetration of political authority internally.

This book attempts to better appreciate the processes behind the empirical developments discussed so far. The aim is to understand how sovereign statehood, as an organisational form, came to take hold across East Asia and elsewhere despite vastly divergent situations. Such less-developed areas of the world are, in the end, replete with examples of polities where sovereign statehood took a firm hold despite largely dissimilar initial conditions. Experiences with organising the state varied tremendously for polities on the Malay Peninsula, Indochina, Borneo, the Philippines, the Ryukyus, Korea, and Japan in periods leading up to sovereign statehood. Incidentally, the wide range of nonsovereign state forms in East Asia historically is particularly permissive of an extension of my findings about state formation to other areas.

Through its focus on Northeast and Southeast Asia, this study also represents an effort at advancing understandings about the circumstances that led nationalism and political identity in polities along the global periphery to find expression in the sovereign state. Such an approach may be especially useful since the long, tumultuous history of nationalist movements in the region suggests that long-term agitation and widespread mobilisation do not necessarily imply the success, or even attractiveness, of the sovereign option. Yet, differences over sovereign claims are now amongst the few enduring issues that have the potential to affect security, stability, and prosperity throughout East Asia and elsewhere outside Europe and North America. By exploring the origins of this phenomenon, I hope to appreciate how one organisational concept was not only adopted, but also gained lasting importance, in vastly different material and social contexts.

STATE FORM AND SOVEREIGN STATEHOOD

Before proceeding further, I wish to clarify several key concepts. First, state form is the institutional configuration that defines a state's internal political structure, as well as its relationship to the external world. These arrangements establish the degree to which governmental powers are centralised hierarchically within the polity, the extent to which internal political structures are subject to external authority, and the degree of autonomy a state enjoys as an actor in world politics. Looking at state form institutionally allows for the possibility that sovereign statehood is not the only means for arranging political order, governance, authority, and power.[27] This is analytically useful for considering changes in the institutional configurations of a polity.

An attempt to explore state form necessarily implicates the relationship between internal and external politics. It entails the existence of a "domestic" sphere where some system of authority, hierarchy, and centralisation, however minimal, exists in contrast to an anarchical "external" world.[28] The concept of state form I present aims to allow for an examination of the different possible institutional means of arranging the political relationship between the external and internal. Nonetheless, I recognise that state form may constitute only one element of sovereignty and acknowledge that this project does not explicitly examine such aspects as changes to the meaning of sovereignty over time and relational dimensions of sovereignty.[29]

[27] Hall, 1986; Van Creveld, 1999.
[28] Anarchy here means the absence of centralised source of authority, what Alexander Wendt terms "Lockean" anarchy and Hedley Bull calls the absence of government. Bull 1977, 44–49; Buzan, Jones, and Little, 1993; Spruyt, 1994, 13; Wendt, 1999, 279–97.
[29] For perspectives on other components of sovereignty, see Bartelson, 1995, 2001; Philpott, 2001; Walker, 1992.

Moulding the Institutions of Governance

Following Charles Tilly, I take sovereign statehood as an organisation form that is contingent on the exercise of coercion and political authority rather than necessary or rooted in particular historical stages. Given that my primary interest is to examine sovereign statehood as a particular means of organising both domestic and external politics, I concentrate less on issues of justice, regime types, development, and society than do the authors of many studies on sovereignty in comparative politics, sociology, and political theory.[30] I look at why political structures in particular polities took the form of the sovereign state at specific moments in time. Such an approach situates sovereign statehood within a range of institutional possibilities for state form, from feudal empires, to suzerains, vassals, colonies, city-states, and city leagues.

To explore sovereign statehood as a type of institution I need to demonstrate variation amongst different types of states. Before I do so, I believe that it is important to outline what I mean by a state, or polity – as opposed to a sovereign state or other state forms. After all, it is in the state where changes in state form occur.

I take a state as an arrangement of political structures that allows the exercise of coercion over a delineated geographical space and population. Within these bounds, the state possesses *prominence* in sectors of social activity pertaining to political authority. Such eminence is relative to other structures of authority and does not necessarily translate into predominance. My classification of state form incorporates empires, vassal states, colonial states, city leagues, city-states, and sovereign states to name just a few examples. It does not include clans, tribes, households, lineages, firms, churches, political parties, administrative subdivisions, and such.[31] This suggests a distinction between an "external" world without a centralised, hierarchical source of government and a "domestic" realm where such conditions exist, even if nominally. Since both *polity* and *state* can capture this sense of political organisation, I use the terms interchangeably unless otherwise stated.

I classify state form along three sets of criteria. They are the degree of territorial exclusivity, the extent of political centralisation, and the level of external autonomy. I believe that these three characteristics best capture the internal and external components of state form this project focuses on. Territorial exclusivity is the degree to which a state limits the direct intervention of outside governments over matters of domestic administration. Political centralisation is the extent to which there is a concentration of governmental powers around a single, hierarchical political structure. The degree to which a central government can veto political, economic, and social developments within a polity determines the level of political centralisation. External autonomy is the level at which an external government or authority oversees the external affairs of the state in question.

---

[30] Ertman, 1997; Kohli, 2004; Weber, 1994a, 1–28.
[31] Tilly, 1990, 1–3.

A sovereign state should rank high on all three criteria. A feudalised state may rank low on territorial exclusivity and political centralisation, but relatively high on external autonomy. The territory of the mediaeval feudal states that formed the Holy Roman Empire, for instance, may have experienced overlapping, parallel lines of authority emanating from the Emperor, Church, and local prince. This, however, did not preclude the prince from entering into binding treaties with, or even declaring war on, the Emperor or Church – or vice versa.[32] Other feudalised states include the fiefdoms, dukedoms, and princedoms, in addition to royal holdings that made up pre- and early-Capetian France.[33]

In contrast, a colonial state may possess high degrees of territorial exclusivity, and even significant centralisation of political and administrative functions independent of the metropole. Lines of authority in such colonial setups are often singular and clearly hierarchical, with the metropole at the apex. The colonial polity, however, can run domestic policy quite independently from the metropole, and have its own central structure of governance – meaning that the colony can have substantial territorial exclusivity and political centralisation. In some instances, such as Canada and Australia up to World War I, metropoles may even permit significant independence of action – that is, external autonomy – to their various local colonial administrations, especially on day-to-day matters. Nonetheless, the metropole retains the final say over external matters of import, making the colony subservient in terms of its fundamental freedom to act over outward affairs.

Such characteristics may be common to traditional land empires as well as overseas empires – all of which I term imperial states. Imperial states, whether traditional continental empires or overseas empires, tend to demonstrate less territorial exclusivity.[34] Empires, like the Romans, Mongols, and Tang, often take as their outer reaches a transitory point of pause for the potentially unlimited, universal expansion.[35] Conquered territories integrated into the imperial state are unable to demonstrate local territorial exclusivity, political centralisation, or external autonomy separate from the empire.

Vassal states accept the influence of a suzerain authority over their external and internal affairs, including leadership selection, but are otherwise independent. Examples include the subordinate positions of Goryeo and Dai Viet vis-à-vis the thirteenth-century Mongol Empire. City-states like ancient Athens, Renaissance Venice, and modern-day Singapore are highly centralised and externally autonomous, but do not have clear areas of control beyond their immediate urban environs and are domestically susceptible to external

---

[32] Spruyt, 1994, 34–57; Tilly, 1990, 53–70.

[33] Spruyt, 1994, 77–108.

[34] For more on the distinctions amongst different forms of empire, see Bull, 1977, 207–20; Doyle, 1986, 30–47, 341–44; Watson, 1992.

[35] What I refer to by the term *traditional land empires* is analogous to what Spruyt calls "universal empires". Kratochwil, 1986, 27–52; Spruyt, 1994, 16–17; Tilly, 1990, 91–95, 167–68.

Moulding the Institutions of Governance

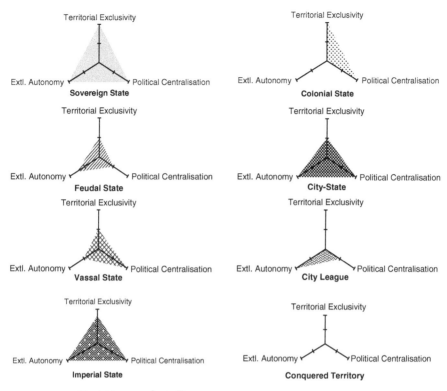

FIGURE 1.1 Variations on State Form

changes.[36] City leagues, like the Hanseatic League, are confederations of city-states that coordinate areas of internal governance and outward affairs even if they are largely self-governing and might not even be contiguous.[37] The diagrams in Figure 1.1 illustrates possible state forms along the lines of territorial exclusivity, political centralisation, and external autonomy.

Figure 1.1 obviously represents ideal types. How a particular polity measures up to each criterion clearly varies by case. To achieve any semblance of accuracy, efforts to estimate variation along the three axes will require an in-depth examination of the polity in question. A polity may approximate any state form at various historical junctures based on its configuration of centralisation, autonomy, and exclusivity, and may even fall between state forms in practice. In this regard, state form is a concept I use to assess the rise of sovereign statehood – as well as other organisational entities – across time and space.

This, of course, leaves us with the question, "who, or what, within the state determines its organisational attributes at particular moments in time?" The

---

[36] Spruyt, 1994, 130–50.
[37] Spruyt, 1994, 109–29.

simple answer is that actors who are able to seize and hold the state have disproportionate influence over state form. They may include organised groups of individuals, households, religious groupings, political parties, and external governments.

This response, however, is incomplete. It leaves open two sets of important and interrelated questions – namely, which actors succeed in taking control of the state, and why? Furthermore, why do actors seek different forms of the state? I believe that accounting for these issues requires a consideration of the influence that competition over access by external powers has on the domestic politics of a state. I develop an argument about the role of foreign intervention in state formation to answer these questions.

Admittedly, the cases included in this study do not represent the full array of possibilities of state form. In fact, the cases I examine sometimes fall between colonial and sovereign statehood and, to a lesser degree, suzerain as well as vassal statehood. The list of possible state forms I have described simply aims to provide a broad perspective on the range of possibilities along my dependent variable. Nevertheless, even a more limited variation should suffice to illustrate the processes driving shifts in state form.

By taking sovereign statehood to be one type of institution amongst many, I consciously follow the lead of others who work on systems change and the nature of units in world politics, notably Charles Tilly and Hendrik Spruyt. In his examination of the rise of modern European states, for instance, Tilly contrasts the national state against the feudal state.[38] When looking at the durability of the sovereign state in Europe, Spruyt compares the sovereign state against city leagues, city-states, and feudal states.[39] These perspectives modify the Weberian approach to sovereign statehood popular in comparative politics by highlighting the "external" elements of statehood and exclusive domestic structures of control, whilst de-emphasising the centrality of legitimacy.[40]

Understanding sovereign statehood as an institutional form differs from several views of statehood and sovereignty common in political science.[41] Many excellent studies in this regard exist, with clear nuances between them, but brevity asks that I group them into several broad categories. I discuss this decision in the text that follows.

The first group is one that takes all corporate actors with some ability to assert territorial control and autonomy in world politics to be sovereign states. This perspective tends not to differentiate amongst empires, feudal states, city-states, or city leagues in terms of how their political institutions vary in regard to political centralisation, territorial exclusivity, and external autonomy. Under such a definition, a polity with unclear spatial boundaries and overlapping lines of authority – such as the feudal fiefdoms of mediaeval Europe – may still

[38] Tilly, 1990.
[39] Spruyt, 1994.
[40] Bendix, 1977; Weber, 1994a, 1–28, 1994b, 309–69.
[41] See Vu, 2010.

Moulding the Institutions of Governance

qualify as a sovereign state.[42] This position is common in international relations scholarship.

A second group holds the international law position, which asserts that sovereignty requires widespread recognition by other juridically sovereign entities, or at least the dominant great powers of the day.[43] Both this approach and the previous one emphasise "external" over "internal" elements of sovereignty, and tend not to concentrate on the nexus between the two.[44] As studies of recognition, as well as failed and quasi-states have indicated, the possession of "external" sovereignty does not naturally imply qualities of "internal" sovereignty, and vice versa.[45] Since my focus is on interactions amongst aspects of "internal" and "external" statehood as played out in the institutions that determine the nature of a polity, an organisational understanding of sovereignty is appropriate for my purposes.

A third perspective is the state-in-society perspective that considers the relationship between state and society across various arenas of interaction.[46] This position examines how contact and contention between government and different parts of society over particular issues can empower certain societal actors and parts of the government while weakening others. These dynamics may be most apparent during times of social transformation. Such a research agenda differs from my attempt to concentrate on states as venues for contention and the resulting shifts in organisational characteristics.[47]

A fourth outlook understands the state in terms of its degrees of paternalism and political openness. Research in this vein considers how forces like the timing and severity of security threats or legacies of colonialism affect sources of state revenue and the openness of the domestic political system.[48] However, the variations in exclusivity, centralisation, and autonomy I explore in this project have little to do with the origins and development of various regime types. After all, the vetoes over domestic politics that central executives, legislatures, and judiciaries of openly competitive federal systems in Germany and the United States wield are highly robust. Conversely, central authorities in paternalistic systems such as Burma and the Soviet Union actually face significant limits on domestic oversight despite substantial territorial exclusivity and external autonomy.[49]

---

[42] Waltz, 1979, 93–97.

[43] Fazal, 2007, 74–88; Krasner, 1999, 14–25; Small and Singer, 1982.

[44] For detailed discussions about the distinctions between different elements of "internal" and "external" sovereignty, see Carlson, 2005; Krasner, 1999. For approaches that are more sensitive to the relationship between aspects of "internal" and "external" sovereignty, see Spruyt, 1994; Tilly, 1990.

[45] Herbst, 2000; Jackson, 1990; Krasner, 1999.

[46] See Migdal, 1988, 1994, 2001.

[47] For a review on how states are the centre of contestation in state formation processes, see Vu, 2010.

[48] Ertman, 1997; Kang, 2002; Kohli, 2004.

[49] Scott, 1985, 1998; Scott and Kerkvliet, 1986.

16 *External Intervention and the Politics of State Formation*

The fifth distinction I wish to make is with the literature that looks at state-building in terms of government capacity. Such work concentrates on the institutional effectiveness of various organs of government, such as taxation, economic development, the administration of various issues, and the effectiveness of coercion.[50] This research agenda clearly relates to issues of bureaucratic and political centralisation. However, the focus here is more on the policy exertions of centralised government rather than degrees of centralisation, territoriality, and autonomy.[51] These issues form a part of my wider concerns in this volume.

When examining state form, my primary concern is the institutional form of governance in practice. This permits me to distinguish institutional structures on the ground from politically or ideologically driven accounts of state form, since such depictions can sometimes depart from the actual exercise of governance. After all, Chinese responses to foreign trade, gunboat diplomacy, foreign intervention, and domestic unrest during the nineteenth century suggest a divergence between the myth of a highly centralised Qing empire and the actual diffusion of governance and authority on the ground.[52] Likewise, claims about persistent political centralisation in Siam differ from the reality of decentralised governance during the eighteenth and nineteenth centuries.[53]

PERIODISATION AND CASE SELECTION

In contrast to Europe, Africa, and Latin America, relatively little systematic scholarly attention has been paid to the development of state form in East Asia in the modern era. Many observers today take sovereignty as given in this part of the world. As such, I approach the empirical component of my project through a comparative perspective that considers variation across time and space. The cases I explore – China, Indonesia, and Thailand – cover many common features of weak polities and intervention between them.

Insights about state formation drawn from my cases are potentially applicable to the similar situations in East Asia and elsewhere. Stephen Krasner observes that:

High power asymmetry is the necessary condition for effective intervention to alter the constitutional arrangements of a target state. The local population can revolt. Externally bolstered rulers are open to accusations of disloyalty. Policing is expensive.

Intervenors have only been successful when their initiatives have not been challenged by a major power rival. If a ruler in a weak state can find an external ally, power asymmetries can disappear. Without great power consensus achieved either though a condominium or mutual recognition of spheres of influence, intervention can be

[50] Brautigam, Fjeldstad, and Moore, 2008; Brautigam and Knack, 2004; Haggard, Kang, and Moon, 1997; Kang, 2002; Kohli, 2004.
[51] Vu, 2010a, 148–51.
[52] Fairbank and American Council of Learned Societies, 1964; Kuhn, 1980, 2002; White, 1998.
[53] Heine-Geldern, 1956; Scott and Kerkvliet, 1986.

Moulding the Institutions of Governance

treacherous. Security has been the most common motivation for the rulers of major powers to intervene to alter the constitutional structures of target states.[54]

China, Indonesia, and Thailand from the late nineteenth to mid twentieth centuries capture these differences and changes in external intervention whilst also featuring characteristics common to weak polities more generally. My case selection permits me to understand such conditions in ways that speak broadly to intervention and state formation in fragile states.

Just as importantly, the polities included in this study are useful for laying out my argument; they are "least likely" cases for external intervention to play a role in fostering sovereign state formation. Common accounts of Chinese and Indonesian history identify sovereignty as reactions against, if not rejections of, outside intervention in domestic politics. Standard narratives of the Thai experience emphasise how the sovereign Thai state arose from indigenous attempts to channel and limit foreign influence. If evidence from these cases do not reject my argument, then it is more likely that outside actors played the active roles in shaping state form that I suggest. Outlining ways in which foreign intervention into domestic politics affect state form for these "least likely" instances could also suggest key dynamics and processes to watch when trying to examine my argument in other contexts.

I use China between the final years of the nineteenth century and the first half of the twentieth century as my main case. This is because the anticipated opportunity costs of intervening in China varied substantially over time for those external powers actively competing for access there, as did their levels of support for local allies. This allows within-case variation on the explanatory variable, making China a highly appropriate case against which to assess my argument. The recent availability of significant archival and secondary historical work on related topics in China is also helpful to my efforts here.

I study China in detail as an extension of the "least likely" approach. The forcefulness and variety of positions asserting the limitations of foreign influence in abetting the formation of the sovereign state, ranging from nationalist to cultural and Marxian, suggest that China may be an especially "hard" case for me. According to these perspectives, outside forces are largely responsible for the division of China if they play any role. I will have more confidence in my argument if the China case does not fundamentally challenge my position. Moreover, the increasing accessibility of archives on Taiwan and the Mainland alongside associated developments in secondary historical work on modern China provide excellent new evidence against which to rigorously assess my argument.

The other two cases I look at are the Dutch East Indies (Indonesia) and Siam (Thailand) from the late nineteenth through mid twentieth centuries. Each case contains external powers competing for access that demonstrate variations in their expected opportunity costs of intervention. Before the mid twentieth

[54] Krasner, 1999, 152–53.

century, the Indonesian archipelago presented low to moderate opportunity costs of intervention to not only the Netherlands, but also Japan. Alternatively, Siam presented high opportunity costs of intervention to France and the United Kingdom, the two foreign powers with most interest in competing over it. Taken together with the China case, such an approach expands the across-case variation on the explanatory variable.

Indonesia and Thailand provide critical, but comparative, "secondary" studies. Alternative claims about state formation for these polities are very strong, though not as dominant as in the case of China. The variations they provide in terms of patterns of foreign intervention are also important for evaluating the generalisability of my argument to other fragile states. They provide opportunities to further test my argument and examine how it may be adapted for application in other circumstances. Unfortunately, space constraints limit my elaboration on the Thai and Indonesian cases. Nonetheless, the detail I consider in these two instances is sufficient for evaluating the key points of my argument.

Additionally, my case selection permits me to control for alternative explanations about change in state form. Political developments in the polities I consider are by-and-large independent from each other in the periods of this study. As issues of sovereignty remain salient for contemporary issues relating to security and cooperation in the international politics of East Asia, it may be useful to analyse the origins of sovereign statehood in that part of the world. Such an exercise may provide new insights into world and East Asian regional dynamics. This is especially true of China, given the continuing salience of its sovereignty concerns for peace, stability, and cooperation in world politics.

To explore variation across time, I consider two periods. The first is from just before the turn of the twentieth century until the end of the World War I peace process in 1922, which occurred with the wrapping up of the Washington Convention. The second begins in the early 1920s and ends with the conclusion of the World War II peace process at San Francisco in the early 1950s.[55] The reason for this choice rests on my claim that the opportunity costs of intervention became uniformly high for intervening external powers at the end of the second period but remained mixed throughout the first. I argue that this development comes from the intensification of systemic competition after World War I.

The two periods I identify also make for good comparisons since they both contained substantial rhetorical support for national self-determination, systemic wars, and significant nationalist mobilisation for polities in both Northeast and Southeast Asia. This enables me to account for such influences. By incorporating East Asian polities with colonial experiences during the first half of the twentieth century, I am setting up hard tests for my argument. Such states tend to be standard cases for arguments about nationalism and self-

---

[55] The World War I peace process began with talks leading up to the 1918 Armistice and concluded with the end of the 1922 Washington Conference. The World War II peace process started with events leading up to Germany's surrender in 1945 and concluded with the coming into force of the San Francisco Treaty in 1952.

Moulding the Institutions of Governance

determination norms. Observers often see China and Indonesia as standard cases for sovereign state creation resulting from the rise and spread of nationalism, for example.

I begin my analysis in 1893, as it is a key historical moment for all three cases. Scholars and governments in China often use the period immediately preceding the 1894–1895 Sino-Japanese War as the baseline against which to measure political and territorial changes in the Chinese polity. In fact, this standard is an important part of contemporary Chinese claims about the status of Taiwan, and was previously applied justify China's jurisdiction over Outer Mongolia. That year also marks the beginning of a major series of modernising government reforms in Siam under King Chulalongkorn and comes just before the launch of the Dutch Ethical Policy, which revamped colonial governance in the Netherlands Indies. Hence, 1893 provides a useful starting point against which to assess changes in state form.

I employ a qualitative small-n research design to highlight the mechanics of outside intervention and state formation processes. Such an approach permits me to evaluate my argument by examining critical aspects of the interactions among intervening actors, their policies, local collaboration, and their effects on state form in detail. The empirical precision such an exercise offers can also advance understandings of these relationships and their key features. This can draw attention to important political dynamics that many existing studies underemphasise. Doing so can point future larger-n research on intervention and state formation toward measures and variables of particular concern.

Tables 1.1 and 1.2 illustrate variation on the independent and control variables, as well as expected values on the dependent variable in the two periods. Case selection allows for the challenging of my argument if actual and predicted outcomes do not cohere.

Data and Evidence

I use secondary historical materials alongside primary sources to accomplish my empirical research and test my claims. If substantial evidence from primary and secondary sources contradicts the predictions of my argument, it is possible to dispute my theoretical claims. I use secondary historical material supplemented by published primary documents to look at both intervening powers' expectations about the opportunity costs of intervention as well as their policies toward the various target polities. Secondary material also provides a means to assess state form, my dependent variable. I examine general areas of agreement about levels of territorial exclusivity, external autonomy, and political centralisation in existing literature for each case.

Specifically, I apply a combination of secondary and primary materials to consider the options available to policymakers when addressing access competition and the possibility of intervention in a target polity. Areas of convergence in these sources are useful for illustrating the rationale behind the decisions and trade-offs taken by those responsible for an outside power's approach toward

TABLE 1.1 *Variations in Antecedent Conditions and Expected Outcomes in Period I*

	China		Dutch East Indies/ Indonesian Archipelago		Siam/Thailand	
Time Period Beginning/Ending	1893	1922	1893	1922	1893	1922
EXPLANATORY VARIABLE						
Opportunity Costs of Intervention by External Powers	Mixed	Mixed	Moderate	Moderate	High	High
EXPECTED OUTCOME						
Expected Level of Political Centralisation	Moderate	Moderate	Moderate	Moderate	Moderate to High	High
Expected Level of External Autonomy	Moderate	Moderate	Low	Low	High	High
Expected Level of Territorial Exclusivity	Moderate	Moderate	High	High	Moderate to High	High
CONTROLS						
Nationalist Movements	Yes		Yes		Yes	
Colonial Experience	Yes (Many metropoles)		Yes (One metropole)		No	

Presence of International "Self-Determination" Norms	Yes (Wilson's Fourteen Points; League of Nations Charter)	Yes (Wilson's Fourteen Points; League of Nations Charter)	Yes (Wilson's Fourteen Points; League of Nations Charter)
Rapid Economic Development	Yes	No	No
War	Substantial Conflict (Sino-Japanese War 1894–1895; Boxer episode, 1899–1901; Civil Wars, 1911–1922)	Minor Conflict (Communist Revolt, 1926)	Minor Conflict (Internal Rebellions, 1902)

TABLE 1.2 *Variations in Antecedent Conditions and Expected Outcomes in Period II*

Time Period Beginning/Ending	China		Dutch East Indies/ Indonesian Archipelago		Siam/Thailand	
	1922	1952	1922	1952	1922	1952
EXPLANATORY VARIABLE						
Opportunity Costs of Intervention for External Powers	Mixed	High	Moderate	High	High	High
EXPECTED OUTCOME						
Expected Level of Political Centralisation	Moderate	High	Moderate	High	High	High
Expected Level of External Autonomy	Moderate	High	Low	High	High	High
Expected Level of Territorial Exclusivity	Moderate	High	High	High	High	High
CONTROLS						
Nationalist Movements	Yes		Yes		Yes	
Colonial Experience	Yes (Many metropoles)		Yes (One metropole)		No	

Presence of International "Self-Determination" Norms	Yes (League of Nations and United Nations Charters)	Yes (League of Nations and United Nations Charters)	Yes (League of Nations and United Nations Charters)
Rapid Economic Development	Ambiguous (Yes until 1937, then No)	No	No
War	Substantial Conflict (Civil Wars, 1923–1949; Sino-Japanese War, 1937–1945; Korean War, 1950–1952)	Substantial Conflict (Pacific War, 1942; Revolution, 1945–1949)	No

24 *External Intervention and the Politics of State Formation*

access in a target polity. If available evidence is incoherent over perspectives on access denial and intervention or contradicts my claims, then it may be possible to challenge the opportunity cost element of my argument. Such an approach enables me to account for the many competing perspectives and narratives relating to strategic concerns, access denial, and intervention.

The more policymakers of a foreign government emphasise the need to devote limited capabilities toward fuller and more complete access denial in a polity over other objectives, the lower the expected opportunity costs of intervention in that polity. The lower the expected opportunity costs of intervention, the closer policies toward a target polity will appear to full intervention. Full intervention occurs if an outside actor can completely deny its rivals access to a target polity by establishing direct and comprehensive vetoes over matters within the polity's territorial boundaries as well as its relations outside these confines. The opposite should hold when expectations about the opportunity costs of intervention become higher.

The choice to use a substantive amount of secondary work to examine the opportunity cost expectations of would-be interveners, their access denial policies, and state form comes from the fact that much excellent research on these issues already exists. Even though disagreements exist within the literature, there is convergence over broad trends and patterns. Areas of consensus that emerge despite interpretive differences provide a good indication of anticipated opportunity costs, policies toward target states, and institutional arrangements, and there is no need to replicate these efforts at this point. My analysis draws together the insights that these disparate bodies of work provide. Primary materials are most useful for highlighting the intricacies of interaction between external and indigenous actors, where a burgeoning but undertheorised literature exists – especially for late-nineteenth- to mid-twentieth-century China.

In my main China cases, I apply primary and secondary sources for process tracing in order to establish variation on the opportunity costs of intervention and the aggregated pattern of major power competition. Supplementing archival data with secondary material, I investigate the nature of any cooperative arrangements that occurred amongst outside and local actors across time. I also use this approach to ascertain the nature and relative degree of external support received by the various local political actors competing in China. For Indonesia and Siam, I investigate the opportunity costs of intervention and bargains between intervening powers and local actors using largely secondary sources complemented by published primary documents. Broad trends and points of convergence in the historical record permit an estimate of changes along the explanatory variable for the Indonesian and Siamese cases.

CONCLUSION

By engaging established theories of sovereign state creation, I am entering several broader conversations. The first is the discussion on sovereignty's past and future. In attempting to develop a theory about change in state form and looking

Moulding the Institutions of Governance 25

at the origins of sovereign statehood, I believe it is possible to better appreciate where the sovereign state may be going. Such an effort can allow greater appreciation for conditions under which state form may change, as well as factors that permit the sovereign state to persist. A reevaluation of such issues may inform discussions on future developments in state form.

The second dialogue I engage is the relationship between power, ideas, and norms. In taking power asymmetries between foreign and local actors seriously, I hope to underscore the relationships amongst force, material considerations, and the success or failure of particular ideas and norms.[56] Various state forms – whether it is the sovereign state, feudal state, or colonial polity – essentially represent organisational ideas that take shape when agents are able to realise them. Incorporating discussions about interactions among power, material factors, and ideas may help in considerations of why some of these organisational approaches appear at particular historical moments and not others.

Much recent discussion on sovereignty and the rise of the sovereign state emphasises the intersubjective, discursive role of ideas and norms ranging from nationalism to Enlightenment ideals, religious ideology, and anticolonialism.[57] These claims at times risk overstating the independence of ideas from power and material calculations, and may underplay the critical effects that authority, force, capabilities, material considerations, and agency can have on ideational factors and the processes of state creation. This line of enquiry deserves further elaboration, even though some of the sovereignty literature does try to take the roles of power and agency seriously.[58] Such an approach can help to further inform and develop efforts to study systems change in world politics.

Another area that this project aims to highlight is the exchange over the relationship between nationalism and collaboration, especially as it pertains to state formation. Recent political science work brings much-needed attention to the mixed, but enduring legacies of colonial rule in many parts of the world formerly under imperial subjugation.[59] This fresh take is a departure from more traditional perspectives that draw sharp distinctions between nationalist mobilisation and resistance on one side and foreign domination and collaboration on the other.[60] However, a growing body of historical research goes even further in probing such divisions by illustrating how agents in subject polities often straddle and traverse the boundaries between collaboration and nationalism.[61] My volume is an attempt to draw on and tie together current developments in historical and political science scholarship.

---

[56] I take power to mean differences in capability. For a discussion on various conceptions of power, see Lukes, 2004.

[57] Anderson, 1991; Bukovansky, 2002; Gorski, 2003; Philpott, 2001.

[58] Acharya, 2009; Adams, 2005; Nexon, 2009.

[59] Haggard, Kang, and Moon, 1997; Kang, 2002; Kuhonta, 2003; Vu, 2010; Vu and Wongsurawat, 2009.

[60] Abdulgani, 1978; Johnson, 1962; Leifer, 2000a, 2000b; Nagazumi, 1972; Sato, 1994.

[61] Barrett and Shyu, 2001; Brook, 2005; Chen, 2004; Duara, 1995, 2003; Jansen, 1954; Kahin, 1952, 1977, 2003; Mitter, 2000.

In a way, I am presenting a modified understanding of the politics of hegemony and domination. My argument attempts to speak to issues of external intervention as well as cases of colonisation and sovereign state formation in the global periphery. By taking seriously the broader conditions behind, and consequences of, foreign intervention, my theoretical framework can inform efforts to understand more recent externally led ventures to institute governance in Iraq, Afghanistan, East Timor, Cambodia, Namibia, Sudan, and elsewhere. World politics and history are replete with examples of the powerful trying to shape domestic developments in weaker states.[62] Such phenomena seem unlikely to abate.

Examining the dynamics of intervention also may aid attempts to understand problems associated with outside efforts to establish order in weak states. After all, low expectations of net return have appeared to dog foreign efforts at addressing instability in Somalia since the 1990s. Similar considerations seemed to forestall timely international action in Rwanda, Burundi, and the Balkans during the mid 1990s.[63] Conversely, higher expectations of net gain appear to have informed foreign attempts at involvement in places like Libya and Egypt during the 2011 Arab Spring. In this respect, this analysis might speak to issues beyond what its focus on Asia may indicate.

---

[62] Berdal and Economides, 2007; Kinzer, 2006.
[63] Barnett, 2002; Berdal and Economides, 2007; Clark, 2001.

CHAPTER 2

Imposing States

Foreign Rivalries, Local Collaboration, and State Form in Peripheral Polities[1]

Wealth and power stand at the heart of competition in world politics. Robert Gilpin observes that "the fundamental nature of international relations has not changed over the millennia. International relations continue to be a recurring struggle for wealth and power."[2] Writing on international cooperation and regimes, Robert Keohane notes that:

[Regimes] are rarely if ever instituted by disinterested idealists for the sake of the common good. Instead, they are constructed principally by governments whose officials seek to further the interests of their states (as they interpret them) and of themselves. They seek wealth and power.[3]

Key to attempts at amassing power and wealth is the ability to secure access to markets and resources. This is particularly important for actors with regional and global ambitions.

If an actor wishes to use the resources it comes to possess, it must be able to shift appropriate amounts of these resources to their proper destinations with minimal disruption. Such action requires a degree of certainty over communication processes. In other words, apart from owning resources, an actor needs to worry about the flow of the resources it controls. Sufficient access to resources enables an actor to remain competitive against rivals. However, when attaining full exclusive access is impossible, it may be enough to prevent rivals from acquiring such privileges. Note that although the focus in this book is primarily on state governments, intervening actors may theoretically be state or nonstate entities.

What drives an actor to intervene in the domestic politics of weak polities is competition over access to these states.[4] This means that rival actors contend

---

[1] I developed part of this chapter from Chong, 2010.
[2] Gilpin, 1981, 7.
[3] Keohane, 1984, 22.
[4] Castex and Kiesling, 1994; Corbett, 1917, 1972; Herbst, 2000, 11–31; Mahan, 1905, 1918, 1957, 1999, 137–357; Richmond, 1934, 1946.

over the relative advantages that may accrue from *denying* adversaries access to a particular area, and hence the resources that pass through that territory. In this regard, I do not simply consider the resource endowments of a polity, but the resources that need to transit the area. Access denial is the basic independent variable shaping state form in weak polities.

In considering competition over access, I am attempting to account for the fact that some areas may be strategically important even if resource poor. Examples include Hong Kong, Singapore, Panama, and Djibouti. After all, ownership of resources may amount to little if an actor cannot move necessary quantities of these assets to areas where and when they are needed – a fact Tsar Nicholas II discovered to his chagrin during the Russo-Japanese War. The inability to control a particular polity may mean that an actor's adversaries can block its ability to employ crucial resources.

Consequently, access denial may have a defining effect on competition amongst various actors. Japan's inability to fully harness and exploit the advantages of controlling resources in Southeast Asia during World War II clearly weakened the Japanese competitive position vis-à-vis its adversaries. This owed much to an American ability to deny open access to sea-lanes of communication in the Pacific.[5] *Ceteris paribus*, an actor would seek direct intervention in and full control of an area to completely shut off access by rivals.

Nonetheless, competing over access inevitably incurs costs, and actors must deal with such constraints. This reality is apparent to those deciding whether and how to secure access. An investment of capabilities to secure benefits in one area means foregoing gains that may accrue from committing those same capacities toward realising other opportunities. Less clear is how such opportunity cost considerations fit into external actors' decisions over involvement in weak polities.

After all, financial, industrial, and military capabilities, however vast, are limited next to the multiple demands for their use. This drives leaders and publics to dispute the trade-offs in net benefits when considering options for the expansion and retrenchment of overseas commitments.[6] Given the complexity of ascertaining actual relative values for particular actions, leaders' opportunity cost expectations tend to shape an actor's approach toward access competition.[7] A government's view on the opportunity costs of intervention in that area as a

---

[5] Taliaferro, 2004, 122; SHAC 18/1513, "Nanyang kaifa wenti zhi taolun" [Discussion on the Development of the South Sea], "Di Wei jiyao di 45, 46 hao" [Key Issues regarding the Enemy and Pseudo-(Governments) Nos. 45–46], No. 46, 21 January 1942; SHAC 18/3276, "Di Wei di 79, 80 ci huiyi guanyu 'Nanyang ziyuan kaifa wenti' zhi dabian" [Question and Answer regarding the Development of Resources from the South Sea in the 79th and 80th Meeting of the Enemy and Pseudo-(Governments)], "Di Wei jiyao 46 hao" [Key Issues regarding the Enemy and Pseudo-(Governments)], No. 46, 21 January 1942.

[6] Barnhart, 1987; Christensen, 1996; Friedberg, 1988; Khong, 1992; Kupchan, 1994; Snyder, 1991; Wohlforth, 1993.

[7] Christensen, 1996; Friedberg, 1988; Gilpin, 1981, 19–21, 55–84; Keohane and Nye, 1989, 80; Khong, 1992; Kupchan, 1994; Wohlforth, 1993.

Imposing States

corporate agent reflects ways leaders decide on access denial over a target polity in the context of competing concerns. Accordingly, I seek to ascertain the degree to which a government prioritises the commitment of capabilities toward intervention in a target polity relative to other goals rather than examine the origins of these differences in relative emphasis.

I take opportunity cost expectations as the understandings political leaders hold about costs, capabilities, and the compromises that pursuing various goals may entail. These views are a starting point for my analysis, which tries to incorporate both misunderstandings and ideological and psychological influences. It is possible for different individuals to vary in their outlooks and calculations over the same polity, especially across governments. Such an approach acknowledges that gaps may exist between reality and what leaders believe to be true, but does not delve into the origins and development of these discrepancies. In this sense, I am consuming existing work on leaders' and governments' positions over the commitment of capabilities and intervention in weak polities rather than trying to develop new arguments about perception and politics.[8]

The intuition behind my use of expectations comes from the appreciation that policymakers would likely avoid the trouble of confronting other governments in various target polities if all actual net costs of access denial were readily observable. They would instead calibrate their actions to avert friction and optimise net gains. Alternatively, variations in knowledge, information, and beliefs can allow for outcomes ranging from conflict to cooperation and coordination. This reasoning follows insights already well established in work on deterrence, coercive diplomacy, strategic interaction, and the causes of war; rehashing such research brings limited value added to this project.[9]

Moreover, I look at expectations because much research persuasively argues that policymakers working under the multiple constraints of time, competing needs, and other pressures face significant difficulties when trying to ascertain true values of cost and benefit.[10] Political leaders often employ assumptions, analogies, experience, ideology, personal preferences, and even discursive framings – consciously or otherwise – as intellectual shortcuts to understand facts and events when making policy.[11] Even if a clear appreciation of particular concerns exist, policymakers may differ substantially over how they understand the costs, consequences, externalities, compromises, and approaches associated with these issues.[12] These dynamics apply to both individual and collective agents, and can occur during crises as well as over protracted periods.

---

[8] For more on perceptions and international relations see, for example, Jervis, 1976; Khong, 1992; Snyder, 1991; Wohlforth, 1993.

[9] Fearon, 1995; Huth, 1988; Kennedy, 2012; Sartori, 2005; Schelling, 1966; Schultz, 2001; Snyder, 1984, 1991; Van Evera, 1999.

[10] Jervis, 1976; Khong, 1992.

[11] Goldstein and Keohane, 1993; Jervis, 1976; Khong, 1992; Risse, 2000; Wohlforth, 1993.

[12] Friedberg, 1988.

In stressing the capabilities at an actor's disposal, my analysis recognises that resources generally require processing before it becomes possible to use them for specific purposes. Resources are less readily usable, fungible, and substitutable than capabilities that may be rapidly redeployed into different applications, a quality that is essential in strategic competition. Naval capabilities, for instance, may be just as adept in safeguarding sea-lanes of communication as in engaging in humanitarian relief, shows of force, blockades, off-shore bombardment, or supporting amphibious landings. Financial capabilities may allow a power to construct military forces, sponsor insurgents, or win over others through aid, investment, and trade concessions.

Given these factors, I expect an external actor to accept less complete and direct forms of denial when its leaders anticipate the opportunity costs of intervening in a polity to rise. As cost expectations grow, the outside actor becomes more willing to work with indigenous partners who can help share the burdens of managing its rivals' access to a target state. In return, these local affiliates receive a degree of control over the polity and the distribution of that state's surpluses. The extent to which the external actor is willing to relinquish oversight of access and control to local associates depends on how expensive it anticipates intervention to be. This spans from complete absorption of local actors when intervention appears cheap, to the sponsorship of indigenous governments at moderate cost, and the creation of pure exchange relationships or cessation of contact when costs seem extreme.

Changes in state form occur as external actors contend over a polity with the assistance of their local partners. Outside actors and their local partners that are constantly able to bring more capabilities to bear than rivals have a greater probability of victory, and can impose their preferred state form on a targeted polity. The extent to which each intervening actor invests in its domestic proxy, however, is not initially evident to the other competitors. This information problem permits commitments to ultimately unsuccessful bids for access denial, as well as the development of stalemates.

A THEORY OF ACCESS, INTERVENTION, AND STATE FORMATION

To address the role of external intervention on state formation, I forward a perspective that takes seriously the collective effects of foreign intervention.[13] I posit that state form in a peripheral polity results from the playing out of efforts by outside actors to compete over access in that locale, conditioned by the expected opportunity costs to intervention facing rival foreign actors. Specifically, when foreign actors come to jointly expect high intervention costs,

---

[13] Note a tension between parsimony and elegance. Elegance emphasises theoretical succinctness and abstraction by allowing more assumptions. Parsimony underscores empirical precision and conciseness in assumptions through greater theoretical specification. Here, I lean toward parsimony. See Audi, 1999, 197–98.

Imposing States

they settle on promoting sovereign statehood in a weak polity as a next best alternative to their least desired outcome, domination of the area by adversaries. The basic condition that drives various powers to intervene in the domestic politics of a target state is the edge they expect to gain over their adversaries through access denial over that polity.[14] Focusing on access denial allows me to account for anticipated benefits from market opportunities to strategic salience as well as material and nonmaterial factors.

Committing capabilities to secure gains in one area means sacrificing benefits that may come from devoting those same capacities toward realising other opportunities. In considering how attempts to address trade-offs in net gains amongst options shape an actor's approach toward access competition, my opportunity cost perspective builds on and adapts standard views about expected utility.[15] Leaders want to optimise net gains when considering policy trade-offs under constraints but operate under bounded rationality.[16] Policymakers simply do not have the time, energy, or ability to appreciate all the implications surrounding an issue given the multiplicity of pressures they constantly face. Consequently, they anticipate opportunity costs through the lenses of simplifications, mental shortcuts, cognitive dissonance, emotive responses, and other perceptual influences rather than careful, exhaustive reasoning and full knowledge of true opportunity cost.[17]

To ascertain opportunity cost expectations, I consider the debates amongst policymakers over the expected net returns from investing a given set of capabilities towards intervention in a polity relative to the net gains from committing to other objectives. Such outlooks on relative net return may involve material and nonmaterial considerations, miscalculation, and misperception. This allows for the possibility of suboptimal decisions even if leaders think they are making the best of their circumstances. Such an approach can provide insight on how decisionmakers weigh capability allocation and access competition over a target polity next to other current and future strategic, political, and economic concerns. I do not delve into the origins of perceptions, cognition, emotions, imperfect information, and strategic interaction, as this re-creates extant research and distracts from efforts to examine the consequences of such dynamics on intervention and state formation.

If anticipated net returns from intervention sufficiently outweigh those of the best alternative, policymakers may still intervene in a polity despite extremely high absolute costs given on-the-ground developments, path dependency, and other considerations. High expectations of net gain persuaded British leaders persecute the 1899–1902 Boer War over domestic and international pressure, robust Boer resistance, more than 97,000 casualties, and a tenfold increase in

---

[14] Corbett, 1917; Herbst, 2000, 11–31; Mahan, 1999, 137–357.

[15] Gilpin, 1981, 19–21, 55–84; Keohane and Nye, 1984, 80.

[16] Christensen, 1996, 17–19; Jervis, 1976; Khong, 1992; Simon, 1982.

[17] Christensen, 1996; Friedberg, 1988; Khong, 1992; Kupchan, 1994; Wohlforth, 1993.

32   *External Intervention and the Politics of State Formation*

national debt that led to a prolonged financial crisis.[18] Expectations about moderate access denial costs led the McKinley, Roosevelt, and Taft administrations to persevere in colonising the Philippines despite the strength of the Filipino nationalist movement and domestic opposition within the United States. At its peak, occupying the Philippines from 1899 to 1913 tied up two-thirds of the U.S. Army, a quarter of the federal budget, and cost more than 7,000 American battle-related casualties.[19] Given the anticipated gains from resisting America, the Chinese Communists too continued to fight in Korea after early 1951, when fighting stalemated and Chinese forces began to sustain many of their roughly 900,000 casualties.[20]

That leaders and governments accept significant absolute costs and substantial risks given expectations of extensive net gain is actually quite intuitive. It is possible to observe such behaviour across a range of actors. State and substate governments commonly accept substantial deficit spending when expected political and economic payoffs sufficiently outweigh other considerations. Firms often raise high levels of debt to finance investments that management and shareholders believe can bring sizeable profits despite having to forgo alternative business opportunities. Individuals and families frequently put off current and future consumption for large home mortgages when they believe this can provide both housing and a source of savings for education and retirement.

Expectations about the opportunity costs of intervention in a target polity inform whether and how an outside actor intervenes in the domestic politics of a weak state. This provides the key intervening variable – the explanatory variable – in my account of state formation. Lower expected opportunity costs about intervention imply that elites attach greater importance to access denial in a polity. Hence, the lower the expected opportunity costs, the more extensively an external actor will seek to absorb and control local political groups to more completely deny rivals access. This logic follows Robert Powell and Joseph Grieco's insights on the costs of war, sensitivity to comparative returns, and relative versus absolute gains.[21]

---

[18] The British combat casualty rate in the Anglo-Boer War was 35.5 percent. Brendon, 2007, 214–48; Cloete, 2000, 342; Ferguson, 2004, 227–39; Friedberg, 1988, 51–52, 106–18; Howard, 1967, 75–95, 1974, 134–173; Kupchan, 1994, 106–7, 126–27; Marix Evans, 2000, 52; Platt, 1968, 249–61; Snyder, 1991, 209–10; Wang, 1979, 187.

[19] Figures exclude the larger numbers that died from disease as well as deaths and injuries from counterinsurgency through 1913. Hunt, 1983, 196–98; Karnow, 1989, 194; Schoonover, 2003, 93; United States, Bureau of the Census, 1975; United States, Dept. of the Treasury, Division of Bookkeeping and Warrants, 1900, 76–85, 106–7.

[20] Tucker and Kim, 2000, 130–41; Yang, 1997, 641–42.

[21] Modifying Grieco, I take an actor's utility from access denial over target polity, U, as:

$$U = V - [E(r/l)][W - V]$$

V is an actor's payoff from access to a target polity and W, its rival's payoff. $[E(r/l)]$ is an actor's coefficient of sensitivity to gaps in payoffs, where r is the anticipated net benefits from complete denial of access over that area to its adversaries through full intervention in a target polity. The

Imposing States   33

To conceptualise how expected opportunity costs factor into intervention decisions, I adapt the reasoning of the "cost of no agreement" and "best alternative to no agreement".[22] For the leaders of an external power, intervention in a polity rests on a choice over denying rivals access to an area and the next best course of action. The more the anticipated net returns of investing in fuller access denial outweighs the expected net gains of committing to an alternative goal, the lower the expected opportunity costs of intervention. In this respect, this project evaluates the degree to which opportunity cost expectations vary rather than explains their origins.

I ascertain expected opportunity costs of intervention by assessing the options policymakers consider when formulating ways to compete for access over a polity. The more political leaders emphasise a need to invest in access denial in a polity at the expense of other objectives, the lower their expected opportunity costs of intervening in that locale. Discussions also should illustrate that policymakers tend to see a government's capabilities as relatively inelastic at any given time, even if they are to some extent divisible. Evidence should also indicate that leaders usually see available capabilities at a particular moment as falling short of the many demands for their use. Table 2.1 summarises the variations in elite expectations about the costs of intervention and the corresponding desired outcomes on access denial.

Rhetoric notwithstanding, it is critical to note that local political groups in weak states often accept foreign aid along with its attendant conditions, as they are price-takers in the market for external support. In highly contentious environments, indigenous political groups vying for control over the polity and a favourable distribution of its surpluses have to quickly gain the wherewithal to hold their own or risk annihilation, even if it means taking foreign assistance. Given the large number of local political groups relative to intervening powers, outside actors can rapidly channel support away from uncooperative local groups and toward their adversaries.

The commitment problem facing indigenous groups in weak states creates an incentive for them to accept foreign backing under terms stipulated by a foreign intervener. After all, both interveners and local actors recognise that the latter have much more to lose should an arrangement fall apart or if one or both sides renege on an agreement. This means that local groups in weak states can and do exercise agency when facing robust intervention, but their individual agency is less consequential in the state formation process. The 2008 "Sunni Awakening" in Iraq is a recent example of such a phenomenon.

---

term l represents the perceived net benefits forgone by not pursuing the next best alternative to committing a given set of capabilities in direct intervention through full access denial over that polity. The coefficient of an actor's sensitivity to gaps in payoffs is the expected ratio of r to l. The smaller the ratio, the less sensitive an actor is to gaps in payoffs and relative gains in access by rivals such that $U = V$ is when an actor focuses on absolute rather than relative gains. See Grieco 1988a; Powell, 1991.

[22] Fisher, Ury, and Patton, 1983; Milner, 1988, 350–76; Moravcsik, 1998; Putnam, 1988.

34 External Intervention and the Politics of State Formation

TABLE 2.1 *Expected Opportunity Costs for an Outside Actor, Approaches toward Access Denial, and Corresponding State Form in a Target Polity*

Expected Costliness of Intervention for an External Power	Approach toward Access Denial over a Target Polity	Corresponding Characteristics of State Form in the Target Polity
Prohibitively High		
Expected net return from full access denial over target polity significantly less than best alternative	Concede access	Not applicable
High		
Expected net return from full access denial over target polity less than or equal to best alternative	Nonprivileged access	High political centralisation High territorial exclusivity High external autonomy
Moderate		
Expected net return from full access denial over target polity outweighs best alternative	Access regulation	Moderate to high political centralisation Moderate to high territorial exclusivity Low to moderate external autonomy
Low		
Expected net return from full access denial over target polity substantially outweighs best alternative	Complete access denial	Low political centralisation Low territorial exclusivity Low or no external autonomy

Expected opportunity costs, though, tell only part of my story of state formation. The way external efforts at access denial interact and aggregate within a polity is also vital.[23] This dynamic provides another intervening variable for my argument. Outside efforts to intervene in and compete for access over a target state collectively shape the nature of its institutions of governance and political authority. Variations in the aggregated patterns of intervention

---

[23] A fragile polity's state form resulting from foreign intervention, S, may be approximated as:

$$S = f[(I|U)_{G1}, (I|U)_{G2}, ..., (I|U)_{Gn}]$$

where S is a function of the interactions amongst intervention policy $[I_{Gn}]$ of each interceding foreign government $[G]$, conditional on the expected utility of intervention into the said locale $[U_{Gn}]$ held by each intervening outside government.

Imposing States

attempts into a polity foist different organisational outcomes on a polity. When one outside actor successfully establishes its preferred approach to access denial over a target state – such as access regulation through colonisation – this simply implies that its rivals ceded access over the polity for the moment.

Accordingly, when the leaders of intervening actors all believe that intervention in a polity is very expensive, a common desire for nonprivileged access promotes the development of sovereign statehood. This occurs as external actors advance the independent ability of one indigenous political group to veto domestic developments in and autonomously determine the foreign relations of the target state, free from direct foreign oversight. The different outside actors view shoring up the independent position of a local central government as a means to prevent each other from enjoying access advantages, even if it spells sacrificing their own claims to such privileges. Alternatively, if external governments commonly see intervention in a polity as prohibitively costly, outside pressure is unlikely to affect state form as all relevant foreign powers shun involvement. This set of conditions may explain the continued anarchy in Somalia since the early 1990s.

Should external powers jointly expect low to moderate costs of intervening in a target state, the polity will likely fragment. This happens as each outside actor tries to work with a cooperative local actor of choice to regulate or fully deny access, but is unable to dislodge the other foreign powers and their local allies. Consequently, different external actors and their respective indigenous partners are only able to forward their desired degree of access denial over part of the polity. Such opposing intervention attempts collectively prompt a fracturing of the target state. The division of indigenous polities by European powers during the nineteenth century "Scramble for Africa" exemplifies this dynamic.

When various outside powers diverge in their expectations about the costs of intervention in a target polity, they generate parallel centrifugal and centripetal forces that foster the development of a feudalised state. To ensure nonprivileged access, powers anticipating high opportunity costs back independent local political groups that can politically centralise the state while securing territorial exclusivity and external autonomy. Outside actors expecting low opportunity costs work toward complete access denial, even as foreign actors perceiving moderate opportunity costs try to regulate access. These cross-cutting forces simultaneously advance the development of central government rule, regional autonomy, and external oversight over matters of domestic governance. This is the case even if external autonomy remains high. The persistence of an enfeebled Ottoman Empire in the face of major power rivalries during the late nineteenth century typifies the effects of such pressures.

Table 2.2 summarises how the aggregated effects of outside intervention affect state form given different configurations in perceived opportunity costs amongst foreign actors.

It may be possible to challenge my argument if outside actors do not seek increasingly indirect means to secure control over a state to manage access when

TABLE 2.2 *Aggregated Pattern of External Intervention Efforts and Outcomes on State Form in a Target Polity*

Aggregated Pattern of Foreign Intervention	Resultant Outcome on State Form
Single Outside Actor Prevails	**Subordinated Statehood/Nonstatehood** Successful attainment of veto over all elements of governance by single external actor
Convergent on Nonprivileged Access	**Sovereign Statehood** Concomitant outside attempts to support rule by a strong, autonomous local centralised government
Divergent	**Feudalised/Fragmented Statehood** Stalemate from simultaneous external push for autonomous centralised government rule and direct administrative oversight through local proxies
Convergent on Full Access Denial	**State Disintegration** Concurrent foreign efforts to achieve direct administrative oversight through local proxies

perceived opportunity costs of intervention grow. My claims are also contestable if intervening actors do not sponsor local actors to pursue sovereign statehood when opportunity costs are high. The same is true if outside powers do not foster local political actors to support collaboration in a colonial project at moderate levels of perceived opportunity cost. Should collective efforts by intervening actors and their local allies to compete over access not affect state form in ways that I expect, it is possible to further question my position.

Another way to cast doubt on the argument is to demonstrate that the support intervening actors provide to particular local actors is for reasons other than to deny access to rivals. It is further possible to contest my argument if external powers do not interfere with the internal politics of weaker outlying polities, or if outside involvement in domestic politics is inconsequential. If foreign actors did not see increasing opportunity costs of intervention after World War II more or less simultaneously, or did not seek indirect control and access denial under such conditions, it is also possible to dispute my argument.

ALTERNATIVE EXPLANATIONS

As Robert Gilpin notes, despite the fact that efforts at understanding the rise of sovereign statehood exist, students of world politics generally do not focus on

Imposing States 37

systems change in world politics.[24] Consequently, I think that it is possible to group the major arguments about sovereign state creation into three broad categories – namely the bellicist, institutional commitment, and ideological approaches. Each presents an alternative to my argument. It is not my intention to reject these explanations. Rather, I suggest that even if they offer good accounts of sovereign state creation and systems change under particular circumstances, further theory development can still supplement understandings of state formation – especially across contexts.[25]

Nationalism, Norms, and Ideology

Amongst the most popular explanations for changes of state form in weak states are those focusing on ideational factors. Such perspectives see ideas and beliefs as key to uniting and mobilising populations behind particular causes. This view often pays particular attention to nationalist ideologies and self-determination norms, even though ideational and normative forces can take other forms. As ideologies about nationalism and self-determination norms spread and take hold amongst a significant section of indigenous elites and publics of a state, they begin to clamour, sometimes violently, for the formation of sovereign statehood.

Changes in state form may occur when local elites and leaders believe that a reorganisation of governance institutions according to international norms forwards their economic and political interests. The view here is akin to the arguments Robert Jackson and Jeffrey Herbst offer on convergences in international and domestic support and their effects on sovereign state creation in Africa. They posit that when promoting sovereign statehood became congenial to the interests of local leaders and the conventions of the international community, sovereign state creation gained widespread support.[26] This was despite the inability of many African states to realise other key conditions of sovereignty. The intuition about the close relationship between interests, power, and ideas presented here similarly informs Stephen Krasner's work on the spread of sovereignty.[27] Also paralleling these perspectives is the view that advancing sovereign statehood in accordance with international norms permits emergent elites in weak polities to assert autonomy vis-à-vis the dominant political forces of the day.[28]

Another argument emphasising the role of ideas and norms in changing state form is the process of isomorphism that John Meyer, John Boli, and others have developed.[29] According to this view, state leaders, following the logic of

---

[24] Gilpin, 1981, 41–42; Ruggie, 1986, 131–57.
[25] In highlighting a different set of causal processes behind sovereign state formation under certain specific circumstances rather than disputing the general validity of other approaches, I attempt to provide what Charles Tilly refers to as an individualising analysis of cases in order to engage in variation-finding. Tilly, 1984, 81–82.
[26] Herbst, 2000; Jackson, 1990, 1993, 111–38.
[27] Krasner, 1999, 1993, 235–64.
[28] Bukovansky, 2002; Nexon, 2004; Philpott, 2001.
[29] Boli and Thomas, 1997, 171–90; Meyer, 1980, 109–37; Meyer et al., 1997, 144–81.

appropriateness, reform institutions along the lines of what they see in other successful states.[30] They do so as they believe that such action legitimates their hold over the state internally and externally.

Other highly influential theories of nationalism, like those developed by Benedict Anderson and Ernest Gellner, provide explanations of sovereign state formation that stress the importance of culture and identity. As members of a state's population experience the standardisation of language through the development of modern education and mass media, they begin to see themselves as a collective cultural and political body that deserves full self-determination.[31] Consequently, they deem the sovereign state as the best political means of expressing this common identity. This spurs indigenous attempts to structure the domestic politics and external relations around sovereign statehood.

A related understanding sees modernisation as a process that encourages a nationalist belief in the necessity of centralising the structures of governance within a polity under local leadership.[32] Accordingly, local political groups share the desire to establish sovereign statehood even if they differ over whom should lead. Popular mobilisation, according to this view, fosters the consolidation of political institutions under tighter indigenous control, making it harder for external forces to intervene in the state. This brand of nationalism may promote the high degrees of political centralisation, territorial exclusivity, and external autonomy central to sovereign statehood. Arguments about global decolonisation after World War II often highlight the connections amongst worldwide nationalist ferment and sovereign state creation and modernisation under colonial rule.

If nationalist and self-determination explanations are correct, sovereign statehood should develop in weak polities when such ideational and normative forces motivate important segments of the elite or population. Further, although ideational and norm-based perspectives focus less on the establishment of other state forms, it is possible to adapt the logic of such positions to explain how institutions like the colonial or feudalised state come about. Should ideas and norms drive variations in the organisational structure of governance and political authority in fragile states, then the effects of purposeful external intervention and competition over access would be minimal.

Nonetheless, even if the effects of ideas, nationalism, and self-determination norms on state formation have limits, these factors may remain highly influential for state-building, conflict, and state collapse. They can affect how regimes may choose to mobilise and even go to war, just as they can help create internal threats that cleave society.[33] Nationalism can also play critical roles in affecting political consolidation, as well as directions in which political liberalisation

---

[30] Anderson, 1998; Bukovansky, 2002.
[31] Anderson, 1991; Gellner, 1983, 39–62.
[32] Gellner, 1983, 19–42; Ruggie, 1982, 1989, 1993, 139–75.
[33] Anderson, 1991, 114–15; Barnett, 2002; Beissinger and Young, 2002; Christensen, 1996; Snyder, 1991.

Imposing States 39

develops.[34] Mobilisation along nationalist lines may be most powerful when a single group seizes full control of a state. This effectively turns commitment problems with both outside actors and other indigenous agents in favour of that group, enabling it to veto political developments relating to the polity. Unfortunately, these large, significant, and highly complex issues lie outside this volume's focus on state formation.

Institutional Commitment and Economic Transformation

Institutional commitment approaches see state form as resulting from a series of institutional bargains and social arrangements between different actors within a state. Different forms of the state are ultimately institutions that bind different domestic political actors together in various cooperative arrangements and social commitments.[35] They do so by redistributing the surpluses resulting from cooperation amongst domestic actors to raise the returns to collaboration. At the same time, the state also reduces the gains of defection and free riding, including through the provision and management of coercion.

By locking various domestic political actors together, the state permits the making of credible commitments with various outside actors. These include holding to agreements, treaties, servicing debt, and responsibilities for self-defence. Various state forms, however, vary on the effectiveness and credibility of the commitments they can offer under different circumstances.

For institutional commitment perspectives, changes in state form often come with transformations in the environmental milieu, which may be economic, social, or political.[36] Such shifts may involve the appearance of new groups of influential political actors. This upsets existing institutional arrangements within a state, as established actors seek to quash, control, or ally with ascendant players in order to hold onto, seize, or expand their influence over the state and the distribution of its surpluses.

Exogenous shocks alter the costs and benefits various domestic actors accrue from extant state forms. A key characteristic of such shocks is that the distribution of surpluses under ongoing institutional arrangements no longer satisfies a significant proportion of the main political actors within a state. Actors can no longer credibly expect the same advantages from cooperation and costs to defection or free riding by adhering to prevailing institutional setups. Consequently, domestic political actors seek alternate state forms that redistribute the gains and burdens of cooperation better as some actors try to improve their lot, whilst others attempt to forestall potential losses.

During periods of environmental change, actors may have different discount rates over the future, be uncertain of their optimal choice, and be unclear about

---

[34] Snyder, 1991, 2000.
[35] Spruyt, 1994, 32.
[36] Collins, 1986; Huntington, 1968; North, 1981, 1990; Ruggie, 1993, 131–57; Spruyt, 1994, 30–31, 61–76; Strayer, 1970; Vogler, 1985.

the probability of attaining their most preferred option.[37] As a result, the compromises domestic political actors in different polities prefer and agree to in terms of state form may display substantial variation even when facing the same exogenous influence.[38] The relative efficiency of these different state forms in providing institutional commitments to both domestic and external actors can determine their ability to persist over time.

According to many institutional commitment arguments, the groundwork for the rise of sovereign statehood comes about as the emergent commercial class allies with actors trying to consolidate control through greater political centralisation. Members of the commercial class provide capital to those advancing the position of central governments by accepting direct taxation. In exchange, central governments offer protection from predation by other political actors and reduce transaction costs for economic activity. The ability of the political centre to muster increasing capital also allows for greater military capability both to defeat domestic rivals and to ensure autonomy vis-à-vis external challengers for political control of the polity. As central governments and the commercial class replicate these coalitions within a geographic space over time, they increase and reinforce territorial exclusivity and political centralisation, moving the state toward sovereign statehood.

Institutional commitment approaches further argue that as sovereign statehood demonstrates greater efficiency in mobilising resources over time, it becomes the dominant state form. This happens through either one of two routes.[39] First, by being better able to muster resources, sovereign states remain more economically vibrant and militarily powerful over time than alternative state forms. In this regard, they weather war better than other state forms. With each subsequent conflict, the number of polities that adopt alternative state forms decreases.

Second, given the political, economic, and military success of sovereign states, leaders in polities with other state forms start learning and mimicking the institutional arrangements found in sovereign states. This enables otherwise underperforming polities to realise the efficiency gains in resource mobilisation that accrue to sovereign states. As polities with alternative state forms have died out through war or adopted sovereign statehood as their approach toward political organisation, the sovereign state has become globally prevalent.

Paralleling the above version of the institutional commitment argument, Marxian perspectives agree that sovereign statehood results from a shift in the environmental milieu brought about by the rise of the capitalist mode of production and a bourgeois class.[40] This is despite disagreements amongst Marxians over the precise causal process behind the emergence of sovereign statehood. Perry Anderson argues that the creation of sovereignty reflects

---

[37] Ikenberry, 2001, 17–20; Spruyt, 1994, 26–27.
[38] Ikenberry, 2001; Spruyt, 1994, 18–26.
[39] Bukovansky, 2002; Rosenau, 1970; Waltz, 1979, 74–77, 127–28.
[40] Engels, 1978, 753–54.

Imposing States

attempts by feudal aristocracy to consolidate control over the state in order to stave off political challenges from ascendant bourgeois capitalists.[41] Others, like Eric Hobsbawm, argue that the institution of sovereign statehood comes about from efforts by the capitalist class to seize the state from the feudal aristocracy.[42]

Regardless of differences over causal accounts, the emergence of the capitalist mode of production and the rise of the capitalist class leads to high degrees of political centralisation, territorial exclusivity, and external autonomy for a state according to many Marxians. Even though Marxians emphasise modes of production, class struggle, and revolution, key factors in both their analyses and their conclusions are consistent with institutional commitment accounts of sovereign state creation. The Marxian logic does not preclude the possibility that capitalist and feudal aristocratic classes may adopt institutional commitment strategies to either seize or maintain control over the state.[43]

It is possible to make an institutional commitment argument if the evidence demonstrates that changes in state form come about through institutional bargains struck by domestic groups in response to a change in the social and economic milieu. Such bargains take place independent of interference from actors outside the polity, and rest on efficiency arguments. If this is the case, it is possible to challenge the argument I am trying to make about outside intervention and state formation.

Bellicism, Capital, and Coercion

Bellicist explanations – based on patterns in the concentration and accumulation of capital as well as coercion – also focus on change in the broader environment to explain transformations in state form.[44] Bellicist arguments, however, identify developments in war-making and the threat of war as key to shifts in state form. Given rising military pressure, state elites seek to adjust their ability to both concentrate and accumulate coercive capacities and capital to address their security concerns. Increasing capital allows for the acquisition of more coercive capacity, whilst expanding coercive capabilities permits greater effectiveness in appropriating capital. State form shifts as elites attempt to reorganise governance structures to meet their coercion and capital needs given variations in security threats.

---

[41] Anderson, 1974a, 15–59, 1974b.

[42] Engels, 1978, 754–55; Hobsbawm, 1984, 1989, 1994, 1996; Marx, 1978a, 18–19, 23–25, 1978b, 186–88.

[43] This logic of economic changes and social conflict leading to transformations of political institutions is prevalent in, but not exclusive to, explicitly Marxian theories. An example is Ruggie's use of Emile Durkheim's concept of "dynamic density" to explain shifts in state form. Ruggie claims that fundamental transformations in property rights and economic production alter the dynamic density of society. This results in pressure to reformulate state form accordingly. Ruggie, 1986, 141–50.

[44] Giddens, 1981, vol. II; Mann, 1986, vols. I and II, 1988; Poggi, 1978, 1990; Tilly, 1990.

Charles Tilly, for instance, identifies three pathways along which states can amass capital and coercion.[45] They are the capital-intensive, coercion-intensive, and capitalised coercion approaches. The capital-intensive approach takes place when rulers form agreements with capitalists to purchase or rent coercive means, such as the hiring of mercenaries. In return, rulers watch out for capitalist interests. The coercion-intensive route has rulers creating structures of extraction and conquest to obtain the capital necessary to wage war, often by empowering loyal elites. Finally, the capitalised coercion path foresees the incorporation of holders of capital as well as coercion into the state.

External pressures from war or the threat of war drives the concentration as well as accumulation of capital and coercion in a state, and occurs when states adopt any of these three approaches. However, the relative efficiency of the capitalised coercion route in concentrating both capital and coercion means that states taking such an approach become predominant in the international system. The outcome of capitalised coercion is the establishment of sovereign statehood.

The reason the capitalised coercion path is most conducive to the creation of sovereign statehood stems from the way in which it centralises coercion and capital. Incorporating coercion into the state's central political structure – often through the establishment of standing armies – allows the central government to quell internal rivals and focus on external threats. Absorbing the means to raise capital into the core political structure of the state by consolidating tax systems permits central governments to directly control sources of revenue and quickly raise large amounts of money.[46] This is more efficient than exacting tribute, collecting rents, or farming out tax collection. These developments spell the beginnings of sovereign statehood.[47]

As sovereign states improve on their ability to wield coercion and extract ever-larger amounts of capital, they are increasingly able to exert their external autonomy. Growing wealth and coercive capabilities further pave the way for conquest and the establishment of territorial exclusivity. In Tilly's words:

Men who controlled concentrated means of coercion (armies, navies, police forces, weapons, and their equivalent) ordinarily tried to use them to extend the range of population and resources over which they wielded power. When they encountered no comparable control of coercion, they conquered; when they met rivals, they made war.[48]

Where fighting stalled, states drew borders inside which their governments held dominion.

An extension of this argument is that as sovereign states demonstrated the efficiency of the capitalised coercion model in war, a learning effect took place. Given the widespread success of sovereign national states in armed conflicts

---

[45] Ertman, 1997; Tilly, 1990, 30–31, 67–95.
[46] Note that by "taxes", I am referring to tariffs, tolls, as well as other regular and legalised forms of government-imposed levies on property, income, and other sources of private wealth.
[47] What I call the sovereign state is equivalent to what Tilly terms the national state.
[48] Tilly, 1990, 14.

Imposing States 43

against polities with other state forms, states either redefined their institutional arrangements accordingly or faced destruction. This meant that polities began to adopt the capitalised coercion approach to organising governance and political authority in order to survive.[49]

Should bellicist approaches be correct, attempts by domestic political actors to both concentrate as well as accumulate capital and coercion in reaction to changes the security environment should lead to changes in state form. As in the case of the institutional commitment argument, this development should take place without having much to do with outside intervention. If dynamics posited by the capitalised coercion approach play out empirically in fragile polities, that presents another challenge to my thesis.

THEORY TESTING

To test my claims, I examine state formation processes in China, the Netherlands Indies/Indonesia, and Siam/Thailand diachronically and synchronically. I adopt within-case diachronic comparisons to examine the effects resulting from changes in expectations amongst foreign actors and aggregated patterns of intervention. This enables me to isolate and trace the consequences of shifts on my explanatory and intervening variables, whilst taking key factors identified by alternative explanations into account. As institutional outcomes on governance and political authority differ at start and end, diachronic comparisons follow the logic of the "method of difference" to highlight causal effects.

Using cross-case synchronic comparisons when looking across the cases of China, Indonesia, and Thailand, I analyse why and how state organisation in these three polities moved toward sovereign statehood *when* they did. This would be during the mid twentieth century for China and Indonesia, and at the end of the nineteenth century for Thailand. Such an adaptation of the "method of agreement" allows me to highlight the dynamics leading to a convergence in institutional outcomes despite cultural and historical dissimilarities. By allowing for variation on factors other than opportunity costs and the aggregated configuration of outside intervention, I can explore key variables behind sovereign state formation in China and Indonesia. This may help to mitigate potential selection biases.

In subjecting the evidence from each case to a series of "standardised, general questions", I focus on evaluating the different possible causal processes that may explain outcomes on state form in my three cases.[50] Hendrik Spruyt notes that such a method is "appropriate when the number of cases is limited and many explanations appear possible".[51] This approach is particularly suited for this study given the number of competing claims about changes of state form in China, Indonesia, and Thailand between the late nineteenth and mid twentieth

[49] Tilly, 1990, 15, 181–87.
[50] George, 1979, 60. For the list of questions I use, see Appendix A.
[51] Spruyt, 2005, 34–36.

centuries. Note that my analysis concentrates on opportunity cost expectations, access denial strategies, and other considerations *leading up to* intervention efforts in a target polity by each relevant outside actor.

Another merit of looking at these three polities across the 1893–1921 and 1922–1951 periods are that they present strong "least-likely" cases for my argument. Many attribute China's political weakness and division to foreign rapaciousness during a "century of humiliation" beginning with the 1839–1842 Opium War, and its development of sovereignty as an indigenous people "standing up" to such pressures. Observers often cast Indonesia's colonial subjugation through World War II and its movement to independence thereafter in similar terms. Alternatively, others tend to see Thailand's ability to remain free from formal foreign subjection as an early example of successful resistance to external ambitions through local cultivation of sovereign statehood. If I can make a good case that variations in foreign intervention were integral to these developments, this would raise confidence in the plausibility of my position and suggest ways to extend my argument.

In this respect, examining the Chinese experience in detail may prove particularly useful. The variety and forcefulness of alternative accounts purporting to explain China's limited fragmentation in the late nineteenth and early twentieth centuries, as well as the rise of a sovereign Chinese state after World War II, make it an especially hard case for me to explain. These range from China's dynastic cycle and culture to the emergence of nationalism and the fundamental restructuring of the social and economic order.[52] Further, the wealth of recently available archival material and secondary historical work on China during these periods provides ample new evidence to evaluate both my argument and prevailing perspectives. An in-depth assessment of the China case may contribute significantly to illustrate specific dynamics in the state formation processes of fragile states and to advance understandings about the history of intervention in an important polity.

STATE FORM AND PERSPECTIVES ON SYSTEMS CHANGE

In exploring changes in state form, I engage parts of the "new sovereignty" literature that explores possibilities for systems change.[53] Much work in this area focuses on normative and ideational issues. I do not deny the importance of such factors, although I focus more on institutional features when I consider states and state formation. In this regard, I hope to make the case that more "traditional" factors – competition amongst external powers and domestic political struggles – remain significant for understanding shifts in state form and systems change.

---

[52] Chiang, 1943; Hu, 1991; Johnson, 1962; Lei, 1968; Skocpol, 1979; Sun, 1945.

[53] Following Robert Gilpin, I take systems change to mean a change in the fundamental nature of the system of world politics. This obviously includes transformations in the basic units that constitute the system. Gilpin, 1981, 41–42. For a review of the "new sovereignty" literature, see Vu, 2010.

Imposing States

By limiting my study to changes in state form from the end of the nineteenth to the first half of the twentieth century, I acknowledge that I do not fully account for the full range of possibilities for nonlinear change. Causes for change in state form earlier in history may not be the same ones driving similar kinds of shifts in a different period, or under a different scope of conditions. Forces behind the emergence of one state form may also differ from those that sustain its existence or account for later strengthening.[54]

By explicitly examining the influence of competition amongst outside powers on domestic politics and the reformulation of the institutional nature of a state, I am trying to add more subtlety to accounts of sovereign state creation in weak states. This augments nationalist perspectives on sovereign state-making that may downplay the full extent of relationships between local actors and outside powers intervening in the polity. Such explanations of sovereign state creation are understandably most prevalent amongst postcolonial polities in the global periphery, given the desires of postindependence elites for postrevolutionary legitimation and mobilisation. Since indigenous nationalist groups were already politically prominent in the cases I consider since at least the late nineteenth century, it may be that nationalism was necessary, but insufficient, for sovereign state creation.

Through an examination of various institutional forms of the state, I further engage the body of work on systems change that examines transformations in the institutional structures that characterise the nature of the "basic" political unit in international relations. My second-image reversed approach attempts to augment explanations of change in state form by highlighting the interactions amongst systemic conditions, external actors, local political groups, and domestic politics. This may illustrate alternative pathways to change in state form under different conditions as well as the contingency of such developments. In this respect, my research speaks to current realities, since outside intervention as well as state-building seem to be persistent features of world politics.

[54] Spruyt, 1994, 20–21.

CHAPTER 3

Feudalising the Chinese Polity, 1893–1922

Assessing the Adequacy of Alternative Takes on State Reorganisation[1]

What is remarkable about China during the late nineteenth and early twentieth centuries is that it held together. It seemed that the polity was hurtling toward disintegration under various internal and external pressures. Population expansion coupled with rebellions, natural disasters, and an erosion of central government capabilities appeared to be pushing at the seams from within.[2] From without, foreign powers looked set to partition the Chinese polity the way they divided much of Africa and Asia. How, then, did the late Qing and early Republican governments maintain sufficient political unity to provide for the later development of a politically centralised, territorially exclusive, and externally autonomous sovereign Chinese state in spite of these forces?

I argue that the key to China's resilience against complete disintegration between the end of the nineteenth century and the first two decades of the twentieth lay in the nature of external competition over and intervention into the polity. That foreign governments active in and around China saw it as an area of secondary import, not worth major armed conflict, brought simultaneous external financial, economic, and military backing for both the central government and various regional regimes. This dynamic kept China whole even as it deepened fractures across the country. It also preserved external autonomy whilst giving foreign powers oversight in certain areas of domestic governance.

That external intervention helped hold China together did not exclude it from contributing to the breakdown in territorial exclusivity and central government rule. The peculiarities of major power competition over the Chinese polity produced two countervailing forces. To exclude rivals from regions of interest, powers like Germany, Japan, Russia, and France extended financial aid, military assistance, and political support to various regional actors in return for a degree of oversight over economic and security matters. These arrangements gave local political agents the wherewithal to stand up to the central government, whether it was under the Qing court or a militarist clique. Simultaneously, largely British

---

[1] This chapter builds on Chong, 2009.
[2] Kuhn, 2002; Luo, 1997; Michael, 1964.

Feudalising the Chinese Polity, 1893–1922   47

and American efforts to avoid disadvantaged access vis-à-vis other major powers saw the provision of financial, material, and political support to those holding sway in the capital. This helped preserve central government rule, limit foreign roles in governance, and sustain China's outward autonomy.

China from 1893 to 1922 provides a particularly apt case to test my argument on external intervention and state formation, since common perspectives see intervention as an unlikely explanation for the polity's survival during that time. After all, the period from the 1894–1895 Sino-Japanese War to the conclusion of the 1921 Washington Conference supposedly represents a high watermark for China's division and subjugation by foreign powers. Many see the Chinese polity's ability to weather such pressures as a standard case for the force of nationalism and common identity. In trying to look at the state as a whole, I recognise that I am trading off important nuances underscored by excellent scholarship on various parts of China. Nonetheless, this approach permits me to explore changes to the polity's general configuration of governance, authority, and rule.

The aims of this chapter are threefold. Its first task is to clarify changes to state form in China from 1893 to 1922. Second, the chapter will establish where existing perspectives on state formation leave off in explaining the China case. Finally, the last section of the chapter will suggest where an account that takes seriously the roles of external intervention and competition amongst outside actors might begin. Rather than a causal explanation, that section provides the groundwork for a closer examination of the relationship between collective external intervention efforts and China's feudalisation in the next chapter.

"SEMICOLONIALISM", FEUDALISATION, AND THE LIMITS OF DISINTEGRATION

China's feudalisation in the late nineteenth and early twentieth centuries was an amplification of fragmentary processes that arguably began late in the eighteenth century.[3] Despite the intensity of domestic and external pressures, central government authority remained intact, even if highly circumscribed. This period also witnessed an expansion in foreign management of commercial activity and the establishment of small leasehold territories along the coast, although Chinese central governments retained their ability to conduct foreign affairs without external oversight. Such developments run counter to straightforward understandings about the division of China as well as the polity's susceptibility to foreign pressure in the late Qing and early Republican periods. In the end, if disintegrative forces were so strong, why China did avert complete collapse and subjugation?

---

[3] Kuhn, 1980, 1–36, 211–25; Luo, 1997; McCord, 1993, 17–45; Michael, 1964; Min, Kuhn, and Brook, 1989; Remick, 2004, 29–37.

Fragmentation and Central Government Authority

To address the host of political, administrative, military, fiscal, and foreign policy problems buffeting its rule from the mid nineteenth century on, the Qing imperial court looked increasingly toward regions and provinces to help bear the burden for reform. The court hoped that decentralising everything from military reform to revenue extraction and even suppressing rebellions could provide the central government some relief from the financial obligations of governance.[4] Devolution, however, spelt disproportionate gains in administrative efficiencies and capacities that benefited provinces and regions more than the imperial government. Even though these reforms aimed to save the empire, the fact that regions and provinces were growing in their independent ability to enact and execute policy softened the ground for an erosion of Beijing's rule.

By the turn of the twentieth century, most regions and even individual provinces were largely responsible for managing their own tax bases.[5] Indeed, local collections of the land tax provided the bulk of revenues for regional and provincial governments both in the late Qing and the early Republican periods.[6] Local regimes could further independently raise "emergency" taxes such as the *pingzhai* or *tankuan* to supplement their income. Notably, although tax remittances to Beijing from some of the richer provinces continued intermittently, especially before 1911, this reflected residual central authority rather than Beijing's ability to coerce regional regimes or extract from local populations directly.[7]

Some more prosperous regions even developed heavy industry and modern arsenals with foreign assistance to meet the economic and military needs of their reform programmes. This was despite official restrictions on regions and provinces taking foreign loans.[8] Governors and governors-general enjoyed such leeway to accumulate capital because administrative changes since the mid nineteenth century left the Qing court with limited direct oversight in, much less active responsibility for, provincial and regional governance.[9]

The growing autonomy of regions and provinces extended to external affairs. As the Boxer episode played out in 1899 and 1900, the foreign powers jointly invaded and occupied areas around Beijing in response to a declaration of war by the Qing court and the unrest caused by Boxer groups. However, governors-

---

[4] Hu and Dai, 1998, 400–05; Kuhn, 2002, 1–24, 114–35; McCord, 1993, 80–118; Richardson, 1999, 88–89.

[5] Billingsley, 1981, 267–71; Duara, 1987, 132–58; McCord, 1993, 17–45, 80–118, 161–204, 272–74; Remick, 2004, 32–39; van de Ven, 1996, 829–68.

[6] Chi, 1976, 152–53; Duara, 1987, 132–58; McCord, 1993, 82, 92, 126–27, 140.

[7] The Qing court used part of the monies sent from the richer provinces to subsidise poorer locales, helping to shore up the central government's position in these areas. Chi, 1976, 167; Hu and Dai, 1998, 400–05; Kuhn, 1980, 211–25, 2002, 114–35; McCord, 1993, 17–45, 80–118; Scalapino and Yu, 1985, 72–277; Sheridan, 1975, 32–40; van de Ven, 1996, 829–68.

[8] Horowitz, 2006, 559–61; Wong, 1997, 155–56; Wright, 1927; Xu, 1962; AS 03/20, collected documents, telegrams, and letters, "Gesheng jiekuan", 1913–1923.

[9] Duara, 1987, 132–58; Scalapino and Yu, 1985, 271–302; van de Ven, 1996, 829–68.

Feudalising the Chinese Polity, 1893–1922

general in central and south China were able to make a separate peace, known as the *Dongnan hubao yundong*, or Southeast Mutual Protection Movement, with the intervening powers.[10] Under the pact, governors and governors-general in south and central China protected the life and property of foreign nationals by controlling and suppressing the Boxers in return for nonintervention.

Through the *Dongnan hubao*, regional administrations in south and central China avoided the invasions and occupations that befell north China. By doing so, these provincial and regional officials departed from the imperial decree to support the Boxers and declare war on all foreign powers active in China, highlighting the capacity of regional and provincial authorities to act independently of the central government.[11] Beijing's inability to rein in administrations in south and central China signalled a decline of imperial control.

For all the decentralisation of government capacities, the Qing court managed to maintain a degree of authority over regional and provincial administrations until the 1911 Revolution, in part due to the personal loyalties of various governors and governors-general. I distinguish authority – influence over and the acknowledged submission of subordinates – from capability – the ability to pursue and implement a certain course of action.[12] So long as Qing authority persisted, power-holders in Beijing – like the Empress Dowager, Cixi, and the Prince Regent, Zai Feng – could change and remove top officials in various localities. Zai Feng and his associates even managed to force an official as important as Yuan Shikai, then-Governor-General of Zhili and Beiyang Minister, into retirement after Cixi's death.[13]

Nevertheless, central government rule in the final years of the Qing became highly dependent on the institutional capacities of various regional and provincial administrations as well as their continued deference to the court. The breakdown of imperial authority following the Wuchang Uprising in 1911, therefore, triggered the collapse of the Qing government.[14] As regional and provincial governments declared independence from the court in late 1911, the Qing court found continued survival increasingly untenable. The final push came when Beiyang military officials, allegedly instigated by Yuan Shikai, indicated their inability to defend the court in a memorial to the Prince Regent.[15] This forced the

---

[10] Hunt, 1983, 194; Lin, 1980, 1–6, 52–134; Twitchett and Fairbank, 1978, 123–24; Wang, 1989, 168–76.

[11] The leaders of the *Dongnan hubao* essentially claimed the imperial decree declaring support for the Boxers and war against the foreign powers to be inauthentic. Heading the movement were some of the most important Qing officials of the day, including Li Hongzhang, Zhang Zhidong, Liu Kunyi, Xu Yingji, Kui Jun, Sheng Xuanhuai, and Yuan Shikai. Li later became the court-appointed negotiator in talks with the foreign powers after the Boxer episode, while 1901 saw Yuan's promotion to Zhili Governor-General and Beiyang Minister. Lin, 1980, 40, 52–134; Wang, 1989, 168–76.

[12] For more extensive treatments of subtle, but highly critical differences between authority, capability, and their relationship with power, see discussions in Arendt, 1970, 35–56; Lukes, 1986.

[13] MacKinnon, 1980, 205–12.

[14] Chan, 1971, 360; McCord, 1993, 66–77, 80–87; Scalapino and Yu, 1985, 260–320; Sheridan, 1975, 34–52.

[15] FHAC 4/239/533, Duan Qirui *et al.* to the Qing Cabinet, "Shou jiaofu shiyi Diyi Jun zongtong guan Duan Qirui deng dian neige", 1911 December; Tang, 2004, 19–28; Wang, 1979, 246–47.

50 *External Intervention and the Politics of State Formation*

Qing court to announce the Xuantong Emperor's abdication and the Empire's dissolution.

The erosion of central rule in the late Qing period spurred further political fragmentation in China following the fall of the empire.[16] Even as Yuan Shikai attempted to reestablish central authority and control after coming to power as President in 1912, regions and provinces provided much of the capacity for an anti-Yuan opposition. Provincial leaders like Jiangxi's Li Liejun and Yunnan's Cai E supplied military forces and leadership to the 1913 Second Revolution against Yuan as well as the Anti-Yuan Campaign of 1916.[17] Following the Second Revolution's failure, Sun Yat-sen and the Nationalists were similarly able to continue their anti-Yuan efforts with help from regional leaders in south China.[18]

Yuan Shikai's ability to install himself into the presidency likewise rested on the support he was able to muster from military leaders and officials in regions and provinces that submitted to his command. It was with the support of forces led by former Beiyang subordinates like Duan Qirui and others that Yuan managed to install himself as president, as well as defeat opponents like those behind the Second Revolution.[19] Yet, when regional and provincial leaders either opposed or shied away from fully supporting Yuan's attempt to enthrone himself as emperor in 1916, Yuan had to annul his ascension.[20] Even at the height of his power, Yuan's central government did not possess unquestioned authority in, much less direct control over, vast areas of China.

With Yuan Shikai's death in 1916, the political fragmentation of the Chinese polity became more extensive even if central government rule persisted, albeit nominally. Without their leader, Yuan's former subordinates and supporters began to assert their own regional, provincial, and local prerogatives even more. Consequently, regional and provincial militarist cliques took on greater prominence.[21] This was despite the fact they still formally acknowledged the preeminence of Beijing central government.[22]

These militarist cliques and their members generally worked to guard and expand areas under their control. Militarist cliques, especially those in north and

---

The term used by the various provinces to declare separation from the Qing court was *duli*, literally "independence".

[16] McCord, 1993, 44–45; Rankin, 1997, 263–74; van de Ven 1997, 357–61.

[17] van de Ven, 1996, 357.

[18] Ch'en, 1968.

[19] Chi, 1976, 15–16, 151; Scalapino and Yu, 1985, 351–89; Tang, 2004, 65–85.

[20] Scalapino and Yu, 1985, 413–18; Tang, 2004, 190–207; Twitchett and Fairbank, 1978, Vol. 12, 249–54.

[21] Ch'en, 1968, 563–600; Chi, 1976, 10–76; Nathan, 1976, 44–58, 226–61; Pye, 1971, 13–59; Scalapino and Yu, 1985, 405–85; Sheridan, 1975, 57–106. For more on different cliques and regional administrations, see, for example, works by Jerome Ch'en, Leslie Chen, Andrew Forbes, Donald Gillin, HE Deqian, Winston Hsieh, Robert Kapp, LAI Xinxia, Diana Lary, LIU Jingzhong, Akira Mizuno, SHAO Weiguo, SHEN Yunlong, James Sheridan, Donald Sutton, TIAN Bofu, Arthur Waldron, WANG Xiaohua, WEN Fei, Allen Whiting, Odoric Wou, Ernest Young, ZHENG Liangsheng, ZHU Hongyuan, as well as the biographies and autobiographies of various militarists.

[22] Li, 2000, 389–98; Pye, 1971, 3–12, 77–153.

Feudalising the Chinese Polity, 1893–1922

central China, would also attempt to seize Beijing in order to access additional revenues from foreign loans, as well as funds left over from foreign administered customs duties after the servicing of external debt.[23] These were among the main prizes that victory in the many wars between different militarist cliques during the 1910s and 1920s seemed to promise.[24]

Militarist cliques in south China likewise fought over territory and resources. Examples include conflicts between the Yunnan, Sichuan, and Hunan militarists, as well as between the militarists controlling Jiangxi and Fujian.[25] Relying as they did on the support of various militarists, these conflicts often embroiled the Nationalists as well. Sun Yat-sen and the Nationalists depended on Chen Jiongming to seize Guangzhou in 1917 when setting up the southern Guangzhou National Government to rival Beijing.[26] When Chen and Sun had a falling out in 1920, the Nationalists allied themselves with the Guangxi Clique to expel Chen from Guangzhou in 1922.[27]

Relations within various militarist cliques too were far from unproblematic. Allies often defected and subordinates, in many instances, turned against their ostensible superiors.[28] Importantly, such realignments could determine the outcome of major conflicts. Liu Xun's unwillingness to pit his forces against his old Zhili Clique allies, for instance, contributed to the defeat of the Anfu Clique in the Zhili-Anfu War of 1920.[29] Feng Yuxiang's defection in the Second Zhili-Fengtian War of 1924 was key in the defeat of Zhili forces and the rise of the Fengtian Clique to national prominence.[30] Even the Nationalists were prone to severe internal divisions. A major reason for ongoing Nationalist reorganisation efforts after 1912 was to address the many serious party splits that emerged following Yuan Shikai's bid for absolute power.[31] This instability in relations amongst and within various political groupings is indicative of the extent of fractures in authority.

Territorial Exclusivity and Foreign Administration

Apart from the obvious decline in political centralisation, the years between 1893 and 1922 witnessed an erosion of China's territorial exclusivity. Despite the fact that much of China's territory and population largely remained under

---

[23] Chi, 1976, 153–60; Nathan, 1976, 59–64; Pye, 1971, 77–166.
[24] Chi, 1976, 153–60; Nathan, 1976, 59–64; Pye, 1971, 21–23, 132–53; Scalapino and Yu, 1985, 426–51, 463–77; Sheridan, 1966, 120–48.
[25] Chi, 1976, 207–08; Pye, 1971, 13–38.
[26] Chen, 1999, 47–163.
[27] Chi, 1976, 215; Lary, 1974, 58–63; Nathan, 1976, 201, 205.
[28] Billingsley, 1981, 235–84; McCord, 1993, 33–45, 220–27, 251–52; Pye, 1971, 13–59, 77–112, 132–53.
[29] Guo, 2003, 87–88; Pye, 1971, 18–21.
[30] Gillin, 1967, 23–24; Guo, 2003, 317–52; Pye, 25–31; Sheridan, 1966, 132–47; Van de Ven, 2003, 77–85; Waldron, 1995, 117–18, 181–207.
[31] McCord, 1993, 164–72; Nathan, 1976, 59–90.

indigenous rule, external actors managed important aspects of domestic governance. The British were essentially in charge of China's Maritime Customs Service since the 1850s, whilst the French and others administered various parts of the Salt Gabelle in areas under their sway.[32] These foreign-run military and police forces controlled and protected major lines of communication, such as the South Manchurian Railway and the Yangzi River.[33]

Due to the granting of extraterritoriality from the mid nineteenth century on, authorities in China had no legal jurisdiction over foreign nationals in the polity. In carving out spheres of influence, various foreign powers also were able to maintain special, and often semiexclusive, economic and political prerogatives over much of China. Foreign law courts even enjoyed final jurisdiction over Chinese nationals living within externally administered regions of China. Such exclusive political and economic privileges were evident in the Japanese, Russian, and French spheres of influence respectively in northeast, northwest, and southwest China, just as they were in German-dominated Shandong. Even the British enjoyed similar concessions in the Lower Yangzi despite not claiming a formal sphere of influence.[34]

External Autonomy and China's Diplomatic Independence

Various internal and external pressures notwithstanding, the Chinese polity managed to retain moderate to high degrees of external autonomy between 1893 and 1922. Central governments from the Qing court and the Nanjing Provisional Government to the Beijing Government of Yuan Shikai, the various Beiyang regimes, and even the Guangzhou National Government were able to avoid being subordinate to any other government or authority outside China.[35]

---

[32] Scalapino and Yu, 1985, 64–65; Spence, 1969, 93–128; KMTPA *Benbu* 13299.2, "British Imperialism in China", 1924, November 18.

[33] Given their administration of the Customs Service, the British oversaw navigation, custom duties and collection, as well as security along the Yangzi. Lian, 2004, 177–324; Scalapino and Yu, 1985, 64, 477–78; Spence, 1969, 93–128; KMTPA *Benbu* 13299.2, "British Imperialism in China"; AS 03/05/047, "Nan Man tielu"; AS 03/05/053, "Ji Chang tielu jiekuan", 1916; AS 03/05/049, "Si-Tao tielu jiekuan'an", 1922.

[34] In 1898, the Qing court formally agreed not to alienate British interests in the Lower Yangzi in favour of any other external power. This arrangement did not guarantee British access regulation over the region as in the case of agreements with other powers. Chan, 1971, 356–58; Kennan, 1984, 22–37; Sun, 1954, 27–48, 120–41; Wang, 1979, 76–115; KMTPA *Benbu* 13299.2, "British Imperialism in China"; AS 03/05/035/01, "Hu-Hang-Jiao, Tong-Qing tielu jiekuan", 1912–1913; AS 03/20/041, Correspondence amongst the Foreign Ministry, Finance Ministry, Japanese Embassy, Agents in Guangzhou, and others, "Min Yue jiekuan'an", 1921; AS 03/20/045, Correspondence amongst the Finance Ministry, Foreign Ministry, British Consulate and others, "Wan sheng Yida yanghang jiekuan", 1917; AS 03/23/134, Foreign Ministry Documents, "Zhong Ying xiuyue digao", 1914–1908.

[35] The various militarist regimes controlling Beijing between Yuan Shikai's death in 1916 and the end of the Northern Expedition in 1928 are collectively termed the "Beiyang Government".

Feudalising the Chinese Polity, 1893–1922

Successive central Chinese governments were even able to represent the polity as an independent actor in the international arena in the face of external pressure. Despite its debt and indemnity obligations, for instance, the Qing court was able to come to its own disastrous decision to declare war on the foreign powers during the Boxer episode. Xu Shichang's government in Beijing could likewise declare war on and make peace with the Central Powers on its own accord during World War I.

Rival claimants to leadership of the central government too managed to create joint missions to represent China in major international conferences such as the Versailles Conference in 1919.[36] As an independent diplomatic actor, representatives of China were able to withhold official recognition of Japanese attempts to occupy Shandong at the Paris Peace Conference.[37] They even managed to elicit support for a withdrawal of Japanese military forces from Shandong at the end of the Washington Conference.

Through its representatives at the convention in Washington, China also managed to acquire *de jure* recognition of her borders from the major powers of the day.[38] As a member of the League of Nations, the Chinese government also secured a degree of international aid and technical assistance.[39] For all its internal turmoil, therefore, China from 1893 to 1922 remained a fully independent corporate actor in world politics.

China as a Feudalised State

Accordingly, the time between 1893 and 1922 marked the feudalisation of the Chinese polity from what was an already decaying imperial state. These three decades witnessed the height of political decentralisation within China, with regional, provincial, and even subprovincial authorities being able to assert ever-increasing political, military, and economic autonomy at the expense of central control. The period too saw the continuation and expansion of foreign administration over key areas of governance in China. Figure 3.1 and the maps shown here approximate variations in state form, my dependent variable.[40]

---

[36] The Chinese mission to the Versailles Peace Conference consisted of representatives of both Xu Shichang's Northern (or Beiyang) Government as well as the Southern Military Government led by the Nationalist Party. The Southern Military Government is also known as the Guangzhou National Government. Koo and Zhongguo shehuikexueyuan. Jindaishi yanjiusuo, 1983, 172–82; Shi, 1994, 151–54, 274–83; SHAC 1039/399 "Zhongguo duiwai zhengce"; AS 03/37/012 "Hehui huiyi jilu", January 1919; AS 03/37/013 "Hehui jishi ji shuotie", February 1919— March 1920; AS 03/37/012/03, "Daibiaotuan ji Dahui renminglu", February 1919; KMTPA *Huanlong Lu* 14006, Wu Tingfang to Tang Shaoyi and Xu Shichang, "Wei Ouzhou heping huiyi shuangfang hui pai daibiao shi".

[37] Nathan, 1976, 3, 158–62; Tang, 1998, 69–81; SHAC 18/3285, "Youguan Bali hehui jianbao", 1946; SHAC 18/3516, "Zhongguo xiwang tiaoyue", May 14, 1919.

[38] Li, 1989, 1–73, 1990, 1–50.

[39] Tang, 1998, 285–347.

[40] Map sources: Wu, 1999; Zhang, 1984; Zhongguo ditu and Xinhai geming Wuchang qiyi, 1991.

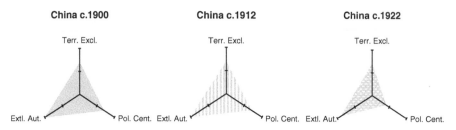

FIGURE 3.1 Feudalising the Chinese Polity, 1900–1922

MAP 1 Chinese Polity under Direct Qing Jurisdiction, c.1893

Given the state of political fragmentation in early twentieth-century China, observers note that the polity resembled world politics more than domestic politics. Historian Lei Haizong characterised China's political structure during this period as a return to the Spring and Autumn and Warring States system of antiquity.[41] Ch'i Hsi-sheng observed that the "Chinese political system of this

---

[41] Chen, 1941, 7–19; He, 1940, 37–42, 1942, 1–8; Hong, 1941, 1–5; Lei 1934, 1941, 1–6; Lin, 1940, 1–8; Lin and Lei, 1971; Nankai daxue. Lishi xueyuan, 2005.

Feudalising the Chinese Polity, 1893–1922

MAP 2 Militarist and Other Regimes in China, c.1917

period more closely resembled an international system than a national system".[42] Certainly, the hold that regional and provincial authorities enjoyed over both internal and external governance made them seem more like independent actors than subordinates of a central government.

All these developments took place in spite of the fact that China's central government maintained nearly singular diplomatic representation regardless of the regime in power, and did so without having to answer to a higher external authority. Likewise, central government rule remained ostensibly unbroken throughout the period despite regular changes in who wielded power in the Beijing. Given the low to moderate levels of political centralisation and territorial exclusivity coupled with a high degree of external autonomy, state form in late-nineteenth- and early-twentieth-century China resembled the feudalised pre-Capetian France and Holy Roman Empire.

CHINA'S FEUDALISATION, COMPETING ACCOUNTS

Extant theories of state formation offer several ways to understand China's feudalisation between the late nineteenth and early twentieth centuries. Even

[42] Chi, 1976, 202.

56 *External Intervention and the Politics of State Formation*

though there is much truth in these accounts, they tend to provide only partial pictures of how the Chinese polity came to experience limited political central- isation and territorial exclusivity alongside substantial external autonomy. This leaves key elements in China's feudalisation from 1893 to 1922 underexplained. By engaging existing explanations, this section underscores the need to take seriously the role that external intervention played in feudalising the Chinese state.

Nationalism and Self-Determination

Nationalism and self-determination offer some promise in laying out the feudal- isation of late Qing and early Republican China, especially the concurrent existence of fragmentary and centralising tendencies. A sense of common iden- tity along with a belief in self-determination could motivate regional leaders, militarist cliques, and political parties to resist erosion of central rule in the face of internal and external pressures. Such sentiments may lead local actors to try to limit foreign involvement in domestic governance and to preserve the polity's external autonomy. Nonetheless, the inability of local actors to resolve differ- ences over parochial interests impeded the attainment of shared goals, and fuelled feudalisation. Nationalist and self-determination arguments do less well in addressing the willingness of local political actors to seek foreign support at the expense of territoriality, autonomy, and even centralisation.

It is certainly possible to make a strong initial case for the force of nationalism and self-determination norms. Efforts by Yuan Shikai, Duan Qirui, Sun Yat-sen and the Nationalists, and the intellectuals of the May Fourth Movement to push for greater centralisation, exclusivity, and autonomy may be consistent with beliefs in national self-determination.[43] Attempts by nationalist revolutionaries to replace the Qing court with a republic, late Qing efforts to maintain the empire, and the 1912 power grab by Yuan Shikai and his Beiyang allies all aimed to create a sovereign Chinese state. Regionally based regimes – especially those based in north and central China – such as Duan Qirui's Anfu Club, the Zhili Clique, and Zhang Zuolin's Fengtian Clique arguably sought to expand their hold over China to do the same.[44] Such actors consistently supported central government rule and external autonomy.

Along these lines, the Qing court and the various Beiyang governments established after Yuan's death tried to expand political and economic control across China. Efforts to whittle away the political foundations, financial base, and administrative autonomy of rivals outside Beijing included attempts control taxation, external relations, foreign borrowing, and the funding and arming of military forces.[45] The Qing court's retirement of Yuan Shikai in 1908 is

---

[43] Chi, 1976, 190–95; Nathan, 1976, 158–62; Pye, 1971, 113–31; Scalapino and Yu, 1985, 451–63, 486–626; Usui and Chen, 1990, 1–3, 39–51, 88–118, 216–27, 277–361.

[44] Chan, 1982, 1–43; Chi, 1976, 190–95; Nathan, 1976, 91–220.

[45] Nathan, 1976, 60–90.

Feudalising the Chinese Polity, 1893–1922

representative of such efforts.[46] Xu Shichang's attempt to broker a negotiated settlement between feuding militarists in north and south China that would unite them under his presidency also exemplifies such political manoeuvring.[47]

Concurrently, the promise of being able to reconstitute the entire polity according to their aspirations encouraged actors out of power at the centre to respect at least nominal authority and avoid permanently dividing China. Hence, many political groups shied away from separating areas under their sway from the rest of China even when under pressure from the central government. This was as true of the Nationalists when they established the Guangzhou National Government to rival Beijing, as it was of the Anfu, Zhili, Fengtian, and other militarist cliques when they did not control the central government.

However, following the nationalist and self-determination logics, local disagreements over who was to lead a unified state, determine the domestic distribution of surpluses, and represent China internationally could also stymie any move toward sovereign statehood. The vision of creating sovereign statehood in the late Qing and early Republican periods led to clashes amongst political actors in China, exacerbating political divisions even if it preserved nominal central government rule. That many political actors were unwilling to see others rule a sovereign Chinese state brought stiff resistance to attempts to create strong central government rule. This dynamic is clear in the tensions between the Nationalist-led southern government and the northern governments of Yuan Shikai, Duan Qirui, and Li Yuanhong as well as between Sun Yat-sen and his erstwhile ally, Chen Jiongming.[48] It is also evident in intraregional conflicts like the 1917 North-South War, the 1920 Zhili-Anfu War, the 1920 and 1924 Fengtian-Zhili Wars, and Zhang Xun's 1917 Qing Restoration attempt.[49]

In spite of any sincere belief in nationalist and self-determination ideals, political actors also did not wish to lose control of the locales they held and the ability to manage the distribution of surpluses in these areas. Groups were ready to resort to arms to protect such privileges. This moved many provincial and regional regimes to defy the writ of the central government, as seen in the 1913 Second Revolution and the 1916 Anti-Yuan Campaign against the Yuan Shikai government.[50] This desire of local regimes to resist encroachments on their prerogatives is also clear in the broad provincial and regional opposition to Zhang Xun's 1917 attempt to restore Qing rule.

It is possible to see Chen Jiongming's decision to turn against Sun Yat-sen and the Nationalists in 1922 as driven by a desire to maintain local prerogatives as well. If Sun and the Kuomintang succeeded in creating a strong central government under their leadership, one of the first things to go would be Chen's

[46] MacKinnon, 1980.
[47] Chan, 1982, 31–43; Nathan, 1976, 138–58.
[48] Chi, 1976, 207–15; Nathan, 1976, 201–05; Pye, 1971, 16–23.
[49] Chan, 1982, 9–30; Chi, 1976, 16–17; Nathan, 1976, 91–92.
[50] McCord, 1993, 205–44.

58   *External Intervention and the Politics of State Formation*

hold over Guangdong and southern Fujian. Accordingly, the Nationalist ascendancy helped give rise to Chen's vehement defence of a federalist ideal that afforded regional administrations significant political and economic privileges.[51] Wars amongst regimes in Guangxi, Yunnan, Sichuan, and Hunan were similarly efforts to secure local surpluses as well as other advantages from control of a population and geographic space.[52] Even Yan Xishan's assiduous avoidance of entanglement in national-level politics was to maintain his hold over Shanxi.[53]

In not attending fully to how various groups acquired the ability to affect domestic politics, the picture of China's feudalisation presented by nationalism and self-determination remains incomplete. Since ideology alone does not produce financing, weapons, training, or organisational capacity, the effectiveness of nationalism and self-determination in state formation processes may require the presence of other forces. Moreover, when considering funding, arms, and military training, almost all groups – including those with explicit nationalist agendas – readily sacrificed national interests to secure advantages vis-à-vis their domestic opponents.[54] So long as actors could enhance their capacity to maintain and extend control over parts of China and the surpluses they promised, almost anything seemed negotiable with almost anyone. This is problematic for nationalist and self-determination views, as supposedly patriotic local actors actively and knowingly undercut territorial exclusivity to forward goals that eroded political centralisation.

This trading of benefits went beyond the Anfu Club and Fengtian Clique's well-known acceptance of Japanese oversight over communications, commercial activity, natural resource extraction, and security in Manchuria for military as well as economic assistance.[55] To acquire funds for the Guangzhou National Government, Sun Yat-sen and the Nationalists were as ready to exchange exclusive railroad, mining, forestry, and minting rights for Japanese funding

---

[51] Chen L., 1999, 165–265.

[52] Chan, 1982, 2–13; Chen L., 1999, 47–56, 86–163; Chi, 1976, 15–35, 201–39.

[53] Gillin, 1967, 21–24.

[54] Chi, 1976, 157–58; Nathan, 1976, 61–81; Richardson, 1999, 88–92; Xu, 4–11, 22–58, 98–100; AS 03/02/090, "Youdian jiaoshe", 1914, AS 03/20/045, "Wan sheng Yida yanghang jiekuan"; AS 02/04/041, "Shanxi kuangwu", July 1914; AS 03/03/002, "Zhong Mei kuangwu", 1921; AS 03/03/018, "Zhong-Ri kuangwu jiaoshe", 1914, AS 03/03/043, "Kuangwu zaxiang", 1922–1923; AS 03/02/071, "Wuxiandian zajian", October 1917; AS 03/30/24, "Makeni wuxiandian-gongsi jiekuan'an", 1918–1925.

[55] Chi, 1976, 27–33, 120–23, 156–68; Guo, 2003, 9–18, 156–57, 219–27; Usui and Chen, 1990, 145–86, 277–82, 365–83; SHAC 18/3043, Wellington V.K. Koo, "Memorandum on Japan's Plots and Schemes against the Unification of China, Document No. 12, Peiping", June 1932; AS 03/23/031, Correspondence amongst the Foreign, Communications, Army, and Finance Ministries, "Zhong Ri chengyue" 1922–1924; AS 03/20/008, Correspondence amongst the Foreign Ministry, Finance Ministry, Army Ministry, and Wartime Governor's Office, "Zhongyang jiekuan", 1919–1925; AS 03/23/135, Foreign Ministry Documents, "Zhong-Ri tiaoyue huibian", 1916–1919; AS 03/05/049, "Si-Tao tielu jiekuan an", 1922.

Feudalising the Chinese Polity, 1893–1922

and arms as Anfu and Fengtian.[56] The Nationalists too had few qualms about trying to win over British, French, and American aid using similar means.[57]

Likewise, Wang Zhanyuan's regime actively sought accommodation with both the British and Japanese in efforts to control Hubei province, whilst Feng Yuxiang was able to dominate Chahar, Suiyuan, and Sha'anxi provinces by cultivating Soviet support.[58] In these cases, political, military, and financial assistance came at the price of permitting significant foreign influence over economic activity and security. Apart from local gentry, economic elites, and peasants, then, foreign powers were simply another potential partner that political groups could cut deals with – even at the expense of sovereign statehood. Nationalist and self-determination arguments need to explain how such "selling out" to foreign powers is consistent with their position to be fully persuasive.

Exogenous Shocks and Patterns of Political Support

It is possible to make a strong case for structural shocks and corresponding shifts in institutional bargains over the distribution of surpluses as key reasons for China's feudalisation between 1893 and 1922. The burdens created by rapid population growth, natural disasters, internal unrest, and foreign pressure since the early nineteenth century led the Qing court to embark on a process of administrative decentralisation to sustain the empire. By increasing the administrative, economic, and military wherewithal of the regional and provincial governments, Qing rulers also laid the groundwork for later challenges to central rule. Nevertheless, this perspective says little about the simultaneous persistence of political centralisation, enduring external autonomy, and the serious, but limited, erosion of territorial exclusivity. Moreover, the fluidity of domestic political support amongst different segments of Chinese society at the time

---

[56] Jansen, 1954; Usui and Chen, 1990, 3–6; Xu, 1962, 224–29; AS 03/20/039, "Gesheng jiekuan", 1923; AS 03/20/042, "Min Yue jiekuan'an", 1922–1924; AS 03/20/041/01/023, Letter from the Office of the *Duban* for War Participation to the Foreign Ministry, "Sun Wen yü Riben Taiping gongsi dijie junqi jiekuan ci shi nengfou shefa jinzu xicha heban liyou", July 1921; AS 03/20/053/ 01/017, "Riren zai Hu shoumai Guangdong Junzhengfu gongzaipiao fu chazhao you", October 1918; SHAC 18/3043, Koo, "Memorandum on Japan's Plots and Schemes against the Unification of China".

[57] Barlow, 1979; Chan, 1982, 32–33; Chi, 1976, 122–23; Huang, 2005, 357–416; Jansen, 1954; Munholland, 1972; Scalapino and Yu, 1985, 223–26; Shen, 2005, 161–62; Zhongguo shehuikexueyuan, 2005, 117–28; KMTPA *Huanlong Lu* 2312, Chen Rongguang to Sun Yat-sen, "Gao Yue caiting weiyuan Lao mou yu Riben mou gongsi ding yue jiekuan, yi Guangzhou dianche lu' wei zuoya", January 28, 1919; SHAC 18/3043, Koo, "Memorandum on Japan's Plots and Schemes against the Unification of China"; AS 03/20/035/03, Correspondence between the Finance and Foreign Ministries, "Er nian gesheng jiekuan'an", 1913; AS 03/20/040, Correspondence amongst the Foreign Ministry, Finance Ministry, Japanese Embassy, and others, "Min Yue jiekuan'an", 1914; AS 03/20/041, "Yue sheng jiekuan'an"; AS 03/20/042, "Min Yue jiekuan'an"; AS 03/20/039/ 04, Correspondence amongst the Foreign Ministry and others, "Min Yue Xiang Dian Su Lu deng sheng shanxing jie waizhai'an", 1913.

[58] McCord, 1993, 237–51, 274–77; Sheridan, 1966, 149–76.

60   *External Intervention and the Politics of State Formation*

makes it difficult to identify the institutionalised arrangements between various political actors, classes, and other segments of society.

According to institutional commitment perspectives, Qing efforts to devolve governance in response to various exogenous shocks facilitated the rise of administrative, coercive, and extractive and revenue-producing capabilities beyond Beijing's direct control.[59] Such circumstances afforded regional and provincial governments substantial autonomy in their actions, even to the extent of being able to contravene the wishes of the central government in Beijing. Accordingly, this rise in regional administrative, economic, and political autonomy enabled regional regimes to strike arms, financing, and political deals with foreign actors that cut against territorial exclusivity, even if Beijing retained its capacity to manage foreign policy.

Focusing on the fragmentary aspects of governance in the late Qing and early Republican periods, however, leaves the persistence of even nominal central government rule unexplained. After all, the logical conclusion of various regions and provinces increasingly pulling away from the centre would be total disintegration. As Edward McCord suggests, broad recognition of Qing authority among regional, provincial, and even local officials existed through the last years of the dynasty even if Beijing lacked the ability to exert direct oversight in most locales.[60] Regional and provincial leaders generally submitted to Qing authority until the Revolution and to Yuan Shikai's presidency during its first years. Titles and positions bestowed on militarist leaders by the central government after the 1911 Revolution even appeared to confer an air of prestige regardless of the regime in Beijing.[61]

Yet, despite the incessant fighting between those in control of the central government and different regional regimes during the early Republican period, attempts to eradicate the central government were notably absent. The Second Revolution, Anti-Yuan Campaign, North-South War, Zhili-Anfu War, and Zhili-Fengtian Wars were conflicts in part over control of the central government rather than its dissolution.[62] In a diminished sense, the authority of the central government persisted into the second decade of the twentieth century under various militarist governments. Institutional commitment perspectives do not sufficiently account for why regional actors did not dismantle central government rule more completely, even if they explain the fragmentary aspects of China's feudalisation.

Further challenging institutional commitment accounts is the noticeable absence of the sorts of long-standing, regularised partnerships amongst political actors and particular social segments that such arguments identify as key to

---

[59] Kuhn, 2002, 1–24, 114–35; Luo, 1997; McCord, 1993, 80–118; Michael, 1964.

[60] McCord, 1993, 17–79.

[61] Chi, 1976, 15–35, 190–95; McCord, 1993, 172–98; Nathan, 1976, 59–90; Sheridan, 1966, 52–54, 84; Waldron, 1991.

[62] Chi, 1976, 153–60; Nathan, 1976, 59–64; Pye, 1971, 13–38, 132–53; Scalapino and Yu, 1985, 426–77; Sheridan, 1966, 120–48, 1975; van de Ven, 1997, 357.

Feudalising the Chinese Polity, 1893–1922

shifts in state form after exogenous shocks. If anything, political groups and members of different social classes proved adept at switching allegiances in light of changing circumstances, complicating efforts to institutionalise relationships. This was despite the fact that structural crises upset preexisting surplus distribution arrangements.

Certainly, nationalist groups drew heavily from an emergent Western-educated professional elite. Many early nationalist leaders, such as Sun Yat-sen and Huang Xing, came from this professional class; Sun was a Western-trained medical doctor, and Huang a Japanese-educated teacher. The many foreign-trained officers within the New Armies in the late Qing period were members of various revolutionary nationalist societies too.[63] Up to perhaps a third of the troops and even more of the officers in Hubei's New Armies belonged to revolutionary groups.[64]

Professional support went beyond nationalists and revolutionaries. Apart from leaders such as Wu Peifu, Duan Qirui, Li Yuanhong, and Feng Guozhang, various militarist cliques also boasted large numbers of modern military professionals.[65] Many civilian professionals also served militarist regimes in Beijing as well as in various provinces and regions. Educator and Chinese Communist Party cofounder, Chen Duxiu, for instance, worked for Guangdong's education system under Chen Jiongming, just as the eminent geologist Ding Wenjiang held various official posts within Sun Chuanfang's regime in the Jiangnan area.[66] Some professionals noted for service in militarist-led Beijing governments are Wellington Koo, Wang Chonghui, and Alfred Sze in the diplomatic corps.[67]

Some nonmilitary professionals even became important powerbrokers in their own right. The Communications and New Communications Cliques, which enjoyed substantial influence over the finances of various Beiyang governments through their roles in banking, railroad, and communications, consisted largely of professional technocrats.[68] Waseda-educated Cao Rulin, a leader of the New Communications Clique, for example, headed the Railroad and Finance Ministries in addition to the semiofficial Bank of Communications as part of several Beiyang cabinets.

As economic modernisation was a largely official effort in China until the early twentieth century, an influential commercial class did not mature until the 1920s. Even then, this emergent commercial class remained small relative to the rest of the population and generally was found in large urban areas along the coast.[69] Actors outside these regions had less opportunity to ally with this segment of society. However, the political persuasion of the commercial class was quite ambivalent.

---

[63] McCord, 1993, 46–79; Shen, 1963.
[64] McCord, 1993, 63.
[65] McCord, 1993, 71; Scalapino and Yu, 1985, 351–53; Shen, 1963; van de Ven, 1997, 356.
[66] Chen L., 1999, 127–28.
[67] Scalapino and Yu, 1985, 355–58.
[68] Nathan, 1976, 239–61.
[69] Richardson, 1999, 25–39; Tang, 1993; Waldron, 1995, 18–19; Zhang, 1996, 1–49.

Business people and commercial concerns worked with actors across the political spectrum, sometimes simultaneously.[70] Even as some business interests in the south assisted the Nationalist Party, others were urging the Feng Guozhang and Li Yuanhong governments in Beijing to take action against the Nationalists.[71] To consolidate their position in Guangdong, the Nationalists even had to suppress widespread opposition from Guangzhou commercial interests that formed an armed militia to resist taxation.[72] During the Zhili-Anfu War, commercial interests generally supported the Wu Peifu-led Zhili Clique rather than Duan Qirui and the Anfu Clique, which controlled the central government in Beijing.[73] Perhaps this political vacillation should not be surprising given the commercial class's need to secure business interests in an environment of constant flux.[74]

Nevertheless, in dealings with political actors, business and commercial concerns played a role in providing some regional and provincial regimes with funding through the purchase of short-term bonds during the late Qing and early Republican periods. Despite the general dearth of information on such transactions, extant studies suggest that short-term debt was an important source of income for many local administrations.[75] However, much of this lending occurred because of speculation, threats, or even coercion, making commercial support often unstable and unpredictable.[76]

Where actors settled into agreements with local social groups, their allies were generally traditional elites and segments of the local population. Apart from being important for establishing order, support from these groups was crucial in providing recruits for the armies of the regional militarist regimes. Traditional elites tended to be landowners and members of the local gentry, as exemplified by the backers of Wang Zhanyuan in Hubei and the many supporters of Yuan Shikai's regime.[77] To dominate regions under their control, the regimes of Yan Xishan in Shanxi, Feng Yuxiang in northwest China, and, to a degree, Zhang Zuolin in Manchuria, worked with peasants, small traditional businesses, and workers.[78] To bolster their political standing the Nationalists similarly cultivated students, workers, landowners, and members of the gentry in localities across China.[79]

Perhaps the only social group that had some political coherence was the overseas Chinese. Members of this group were active in supporting centralising

---

[70] Pye, 1971, 160–66; Yu, 1993, 261–322.

[71] Yu, 1993, 286–91.

[72] Chan, 1982, 106–7; Chi, 1976, 174–75; Huang, 2005, 571–620.

[73] Guo, 2003, 84–86; Yu, 1993, 291–301.

[74] Pye, 1971, 160–66; Tang, 1993; Usui and Chen, 1990, 190; Yu, 1993, 261–322; Zhang, 1996, 249–311.

[75] Chi, 1976, 160–61, 262n26.

[76] Chi, 1976, 160; McCord, 1993, 272–77; Tang, 1993; Zhang, 1996.

[77] Chi, 1976; McCord, 1993, 237–52, 271–73; Nathan, 1976, 18, 100; Skocpol, 1979, 238–42.

[78] Gillin, 1967, 30–102; Nathan, 1976, 100; Sheridan, 1966, 149–76; Skocpol, 1979, 238–42.

[79] Bianco, 1971, 15; Skocpol, 1979, 242–51.

Feudalising the Chinese Polity, 1893–1922

nationalist groups, in terms of both funding and membership.[80] In fact, significant funding for the activities of the various nationalist groups both before and after the 1911 Revolution came from overseas Chinese donations.[81] There was, however, also an important minority amongst overseas Chinese that supported Qing rule. They included reformer Wing Yung (Rong Hong), lawyer and diplomat Wu Tingfang, physician Wu Lien-teh, and philosopher Gu Hongming amongst others.[82] Nevertheless, general physical absence from China and relatively small numbers limited the direct political influence of overseas Chinese.

Popular support for different political actors varied greatly. From militarist cliques to nationalist groups, patterns of support looked similarly mixed and fluid. As a result, institutionalised relationships amongst political groups and different parts of society were difficult to achieve and sustain. For groups competing over the Chinese polity, almost everyone was fair game as targets for soliciting support as and when necessary. This complicates the ability of actors to maintain the kinds of stable, long-term relationships necessary for successful institutionalised arrangements.

Regional Accumulation of Capital and Coercion

Bellicist arguments do well in depicting how political groups in China developed the independent ability to accumulate both capital and the tools of coercion that enabled them to assert increasing autonomy from the central government. Many of the more competitive militarist cliques and political parties maintained their viability on the financial and coercive capabilities initially inherited from nineteenth-century Qing responses to both internal and external security pressures. However, standard bellicist arguments are much better at addressing fragmentation in late Qing and early Republican China than how centralisation and external autonomy persisted alongside eroding territorial exclusivity.

A legacy of Qing reform efforts in the mid nineteenth century was to give regional and provincial regimes an independent means to supplement their income. Central to the Qing's Self-Strengthening Movement was the development

---

[80] There was also overseas Chinese support for the Qing court, the various Beiyang governments, and even particular regional regimes in their home provinces. Scalapino and Yu, 1985, 148–259; Zhang and Chen, 1997; KMTPA *Huanlong Lu* 3550–3551, Commander-in-Chief of Northeastern Forces to Sun Yat-sen, "Nanyang Huaqiao Shituan"; KMTPA *Hankou* 16351.3, Central Executive Committee to Jiang Jieshi, Commandant, Army Officer Academy, "Jieshao Huaqiao tongzhi Duan Yuanmou ru Huangpu Junguan Xuexiao", December 4, 1924; KMTPA *Hankou* 16356.1, Zhang Yongfu in Singapore to Lu Zhenliu, "Jieshao Chen Chouxin deng ershi ren ru junxiao", February 3, 1925.

[81] Bianco, 1971, 14; Jansen, 1954, 126–27; Liu, 1999; Scalapino and Yu, 1985, 148–259; Spence, 1999, 227, 238, 258; Zhang and Chen, 1997; KMTPA *Huanlong Lu* 2828, Song Ren to Sun Yat-sen, "Jie Hu Hanmin jie wei Nanyang kuan xuhui Dongjing, zhi ling ren shou lei", KMTPA *Huanlong Lu* 4826–4828, Lu Yaotang to Sun Yat-sen, "Baogao choushang Xinjiapo dangwu, bing He shu tongzhi zhijie huikuan shi", August 28, 1914; KMTPA *Huanlong Lu* 7618, "Wei Huaqiao choukuan ju yougan".

[82] Du, 2009; Pomerantz-Zhang, 1992; Wu, 1995; Yung and Twichell, 1909.

64   *External Intervention and the Politics of State Formation*

of heavy industry under the oversight of regional and provincial governments.[83] This saw local regimes control major industrial concerns such as the Hanyeping Company, Jiangnan Shipyard, Fuzhou Shipyard, Jiangnan Arsenal, and other metalworking, chemical, and railroad-related businesses.[84] The operations of these corporations gave regional and provincial governments an additional revenue stream. Even when foreign governments or private business owned and ran such facilities, local administrations could tax their use.[85] These operators generally accepted such taxation to minimise disruption to business.[86]

Local regimes further augmented their independent access to capital with the growing delegation of tax collection responsibilities to provincial and regional governments around the turn of the twentieth century.[87] The *lijin* transit tax provides perhaps the best example of local regimes' rising extractive autonomy from 1893 to 1922.[88] According to historian Ch'i Hsi-sheng, even though the number of official *lijin* stations remained at 735 throughout the late Qing and early Republican periods, the number of locally administered points where the tax was collected had grown several fold by the early 1920s.[89] There was often a *lijin* station every sixty to seventy miles of railroad or major road.

Between 1916 and 1928, estimated annual *lijin* revenues totalled between Mex.\$96 million and Mex.\$240 million.[90] Since total annual expenditures by governments across China was roughly between Mex.\$500 and Mex.\$600 million, the income that came from the *lijin* tax was no trifling amount.[91] In contrast, estimates put contemporaneous total yearly outlays by the central government in Beijing at about only Mex.\$52 million.[92] Local taxes were in fact a major source of regular income for regional and provincial governments, and by extension, those running these regimes.[93]

By taking charge of tax collection as well as advancing industrial development, regional and provincial authorities were largely financially independent.

---

[83] Hu and Dai, 1998, 19–20, 406–08; Rawski, 1989, 12–32; Richardson, 1999, 88–92; Xu and Wu, 1990, 333–501, 576–630, 787–900, 1993, 22–185.

[84] Perkins, 1967, 478–92; Richardson, 1999, 88–92; AS 03/05/075, "Luzheng zaxiang", 1922.

[85] McCord, 1993, 272–77; Rawski, 1989, 12–32; Richardson, 1999, 88–92; Xu and Wu, 1990, 22–58, 1993, 527–76, 717–86.

[86] McCord, 1993, 275–76.

[87] Chi, 1976, 152–67; Liu, 2005; McCord, 1993; Scalapino and Yu, 1985, 46.

[88] The *lijin* was a local levy on goods transported across local jurisdictions. Like the Salt Gabelle and other local taxes, part of the *lijin* theoretically went to the central government. However, local administrations withheld an increasing proportion of the levy, especially after 1911. Remick, 2004, 32–39; Skocpol, 1979, 76–77.

[89] Chi, 1976, 156. Economist Ma Yinchu estimated that *lijin* collection offices across China employed as many as 1.5 million people during the early Republican era. Ma, 1932, Vol. 3, 292–93.

[90] Chi, 1976, 156; *The China Weekly Review*, 1923 (August 7, 1926): 251.

[91] I follow Andrew Nathan in denoting currency in Mexican silver dollars. This helps to simplify the conversion rates between the different local and central currencies circulating at the time, since most were silver-backed. Nathan, 1976, 70.

[92] Nathan, 1976, 70.

[93] Chi, 1976, 166–67; Duara, 1987, 132–58; van de Ven, 1996, 829–68.

Feudalising the Chinese Polity, 1893–1922

Ch'i Hsi-sheng further notes that resulting from these developments, collectively:

[T]he financial resources at the disposal of the local militarist regimes [collectively] far exceeded those of the central government at Peking. … With the exception of the surplus from the customs service, and to a lesser extent the Salt Gabelle, the central government held no visible advantage over the local regimes.[94]

Whether they were militarists or nationalists, so long as political actors controlled provincial or regional governments, they were in a position to expand their ability to engage in organised coercion and challenge the position of rivals.

With their growing wealth, regional and provincial regimes went about building up their military prowess. Using funds collected by their respective provincial and regional administrations in the Zhili and Liangjiang regions, Yuan Shikai and Zhang Zhidong established the first of the modern, foreign-trained New Armies in 1895.[95] Subsequent late Qing New Armies like the Beiyang Army and the various provincial standing armies created in and after 1901 similarly drew from the enlarged revenue base of local governments.

As rivalries amongst domestic political actors intensified, the use of provincial and regional finances to build military forces continued into the 1920s and beyond. Part of the Fengtian Clique's military might during the 1910s and early 1920s, for example, came from its ability to harness economic growth in the Chinese northeast as a steady source of revenue on which to build coercive capabilities.[96] This situation repeated itself amongst domestic political actors across China. Whether from taxation, rents from industrial and commercial development, or even the sale of opium, revenues raised by local governments financed a range of political groups, their armies, and their wars. Control of regional and provincial administrations gave local political actors the financial and coercive wherewithal to resist, challenge, and even replace central political authority.

Changes in the relative concentration and accumulation of coercion and capital in China due to growing internal and external security pressures clearly provide a strong explanation of political decentralisation in the late Qing and early Republican periods. However, such a perspective can afford a better account of the persistence of central government authority and rule, even if nominal. After all, the logical conclusion of rising fragmentation would be the dissolution of the polity, an eventuality that never occurred. Looking at changes in capital, coercion, and competitive security pressures alone also says little about external autonomy and territorial exclusivity, which are also important elements of state form.

[94] Chi, 1976, 167.
[95] McCord, 1993, 33–34.
[96] Chan, 1982, 112–16; Chi, 1976, 162–77; van de Ven, 1997, 359–60; Waldron, 1995, 125.

EXTERNAL INTERVENTION AND CHINA'S FEUDALISATION

Given the limitations of existing state formation perspectives in explaining China's feudalisation, it may be useful to revisit the role of foreign intervention to better appreciate the concurrent fragmentation and centralisation in the late Qing and early Republican periods. If nothing else, considering intervention permits a better appreciation of China's feudalisation between the late nineteenth and early twentieth centuries. These dynamics suggest that external intervention can help provide an explanation for variations in state form in the Chinese case. The next chapter follows up on this issue and examines the details surrounding foreign intervention into China's domestic politics in this period.

Outside economic, military, and political support gave provincial as well as regional regimes the capacity to pull away from central government control in return for accepting direct foreign management of certain areas of governance. However, by consistently channelling funds, arms, and political support to the central government, foreign actors also limited the erosion of political centralisation and territorial exclusivity whilst shoring up external autonomy. Apart from its traditionally ascribed function of abetting fractionalisation, external intervention contributed substantially to holding China together.

Centralisation, Fragmentation, and Major Power Influence

Going into the Republican era, external pressure was key in fostering negotiations and pauses in fighting that helped to prevent the complete collapse of central authority. These include the 1912 North-South Armistice between the "independent" revolutionary provincial regimes and nonrevolutionary forces, which permitted the creation of Yuan Shikai's presidency after the collapse of the Qing regime.[97] Similarly, British and American diplomatic pressure on the various belligerents, notably the Duan Qirui cabinet, gave rise to the 1919 Shanghai Peace Conference between the Beijing government and various regional regimes.[98] This forestalled an exacerbation of the armed conflict resulting from Duan's armed unification efforts between 1918 and 1919. In helping to compel Yuan Shikai and Zhang Xun to respectively retreat from imperial ascendancy and restore the Qing, joint foreign political pressure also was useful in defusing threats to central authority caused by strong domestic resistance to such moves.[99]

Involvement of the powers in domestic politics was also important in making the continued survival of central political authority, albeit in reduced form, attractive to many competing factions within China. Since only central governments in Beijing received official foreign diplomatic recognition, actors holding

---

[97] Chan, 1971, 355–72; Usui and Chen, 1990, 26–42; Wang, 1979, 233–50.
[98] Chan, 1982, 33–39; Nathan, 1976, 129–30, 42–51; Usui and Chen, 1990, 204–07; AS 03/23/029/03/038, Telegram from Foreign Minister Lu (Zhengxiang) in Paris to the Foreign Ministry, "Nan Bei tiaohe de muqian qingxing", January 1919.
[99] Chan, 1982, 8–9; Usui and Chen, 1990, 124–41.

Feudalising the Chinese Polity, 1893–1922

sway in the capital were able to retain a sense of legitimacy.[100] This enabled those who controlled the Beijing government to negotiate over foreign loans, railroads, and treaty ports, and even to confer official recognition on regional regimes.[101] Such talk and bestowal of titles allowed groups to manipulate domestic politics by playing to nationalist feelings or showing support to particular actors.

Control of the central government spelt access to large external loans secured on national assets like the railroads under the Ministry of Communications, as well as surpluses from customs and salt revenues remitted exclusively to the central government.[102] Such income enhanced the fortunes of the faction controlling Beijing. Central government status could also avail an actor to more foreign loans and arms given the presence of foreign embargoes on arms and foreign loans to nonofficial groups in China.[103] Foreign support for the central government helped make it into a prize for contending domestic actors to seize. Hence, groups with major political pretensions were unwilling to see the disappearance of all central authority. This helped preserve a degree of central government rule.

Nevertheless, external intervention was also a key driver behind the rising ability of a growing number of actors in China to accumulate capital and coercion from 1893 to 1922, and consequently resist central government rule. Efforts at economic, administrative, and military modernisation throughout early-twentieth-century China were underwritten to an important degree by foreign funds and expertise. From foreign investments to direct loans and the floating of bonds, external financing was central to projects under official-led economic modernisation efforts in China since the mid nineteenth century. These included attempts to develop telegraph networks, mines, shipyards, and arsenals.[104]

Critically, many of the assets resulting from these modernisation efforts fell under the oversight of various regional governors-generalship and provincial governorships. This allowed regional and provincial jurisdictions important and substantial infusions of capital and financial resources independent of the central government. Much of the Hanyeping Company's capital was provided by loans from British, French, Russian, German, and Japanese firms through the support of their respective governments, just as foreign funds accounted for a significant

---

[100] Chan, 1982, 33–38; Nathan, 1976, 59–60; Pye, 1971, 13–59, 77–166.
[101] Chi, 1976, 156–57; Nathan, 1976, 59–60; SHAC 1039/553, "Zhong wai tiaoyue, geguo guanyu Zhongguo suoding xieyue, geguo yuezhang chuanyao, Zhong wai yuezhang zhaiyao deng wenjian"; SHAC 1039/559, "Zhong Ri gezhong tiaoyue, tongshang hangchuan xinyue ji ci Zhong Ri Meng Man tiaoyue shanhou huiyi jueyi'an deng zhajian"; SHAC 1039/560, "Geguo guanyu Zhongguo suoding tiaoyue deng wenjian", 1919.
[102] Nathan, 1976, 60–64; Pye, 1971, 132–53; Wright, 1927, 161–92.
[103] Chan, 1982, 59–65; Chen, 1983, 68–75; SHAC 1039/553, "Zhong wai tiaoyue, geguo guanyu Zhongguo suoding xieyue, geguo yuezhang chuanyao, Zhong wai yuezhang zhaiyao deng wenjian".
[104] Davis, 1982, 236–64; Scalapino and Yu, 1985, 63–64; Xu, 1962, 6–11, 28–57.

68   *External Intervention and the Politics of State Formation*

proportion of the China Merchants' Steam Navigation Company's capital.[105] Borrowed foreign funds paid for the establishment of the Jiangnan Arsenal and Shipyards under the Liangjiang Governors-generalship, while German, French, and British money financed the development of the Beiyang Army and Navy.[106]

Apart from infusing financial support, outside backing gave local political actors added means to generate revenue. Development and industrialisation projects drew heavily on the expertise provided by foreign governments through official and unofficial advisors. Modern economic concerns in late-nineteenth and early-twentieth-century China relied heavily on foreign training, advisors, and consultants for their establishment and operation.[107] British and American engineers, for instance, ran the Beijing-Hankou-Guangdong Railroad, while French experts managed the Sichuan-Yunnan-Guangxi Railroads.[108] This was despite the fact the central government ostensibly owned these rail lines. Critically, the collection of taxes along railroads in the various provinces and regions became important sources of funds for actors in control of regional and provincial regimes.

External funding too was important to other income-generating modernisation projects across China. These included both British and later American and Japanese loans that went toward the construction of telegraph networks and the development of air transport links, notably in East and South China.[109] The development of modern mining concerns around China, which involved revenue-sharing arrangements with various provincial administrations, likewise witnessed substantial foreign financial backing.[110] Notably, although much external financing came from corporations, many had official ties, and still more secured business through assistance from their home governments.

Foreign actors also featured prominently in allowing regional and provincial regimes to acquire means of coercion beyond what local extraction and economic development could provide. German, British, and Japanese arms,

---

[105] Chan, 1971, 356–57; Feuerwerker, 1958, 124–37; Hu and Dai, 1998, 406–08; Kirby, 1997, 456–57; Wright, 1980, 711–27; Xu, 1962, 36–54; AS 03/03/030, "Hanyeping Gongsi'an", 1912.

[106] Lee, 1999, 219–45; Qian, 2004; van de Ven, 1997, 355–57; Wang, 1979, 108–15; Xu, 1962, 4–11, 28–29, 48–57.

[107] Guo, 1987, 33–47; Iriye, 1967, 80, 95–96; Kirby, 1997, 456–57; Rawski, 1980, 6–28; Usui and Chen, 1990, 198–200; Wang, 1997, 249–93; Xu and Wu, 1990, 333–501.

[108] Chan, 1971, 358–59; Wang, 1997, 256–62; AS 03/05/065, Correspondence between the Ministry of Communications and the Foreign Ministry, "Zhong Mei, Zhong Fa, Zhong Ao tielushiyi", 1923.

[109] Wang, 1979, 108–20; Xu, 2001; KMTPA *Benbu* 13299.2, "British Imperialism in China"; AS 01/21/056/03, Correspondence between French and Chinese officials, "Zhong Fa tongshang zhangcheng; xüyi jiewu zhuantiao; Zhong Fa Dian-Yue; bianjie lianjie dianxian zhangcheng", October 1913–January 1914.

[110] AS 02/04/041, "Shanxi kuangwu"; AS 03/03/002, "Zhong Mei kuangwu"; AS 03/03/018, "Zhong Ri kuangwu jiaoshe"; AS 03/03/043, "Kuangwu zaxiang", 1922–1923; AS 03/02/071, "Wuxiandian zajian"; AS 03/30/24, "Makeni wuxiandiangongsi jiekuan'an"; AS 01/21/056/03, "Zhong Fa tongshang zhangcheng; xüyi jiewu zhuantiao; Zhong Fa Dian Yue; bianjie lianjie dianxian zhangcheng".

Feudalising the Chinese Polity, 1893–1922

equipment, and military and technical expertise provided foundations for the regional New Armies established in the last decade of Qing rule.[111] Expertise, technology equipment, and, to a degree, funds from Germany, France, and Britain, for example, lay behind the establishment and maintenance of the Beiyang Army and Navy.[112] New Armies under governors-general and governors elsewhere in China too were established on foreign advice and funding. As internal conflicts mounted from the 1910s to early 1920s, so did demand for using foreign loans, arms, and expertise to build up regional and military capabilities.[113]

In examining the early-twentieth-century arms trade, Anthony Chan notes that few domestic arsenals could produce armaments of adequate quality and quantity to equip the various armies in China by the 1910s.[114] Even the largest and most advanced arsenals at Shenyang, Taiyuan, and Hanyang were only capable of arming little more than a regiment, and at most a brigade. Moreover, the general quality of their output was inferior to even used foreign equipment. Through official trade agents working out of the legations as well as more shady middlemen, then, weapons, ammunition, and equipment from Britain, Japan, Germany, Italy, and elsewhere began to flow to various regional and provincial regimes.[115]

The Anfu Clique under Duan Qirui and the Fengtian Clique, for example, received much funding, military training, and war material from Japan.[116] These included active strategic and tactical advice, light arms, heavy machine guns, artillery, and even light aircraft. The French provided similar assistance to Tang Jiyao in Yunnan and Lu Rongting in Guangxi, while Soviet Russia later did the same with Feng Yuxiang's Guominjun in Northwest China and the Chinese Nationalists in Guangdong.[117] Simply, the ability of political actors in early-

---

[111] Chi, 1976, 107; McCord, 1993, 31–39; Spector, 1964, 162–94; Twitchett and Fairbank, 1978, 47–69, 204–11; Weng and Weng, 2003, 53–56, 227–44; AS 02/10/005, "Ri E zhanzheng hou Dongbei, Neidi fangwu", 1906–1907; AS 02/02/002, "Goumai junhuo", 1906–1908, AS 02/01/002, "Yunru junhuo", 1909; AS 02/10/010, "Dongbei Zhili fangwu", April—June 1908; AS 03/011/016, "Geguan huiwu wenda", 1913.

[112] Lee, 1999, 219–45; Qian, 2004; van de Ven, 1997, 355–57; Wang, 1979, 108–15; Xu, 1962, 6–11, 28–29, 48–57.

[113] Chan, 1982, 67–108; Chen, 1983, 8–19; Chi, 1976, 116–42; AS 03/011/016, "Geguan huiwu wenda"; AS 03/20/011, "Shanhou dajiekuan'an", 1913.

[114] Chan, 1982, 110–15; Chi, 1976, 78.

[115] Chan, 1982, 49–91; Chen, 1983, 19–31; AS 03/18, "Junhuojinyun", 1912, AS 02/01/002, "Yunru junhuo"; AS 03/20/008, "Zhongyang jiekuan"; AS 03/20/039/04, "Min Yue Xiang Dian Su Lu deng sheng shanxing jie waizhai'an".

[116] Li, 2000, 249–84, 306–11; Usui and Chen, 1990, 3–6, 22–26, 78–98, 145–90; Wang, 1979, 76–115, 128–32, 192–97; Wright, 1980, 711–27; Xu, 1962, 30–45, 116–23, 148–89; SHAC 18/3043, Koo, "Memorandum on Japan's Plots and Schemes against the Unification of China".

[117] Chamberlain, 1946, 7–10; Chan, 1982, 54–63, 83–84, 102–04; Chi, 1976, 121; Liu and Tian, 2004, 116–31; Zhu, 1995, 131–40; AS 03/20/039/04/011–012, Telegram from Governor Wu [Peifu] at Luoyang to the Foreign Ministry, "Tang Jiyao yi ge jiuchang digou qiangdan you", April 1923; AS 03/20/039/04/014, 018, Telegram from Governor Wu [Peifu] at Luoyang to the Foreign Ministry, "Yunnan siyungou junhuo shi", May 1923; AS 03/18/101/01, Correspondence between

70   *External Intervention and the Politics of State Formation*

twentieth-century China to accrue the coercive capabilities that kept them competitive rested on a capacity to access external support.

Further, revenue brought about by external involvement in the economy meant ready funds with which local regimes could purchase coercion. This accelerated the potentially generations-long process of accumulating economic and military capabilities Charles Tilly and others deem key to political power.[118] Once Qing central authority started to increasingly waver, the availability of external economic and military resources enabled those controlling various localities to assert autonomy.

By reducing barriers to the attainment of independent tools of coercion and wealth creation, external intervention permitted more assertion of political prerogatives by a growing number of domestic actors. Foreign backing spelt an increasing ability by groups in China to face off against adversaries within China's domestic political milieu, including from those claiming central authority. The numerous civil wars between Yuan Shikai's presidency and the Second Zhili-Fengtian War exemplify this fracturing of politics.

Outsiders and the Preservation of Limited Territorial Exclusivity

Outside intervention between 1893 and 1922 brought limited territorial exclusivity. During this time, external powers continued to administer various functions of government within China, which they seized over the course of the previous century. Most notable was the Maritime Customs Service. Foreign administration of customs meant that governments in China could not set tariffs without prior consultation with and approval by the relevant external powers, and that the ability to police ports, as well as coastal and inland shipping, was ceded to outside actors.[119]

Other areas of governance under foreign control were the postal, Salt Gabelle, and telecommunications services. Chinese central governments and regional regimes often did not have full oversight and control over the major railroads

---

the Foreign Ministry and Yunnan Governor Cai E, "Fa shi qing zhun Yunnan tielu gongsi yunru gongcheng yong zhayao'an", November 1912; AS 01/21/056/03, "Zhong Fa tongshang zhangcheng; xüyi jiewu zhuantiao; Zhong Fa Dian Yue; bianjie lianjie dianxian zhangcheng"; AS 03/30/039/04/014–018, Telegrams between the Foreign Ministry and the Governor Wu at Luoyang, "Yunnan gou junhuo shi", May 1923; AS 03/18/101/01/009–011, "Dian Yue gongsi bao yun zhayao ying zhao ci bu dingban fazhi shiyong cunchu gejie ying zhaozhang qudi".

[118] Tilly, 1990, 192–201, 18–24.

[119] Lian, 2004, 87–112, 77–324; Nathan, 1976, 60–63; Scalapino and Yu, 1985, 64–65, 477–78; Spence, 1969, 93–128; Tilly, 1990; Usui and Chen, 1990, 300–61; KMTPA *Benbu* 13299.2, "British Imperialism in China"; AS 03/05/047, "Nan Man tielu"; AS 03/05/053, "Ji-Chang tielu jiekuan"; AS 03/05/049, "Si-Tao tielu jiekuan'an"; SHAC 1039/158, "Guomin Waijiao wei zhengqu guanshui zizhu shouhui Qingdao deng wenti zhi Bali hehui daibiao dian", March 1919; SHAC 1039/159, "Sun Baoqi guanyu jiashui mianli haiguan zizhu xiang waizhang Lu Zongyu jianyi han", May 1919; SHAC 1039/160, Foreign Minister Shen Ruilin, "Guanyu haiguan zizhu huiyi zhi luji gexiang ziliao", August 1924.

Feudalising the Chinese Polity, 1893–1922

either.[120] Despite efforts by central and regional authorities in China to reclaim the ability to manage agencies responsible for these functions during the first two decades of the twentieth century, foreign opposition meant that they at best met with only partial success.[121] This was perhaps most evident with attempts to reclaim railroad rights. Despite efforts across China, most of the more than 13,000 kilometres of railroad built between 1876 and 1927 remained under foreign ownership and management either in part or in whole.[122] This was also the case with the other government functions discussed previously.

Outside funding, expertise, and equipment came at a price. This is clear when looking at the agreements that sealed foreign support in the 1910s and 1920s. External financing, advice, and equipment were almost always either conditional on exclusive access privileges over raw materials, markets, and communications networks, or secured on key assets and internal revenue streams.[123] Given the high degrees of political and economic instability across most of China, arrangements between domestic groups and foreign players usually translated into foreign management of the official organs overseeing the various assets used as guarantees.[124] External actors had interests to forward and preserve too.

---

[120] Foreign powers oversaw security in the areas surrounding the railroads, and foreign jurisdiction extended to mineral and other resources in areas adjacent the railroad. China. Dept. of Railways and Wang, 1916; Lee, 1977; Sun E., 1954; SHAC 1039/158 "Guomin waijiao wei zhengqu guanshui zizhu shouhui Qingdao deng wenti zhi Bali hehui daibiao dian".

[121] Li, 1994, 149–55; Sun E., 1954, 88–89, 21–23; Zhang, 1989; Zhongguo tielushi bianji yanjiu zhongxin, 1996; KMTPA *Huanlong Lu* 516, Express telegram from the Sichuan Provincial Assembly to Premier Sun Yat-sen, "Qing Beifang zhengfu jianjü woguo tielu you wairen guanli huo she zuqi jian", August 29, 1919; FHAC 329/4/50/406, "Wen Qing, Rui Liang deng guanyu bu pingdeng tiaoyue de xiuding, peikuan, geguo zai Hua zujie ji youguan lingshi zhuquan jiaoshe fangmian zouzhe", 1908; SHAC 1039/158, "Guomin waijiao wei zhengqu guanshui zizhu shouhui Qingdao deng wenti zhi Bali Hehui daibiao dian"; SHAC 1039/160, Foreign Minister Shen Ruilin, "Guanyu haiguan zizhu huiyi zhi luji gexiang ziliao"; SHAC 18/3516 "Zhongguo xiwang tiaoyue"; SHAC 18/3518, Jin Hua and Xu Dongfan, "Shandong wenti yü Guoji Lianmeng kangyi Lu an zhi wenzhang", November 4, 1920; SHAC 1039/380, "Guan yu Shandong wenti ruhe jiao Guoji Lianhehui ji youguan Shandong wenti zhi shuotie", 1921; SHAC 1039/339, "Zhonghua Minguo kaiguo zhi Bali Hehui qianxi zhi waijiao zhengce", 1918–1919; SHAC 1039/375, "Taipingyang Huiyi shanhou weiyuanhui taolun caibing jiaohui Guangzhou Wan, jiejue Shandong xuan'an deng wenti laiwang wenshu ji canyu Huashengdun Huiyi wenjian", 1918–1922; SHAC 1039/651, "Beiyang zhengfu Taipingyang Huiyi Weihaiwei wenti", 1923; AS 03/08/013/02/012, Representatives Gu, Shi and Wang in London to the Foreign Ministry, "Niti guanyu yuanzhu Zhong jiao liang xingshi", November 1921; AS 03/39/032/05, "Huashengdun huiyi qian ding zhi gexiang tiaoyue xieding ji jueyian", December 1921; AS 03/39/036/04/001–020, telegrams between the Foreign Ministry and Shi Zhaoji (Alfred Sze), Chinese Consul to the United States, "Huashengdun huiyi suo ding zhi guanyu Zhongguo shijian tiaoyue shi", January 1926.

[122] Jin and Xu, 1986, 581–603; Li, 1994, 590–606; Mi, 2002; Sun E., 1954, 22; Zhang, 1989, 3–76, 1997; Zhongguo tielushi bianji yanjiu zhongxin, 1996.

[123] Assets used as security included mines, railroads, mints, factories, and the like, whilst internal revenue streams offered up as collateral included local sales taxes, income taxes, and internal customs duties like the *lijin*. Chi, 1976, 157–58.

[124] Chi, 1976; Xu, 1962.

72   *External Intervention and the Politics of State Formation*

The most well known example of a foreign-run agency was the Maritime Customs Service.[125] The years between 1894 and 1901 saw the pledging of customs and salt revenues to service loans undertaken to pay for wars and indemnities incurred by the Qing.[126] Customs revenues also secured many of the subsequent foreign loans taken out by central governments in Beijing into 1922.[127] To ensure proper collection of customs duties and the remittance of revenues, the central government's main creditors, notably Britain, France, and the United States, further placed Chinese customs under their joint supervision, with Britain effectively administering the service.[128]

In the regions and provinces, entities related to foreign governments ran mines and other raw material extracting concerns, just as advisors from these countries managed policing and military affairs. In addition to Russian-owned railroads, the Russian government ran, guarded, and policed mines in South Manchuria whilst overseeing police, military, and administrative affairs in the area until the Japanese took over this role in 1905.[129] Even then, St. Petersburg maintained such privileges in areas of northern Manchuria not under Japanese influence.[130] These were amongst the conditions for Russian and Japanese financial and military assistance to both regimes in Manchuria and central governments in Beijing.[131]

---

[125] Other foreign-run Chinese central government agencies included the postal service, which was initially part of the customs service, the telegraph service, and the Salt Gabelle. Fairbank, 1964, 285–368; Fox, 1940; Lian, 2004, 87–112; Nathan, 1976, 60–63; Spence , 93–128; KMTPA *Benbu* 13299.2, "British Imperialism in China"; AS 03/02/090, "Youdian jiaoshe".

[126] Brunero, 2006, 19; Nathan, 60–64; Wang, Zhen, and Sun, 2002, 53–55; Wright, 1927, 91–126, 1939, 109–19, 1950, 656–57, 744–48; Xu, 28–35.

[127] Brunero, 2006, 19; Wang, Zhen, and Sun, 2002, 53–55; Wright, 1927, 59–80, 127–59, 1950, 653–66; Xu, 1939, 114–29, 48–97.

[128] Brunero, 2006, 9–53; Lian, 2004, 113–43; Scalapino and Yu, 1985, 64; Skocpol, 1979, 76; Wang, Zhen, and Sun, 2002, 55–62; Wright, 1927, 1–59, 1939, 33–147, 1950, 639–883; KMTPA *Benbu* 13299.2, "British Imperialism in China"; AS 03/19/011/04, Correspondence between the Tax Bureau and Foreign Ministry, "E junguan faling ganshe Zhongguo shuiguan chayanquan'an", October 1904.

[129] Chi, 1976, 107; Wright, 1980, 711–27; SHAC 18/3043, Koo, "Memorandum on Japan's Plots and Schemes against the Unification of China"; AS 03/05/062, Documents and correspondence between the Communications and Foreign Ministries, "Zhong-Ri tielu shiyi", 1914; AS 03/32/480, Foreign Ministry documents and correspondence, "Zhong-E gexiang yuezhang", 1922; AS 03/32/517, Documents of the Foreign Ministry, "E yu Ri dingyue", 1921; AS 03/33/124, Correspondence amongst the Foreign Ministry and provincial officials, "Jiaozhou'an", May 1919; AS 03/33/146, Correspondence amongst the Foreign Ministry, the Delegation at Paris, provincial officials, and local negotiators, "Bali hehui", April 1919; AS 03/33/150, Correspondence amongst the Foreign Ministry, provincial officials, and local negotiators, "Shandong wenti", April 1919; AS 03/33/161, Correspondence amongst the Foreign Ministry and provincial officials, "Lu'an", 1922.

[130] AS 03/32/231/01, Correspondence between the Foreign Ministry and Governor Bao, "Zhongdong tielu jiaoshe", 1920; AS 03/33/092, Foreign Ministry documents, "Ri-E xieyue", 1916; Li, 329–65.

[131] Li, 2000, 249–84, 306–11; Usui and Chen, 1990, 3–6, 22–26, 78–98, 145–90; Wang, 1979, 76–132, 92–97; Wright, 1980, 711–27; Xu, 1962, 30–45, 116–23, 48–61, 78–89; SHAC 18/3043, Koo, "Memorandum on Japan's Plots and Schemes against the Unification of China".

Feudalising the Chinese Polity, 1893–1922

Such relationships saw replication across China, with the Germans in Shandong until 1914 and the French in Yunnan as well as parts of Sichuan until the early 1930s being just two examples.[132] On the other hand, even though the British government took a less area-specific and intrusive approach, they were still able to similarly extend their influence over the management of trade, transportation, and communications in China between 1893 and 1922.[133] They did so by similarly linking financial and military assistance to provincial, regional, or central governments with the ownership or operation of railroads, telegraph networks, and transportation systems by British firms.[134]

External Autonomy

By supporting the persistence of central authority, even in diminished form, the major outside powers enabled the Chinese polity to retain a relatively high degree of external autonomy between 1893 and 1922. British, American, and intermittent Japanese and Russian insistence on the autonomy of the Chinese polity allowed central governments from the Qing court to the Xu Shichang government to remain fully responsible for official external relations.[135] To be sure, material inadequacies, political divisions, and conditions set by agreements of various sorts hindered the ability of various central governments to negotiate with other external actors. Nevertheless, the Qing and various Republican regimes that represented China's central government between 1893 and 1922 were not subject to any higher sources of authority in their foreign relations.

The fact most major powers were only willing to deal with one central Chinese government in external, as opposed to domestic, affairs forced competing groups within China to present a single external front. To have any claim on central authority, the different domestic political actors needed foreign governments to treat them as such. Part of this lay in being able to represent more than the narrow interest of the group holding power in Beijing.[136] This led to the formation of joint delegations approved by at least some of the major factions, and ostensibly representing a single "China" at major diplomatic events.[137]

---

[132] Usui and Chen, 1990, 198–200; Wang, 1979, 83–89, 100–12, 141–48, 192–220; AS 03/20/039/ 04, "Min, Yue, Xiang, Dian, Su, Lu deng sheng shanxing yajie waizhai'an"; AS 01/21/056, "Sino-French Treaty", October, 1913; AS 03/20/039, "Gesheng jiekuan"; AS 03/18/101, "Junhuo jinyun", 1912.

[133] Scalapino and Yu, 1985, 56–57; Wang, 1979, 76–115; KMTPA *Benbu* 13299.2, "British Imperialism in China"; AS 03/20/045, "Wan sheng Yida yanghang jie kuan"; AS 02/04/008, Correspondence between the British Embassy and Foreign Ministry, "Shanxi kuangwu", 1914.

[134] Wang, 1979, 108–20; KMTPA *Benbu* 13299.2, "British Imperialism in China".

[135] Chan, 1982, 33–38; Nathan, 1976, 59–64; Wang, 1979, 116–50.

[136] Chi, 1976, 190–95; Nathan, 1976, 59–64.

[137] KMTPA *Huanlong Lu* 659, Urgent telegram from the Sichuan provincial assembly to Premier Sun Yat-sen, "He daibiao woguo fu Fa canjia heping huiyi", February 21, 1919; SHAC 1039/ 339, "Zhonghua Minguo kaiguo zhi Bali hehui qianxi zhi waijiao zhengce".

74 *External Intervention and the Politics of State Formation*

The Chinese delegation to the 1919 Paris Peace Conference is representative of this phenomenon. The personnel makeup as well as the positions that the "Chinese" delegation took were the result of negotiations amongst the major political actors in China, notably the Beiyang government of Xu Shichang and the Guangzhou National Government.[138] The backbone of the Chinese delegation to the Versailles Conference was Lu Zhengxiang, Wellington Koo, Wang Zhengting, and Alfred Sze, who, on top of their expertise and experience as professional diplomats, were individuals acceptable to local powerbrokers.

CONCLUSION

To claim that competition for access amongst outside actors led collectively to China's late-nineteenth and early-twentieth-century feudalisation on the basis that intervention provides a fuller account of changes in state form is clearly insufficient. Even though foreign financial, military, and political support to local actors limited centralisation and territorial exclusivity whilst preserving autonomy in China, this could be due to reasons other than the aggregation of foreign attempts to secure access. Concerns for immediate economic gains or ideology rather than access denial may lie behind such assistance. Hence, a thorough consideration of the contours and consequences of external intervention is critical for understanding the dynamics of state formation in modern China.

For my argument to be plausible, there should be evidence that external powers backed particular indigenous actors to exclude rivals from China in ways consistent with their opportunity cost perceptions. It means that simultaneous support for the central government and regional regimes came from a divergence in expected costs of intervention amongst outside actors. The next chapter examines external actors' opportunity cost perceptions and the relationships between foreign actors and domestic political groups to ascertain if this was indeed the case. If not, then it is possible to undermine my argument.

---

[138] AS 03/37/012, "Hehui huiyi jilu"; AS 03/37/013, "Hehui jishi ji shuotie"; AS 03/37/012/03, "Daibiaotuan ji dahui renminglu"; KMTPA *Huanlong Lu* 14006, "Wei Ouzhou heping huiyi shuangfang hui pai daibiao shi"; SHAC 1039/339, "Zhonghua Minguo kaiguo zhi Bali hehui qianxi zhi waijiao zhengce"; Koo and Zhongguo shehuikexueyuan. Jindaishi yanjiusuo, 172–82; Shi, 151–54, 274–83.

CHAPTER 4

External Influence and China's Feudalisation, 1893–1922

Opportunity Costs and Patterns of Foreign Intervention

The late-nineteenth, early-twentieth-century struggle over China amongst various external powers reflected disparate attempts to address broader concerns over security, economic, and other interests. Even though most leaders in various foreign capitals generally wished to avoid major conflict in China, they differed about how access in China fit within broader systemic concerns. Such dissimilar expectations about the relative return from investing limited capabilities in China brought substantial variation in foreign involvement with Chinese domestic politics and local actors. China's feudalisation from 1893 to 1923 was the collective result of interactions between these cross-cutting intervention efforts.

I begin with an assessment of the opportunity cost expectations held by the main intervening parties in China between the late nineteenth and early twentieth centuries, and the corresponding approaches they took toward access denial. I then lay out how these intervention efforts together affected state form along the lines of political centralisation, territorial exclusivity, and external autonomy. As indicated earlier, I derive the opportunity cost expectations of the intervening actors from points of agreement in established secondary scholarship and supplemented by primary sources. I do so to highlight the considerations, incentives, and constraints various outside governments faced as they looked toward interceding into Chinese politics rather than to explain motivations. This enables me to concentrate on building off and drawing together established research whilst keeping succinct an otherwise expansive and potentially unwieldy discussion.

RELATIVE DECLINE AND BRITAIN'S EFFORTS TO KEEP AN OPEN DOOR AJAR

British leaders faced an array of pressing, competing demands on their government's capabilities between the late nineteenth and early twentieth centuries. Even as the perceived needs of defending their global empire grew, Germany's rising prominence and assertiveness in Europe seemed to warrant a substantial reorientation toward homeland defence. Fiscal crises and prolonged economic uncertainty further dampened the appetite amongst elites and the public for a

76 *External Intervention and the Politics of State Formation*

heavy commitment toward security. The expected net gains from investing substantial capabilities toward denying other powers access to China more fully seemed comparatively small beside these considerations. That China was mostly an afterthought led London to settle for nonprivileged access over China through support for autonomous central government control over the polity and its outward relations.

Growing concerns about Britain's worsening strategic position captured the attentions of many key British policymakers. The rapid modernisation and expansion of American, French, Japanese, and especially German navies seemed especially threatening to British shipping and communications.[1] Intensifying competition also made it seem increasingly difficult to maintain the two-power naval standard and global deployment, traditionally deemed central to Britain's security.[2] In fact, the Royal Navy was only about 60 percent larger than the next largest navy, the German Kaiserliche Marine, on the eve of World War I.[3] Adding to such woes was Germany's growing assertiveness on continental Europe.

Moreover, industrialisation in Imperial Russia gave St. Petersburg a new eastward focus, which saw the construction of railways that could transport Russian troops to the frontiers of British India.[4] Difficulties from the 1897–1903 Boer War tied down British forces in Africa, and left successive cabinets with a financial crisis that took years to resolve.[5] Fighting World War I only depleted British military and financial capabilities more.[6] Concerns about these developments started with senior Admiralty, War Office, and Colonial Office officials, but spread to leading Conservatives like Joseph Chamberlain and Winston Churchill as well as prominent Liberals such as Herbert Asquith and David Lloyd George.[7]

Making matters appear even more disconcerting was a common belief about persistent economic weakness, which became increasingly apparent from the 1890s. This position was common not just amongst a number of leading Conservatives, but within the Treasury, Customs Board, and Board of Trade.[8] Several trends lay behind this view. British share of world manufacturing output fell from an estimated 22.9 percent to 9.9 percent and its share of world trade from 23.2 percent to 14.1 percent between 1880 and 1928.[9] British holdings of

---

[1] Herman, 2004, 480–91.

[2] Ferguson, 2004, 240–43; Friedberg, 1988, 152–84, 84n75, 206, 300; Howard, 1967, 75–95, 1974, 134–73.

[3] Ferguson, 2004, 227–42; Herman, 2004, 473–503; Kupchan, 1994, 120–21.

[4] Friedberg, 1988, 215–78; Platt, 1968, 181–248.

[5] Initial estimates put war expenses at £5 million, but this ultimately came to almost half a billion pounds. Brendon, 2007, 214–48; Friedberg, 1988, 51–52, 106–18; Kupchan, 1994, 106–07, 126–27; Platt, 1968, 249–61; Snyder, 1991, 209–10; Wang, 1979, 187.

[6] Brendon, 2007, 249–88; Ferguson, 2004, 273–75; Herman, 2004, 519–28.

[7] Howard, 1967, 14–173, 1974, 75–95; Platt, 1968, 276–307; Wang, 1979, 116–28, 149–55.

[8] Friedberg, 1988, 21–134; Ikenberry, 2001, 277–78; Kennedy, 1987, 228–29; Maddison and Organisation for Economic Co-operation and Development, Development Centre, 2003, 46–51, 71, 84–85; Platt, 1968, 276–307; Wohlforth, 1999, 12–14.

[9] Ferguson, 2004, 240; Imlah, 1958, 190–93.

External Influence and China's Feudalisation, 1893–1922

foreign capital stock, whilst still larger than other major powers, were declining too. Britain's outward investment peaked at around 40 percent of the world total in 1914 and fell steadily thereafter, especially next to the United States.[10]

The turn of the century also saw the British economy just emerge from a prolonged, thirty-year period of economic uncertainty from 1872 to 1898.[11] At a cost of £10 billion, fighting World War I increased Britain's national debt tenfold.[12] Paying for that war and the absorption of territories in the Middle East and Central Asia took up almost half of government spending until the mid-1920s.[13] The postwar growth in trade union influence coupled with deflationary policies aimed at returning the pound to the gold standard at overvalued 1914 rates created yet more economic strain.

Certainly, Britain had large commercial stakes in China at the time. British-owned firms accounted for about half of external trade, 41 percent of coastal trade, and 37.7 percent of foreign investment as late as 1913, even as the absolute value of British business interests in China continued to rise steadily.[14] Stressing China's economic importance, British businesses with interests in China lobbied Parliament, the Foreign Office, and successive cabinets to intervene strongly in the polity to prevent non-British competitors from gaining ground.[15] They argued that the British government should act resolutely to preserve Britain's slipping relative economic importance, given efforts by other foreign firms to make inroads into a growing Chinese economy.[16]

However, China trade only accounted for roughly 3 to 4 percent of total British trade going into the early twentieth century.[17] Investment in China never exceeded much more than 3 percent of total British foreign investment at the time.[18] This was despite the large absolute value of economic exchanges with

[10] Ferguson, 2004, 202–03, 65, 71; Kupchan, 1994, 133–37; Maddison and Organisation for Economic Co-operation and Development, Development Centre, 2001, 99.

[11] Friedberg, 1988, 21–134.

[12] Ferguson, 2004, 265.

[13] Ferguson, 2004, 271–72.

[14] China Dept. of Railways and Wang, 1916, 79–126, 169–86, 221–84, 325–514, 537–604, 691–718, 759–831; Sun E., 1954; Wang, 1979, 228–30; AS 03/20/025, exchanges amongst the Foreign and Finance Ministries and the British Embassy, "Makeni wuxiandian gongsi jie-kuan'an", February 1922; AS 03/05/042, exchanges amongst the Foreign, Communications, and Finance Ministries and the British Embassy, "Guang-Jiu tielu jiekuan'an", June 1913.

[15] Support for British firms in China included many prominent politicians. Examples were Lord Salisbury, Arthur Balfour, George Curzon, Michael Hicks Beach, Viscount Cranborne, Ellis Ashmead-Bartlett, William St. John Brodrick, Robert Armstrong Yerburgh, James Lowther, and Charles Beresford on the Conservative side. Amongst the Liberal supporters were Lord Rosebery, William Harcourt, Joseph Chamberlain, Lord Kimberley, Edward Grey, Henry Labouchere, Thomas Gibson Bowles, Charles Dilke, Samuel Smith, and Joseph Walton. Wang, 1979, 116–28, 149–55.

[16] Schoonover, 2003, 112; Wang, 1979, 117–18, 228–30.

[17] Bickers, 1999, 12; Maddison and Organisation for Economic Co-operation and Development, Development Centre, 2001, 99; Mitchell, 1962, 315–27.

[18] Bickers, 1999, 12; Imlah, 1952; Maddison and Organisation for Economic Co-operation and Development, Development Centre, 2001, 99.

78   *External Intervention and the Politics of State Formation*

China, which actually continued to grow into the early twentieth century. British firms continued to account for about half of China's external trade going into the early twentieth century, 41 percent of coastal trade, and 37.7 percent of foreign investment as late as 1913.[19] To be sure, these proportions were down from the historic highs of the mid nineteenth century, when Britain dominated China's foreign trade and investment, particularly in the Lower Yangzi region.[20]

In terms of security, China did not appear vital for either securing maritime access or defending key possessions like India.[21] Bases in Singapore, Hong Kong, and Weihaiwei seemed sufficient to an Admiralty led by Winston Churchill and Jackie Fisher for maintaining a naval presence in the Far East.[22] In this sense, seriously contending for access in China appealed largely to a small, but vocal, minority in British politics.

Given Britain's broader strategic concerns and the need to place access to China within this context, bureaucrats and politicians across the political spectrum mostly took a view that emphasised limited but robust British involvement. Parliamentary debates and policy discussions indicated a growing worry that overly committing capabilities to China could mean sacrificing more pressing needs.[23] By 1898, Parliamentary opinion clearly began shifting away from Joseph Chamberlain's view "that the doors [to China] should be kept open at the risk of war".[24] Rather than the potentially expansive intervention allowed by Chamberlain's position, prevailing sentiment veered towards Arthur Balfour's position that "what is good for one [power in

---

[19] British foreign investment includes direct investments, especially in railroad and telecommunications, as well as portfolio investments from loans. These accounted to about US$1.6 billion. The value of the British share of China's external trade was roughly 803 million Chinese Customs Taels (about US$648 million). Britain's GDP in 1915 was estimated at around US$234 billion. British-owned firms prominent in China included Jardine, Matheson, and Company, the Hong Kong and Shanghai Banking Corporation, John Swire and Sons Limited, Hutchinson International, Hong Kong and Whampoa Docks, the Anglo-Chinese Company, as well as the British and Chinese Corporation, Messrs. Pauling and Company, Chinese Central Railways, Limited, the Pekin Syndicate, Limited, amongst others. China Dept. of Railways and Wang, 1916, 79–126, 169–86, 221–84, 325–514, 537–604, 691–718, 759–831; Ikenberry 2001, 278; Sun E., 1954; Wang, 1979, 228–30; AS 03/20/025, exchanges amongst the Foreign and Finance Ministries and the British Embassy, "Makeni wuxiandian gongsi jiekuan'an", February 1922; AS 03/05/042, exchanges amongst the Foreign, Communications, and Finance Ministries and the British Embassy, "Guang-Jiu tielu jiekuan'an", June 1913.

[20] Firms from the British Isles alone took up 80 percent of Chinese external trade in the 1860s, and corporations from the rest of the empire accounted for about 84 percent of China's foreign trade in 1894 and 60 percent of coastal trade as late as 1899. The subsequent drop in the British empire's share of the Chinese economy represented an overall increase in the volume of China's trade and investment in the early twentieth century. British firms actually enjoyed an increase in the absolute value of their China business despite a fall in market share. Platt, 1968, 276–307; Schoonover, 2003, 112; Wang, 1979, 117–18, 228–30.

[21] Kupchan, 1994, 121; Wang, 1979, 113–22.

[22] Friedberg, 1988, 176–83; Herman, 2004; Wang, 1979, 28–108.

[23] Doyle, 1986, 297; Wang, 1979, 156–59.

[24] Quoted in Wang, 1979, 142.

External Influence and China's Feudalisation, 1893–1922 79

China] is not necessarily bad for the other".[25] Balfour's approach called for indirect support of central government rule through loans, arms sales, and the remittance of customs surpluses.[26]

The outlook that emerged across party lines and within official circles saw working through China's central government as permitting the continued accrual of commercial benefits without substantial capability commitments. So long as a stable, independent central government could resist the division of China and offer most-favoured nation treatment, London would have a potential partner to help prevent other powers from acquiring access advantages over Britain.[27] After all, most-favoured nation status meant that all privileges any outside actor secured with China's central government would automatically extend to Britain. This could free diplomatic and military capabilities for use in more pressing circumstances, and put exposure in China in line with the economic and other gains British leaders expected to accrue there. The servicing and retiring of loans to China's central government could also bring financial returns both for London and for British firms.[28]

Notably, more extensive access denial efforts were absent from mainstream British discussions about China policy, as was complete withdrawal. This was a departure for a power that was a belligerent party in the 1839–1842 and 1856–1860 Opium Wars, two of the Qing Empire's major nineteenth-century wars. The change of tack further suggests the diminished, but continuing, value of securing access in China within the corridors of power in London. British policymakers between the late nineteenth and early twentieth centuries generally seemed to understand competing over access in the Chinese polity as an issue to manage with moderate capability commitments rather than heavy investment.

BRITAIN'S REVISED OPEN DOOR

Given prevailing views in London, the Foreign Office took a three-pronged approach to neutralise access advantages other major powers obtained in China between 1898 and 1922. This incorporated consistent support for the central government in China, seeking of corresponding "compensation" for access advantages accrued by other major powers, and encouraging more outside actors to be actively involved in China. The belief was that such action could maintain Britain's leading position in China by preventing any single power from obtaining access privileges not enjoyed by London whilst minimising British capability commitments in China.

First, British policy sought to sustain official support for a central government that could maintain a semblance of stability, regardless of the domestic actor in

[25] Quoted in Wang, 1979, 151.
[26] Platt, 1968, 276–307; Wang, 1979, 117–28, 148–51, 228–30, 241–50.
[27] Joseph, 1928, 285–414; Wang, 1967.
[28] Davis, 1982; Wang, 1979, 117–28, 228–50.

80 External Intervention and the Politics of State Formation

power.[29] Even in the aftermath of the 1911 Revolution, Foreign Secretary Edward Grey stressed the need to avoid direct intervention except to safeguard British subjects and their property.[30] Moreover, the British government would provide political support assistance to whoever could ensure unity and political stability. London applied diplomatic pressure as well as its control of China's maritime customs to ensure that surplus customs revenues continually went to central government coffers during both the last years of Qing rule and the early Republic.[31] For those in power in Beijing, this provided welcome regular income that could help fund the suppression of domestic rivals.[32] British leaders believed that their approach could serve British interests in China without affecting their capacity to act elsewhere.

When Foreign Office officials determined Yuan Shikai to be the best candidate for maintaining China's stability and unity after 1911, the Liberal Asquith government helped muster both the political support behind his regime as well as the financing that kept it liquid.[33] British pressure likewise facilitated the North-South Armistice that brought about the ascendancy of Yuan's regime in 1912 and undermined the anti-Yuan Second Revolution of 1913.[34] Official British lobbying also gave rise to the international financial consortia that provided the 1913 Re-Organisation Loan that helped keep Yuan's government liquid. Nonetheless, when Yuan's attempt to install himself as emperor in 1916 threatened to undermine stability and central authority, the British government was quick to apply the pressure that helped force Yuan to backtrack.[35] This was despite the fact that John Jordan, Britain's envoy to China, initially intimated sympathy for Yuan's ascension.[36]

---

[29] SHAC 1039/194, "1913–1916 nian jian Zhongguo zhengfu wei jiaru dierci baohehui de gexiang tiaoyue bing dui xiuzheng luzhan fagui ji guanli tiaoyue qianshu yijian de wengaobu", 1905–1916; SHAC 1039/195, "Baohehui huiyilu", 1911.

[30] Huang, 2005, 292–303.

[31] Nathan, 1976, 60–81, 206; Twitchett and Fairbank, 1978, Vol. 12, 179–87; Wright, 1927, 131–32; SHAC 1039/502, "Tongshang tiaoyue xiugai, haiguan shuize yu neidi shuixiang, haiguan wenti ji zhengshou waishang gang di shui tong Caizhengbu, zhu Hua shiguan deng laiwang wenjian", 1919; AS 03/23/134, agreements, contracts, and related documents, "Zhong Ying xiuyue digao".

[32] Chi, 1976, 156–60; Nathan, 1976, 60, 69; SHAC 1039/467 "Ji Chang Lu jiekuan hetong xieyue gaiding, Guang-Jiu Hu-Ning Bo-Shen lu jianzhao xieyi de hanjian, ji Zhongguo tielu fazhan deng wenjian", 1919; SHAC 1039/467, "Kaikuang zhulu, Ying shi kangyi daoqu Dao Qing lu kuan, quxiao Lüyü lin kuang quan, ji Chifeng kaifu'an deng wenjian".

[33] Chan, 1971; Nathan, 1976, 62; Usui and Chen, 1990, 28–38; SHAC 1039/502, "Tongshang tiaoyue xiugai, haiguan shui ze yu neidi shuixiang, haiguan wenti ji zhengshou waishang gang di shui tong Caizhengbu, zhu Hua shiguan deng laiwang wenjian".

[34] SHAC 1039/194, "1913–1916 nian jian Zhongguo zhengfu wei jiaru dierci baohehui de gexiang tiaoyue bing dui xiuzheng luzhan fagui ji guanli tiaoyue qianshu yijian de wengaobu"; SHAC 1039/195, "Baohehui huiyilu".

[35] Many of Yuan's Beiyang militarist supporters did not support his ascension. To force Yuan to retreat, the British threatened to withhold funds to his government. McCord, 1993, 198–227; Tang, 2004, 194–96; Twitchett and Fairbank, 1978, Vol. 12, 253; Wright, 136–38.

[36] Tang, 2004, 159–64.

External Influence and China's Feudalisation, 1893–1922   81

British actions also helped buffer central authority from fragmentary challenges. London was, for example, the political force behind the 1919–1929 arms embargo regulating weapons and ammunition sales to China.[37] Despite the embargo's lack of success, it privileged the relative coercive capabilities of central governments by reducing arms available to local regimes.[38] General goodwill towards Wu Peifu and his Zhili Clique notwithstanding, London also refrained from supporting the Zhili opposition to the central government of Duan Qirui and the Anfu Clique to limit fragmentation.[39]

Official British efforts to contain fragmentation went beyond militaries factions. At Beijing's request, London pressured British firms to stop lending to regional regimes that seemed especially threatening to the central government, as was the case with loans to the Guangzhou National Government in 1922.[40] Stanley Baldwin's Conservative government even threatened the use of force to halt efforts by Sun Yat-sen and the Nationalists to seize the administration of salt taxes and customs in Guangdong.[41]

Moreover, the British government through the Foreign Office restricted official recognition to the central government regardless of the regime in power, and publicly insisted on Beijing's leadership in all Chinese diplomatic efforts. As a result, Chinese participation at international conventions, such as the Paris Peace Conference and the Washington Conference, required representation by the government in Beijing even if the delegation included representatives of other domestic actors.[42] British pressure was also partially responsible for efforts at forcing Tokyo's acceptance of Chinese participation in the Versailles Conference and an end to the Japanese military occupation of Shandong during the Washington Conference.[43]

---

[37] Chan, 1982, 49, 51, 65, 131; Chen, 1983, 54–68; Chi, 1976, 59–62; AS 03/18/104/02, Correspondence amongst the Foreign Ministry, Army Ministry, Navy Ministry, Secretariat of the State Council, and the Office of the *Duban* for War Participation, "Geguo jinyun junxie lai Hua'an", July 1919; AS 03/18/104/03, Correspondence between the Navy and Foreign Ministries, "Haijunbu han xün wairen junhuo jinyun lai Hua'an", May 1919; AS 03/18/104/04–05, Correspondence amongst the State Council, Foreign Ministry, and various foreign embassies in China, "Jinyun junxie lai Hua'an", May 1919.

[38] Chan, 1982, 131–37; Chen, 1983, 68–95, 128–37, 165–232; Chi, 1976, 121–22; AS 03/18/104/02, "Geguo jinyun junxie lai Hua'an"; AS 03/18/104/03, "Haijunbu han xün wairen junhuo jinyun lai Hua'an"; AS 03/18/104/04–05, "Jinyun junxie lai Hua'an".

[39] Chan, 1982, 45–65, 129–37; Chi, 1976, 123.

[40] AS 03/20/041–042, "Yue sheng jiekuan'an"; AS 03/20/042/03, Exchanges amongst the Foreign Ministry, Secretariat of the President of the Republic of China, and the American and British Embassies, "Sun Wen xiang geguo jiekuan choubei junshi'an", March 1922.

[41] AS 03/19/012/04, Correspondence between Sir John Jordan, British Ambassador to China, and the Foreign Ministry, "Sun Wen shouguan Yue haiguan shi", December 1923; AS 03/04/008/01, Minutes from meetings between various foreign embassies and the Foreign Ministry, "Guangzhou Junzhengfu kouliu yankuan geguo zhi wei Shanhou Jiekuan hetong shi", June–October 1918.

[42] Liu and Li, 1962, 542; Nathan, 1976, 3, 158–62; Tang, 2004, 69–81; SHAC 18/3285 "Youguan Bali hehui jianbao"; SHAC 1039/339, "Zhonghua Minguo kaiguo zhi Bali hehui qianxi zhi waijiao zhengce"; SHAC 18/3516, "Zhongguo xiwang tiaoyue".

[43] Li, 1966, 1994; SHAC 18/3285 "Youguan Bali hehui jianbao"; SHAC 1039/648, "Waijiaobu wendu: Zhong Ri jiejue Shandong xuan'an linshi huiyilu (xia)"; SHAC 1039/653, "Taipingyang

82   *External Intervention and the Politics of State Formation*

Second, in the event that British leaders felt that another external power was gaining an edge in access, they demanded compensatory concessions from China's central government to nullify any disadvantage.[44] Following the Scramble for Concessions, for instance, the Salisbury cabinet secured ninety-nine-year leases over Weihaiwei and Kowloon, in addition to promises not to grant access privileges in the Lower Yangzi area to other powers.[45] This aimed to counter Russian, German, and French advances in China, and permit the British government to trade access privileges in the Lower Yangzi region for reciprocal arrangements with the other external powers.[46] The Salisbury, Balfour, and Campbell-Bannerman cabinets believed that this could forestall a formal carving up of China, and allow British interests to retain a foothold if partition occurred.

Third, London undertook to promote competition over access by more outside actors in the hope that this could prevent other foreign powers from gaining exclusive access whilst minimising British capability investments in China.[47] Facing the creation of Russian, German, and French spheres of influence after the Sino-Japanese War, the Salisbury cabinet pushed to neutralise the advantages in access such inroads might bring for the other powers. To this end, London acquiesced to Japan's creation of a sphere of influence in Fujian in 1898, supported Japan in the Russo-Japanese War, and recognised Tokyo's interests in Manchuria at the Washington Conference.[48] In return, the Conservative Salisbury government and Foreign Office sought Japanese support for a less restrictive application of the Open Door principle that permitted the exchange of access privileges across the spheres of influence. London also tried to gain American sympathy for its modified Open Door approach, which saw partial fruition in U.S. Secretary of State John Hay's circulation of the Open Door Notes from 1899 to 1900.

British leaders also advanced economic cooperation with France in southern and southwest China as part of an attempt to foster the exchange of access privileges.[49] This move aimed to increase competitive pressure on powers that held exclusive spheres of influence. Further, British policymakers consistently attempted to give other powers a stake in China's continued centralisation by

---

huiyi shanhou weiyuanhui caibing banfa dagang; Shandong wenti shanhou huiyi"; AS 03/33/165, "Huashengdun huiyi Lu'an yilu"; AS 03/39/032/05, "Huashengdun huiyi qianding zhi gexiang tiaoyue xieding ji jueyi'an"; AS 03/39/036/04/001–020, "Huashengdun huiyi suoding zhi guanyu Zhongguo shijian tiaoyue shi".

[44] Joseph, 285–414; Wang, 67–68, 116–28, 48–59, 92–97; AS 03/23/134, "Zhong Ying xiuyue digao".

[45] SHAC 1039/651 "Beiyang zhengfu Taipingyang huiyi Weihaiwei wenti"; AS 03/23/134, "Zhong Ying xiuyue digao".

[46] AS 03/23/134, agreements, contracts, and related documents, "Zhong Ying xiuyue digao".

[47] Davis, 1982; Edwards, 1966; McLean, 1973; Platt, 276–307.

[48] Barnhart, 1995, 26–37, 77–78; Schneider, 1998, 161–82; Wang, 1979, 106–08, 136–41; AS 03/33/165, "Huashengdun huiyi Lu'an yilu"; AS 03/39/032/05, "Huashengdun huiyi qianding zhi gexiang tiaoyue xieding ji jueyi'an"; AS 03/39/036/04/001–020, "Huashengdun huiyi suoding zhi guanyu Zhongguo shijian tiaoyue shi".

[49] Edwards, 1971; Joseph, 1928, 315–42; Wang, 1979, 187–97.

External Influence and China's Feudalisation, 1893–1922   83

engaging in joint efforts to prop up the central government. London's attempts to coordinate a multinational response to the Boxer episode, which included an international military expedition and a multilateral loan to help the Qing court pay the Boxer indemnity, exemplifies such efforts.

ACCESS AND CENTRAL GOVERNMENT RULE: CHINA AND AMERICAN ASCENDANCE

Like the British, U.S. policy towards China between 1893 and 1922 generally supported a central government that wielded authority across the polity and whose ability to engage external actors was free from foreign domination. Despite China's commercial and strategic attractions, as well as America's growing prominence, U.S. leaders believed that securing access in China did not warrant a diversion of capabilities away from other strategic concerns. Due to such perspectives about the high costs of intervention in China, American administrations from McKinley to Harding focused on preserving a degree of nondiscriminatory access relative to the other powers. This meant helping China's central government to maintain rudimentary degree of political integration and autonomy even if outside powers continued to perform certain functions of domestic governance.

There was a persistent belief in China's large commercial and growing strategic importance amongst many U.S. leaders in the late nineteenth and early twentieth centuries. Development of the China market was an ongoing temptation for American business people since the founding of the American Republic.[50] China's then 400 million plus inhabitants, its natural resources, and its need for infrastructure development and financing remained attractive for American business. This promise of a huge potential market motivated the Taft administration to push especially hard for the creation of opportunities for U.S. commercial interests in Manchuria and elsewhere in China.[51] Administrations from McKinley to Harding also viewed China as potentially useful for balancing potential threats in the Far East, especially given increasing Russian and Japanese assertiveness in the area.[52]

In this regard, a number of prominent American leaders hoped to tap into China's economic and strategic potential by helping to realise its development into a strong, centralised, and autonomous state. These included Presidents Taft, Wilson, and Harding, Secretaries of State Philander Knox and Robert Lansing, William Jennings Bryan, and business and missionary leaders like William

[50] Hunt, 1983, 2–40, 143–54, 202–16, 273–85; Iriye, 1967, 3–4; Schoonover, 2003, 12, 61–76.
[51] Cohen, 2000, 36–89; Iriye, 1967, 123; Schoonover, 2003, 76; Wang, 1979, 132–36, 159–86.
[52] Proponents of this view included Alfred Thayer Mahan, Brooks Adams, as well as American Ministers in Beijing, William W. Rockhill and Paul S. Reinsch. Chen, 2005, 121–29; Hunt, 1983, 189–226; Iriye, 1967, 78–89, 102–08, 118–41; Kennan, 1984, 14–37; Schoonover, 2003, 73–88; Tompkins, 1949, 19–24.

W. Rockhill, Willard Straight, and E.H. Harriman.[53] They felt that cooperating with a strong and centralised Chinese central government could help U.S. firms overcome the disadvantages of late market entry in China whilst bolstering stability in the Far East. Proponents of this view thought they could facilitate this outcome by extending loans, diplomatic recognition, and political support to shore up central government rule.[54] Alternatively, China's domination by another power or partition by several powers threatened discrimination against if not outright exclusion of American interests, which could prove highly detrimental going forward.

However, broader economic and strategic concerns facing Washington curbed the enthusiasm of all but the most fervently optimistic American leaders. A brief boom in U.S. economic ties with China during the 1890s slowed by the time the United States was ready to play a major role in the Asia-Pacific at the turn of the century.[55] Coinciding with this change were inroads by American firms into more stable and profitable markets within the United States, Oceania, Latin America, the Caribbean, and Europe.[56] Moreover, as relative latecomers, American businesses realised that they had to battle British, Japanese, and other corporations with established market positions.[57] This was especially true of the lucrative financial, telecommunications, and railway industries.[58]

Dampening of the general American economic outlook on China encouraged policymakers and business leaders alike to take a more conservative position on securing access in the polity. It eased pressure for a more active and robust U.S. government role in China from business-related groups like the American Asiatic Society.[59] Such trends led Presidents William McKinley and Theodore Roosevelt, Secretaries of State John Hay and Elihu Root, and politicians like Henry Cabot Lodge to become more cautious about heavy involvement in China, even if their enthusiasm about its potential remained.

American leaders further understood that the U.S. government was strategically not in a position to force its way into China. Despite rapid growth in its capabilities during the late nineteenth and early twentieth centuries, the U.S. military could not project force in China in way sufficient to challenge the other foreign powers entrenched there.[60] Theodore Roosevelt pointed out that the

---

[53] Other supporters of strengthening China included Secretary of State Charles Evans Hughes, Hughes' principal advisor, J.V.A. MacMurray, American Minister to China Jacob Gould Schurman, and other State Department officials like E.T. Williams. Chen, 2005, 121–39; Davis, 1982; Hunt, 1983, 154–83, 216–26, 258–98; Iriye, 1967, 79–82, 102–08, 116–45; Jespersen, 1996, 1–10; Schoonover, 2003, 70, 86–87, 106; Zhang, 2001, 447–48, 490–96, 2004, 339–59.

[54] Schoonover, 2003, 112–13; Zhang, 2004, 150–51, 85–87.

[55] About 8 percent of U.S. GNP from this period came from foreign trade. With the exception of a small spike to 3.5 percent in 1905, American exports to China between 1900 and 1920 stood at between 0.7 and 1.8 percent of total U.S. exports. Iriye, 1967, 108–10; Schoonover, 2003, 61–64.

[56] Kennan, 1984, 14–19; Schoonover, 2003, 116, 20.

[57] Schoonover, 2003, 52, 69.

[58] China Dept. of Railways and Wang, 1916, 537–604; Zhang, 2004, 225–35.

[59] Cohen, 2000, 36–93; Hunt, 1983, 235–49, 261, 275–85; Iriye, 1967, 80–97, 102–20.

[60] Schoonover, 2003, 66–75, 113; Zhang, 2004, 188–89.

External Influence and China's Feudalisation, 1893–1922   85

Great White Fleet would face problems against Japanese naval superiority in Northeast Asia, especially after the Russo-Japanese War.[61] By 1906, concerns were also building within the U.S. Navy and government about both a potential Japanese threat to the Philippines and the possibility of a German attempt to seize control of the Caribbean.[62]

Additionally, the dragging on of the Philippine War from 1899 tied up about two thirds of the entire U.S. Army at the time, and cost about US$600 million between 1899 and 1902 – about a quarter of the federal budget for the period.[63] In fact, the commander of American forces in Asia did not support participation in the China Relief Expedition during the Boxer episode given concerns about its negative impact on troop strength in the Philippines.[64] Concurrent interventions across the Western Hemisphere, Guam, and Hawaii stretched any remaining U.S. military capabilities until the mid 1910s.[65] When fighting in these areas finally subsided, World War I soon drew American energies toward Europe.[66]

Further limiting U.S. involvement in China after the war was the rise of already strong isolationist sentiments within Congress and amongst the American public.[67] Consequently, U.S. leaders between 1893 and 1922 had little funding and only a few assets to employ for projecting American power into China. Given alliance patterns and major power interests, American leaders also expected little support from the other major powers for an enhanced U.S. economic and political role in China.[68]

Key American policymakers had neither the appetite for intensive intervention in China nor an aspiration for complete noninvolvement, much like their British counterparts. There was little consideration of these options during serious policy discussions. The U.S. Navy toyed with the possibility of establishing a naval station on Sansha Bay in Fujian between 1900 and 1907.[69] This could put the United States in a more serious position to compete for access along China's southeast coast. However, the Roosevelt and McKinley administrations never treated the idea with much gravity, in part because Sansha Bay fell well within

---

[61] Hunt, 1983, 182, 202–07.

[62] Hunt, 1983, 196–98, 224; Iriye, 1967, 78, 107, 120, 135–36; Kennan, 1984, 14–19.

[63] Schoonover, 2003, 93; United States Bureau of the Census, 1975; United States Dept. of the Treasury, Division of Bookkeeping and Warrants, 1900, 76–77, 84–85, 106–07; Government Printing Office, "Table Ea636–643 – Federal government expenditure, by major function: 1789–1970" in *Historical Statistic of the United States: Millennial Edition Online* (Cambridge: Cambridge University Press) stable URL: <http://hsus.cambridge.org/HSUSWeb/toc/tableToc.do?id=Ea636–643> (accessed April 6, 2007).

[64] Schoonover, 2003, 69, 95–96, 121.

[65] Between 1900 and 1922, U.S. forces engaged in major military operations in Cuba, Haiti, Panama, the Dominican Republic, and Mexico in addition to the Philippines and Europe. Cohen, 2000, 36–53; Iriye, 1967, 87–88, 128; Kennan, 1984, 14–19; Schoonover, 2003, 89–95.

[66] Hunt, 1983, 177–226.

[67] Ikenberry, 2001, 148–60; Iriye, 1967, 141–45; Wang, 1979, 159–86.

[68] Schoonover, 2003, 112–17.

[69] Braisted, 1968; Cohen, 2000, 37–50, 62–94; Hunt, 1983, 368n18; Iriye, 1967, 87, 129–45; Shippee, 1936; Zhang, 2004, 188–89.

86 *External Intervention and the Politics of State Formation*

the Japanese sphere of influence. They believed that such a move could bring about a costly and potentially pointless confrontation with Tokyo.

As a result, neither overt access regulation over parts of China nor complete withdrawal appealed to Washington from 1893 to 1922, suggesting the predominance of perceptions about the high opportunity costs of intervention there.[70] American administrations from Roosevelt on believed that the United States could ill afford a robust China policy given the broader circumstances of world politics during the early twentieth century.[71] United States leaders viewed involvement in China as an issue over the degree to which they should lend limited financial and political support for political centralisation and external autonomy, but would close an eye on issues of external autonomy.[72] They believed that this could maintain sufficient order in China to prevent its dismemberment by other external actors and subsequent discrimination against American access.[73]

America's Open Door Option

The American approach to China meant finding just enough support for a central Chinese government that could hold the polity together in a way that would not provoke the concerted opposition by other outside powers. United States government involvement in China in the first two decades of the twentieth century generally translated into the provision of political and financial support to central authorities under terms that averted discrimination against American access. This aim motivated the American Open Door Notes of 1900, as well as the Taft administration's rapid recognition of Yuan Shikai's government and support for its consolidation of power after the 1911 Revolution.[74] Similar concerns drove the Wilson administration's call for official Chinese participation in World War I and the Versailles Conference, as well as the Harding administration's support for Beijing's representation at the Washington Conference.[75] In this regard, the McKinley and Roosevelt administrations even tried to calibrate American military and diplomatic actions between the Boxer episode and the Russo-Japanese War to balance the relative access advantages amongst outside powers active in northern China.[76]

Woodrow Wilson's efforts to bolster central governments under Duan Qirui and Xu Shichang domestically also sought to preserve central authority. By

---

[70] Braisted, 1968; Hunt, 1983, 368n18; Shippee, 1936.

[71] Iriye, 1967, 80–90, 102–45.

[72] Chen, 2005, 88–94; Cohen, 2000, 36–91; Schoonover, 2003, 66, 69.

[73] Iriye, 1967, 78–90, 102–45; Kennan, 1984, 21–37; Zhang, 2004, 137–53, 185–88.

[74] Chen, 2005, 95–103; Davis, 1982; SHAC 1039/194, "1913 – 1916 nian jian Zhongguo zhengfu wei jiaru dierci Baohehui de gexiang tiaoyue bing dui xiuzheng luzhan fagui ji guanli tiaoyue qianshu yijian de wengaobu"; SHAC 1039/195 "Baohehui huiyilu".

[75] Chen, 1983, 121–39; Iriye, 1967, 83–102, 127–29, 141–45; Zhang, 2004, 275–82.

[76] Barnhart, 1995, 38–40; Cohen, 2000, 47–55; Hunt, 1983, 196–207, 70, 369n23; Schoonover, 2003, 110; Wang, 1979, 195–96.

External Influence and China's Feudalisation, 1893–1922   87

helping to support an arms embargo over China, the Wilson administration sought to lock in the financial and military advantages enjoyed by Duan's government as it faced off against regional regimes in the south.[77] At the behest of China's central government, the Wilson administration even stepped in to block private American financing of regional regimes such as the Nationalists in Guangzhou.[78] Washington hoped that such action would encourage accommodation of the Beijing central government during the Shanghai Peace Conference, of which the U.S. government was a cosponsor.[79]

Moreover, the U.S. government also attempted to partially fund efforts by Chinese central governments to bring the rest of the polity to heel. With the partial exception of Wilson, U.S. administrations from Taft onward tended to be strong supporters of financial concerns like the American Group, which provided large loans to the central government.[80] These included financing for the 1901 Boxer Indemnity, the Old Consortium Loans to the Qing court in 1909, the 1913 Re-Organisation Loan to the Yuan government, and the abortive 1919 New Consortium Loan to Xu Shichang's government.[81] American capital was also significant in the construction of the important Hu-Guang railroad.[82]

In return, American financing came with conditions stipulating the nonalienation of U.S. interests.[83] Contracts often required the use of American firms in constructing and operating related projects as well.[84] This is evident in the contracts from the Hu-Guang Railway to financing projects with U.S. participation like the New and Old Consortium as well as Re-Organisation Loans.[85]

---

[77] Chen, 1983, 68–75, 107–25, 2005, 129–39; Zhang, 2004, 313–23; AS 03/18/104/02, "Geguo jinyun junxie lai Hua'an"; AS 03/18/104/03, "Haijunbu han xün wairen junhuo jinyun lai Hua'an"; AS 03/18/104/04–05, "Jinyun junxie lai Hua'an".

[78] AS 03/20/041/01/028, Minutes of Meeting between Foreign Ministry and American Embassy representatives, "Guanyu benguo ren yu Sun Wen qianding hetong jiekuan yishi yijiang laizhao chengsong benguo zhengfu bing shichi zhu Guangzhou benguo lingshi qing chazhao you", December 1921; AS 03/20/042/03, "Sun Wen xiang geguo jiekuan choubei junshi'an".

[79] Chan, 1982, 33–39; Chen, 1983, 47–68, 2005, 129–39; Nathan, 1976, 129–51; AS 03/23/029/03/038, Telegram from Foreign Minister Lu in Paris to the Foreign Ministry, "Nan Bei tiaohe de muqian qingxing".

[80] Chen, 2005, 105–10; Cohen, 2000, 60–78; Hunt, 1983, 211–16, 79; Iriye, 1967, 121–24; Scheiber, 1969; Zhang, 2004, 327–35; AS 03/12/007/03/010, Telegram from the Foreign Ministry to the Embassy to the United States, "Zhong De juejiao caizheng jiang shou yingxiang wang Meiguo yuanzhu ji dian qingda Mei waibu you", March 1917; AS 03/12/008/01/079, Telegram from the Foreign Ministry to the Embassy to the United States, "Yu waibu jieqia she fa yuanzhu shi", November 1918; AS 03/05/065, "Zhong-Mei, Zhong-Fa, Zhong-Ao tielu shiyi".

[81] Cohen, 2000, 37–91; Davis, 1982; Hunt, 1983, 143–216, 273–85; Iriye, 1967, 75–80, 95–96, 121–25; Li, 2000, 356; Zhang, 2004, 151–53, 185–87, 327–35.

[82] China Dept. of Railways and Wang, 1916, 537–604; AS 03/05/065, "Zhong-Mei, Zhong-Fa, Zhong-Ao tielu shiyi"; AS 03/05/067, exchanges amongst the Foreign, Finance, and Communications Ministries, and the American Embassy, "Xiang Mei shang Yuzhong gongsi jiekuan zhulu", June 1918—August 1922.

[83] Iriye, 1967, 151–52.

[84] Davis, 1982; Zhang, 2004, 151–53, 85–89, 327–35.

[85] China Dept. of Railways and Wang, 1916, 537–604; AS 03/32/132/01/014, "1920 nian 4 yue xiurui yunhe Huaqi yinhang shi wan yuan jiekuan hetong", April 1920.

88   *External Intervention and the Politics of State Formation*

Concurrently, American administrations tried to avert opposition from and potential confrontation with other foreign actors in their attempts to ensure non-discriminatory access. Even as they tried to shore up China's central government, U.S. leaders and diplomats tried to obtain the acquiescence of major external powers over the nonpartition of the polity.[86] A key argument put forward by U.S. officials espousing the benefits of such an approach was the guarantee of non-discriminatory access opportunities in the China market.[87] Significantly, pronouncements from the Open Door Notes to the 1922 Nine Power Treaty came with limited or no consultation with China's central government.[88]

Washington wished to support the central government to ensure nondiscriminatory access in China, but was unwilling to directly challenge entrenched outside powers to do so.[89] This attitude became especially strong after joint Russian-Japanese pressure forced Philander Knox and the Taft administration to abort plans to build and operate the Jinzhou-Aihun railroad for the Qing court in 1909.[90] Subsequent officially supported American initiatives in China tended to first seek sanction by the other major external powers. For all its misgivings about Russia and Japan, Washington sought their cooperation in the 1909 Old Consortium Loan, 1913 Re-Organisation Loan, and the proposed 1919 New Consortium Loan.[91]

The circulation of John Hay's Open Door Notes, too, came with support from the British and Japanese governments.[92] The Wilson administration similarly sought to work with the British to promote the arms embargo and the 1919 North-South Peace Talks in Shanghai.[93] Ending Japan's occupation of Shandong likewise occurred in conjunction with pressure from other major powers at the Washington Conference.[94]

---

[86] Iriye, 1967, 78–82, 102–45.

[87] Wang, 1979, 175–86.

[88] Iriye, 1967, 144–45; Kennan, 1984, 21–54; Schoonover, 2003, 112–13.

[89] The original intent of Hay's Open Door notes was to placate domestic groups arguing against the partition of China, whilst at the same time minimising possible U.S. government involvement. Hay carefully avoided official U.S. commitments as well as impinging on the interests of the major external powers active in China. It is a later reading that gives the notes a seemingly pro-China, anti-imperialist flavour. Hunt, 1983, 153–54, 182–226, 874–79; Iriye, 1967, 78–145.

[90] Li, 2000, 349–56; Tompkins, 1949, 16–29.

[91] Davis, 1982; Tompkins, 1949, 30–42; Zhang, 2004, 151–53, 85–87, 327–35.

[92] Cohen, 2000, 38–48; Hunt, 1983, 153–54, 183–97; Iriye, 1967, 80–82; Wang, 1979, 175–86.

[93] The U.S. government also did little to stem the flow of American-made arms to the various warring parties in China during the embargo. Chan, 1982, 45–65; Chen, 1983, 47–125, 2005, 129–39; Zhang, 2004, 313–23; AS 03/18/104/02, "Geguo jinyun junxie lai Hua'an"; AS 03/18/104/03, "Haijunbu han xün wairen junhuo jinyun lai Hua'an"; AS 03/18/104/04, "Jinyun junxie lai Hua'an"; AS 03/23/029/03/038, "Nanbei tiaohe de muqian qingxing".

[94] Barnhart, 1995, 73–78; Cohen, 2000, 87–89; SHAC 1039/375, "Taipingyang huiyi shanhou weiyuanhui taolun caibing jiaohui Guangzhouwan, jiejue Shandong xuanan deng wenti laiwang wenshu ji canyu Huashengdun huiyi wenjian"; SHAC 1039/648, "Waijiaobu wendu: Zhong Ri jiejue Shandong xuanan linshi huiyilu (xia)"; SHAC 1039/653, "Taipingyang huiyi shanhou weiyuanhui caibing banfa dagang; Shandong wenti shanhou huiyi"; AS 03/33/165, "Huashengdun huiyi Lu'an yilu"; AS 03/39/032/05, "Huashengdun huiyi qianding zhi gexiang

External Influence and China's Feudalisation, 1893–1922 89

Given that insisting on territorial exclusivity could spell direct confrontation with other foreign actors, however, the U.S. government was willing to compromise on this issue so long as they enjoyed a level of nondiscriminatory access. Despite Hay's Open Door declaration, Washington did little to challenge the German position in Shandong, France's sway over the Southwest, or British influence of the Lower Yangzi between 1893 and 1922. When it did seek to disrupt Russian and Japanese efforts to seize Manchuria, it was in cooperation with the British and in the wake of Japanese military successes in the Russo-Japanese War.[95] Even in doing so, the United States acknowledged Japanese control over southern Manchuria and continuing Russian influence in northern Manchuria. Washington also remained quiet over the Twenty-One Demands despite Yuan Shikai's efforts to elicit official American support against Japan.[96]

At Versailles, Wilson was willing to trade opposition to Japanese domination in Shandong and Manchuria for Tokyo's support for the League of Nations.[97] In spite of calls to support China's political unity, external autonomy, and territorial exclusivity, the Washington Conference concluded with *de facto* U.S. recognition of Japan's domination over Manchuria. Moreover, Washington's efforts to secure Japan's military withdrawal from Shandong gave Tokyo special privileges that effectively put the area under Japanese economic domination.[98] Until the mid 1920s, Washington was also notably silent about British administration of the Chinese Maritime Customs.

JAPAN AND INFORMAL IMPERIALISM IN CHINA

Tokyo had several opportunities to intervene in China between 1893 and 1922. These included the 1894–1895 Sino-Japanese War, the Boxer Protocol, the Russo-Japanese War in Manchuria, following the 1911 Revolution, and after the start of World War I. Evidence indicates that whilst markets, resources, and proximity to Japan made full access denial over parts of China seem highly attractive, broader strategic concerns and a strong desire to minimise friction

tiaoyue xieding ji jueyi'an"1; AS 03/39/036/04/001–020, "Huashengdun huiyi suoding zhi guanyu Zhongguo shijian tiaoyue shi".

[95] Barnhart, 1995, 38–41; Cohen, 2000, 38–76; Hunt, 1983, 370n34; Kennan, 1984, 38–46; Li, 329–38.

[96] Chen, 2005, 111–20; SHAC 1039/339 "Zhonghua Minguo kaiguo zhi Bali hehui qianxi zhi waijiao zhengce".

[97] Barnhart, 1995, 67–68; Cohen, 2000, 79–80; SHAC 1039/648, "Waijiaobu wendu: Zhong-Ri jiejue Shandong xuanan linshi huiyilu (xia)"; SHAC 1039/653, "Taipingyang huiyi shanhou weiyuanhui caibing banfa dagang; Shandong wenti shanhou huiyi".

[98] Barnhart, 1995, 76–77; SHAC 1039/375, "Taipingyang huiyi shanhou weiyuanhui taolun caibing jiaohui Guangzhouwan, jiejue Shandong xuanan deng wenti laiwang wenshu ji canyu Huashengdun huiyi wenjian"; SHAC 1039/648, "Waijiaobu wendu: Zhong-Ri jiejue Shandong xuanan linshi huiyilu (xia)"; SHAC 1039/653, "Taipingyang huiyi shanhou weiyuanhui caibing banfa dagang; Shandong wenti shanhou huiyi"; AS 03/39/032/05, "Huashengdun huiyi qianding zhi gexiang tiaoyue xieding ji jueyian"; AS 03/39/036/04/001–020, "Huashengdun huiyi suoding zhi guanyu Zhongguo shi jian tiaoyue shi".

with other major powers prompted caution.[99] Stemming from such perspectives about the moderate opportunity costs of intervening in China during the late nineteenth and early twentieth century, Tokyo restricted intervention to access regulation over areas that appeared most strategically and economically important.

Elite arguments advocating intervention and full access denial over China were common in Japan throughout this time. Proponents of fuller access denial, including Prime Ministers Okuma Shigenobu, Kato Takaaki, and many senior Imperial Army officers, argued that the most pressing concern for Japan at the time an increasingly vigorous Russia. They pointed to growing Russian assertiveness in Northeast Asia around the turn of the century as St. Petersburg began to shift focus away from Southern Europe and Central Asia.[100] This took shape in the Trans-Siberian Railroad – with its extensions into Manchuria, sharply increased Russian naval presence in Liaodong, and the purported Russian plans to expand into Korea and parts of China south of the Great Wall.[101] Supporters of a more interventionist policy believed that these developments threatened to erase Japan's gains from the Sino-Japanese War, exclude Japan from Manchuria and Korea, and even menace the Home Islands and Japanese sealanes of communication.[102]

Given these strategic concerns, the more aggressive Japanese civilian and military leaders lobbied for the outright occupation of Manchuria and Korea.[103] Trying to take advantage of the chaos following the 1911 Revolution in China, the Imperial Army called for military action and support of the revolutionaries to secure an independent Manchuria subservient to Japan.[104] In comparison, the *genro* considered aiding the Qing court in exchange for control of Manchuria. Hara Kei and his political party, the Seiyukai, wished to aid both the revolutionaries and Qing court to put Japan in a position to cut a deal for Manchuria no matter which side won.[105]

Using the distraction that World War I presented to the other major powers, Foreign Minister Kato Takaaki even sought to engineer the occupation of Shandong beyond the German-held areas around Jiaozhou Bay in 1914. This was on grounds of being an Allied Power.[106] Kato further attempted to force the Yuan Shikai government to accept its Twenty-One Demands in 1915.[107] Apart from formalising existing advantages, the Demands aimed to establish Japanese

---

[99] Barnhart, 1995, 30.

[100] Li, 2000; Satow and Lensen, 1966; Wang, 1979, 89–90, 128–32; Zheng, 2001, 518–27.

[101] Barnhart, 1995, 25–37; China Dept. of Railways and Wang, 1916, 1–12, 187–210; Fuller, 1992, 367–70; Iriye, 1967, 97–98; Shen, 2005, 113–17; Wang, 1979, 197–209.

[102] Joseph, 1928, 101–21; Satow and Lensen, 1966; Zheng, 2001, 390–92, 419–31.

[103] Iriye, 1967, 97–101; Shen, 2005, 115–17, 128–30, 155–56.

[104] Barnhart, 1995, 48; Usui and Chen, 1990, 3–6, 17–26; Zheng, 2001, 513–27.

[105] Barnhart, 1995, 19–50; Li, 2000, 318–19; Usui and Chen, 1990, 15–26; Zheng, 2001, 505–15.

[106] Barnhart, 1995, 69; Shen, 2005, 188–205; Usui and Chen, 1990, 58–73.

[107] Li, 1966; Shen, 2005, 192–205; Snyder, 1991, 125; Tang, 2004, 140–46; Usui and Chen, 1990, 30–87; SHAC 1039/645, Chinese Consulate in Japan, "Zhong Ri jiaoshe shimo", 1915.

External Influence and China's Feudalisation, 1893–1922   91

oversight over military, political, economic, cultural, and religious activities in China by placing Japanese advisors in key central government positions.[108]

Moreover, Hara Kei's cabinet advocated the formal absorption of Manchuria and at least the former German-leasehold areas of Shandong into the Empire in 1919. In return, they offered Japanese support for the League of Nations at the Versailles Conference.[109] The Imperial Army also opposed international support for development projects in Manchuria and Inner Mongolia discussed in Paris, lest they weaken Japan's position.[110] At the 1921 Washington Conference, the Imperial Army and leading political figures like Inukai Tsuyoshi and Goto Shimpei further pressed for the formal annexation of Manchuria and Shandong.[111]

Japanese leaders of the early twentieth century, however, had other strategic worries too. Growing American influence and continuing British prominence in the Far East were major causes for concern. With its annexation of Hawaii and the Philippines in 1898, the United States established a forward presence in the Asia-Pacific that was uncomfortably close to Japan's colony on Taiwan.[112] This new position in the Pacific along with its growing economic weight permitted a more active American role in the Chinese economy as well as a rising ability to influence domestic politics in China.[113]

For all its problems, Britain looked to remain prominent in East Asia. The Royal Navy was still the world's largest and most advanced fleet at the beginning of twentieth century, and Britain could control strategic points along the China coast through its presence in Hong Kong, Shanghai, and Weihaiwei.[114] Through the 1920s, Britain was the preeminent player in the Chinese economy, especially in terms of private loans and investment.[115] Britain also continued to police trade along China's coast and major waterways through its influence over maritime customs. For Japanese leaders close to the country's large commercial conglomerates, British and American economic prominence in China appeared to come at Japanese expense.[116]

Further complicating matters was German control of Jiaozhou Bay in Shandong until 1914, and a reemergence of the Russian threat that temporarily subsided after the Russo-Japanese War. Not only did the internal problems that distracted the Tsarist regime after the Russo-Japanese War ebb with the

---

[108] Barnhart, 1995, 52–53; Iriye, 1967, 133–34; Usui and Chen, 1990, 89–106; SHAC 1039/339 "Zhonghua Minguo kaiguo zhi Bali hehui qianxi zhi waijiao zhengce".

[109] Barnhart, 1995, 68–69; Shen, 2005, 229–36; Usui and Chen, 1990, 197–216, 32–34.

[110] Barnhart, 1995, 76–78; Usui and Chen, 1990, 228–36; AS 03/18/026/03/002, Telegram from the Embassy in Japan to the Foreign Ministry, "Zhong-Ri jingji tongmeng shizhi zai pohuai Ying-Fa Mei Ri lianhe yuanzhu Zhongguo zhiyi", July 1921.

[111] Barnhart, 1995, 68–69; Shen, 2005, 237–44; Usui and Chen, 1990, 246–68.

[112] Iriye, 1967, 114–17, 131–33.

[113] Iriye, 1967, 87–88, 116–23, 175–86; Shen, 2005, 237–44; Wang, 1979, 159–86.

[114] Barnhart, 1995, 45; Wang, 1979, 89–120, 136–59, 220–26.

[115] Davis, 1982; Shen, 2005, 237–44.

[116] Lian, 2004, 87–112, 177–324; Scalapino and Yu, 1985, 64–65; Usui and Chen, 1990, 158–59; Wang, Zhen, and Sun, 2002, 53–55; Wright, 1927, 59–80, 127–59, 1950, 653–66; Xu, 1962, 114–29, 148–97.

External Intervention and the Politics of State Formation

Bolshevik Revolution's success, but the consolidation of Soviet control in Russia and Siberia also portended the spread of radical leftist ideas into Japan.[117] Japanese policymakers believed that this seriously threatened the imperial system and major commercial concerns that undergirded Japan's political and economic system.

Consequently, a significant portion of top leaders, especially senior naval officers and members of the *genro* such as Ito Hirobumi believed that overcommitment in China would undercut Japan's ability to safeguard its broader interests.[118] Moreover, Japan's relative dearth of economic, financial, and military capabilities next to other major powers was widely known.[119] With their naval presence in the region, the Americans, British, and Germans could easily endanger Japan's maritime access to northern China, Taiwan, and the Pacific. Even some of those most wary of a Russian threat, like Okuma and Hara, acknowledged the risks of overinvesting in China.[120]

Japanese leaders from Hara Kei and Admiral Kato Tomosaburo to hardliners like Foreign Minister Goto Shimpei saw any successful attempt to secure access in China to require an avoidance of joint resistance from other major powers.[121] They judged that overcoming combined major power opposition required a level of capability commitment that was impossible without sharp sacrifices to other objectives.[122] Even then, there was no guarantee of success. It was also easy for Japanese policymakers to envision circumstances where rivals could act collectively to thwart Japan. The Franco-Russian-German Triple Intervention following the Sino-Japanese War, after all, denied Japan control of the Liaodong Peninsula and weakened Japan's ability to secure access over Korea despite its resounding military victory.[123] Just as joint American, British, and German opposition forced Japan to reduce its post-Boxer presence in Fujian, concerted international pressure at the Washington Conference fostered the Imperial Army's withdrawal from Siberia in 1921.[124]

Adding to the burdens on Japanese leaders was the acknowledgement of Tokyo's spare financial resources. Government revenues in the first two decades of the twentieth century were stable, but a desire to quickly retire the public debt that financed the Sino-Japanese and Russo-Japanese Wars created substantial

---

[117] Barnhart, 1995, 57, 65.

[118] Barnhart, 1995, 16–19, 28–45, 68–76; Ishikawa, 1995, 4–104; Shen, 2005, 125–40, 156.

[119] Even the Japanese war effort during the Russo-Japanese War relied heavily on foreign loans, with roughly half coming from the United States and the other half from Britain. Iriye, 1967, 99–100; Kennedy, 1987, 199–209; Li, 2000, 318–19; Usui and Chen 1990, 28–46.

[120] Satow and Lensen, 1966.

[121] Barnhart, 1995, 62–71; Iriye, 1967, 142–45; Shen, 2005, 157; Usui and Chen, 1990, 113–16, 152–62, 228–39; Zheng, 2001, 463–75.

[122] Barnhart, 1995, 19–50, 62–63.

[123] Barnhart, 1995, 25; Fudan daxue (Shanghai China), "Sha E qin Hua shi" bianxie zu, 1986, 224–82; Iriye, 1967, 131–33; Joseph, 1928, 124–87; Mutsu, 2005, 141–75; Shen, 2005, 106–08; Zheng, 2001, 351–57.

[124] Iriye, 1967, 114–15, 142; Zheng, 2001, 407–08.

External Influence and China's Feudalisation, 1893–1922   93

financial pressure.[125] This belief in financial prudence weighed especially heavily on successive cabinets led by Ito Hirobumi, Okuma Shigenobu, Yamagata Aritomo, Saionji Kinmochi, and Katsura Taro.

A realisation of the need to account for the array of competing interests tempered Japanese leaders' approach toward access denial in China. Cognizant of international wariness toward independent Japanese action and Japan's own financial limitations, the Saionji, Katsura, and Yamamoto cabinets decided against seeking full access denial over Manchuria and Shandong after the Boxer episode and the 1911 Revolution.[126] This was in spite of objections by the Army, public, and some members of the *genro*. Instead, they sought to regulate access in these areas by acquiring local actor support whilst purchasing acquiescence from China's central government and seeking accommodation with other powers.

JAPAN'S CAUTIOUS ACCESS REGULATION

Tokyo's efforts to regulate access in partnership with local actors saw successful application in South Manchuria, eastern Inner Mongolia, coastal Fujian, and Shandong.[127] The Japanese government and Imperial Army provided financial and military support to local actors that controlled these areas, such as Zhang Zuolin and the Fengtian Clique, as well as Li Houji and later Xu Shuzheng in Fujian.[128] So long as the partnership between the Japanese government and those heading key regional and provincial governments held, Japan could regulate access over these areas. Japanese assistance generally went toward military modernisation, infrastructural development, arms sales, and military training in

---

[125] Usui and Chen, 1990, 15–26; Zheng, 2001, 505–15.

[126] Saionji's foreign minister, Uchida Yasuya, and the *genro* called for aid to the Manchu government in exchange for recognition of Japan's position in Manchuria. Hara Kei and his political party, the *Seiyukai*, wanted to aid both the revolutionaries as well as the Manchu court to ensure that China would be friendly to Japan regardless of which side won. The Imperial Army wanted to aid the rebels in exchange for an independent Manchuria that Japan could directly oversee.

[127] Zheng, 2001, 396–401, 446–52, 511–41; SHAC 18/3043, Koo, "Memorandum on Japan's Plots and Schemes against the Unification of China"; SHAC 1039/559, "Zhong Ri gezhong tiaoyue, tongshang hangchuan xinyue, ji ci Zhong Ri Meng Man tiaoyue shanhou huiyi jueyian deng zajian"; SHAC 1039/648, "Waijiaobu wendu: Zhong Ri jiejue Shandong xuanan linshi huiyi lu (xia)"; SHAC 1039/653, "Taipingyang huiyi shanhou weiyuanhui caibing banfa dagang; Shandong wenti shanhou huiyi"; AS 03/23/135, "Zhong Ri tiaoyue huibian".

[128] Gillin, 1967, 208–18; Schneider, 1998, 161–82; Shen, 2005, 138–70, 227–29, 257–64; Sheridan, 1966, 29, 69, 140–56, 77–84; Usui and Chen, 1990, 22–26, 78–99; Wright, 1980; Zheng, 2001, 397–409, 463–98; SHAC 18/3043, Koo, "Memorandum on Japan's Plots and Schemes against the Unification of China"; SHAC 1039/559, "Zhong Ri gezhong tiaoyue, tongshang hangchuan xinyue, ji ci Zhong Ri Meng Man tiaoyue shanhou huiyi jueyian deng zajian"; AS 03/23/135, "Zhong Ri tiaoyue huibian"; AS 03/23/029/03/001, Telegram from Consul Hu in France to the Foreign Ministry, "Zhong Ri gexiang miyue'an", January 1919; AS 03/05/049/02/15, Correspondence from the Army Ministry to the Foreign Ministry, "Ju micheng Zhang Zuolin yi Si-Tao tielu zuodi jie Ri kuan shichao song yuanjian qing chazhao you", October 1922.

94   *External Intervention and the Politics of State Formation*

return for exclusive economic privileges and oversight of these regional authorities, particularly over railroads, mining, and forestry.[129]

Critically, the Japanese government could place advisors in key parts of the
police, military, administrative, and economic units of the local regime.[130] These
advisors had oversight of operations, and reported to the Japanese administrative or military hierarchy rather than the regular chains of command in their host
units.[131] Supplementing such administrative influence were Japanese troops and
police stationed to secure key locations and installations such as railway lines,
mines, and other key transport nodes.[132] Other powers hoping to gain a share of
the markets, raw materials, communications, and strategic advantages in an area
needed at least Tokyo's acquiescence, as most were unwilling to openly confront
Japan over China.[133]

To further ensure an ability to regulate access over areas of interest, Japanese
leaders tried to buy acceptance if not support for Japan's exclusive positions
from regimes that controlled the Chinese central government.[134] Such thinking
moved the Saionji cabinet to participate in the 1913 Re-Organisation Loan
despite having to raise funds from abroad.[135] Japanese provision of weapons

[129] Barnhart, 1995, 43–84; China Dept. of Railways and Wang, 1916, 123–69; Iriye, 1967, 132;
SHAC 1039/469, "Guanyu zhulu, jiuzai xiangwai jiekuan, ji jiaotong yanxian zhujun qingkuang, yanlu fasheng chexian, daoqie deng shi zhi hanjian", 1919; SHAC 1039/559, "Zhong Ri
gezhong tiaoyue, tongshang hangchuan xinyue, ji ci Zhong Ri Meng Man tiaoyue shanhou huiyi
jueyian deng zajian"; AS 03/23/135, "Zhong Ri tiaoyue huibian"; AS 03/23/029/03/001,
"Zhong Ri gexiang miyue'an".

[130] Chi, 1976, 107; Shen, 2005, 122–23, 138–58, 227–29, 257–64; SHAC 18/3043, Koo,
"Memorandum on Japan's Plots and Schemes against the Unification of China"; SHAC 1039/
469, "Guanyu zhulu, jiuzai xiangwai jiekuan, ji jiaotong yanxian zhujun qingkuang, yanlu
fasheng chexian, daoqie deng shi zhi hanjian"; SHAC 1039/559, "Zhong Ri gezhong tiaoyue,
tongshang hangchuan xinyue, ji ci Zhong Ri Meng Man tiaoyue shanhou huiyi jueyian deng
zajian"; AS 03/23/135, "Zhong Ri tiaoyue huibian"; AS 03/23/029/03/001, "Zhong Ri gexiang
miyue'an".

[131] Zheng, 2001, 483–89; SHAC 18/3043, Koo, "Memorandum on Japan's Plots and Schemes
against the Unification of China"; SHAC 1039/469, "Guanyu zhulu, jiuzai xiangwai jiekuan, ji
jiaotong yanxian zhujun qingkuang, yanlu fasheng chexian, daoqie deng shi zhi hanjian"; SHAC
1039/559, "Zhong Ri gezhong tiaoyue, tongshang hangchuan xinyue, ji ci Zhong Ri Meng Man
tiaoyue shanhou huiyi jueyian deng zajian"; AS 03/23/135, contracts, agreements, treaties, and
related documents, "Zhong Ri tiaoyue huibian"; AS 03/23/029/03/001, Telegrams amongst
Consul Hu in France, the Foreign Ministry, and the delegation at Paris, "Zhong Ri gexiang
miyue'an".

[132] China Dept. of Railways and Wang, 1916, 127–68, 515–36.

[133] Usui and Chen, 1990, 78–84, 145–90; Zheng, 2001, 397–409, 83–96; SHAC 1039/559,
"Zhong Ri gezhong tiaoyue, tongshang hangchuan xinyue, ji ci Zhong Ri Meng Man tiaoyue
shanhou huiyi jueyian deng zajian".

[134] Shen, 2005, 134–37, 157–87, 222–27; SHAC 18/3043, Koo, "Memorandum on Japan's Plots
and Schemes against the Unification of China"; SHAC 1039/559, "Zhong-Ri gezhong tiaoyue,
tongshang hangchuan xinyue, ji ci Zhong-Ri Meng Man tiaoyue shanhou huiyi jueyian deng
zajian"; AS 03/23/135, "Zhong-Ri tiaoyue huibian".

[135] Usui and Chen, 1990, 30–34; SHAC 18/3043, Koo, "Memorandum on Japan's Plots and
Schemes against the Unification of China"; AS 03/23/029/03/001-023, "Zhong-Ri gexiang
miyue'an".

External Influence and China's Feudalisation, 1893–1922

and the War Preparation and Nishihara Loans to the Beiyang governments of Duan Qirui and Zhang Zuolin followed a similar reasoning.[136] When partners in the central government proved uncooperative, Tokyo reduced support.[137] So, when Duan and Zhang's central governments tried to extend their hold over the rest of China in spite of Tokyo's reservations, Japanese support became much less forthcoming.

Moreover, Tokyo worked to distract central authorities in China from challenging their ability to regulate access over certain regions. The Imperial Army, in particular, provided financial and material assistance to militarists in Yunnan and Guangdong in the south and to Gansu, Shanxi, Suiyuan, and Chahar in the north, whilst instigating uprisings in Shanghai and Guangdong.[138] Between 1912 and 1917, Japan even provided the Nationalist Party with loans and arms to oppose central governments in Beijing.[139] However, when working with local political actors outside its core areas of interest, the Japanese government generally provided less to these groups than its partners in Manchuria, and was careful to avoid upsetting other powers.[140] Tokyo correspondingly asked less of these groups.

Tokyo also sought accommodation with the other major powers to safeguard the Japanese position in areas of interest. This took the form of Japanese participation in activities such as the international consortium that provided the 1913 Re-Organisation Loan to the Yuan government. Such a move allowed greater Japanese oversight of governance in the Chinese northeast without a

---

[136] Chan, 1982, 45, 129–31; Chi, 1976, 26–30, 120–23, 56–68; Iriye, 1967, 131–32; Liu and Tian, 2004, 157–65; Pye, 1971, 18–37; Sheridan, 1966, 29, 69, 147, 177–79; Sunaga, 1988, 63–100; Usui and Chen, 1990, 145–90, 365–83, 1994, 71–82; Zheng, 2001, 539–41; SHAC 18/3043, Koo, "Memorandum on Japan's Plots and Schemes against the Unification of China"; SHAC 1039/559, "Zhong-Ri gezhong tiaoyue, tongshang hangchuan xinyue, ji ci Zhong-Ri Meng Man tiaoyue shanhou huiyi jueyian deng zajian"; AS 03/18/104/03/001, Letter from the Navy Ministry to the Foreign Ministry, "Dinggou riben haijun gongchang buqiang'an", May 1919; AS 03/23/135, "Zhong Ri tiaoyue huibian"; AS 03/20/071/03/010–011, correspondence between the Army and Foreign Ministries, "Chaosong guanyu junqi qianjia yu Dacangzu ding zhuanqi zuijia tiaojian qing zhuan Riben shiguan you", April 1903; AS 03/23/030, Exchanges amongst various governors and ministries, "Zhong Ri chengyue", January 1922; AS 03/23/029/03/001–023, "Zhong Ri gexiang miyue'an".

[137] Shen, 2005, 206–11; Tang, 2004, 140–46; Usui and Chen, 1990, 124–41; SHAC 18/3043, Koo, "Memorandum on Japan's Plots and Schemes against the Unification of China".

[138] Gillin, 1967, 108–19, 136–37, 208–09; Pye, 1971, 18–37, 47–51; Shen, 2005, 206–11; Usui and Chen, 1990, 71–82, 1994, 3–13, 28–42; SHAC 18/3043, Koo, "Memorandum on Japan's Plots and Schemes against the Unification of China".

[139] Jansen, 1954; SHAC 18/3043, Koo, "Memorandum on Japan's Plots and Schemes against the Unification of China"; AS 02/20/039/04/030–032, Telegram from Governor Wu (Peifu) at Luoyang to the Foreign Ministry, "Guangdong zaobichang'an", October 1923; AS 03/20/041/01/023, "Sun Wen yü Riben Taiping gongsi dijie junqi jiekuan ci shi nengfou shefa jinzu xicha heban liyou"; AS 03/20/053/01/017, "Riren zai Hu shoumai Guangdong Junzhengfu gongzai-piao fu chazhao you".

[140] Barnhart, 1995, 43–76; SHAC 18/3043, Koo, "Memorandum on Japan's Plots and Schemes against the Unification of China"; AS 03/23/029/03/001–023, "Zhong Ri gexiang miyue'an".

96 _External Intervention and the Politics of State Formation_

costly military takeover that risked intense international opposition.[141] This echoed the Yamagata cabinet's decision during the Boxer episode to block Russian control of northeast China through participation in an international intervention force.[142] Here, Yamagata overcame appeals by the Army, elites, and the public to unilaterally occupy Manchuria and parts of northern China, as well as a call by the Taiwan Government-General to occupy Xiamen on China's southeast coast.[143]

Similarly, despite stunning victories against Russian forces, the Katsura cabinet and Imperial Army decided to quickly end the Russo-Japanese War in June 1905 through American mediation despite Japanese elite and popular opposition.[144] In subsequent negotiations, Japanese leaders even agreed to forgo a much-needed indemnity, and settle for the transfer of exclusive Russian rights in Manchuria and control of south Sakhalin.[145] This paved the way for subsequent cooperation with Russia over excluding other powers from Manchuria and Mongolia, even though it left Japanese financial and military capabilities near exhaustion.[146] Worries about antagonism from other capitals likewise prompted Japanese leaders drop their most expansive "wishes" in the Twenty-One Demands, and led the Imperial Army to avoid clashes with Chinese troops during Japan's 1919–1921 Siberian Expedition.[147]

Prime Minister Hara Kei, Admiral Kato Tomosaburo (Japan's Chief Delegate and soon-to-be Prime Minister), and the Navy were likewise ready compromise with other powers in Washington to secure international acceptance of Japan's position in Manchuria. They essentially traded military occupation of Shandong and Japanese involvement in Siberia for formal recognition and acceptance of Japan's ability to regulate access over Manchuria and to maintain an ability to meet any potential American naval challenge.[148] This was in spite of the immense unpopularity of such a move amongst the public, Army, and other constituencies who wished to limit foreign influence on the Asian mainland even further.[149]

---

[141] Barnhart, 1995, 38–41; Wang, 1979, 227–50; Zheng, 2001, 515–19, 34–36.

[142] Barnhart, 1995, 31–41.

[143] Iriye, 1967, 114–17, 131–33; Jansen, 1954, 99–103; Schneider, 1998, 161–66.

[144] Iriye, 1967, 99–102; Li, 2000, 329–35; Zheng, 2001, 445–46.

[145] Hara, 1995, 55–65; Li, 2000, 254–83, 335–38; Shen, 2005, 135–37; Zheng, 2001, 446–52.

[146] Barnhart, 1995, 38–54; Hunt, 1983, 202; Li, 2000, 341–65; Tompkins, 1949, 30–43; AS 03/32/517, "E yu Riben dingyue"; AS 03/33/078, "Ri E xieyue".

[147] Barnhart, 1995, 60–63; Iriye, 1967, 131; Ishikawa, 1995, 80–104; Tang, 2004, 140–46; Usui and Chen, 1990, 107–13; AS 03/32/036/01/004, Telegram from Secretary Zheng in Russia to the Foreign Ministry, "Zhong-E shangding miyue shi", May 1918; AS 03/32/078, Correspondence amongst the Foreign Ministry, various foreign embassies in China, and Chinese consulates abroad, "Zhong-Ri gongtong fangdi", April 1918.

[148] Barnhart, 1995, 70–78; Ishikawa, 1995, 4–7; Shen, 2005, 244–5; Zheng, 2001, 539–41; AS 03/33/165, "Huashengdun huiyi Lu'an yilu"; AS 03/39/032/05, "Huashengdun huiyi qianding zhi gexiang tiaoyue xieding ji jueyi'an".

[149] Ishikawa, 1995, 80–104; Usui and Chen, 1990, 252–68.

External Influence and China's Feudalisation, 1893–1922   97

The only real deviation from Japan's overall approach towards securing access in China was Taiwan and the Pescadores, which passed into Tokyo's jurisdiction with the Treaty of Shimonoseki that concluded the Sino-Japanese War.[150] In contrast to the mainland, the Japanese government attempted to first regulate access over these islands and then incorporate them into the metropole.[151] Here, Tokyo cultivated local elites whom it could use to assist in the administration of the colony in the years between 1893 and 1922, whilst forcefully repressing opposition to Japanese rule.[152] Nonetheless, that no other external power was willing or able to seriously challenge the Japanese position on Taiwan and the Pescadores clearly contributed to Tokyo's success in absorbing these areas.

RUSSIA AND THE ENDS OF EMPIRE

Between 1893 and the October Revolution, Russian leaders generally expected the opportunity costs of intervention in China to range between low to moderate levels. Certainly, policymakers led initially by A.M. Bezobrazov, Army Minister Prince Alexey Kuropatkin, and Far East Governor-General Evgenii Alexeyev called for the absorption of Manchuria, Mongolia, northern Xinjiang, and parts of Inner Mongolia.[153] Arrayed against them was a group best represented by Finance Minister Sergius Witte and senior military leaders, who were more sensitive to the multiple pressures then facing Russia – even if they too wished to restrict access into northern China.[154] Ultimately, a growing perception that Russia needed to direct its limited capabilities toward addressing more urgent threats in Europe moved St. Petersburg toward the more conservative second view. This paved the way for a long-standing policy of working with local political groups to regulate access in areas from Xinjiang through Manchuria – with Tuva and Hulunbei'er as the exceptions.

At the close of the nineteenth century, Russian efforts to expand southward seemed to be stalling. Despite bringing large areas of Eastern and Southern Europe under its sway, British actions in Turkey, Iran, Afghanistan, northern India, and Tibet made further expansion in these areas seem increasingly difficult to St. Petersburg.[155] Tsar Nicholas II and other Russian leaders started looking to Siberia, the northern extremes of the Qing Empire, and the Korean Peninsula to satisfy their desire for access to resources and markets.[156] Russia seemed particularly poised to extending its influence over the Northeast Asian mainland by the turn of the twentieth century. The port of Vladivostok was developing well, whilst the Trans-Siberian Railroad, with its branch lines running across

[150] Iriye, 1967, 66–67; Joseph, 1928, 101–21; Shen, 2005, 104–10.
[151] Ching, 2001; Copper, 1999, 31–32; Ka, 1995, 2003; Lamley, 1999, 209–48.
[152] Ching, 2001, 133–48; Katz, 2005; Lamley, 1999, 203–08; Zheng, 2001, 363–69.
[153] Fuller, 1992, 328–29, 350–451; Li, 2000, 282–83, 311–12; Schimmelpenninck van der Oye, 2001, 24–103; Wang, 1979, 71–99, 112–32, 206–09.
[154] Barnhart, 1995, 19.
[155] Barnhart, 1995, 18–35; Ferguson, 2004, 144–45, 193, 247–48.
[156] Fuller, 1992, 328–29, 50–451.

98 *External Intervention and the Politics of State Formation*

Manchuria and Russian troops stationed along its length, was near completion.[157] Backing these developments were Russia's steady industrialisation and growing economy, a huge population, and the largest military amongst the major powers.[158]

Unsurprisingly, Russia made substantial headway given its many strengths. Following the end of the Sino-Japanese War, St. Petersburg stalled the extension of Japanese influence into South Manchuria through the Triple Intervention together with France and Germany.[159] This enabled Tsarist government secured ninety-nine-year leases over Dalian and Port Arthur in Liaodong from the Qing court.[160] Moreover, Russia concluded a secret alliance with the Qing court in 1896 that saw Beijing promise not to grant any other outside power access privileges in Manchuria in return for a Russian security guarantee.[161] Russian influence in the officially independent, post-Sino-Japanese War Korean court was also growing. The Russian Navy even secured a coaling station at Masampo on Korea's south coast.[162]

The next step for Russian leaders seemed to be how to consolidate and further these gains. Indeed, this was the rallying cry of policymakers advocating a more robust Russian role in the Far East. A number of Russian civilian and Army leaders, including Prime Minister Pyotr Stolypin, saw a need to quickly secure the area south of Lake Baikal between the turn of the century and the immediate aftermath of the Russo-Japanese War.[163] St. Petersburg's hold over Siberia and influence over Manchuria rested on the ability of the Trans-Siberian Railroad to traverse this region, projecting Russian presence.[164] This meant augmenting Russian dominance over Xinjiang whilst preventing other powers from entering Manchuria and areas north of the Gobi Desert.[165]

Wary of the response by the other major powers active in China to increased Russian assertiveness in the area, however, Witte and senior members of the Russian Army and Navy called for restraint.[166] After all, no power opposed America's Open Door pronouncement and its call for external actors to uphold

[157] China Dept. of Railways and Wang, 1916, 1–12, 187–210; Ferguson, 2004, 247–48; Joseph, 1928, 124–87, 387–96; Li, 2000, 261–82; Wolff, 1995, 40–52.

[158] Li, 2000, 317–20; Wohlforth, 1987, 353–81.

[159] Fudan daxue (Shanghai China), "Sha E qin Hua shi" bianxie zu, 1986, 224–82; Li, 2000, 250–55; Zhou, 2001, 450–58.

[160] Fuller, 1992, 366–73; Joseph, 1928, 124–87, 222–81, 387–96; Li, 2000, 255–77; Satow and Lensen, 1966, 101–24; Schimmelpenninck van der Oye, 2001, 118–46; Wang, 1979, 89–99, 112–15.

[161] Li and Zhongguo renmin zhengzhi xieshanghuiyi. Heilongjiang Sheng weiyuanhui. Wenshi ziliao yanjiu weiyuanhui. Bianjibu, 1989; Zhou, 1997, 450–58.

[162] Barnhart, 1995, 24–37; Li, 2000, 313–18, 339; Satow and Lensen, 1966, 43–100, 220–82.

[163] Fuller, 1992, 329, 366–70, 408–23.

[164] China Dept. of Railways and Wang, 1916, 1–12, 187–210; Cohen, 2000, 341–98; SHAC 18/3440, "Zhong-E jiejue xuan'an dagang zhan xingying guanli Zhongdong tielu xieding qi fujian".

[165] Li, 2000, 341–74, 397–427; Wang, 1979, 121–32.

[166] Fuller, 1992, 328–29, 350–451; Schimmelpenninck van der Oye, 2001, 118–46; Wang, 1979, 69–99, 128–32, 184–85, 204–20.

External Influence and China's Feudalisation, 1893–1922 99

nondiscriminatory access across China. Britain and Japan even displayed open support.[167] These more cautious leaders warned that an overcommitment in China and the Far East could place other key interests at risk.[168]

Germany's rapidly growing military and economic strength, as well as the apparent anti-Russian nature of the partnership amongst Germany, Austria-Hungary, and Ottoman Turkey created a potential threat in Europe that St. Petersburg could ill afford to ignore.[169] Even the conclusion of the Triple Entente in 1907, which brought Britain into the existing defensive arrangement between Russia and France, seemed to reduce pressures in Europe only slightly.[170] The outbreak of World War I further suggested to many Russian leaders that committing capabilities to the Far East over Europe might not be the wisest decision.

Additionally, Russia did not appear to be quite as strong as its geographical size, population, and the confidence of its more assertive leaders suggested. Those urging prudence believed that Russia's economy lagged behind the more advanced European economies, and the physical size of its military forces belied inadequate training, discipline, and equipment.[171] These deficiencies appeared all the more apparent after Russia's defeat by Japan, which led to a financial crisis that placed the St. Petersburg government heavily in debt and spurred an upsurge of revolutionary activity.[172] The stalemate with Germany during the Great War, as well as the financial, military, and human costs of the fighting, hampered Russian leaders' appetites for expansion into China even more.

Nevertheless, to Bezobrazov, Kuropatkin, Alexeyev, their allies, and successors, the belief in Russian military and economic superiority over China, coupled with physical proximity, made the northern reaches of the Chinese polity seem ripe for the picking.[173] Those in favour of a more forceful stance posited that full control over such areas promised access to strategic assets, resources, and territory that could help alleviate both Russia's concerns in Europe and some of its domestic problems.

To this end, policymakers pushing for a more assertive approach toward China proposed a significant expansion of Russia's military presence in Manchuria, as well as the occupation of areas in Xinjiang and Inner Mongolia bordering Russia. This would accompany efforts to secure the allegiance of the major tribes in Outer Mongolia. Such a move aimed to replace Qing rule with Russian political, economic, and military administration.[174] This could pave the

---

[167] Barnhart, 1995, 31–32; Wang, 1979, 175–86.

[168] Li, 2000, 313–20, 341–45, 363–65.

[169] Ferguson, 2004, 247–49, 251; Fuller, 1992, 362–93, 413–51; Kissinger, 1994, 201–17.

[170] Ferguson, 2004, 240–51; Fuller, 1992, 379–93, 413–51; Kissinger, 1994, 201–17; Li, 2000, 363–65; Wang, 1979, 71–76.

[171] Li, 2000, 359–66, 384–98; Wohlforth, 1987, 353–81.

[172] Fuller, 1992, 362–93, 397–418.

[173] Li, 2000, 265–77, 285–312, 341–98; Schimmelpenninck van der Oye, 2001, 24–41, 82–103; Wang, 1979, 77–79.

[174] Nakami, 1995, 69–77; Wang, 1979, 121–32, 206–09.

External Intervention and the Politics of State Formation

way for the full incorporation of these areas into the Russian Empire, enabling St. Petersburg to completely seal off access by other powers.[175]

With defeat in the Russo-Japanese War, Russian leaders began to resolve their differences by calibrating intervention in different parts of China according to variations in the risk of resistance from other major powers. Where intervention was likely to affect Russia's strategic position in Europe by aggravating allies or forcing a significant redeployment of capabilities, St. Petersburg sought to regulate rather than fully deny access.[176] Concurrently, St. Petersburg would redeploy forces already in the Far East to occupy and completely deny access over less risky regions.

ACCESS REGULATION BY PROXY

With the exception of areas where the costs of intervention seemed relatively cheap, Tsarist Russia attempted to regulate access by imposing oversight through local proxies. In Manchuria and Inner Mongolia, where Russian interests clearly butt up against those of other external powers, St. Petersburg sought accommodation with rivals, the acquiescence of China's central government, and local collaboration. This brought a moderation of efforts to control Manchuria and other areas in northern China through *de facto* occupation and the cultivation of local complicity between 1896 and 1905.[177]

Rather than occupation and complete access denial, leaders in St. Petersburg sought to regulate access to Manchuria and Inner Mongolia in conjunction with other powers. The Tsarist government's unwillingness to accept exclusionary Japanese access over Northeast China coupled with a desire to avoid a major power war in the Far East led St. Petersburg to initiate the 1896 Triple Intervention with Paris and Berlin. By funding the Qing court's indemnity payment to Tokyo, the three powers averted Japanese annexation of Shandong and South Manchuria while securing for themselves the opportunity to develop access regulation in these areas and elsewhere in China.[178] St. Petersburg reinforced its position in Manchuria in the aftermath of the Boxer episode through the conclusion of a secret defence treaty with an enfeebled Qing court.[179] The

---

[175] Fuller, 1992, 377–93, 408–18; Fudan daxue (Shanghai China), "Sha E qin Hua shi" bianxie zu, 1986, 414–53.

[176] Wang, 1979, 69–99, 128–32, 184–85, 204–20.

[177] Barnhart, 1995, 35; Fudan daxue (Shanghai China), "Sha E qin Hua shi" bianxie zu, 1986, 462–70; Joseph, 1928, 173–87, 264–81, 387–96; Li, 2000, 249–320; Satow and Lensen, 1966, 127–219; Schimmelpenninck van der Oye, 2001, 111–211; Usui and Chen, 1991, 28–38; SHAC 18/3440, "Zhong-E jiejue xuan'an dagang zhan xingying guanli Zhongdong tielu xieding qi fujian", 1924; AS 03/19/011/04, "E junguan faling ganshe Zhongguo shui guan chayan quan'an".

[178] Barnhart, 1995, 25; Fudan daxue (Shanghai China), "Sha E qin Hua shi" bianxie zu, 1986, 224–350; Iriye, 1967, 131–33; Joseph, 1928, 124–87; Mutsu, 2005, 141–75; Shen, 2005, 106–08; Zheng, 2001, 351–57.

[179] Fudan daxue, "Sha E qin Hua shi" bianxie zu, 1986, 224–350, 462–70; Li, 2000, 249–320; Zhou, 2001, 459–77.

External Influence and China's Feudalisation, 1893–1922   101

pact expanded and strengthened Russian oversight of governance in Manchuria, and was backed by troops stationed in Port Arthur and along the China Eastern and South Manchurian railways.

When the Russo-Japanese War made it seem that winning a major power war over access in China required a substantial reallocation of capabilities around the empire, leaders in St. Petersburg readily set aside differences with Japan.[180] Rising concerns over Germany leading up to and resulting from the outbreak of World War I, coupled with a host of domestic political and financial difficulties between 1905 and 1917 meant that Russian leaders were not ready for another war with Japan.[181] As such, the Tsarist government concluded a series of secret treaties with Tokyo in 1907, 1909, 1912, and 1916 to safeguard access to the railways in and raw materials of northern Manchuria and Inner Mongolia.[182] The Russian and Japanese governments agreed to respect each other's existing dominance over different parts of Manchuria and Inner Mongolia, whilst preventing third parties from obtaining economic and strategic gains into these areas.[183] For St. Petersburg, this meant consolidating oversight of security, political, and economic matters by coercing and buying off the Qing court, its successors, and local authorities.[184]

In comparison, St. Petersburg sought access regulation through the sponsorship of pliant local groups in areas where major power opposition was negligible.[185] By seizing on opportunities presented by local opposition to Qing

---

[180] The Russian government maintained a 20,000-strong occupation force in Manchuria after the Boxer episode. This force grew to more than 126,000 during the Russo-Japanese War. Russian leaders soon realised that keeping down badly equipped and poorly trained Chinese armies and irregulars was completely different from operating against well-equipped, -organised, and -led Japanese forces. Li, 2000, 329–65.

[181] Ferguson, 2004, 247–51; Li, 2000, 341–65.

[182] Barnhart, 1995, 41–44, 54; Fudan daxue (Shanghai China), "Sha E qin Hua shi" bianxie zu, 1986, 351–470; Hunt, 1983, 202; Tompkins, 1949, 30–43; AS 03/32/517, "E yu Riben din-gyue"; AS 03/33/078, "Ri-E xieyue".

[183] The specific target of these treaties at the time was the United States, given the Taft administration's efforts to make commercial inroads into Manchuria. Hunt, 1983, 202–16; Tompkins, 1949, 16–42; SHAC 18/3440, "Zhong E jiejue xuan'an dagang zhan xingying guanli Zhongdong tielu xieding qi fujian".

[184] Given the 1896, 1898, and 1902 Sino-Russian agreements, the Qing government could only deploy and mobilise the military and police in these regions with Russian consent, whilst the appointment of Qing civil officials in these regions as well as official permission for economic development areas required Russian approval. Conversely, Russian activity in these areas could proceed without the Qing government's agreement or oversight. Fudan daxue (Shanghai China), "Sha E qin Hua shi" bianxie zu, 1986, 224–474; Li, 2000, 258–60, 73–74, 310–11; SHAC 18/3440, "Zhong E jiejue xuanan dagang zhan xingying guanli Zhongdong tielu xieding qi fujian"; SHAC 1039/131, "Duban Zhong E jiaoshe huiyi gongshu shenyichu shoufa wenjian shiyou zongbu ji leibu", May 1923—March 1924; SHAC 1039/140, "Heilongjiang sheng yu Yuandong gongheguo qianding jiaotong xieding cungao".

[185] Li, 2000, 367–98; Li and Wu, 1987; SHAC 1039/427/1, "E qing zhuan zhi Wai Meng huiyi zhuanshi; Wai Meng guanshui wenti wu zai jianchi you, February 10, 1915; AS 03/32/138, Exchanges amongst the Foreign Ministry, foreign embassies, and various officials, "Tangnuwulianghai'an", May 1926.

attempts to consolidate control over Outer Mongolia and the chaos resulting from the 1911 Revolution, Russian officials worked with cooperative Mongolian leaders to dominate Outer Mongolia.[186] This gave Russia oversight over all military, political, and economic affairs in Outer Mongolia even though it remained formally part of China.[187] It was only wariness of British and American opposition after Russia's violation of the Open Door in Manchuria that led the Tsar's government to shy away from plans to bribe and coerce Mongol tribes in the region into openly accepting Russian suzerainty.[188] In Tuva and Hulunbei'er, where major power opposition was of little concern, St. Petersburg engineered the replacement of Chinese jurisdiction with direct Russian rule by cultivating local allies who abetted outright Russian military occuption.[189]

Tsarist Russia's involvement in China ended with the Bolshevik Revolution in 1917 and subsequent Russian Civil War. Political upheaval in Russia brought a pause to official Russian attempts to intervene in Chinese domestic politics.[190] This situation lasted until the mid 1920s, when the government of Soviet Russia, fresh on the heels of the Bolshevik consolidation of power, began to intervene in China in a very different way. This was the start of Soviet involvement with the Chinese Nationalist and Communist parties.

GERMANY, FRANCE, AND OTHER CONTENDERS

Germany

In 1897, the Imperial German government forced the Qing court to lease Jiaozhou Bay during the Scramble for Concessions, giving it exclusive access

---

[186] Fudan daxue (Shanghai China), "Sha E qin Hua shi" bianxie zu, 1986, 414–52; Li, 2000, 370–84; Sheridan, 1975, 44fn, 296n5; SHAC 1039/427/1, "E qing zhuan zhi Wai Meng huiyi zhuanshi; Wai Meng guanshui wenti wu zai jianchi you"; AS 03/32/201, Correspondence between Governor Wu (Peifu) at Luoyang and the Foreign Ministry, "Shouhui Kuqia yu chetui zhu Meng Hongjun zhijiao she", January 1923.

[187] Li, 2000, 384–89; SHAC 18/3440, "Zhong E jiejue xuanan dagang zhan xingying guanli Zhongdong tielu xieding qi fujian"; SHAC 1039/427/1 "E qing zhuan zhi Wai Meng huiyi zhuanshi; Wai Meng guanshui wenti wu zai jianchi you"; AS 03/32/203/03/010, Army Supplies Superintendent Li to the Foreign Ministry, "Yu qing gejie zhukuan yuanzhu zheng Meng shi", September 1922; AS 03/32/205/03, "Zhu Meng Hongjun chetui shi jiaoshe'an (Wai Meng baogao)", 1925; AS 03/32/201, "Shouhui Kuqia yu chetui zhu Meng Hongjun zhi jiaoshe".

[188] Tompkins, 1949, 16–29.

[189] AS 03/32/201, "Shouhui Kuqia yu chetui zhu Meng Hongjun zhi jiaoshe"; AS 03/32/157, Exchanges between the Army and Foreign Ministries, "Kulun duli'an", March 1913; AS 03/32/163/04/007, Official correspondence from the Finance Ministry to the Foreign Ministry, "Ku-E siding miyue ji hezu gongsi shi guibu dian Mo zonglingshi micha qing dafu", November 1922; AS 03/32/169/01/019, Letter from the Marshal's Office to the Foreign Ministry, "Ju bao E yu Meng ding miyue jiekuan yu Mengbing maigei junqi yaoqiu Wai Meng tieluquan", November 1914; AS 03/32/138, "Tangnuwulianghai'an".

[190] Yang, 1997, 16–67; SHAC 1039/559, "Zhong-E xieyue E yue yanjiu huiyi ji luji, Zhong E huiyi cankao wenjian".

External Influence and China's Feudalisation, 1893–1922   103

over the region.[191] Berlin further obtained an agreement from the Qing court promising not to alienate political, strategic, or economic privileges in Shandong to any other external power, having failed to acquire exclusive privileges in the Lower Yangzi due to British opposition.[192] Until Japan's seizure of Shandong in 1914, the Wilhelmine government enjoyed the sole right to construct railway, mining, and telegraph networks in the province, which it tried to fully exploit by working with local Chinese officials.[193] This saw the development of Qingdao port into a major gateway to the markets and resources of Shandong, as well as a Far Eastern base that augmented the Kaiserliche Marine's aims of challenging British naval supremacy.

Wilhelmine Germany's attempts to establish direct regulation of access in China from the close of the nineteenth century to the start of World War I fell within the German government's larger approach to foreign policy at the time. Berlin's assertive colonial strategy and military build-up were a result of domestic political logrolling amplified by British, French, and Russian responses to these actions.[194] Backed by expanding economic and military capabilities, these developments raised the gains German leaders expected from regulating economic, political, and strategic access over part of China.[195] Anglo-German talks over Shandong suggest that German leaders generally felt such an outcome to be preferable to the nondiscriminatory access opportunities in China promised by the Open Door. However, continuing concerns about the threats posed by Russia, France, and Britain discouraged Berlin from expanding access regulation to other parts of China.

France

Just as the German government was gaining its foothold in Shandong, leaders of the Third Republic were trying to make inroads into directly regulating access over south China. In 1898, the French government pressured the Qing court to grant Paris the right of first refusal over foreign access to Guangxi, Yunnan, and parts of Sichuan, as well as a ninety-nine-year lease over the port of Guangzhou.[196] The desire to exclude other powers from these regions stemmed,

---

[191] Joseph, 1928, 124–217; Platt, 1968, 376–07; Zhang and Liu, 1933.

[192] The exception was the British leasehold of Weihaiwei on Shandong's northern coast, which the Kaiser's government accepted in exchange for the withdrawal of British objections to the German position in Shandong. Lu, 2001, 12–15, 141–48; Qingdao shi bowuguan, Zhongguo di 1 lishi dang'anguan, and Qingdao shi shehuikexue yanjiusuo, 1987, 391–427; Schimmelpenninck van der Oye, 2001, 147–58; Wang, 1979, 82–89, 112–20, 141–48; SHAC 1039/560, "Zhong De xieyue ji qita wenjian".

[193] China Dept. of Railways and Wang, 1916, 395–466; Koo and Zhongguo shehuikexueyuan, Jindaishi, 1983, 20–32; Lu, 2001, 15–33; SHAC 1039/560, "Zhong De xieyue ji qita wenjian".

[194] Doyle, 1986, 219–31; Ferguson, 2004, 248–49; Kupchan, 1994, 385–417; Snyder, 1991, 66–111.

[195] Tahara, 1928, 402–08; Wang, 1979, 206–20.

[196] Wang, 1979, 81–82, 100–08, 185.

104   *External Intervention and the Politics of State Formation*

in part, from French concerns that British influence from eastern Guangdong and Burma could threaten French colonial interests in Indochina.[197]

From French-held Vietnam, the French government constructed railroads into Guangdong, Guangxi, Yunnan, and Sichuan that allowed management of access to these areas.[198] French leaders further secured mining and telegraph construction rights in these southern provinces from central and local authorities.[199] To ensure successful attainment of these goals, French officials sought active cooperation from local authorities to regulate access in these regions. In return, Paris offered armaments and supplies to local regimes like Tang Jiyao's Yunnan militarists and Lu Rongting's Old Guangxi Clique.[200]

Behind such limited French efforts to regulate access over south China were tensions in Paris over concerns about a growing German threat. Throughout the latter half of the nineteenth century, the *parti colonial* drove French efforts to incorporate large areas of Africa and Indochina into the metropole.[201] However, when leaders in Paris began to look seriously at access denial in southern China at the turn of the century, German military and economic expansion was already a major challenge to French security. Despite promises of economic gain, the importance of regulating access in south and southwest China paled in comparison, which made a limited investment of capabilities into creating a sphere of influence in these areas seem more attractive than fuller access denial through colonisation.[202]

Further reducing the need for Paris to completely control access to southern China was the easing of tensions with London. The 1904 Anglo-French understanding resulting from the Entente Cordiale, in particular, eased concerns about potential British threats to French Indochina. Moreover, building on the 1894 Salisbury-Courcel and 1896 Anglo-French Agreements, both sides agreed to jointly develop parts of Sichuan and Yunnan at the exclusion of third parties.[203] Consequently, there was no need to expend capabilities on incorporating parts of south and southwest China into the French empire more formally.

---

[197] Kupchan, 1994, 210–11.

[198] China Dept. of Railways and Wang, 1916, 719–58; Joseph, 1928, 124–87; Zhu, 1995, 140–46, 323–456; AS 01/21/056/03, "Zhong Fa tongshang zhangcheng; xüyi jiewu zhuantiao; Zhong Fa Dian Yue; bianjie lianjie dianxian zhangcheng".

[199] Chan, 1982, 54–63, 83–84, 102–04; Joseph, 1928, 124–87; AS 03/05/065, "Zhong Mei, Zhong Fa, Zhong Ao tielu shiyi"; AS 01/21/056/03, "Zhong Fa tongshang zhangcheng; xüyi jie wu zhuantiao; Zhong Fa Dian Yue; bianjie lianjie dianxian zhangcheng".

[200] Chi, 1976, 121; Zhu, 1995, 131–40; AS 03/20/039/04/011–012, "Tang Jiyao yi ge jiuchang digou qiangdan you"; AS 03/20/039/04/014, 018, "Yunnan si yungou junhuo shi"; AS 03/18/101/01, "Fa shi qingzhun Yunnan tielu gongsi yunru gongcheng yong zhayao'an"; AS 01/21/056/03, "Zhong Fa tongshang zhangcheng; xüyi jiewu zhuantiao; Zhong Fa Dian Yue; bianjie lianjie dianxian zhangcheng"; AS 03/30/039/04/014–018, "Yunnan gou jun huo shi"; AS 03/18/101/01/009–011, "Dian Yue gongsi bao yun zhayao ying zhao ci bu dingban fazhi shiyong cunchu gejie ying zhaozhang qudi".

[201] Doyle, 1986, 316–19.

[202] Kupchan, 1994, 185–213.

[203] Edwards, 1971.

Other Powers

Also present in the struggle for access within the Chinese polity at the time were Italy, Austria-Hungary, and Belgium. They had particular interests in the markets for loans, banking, and railway and telegraph construction.[204] In 1898, Italian leaders attempted to seek an exclusive sphere of influence in Zhejiang province, but withdrew such notions in light of British disapproval. Leaders in Vienna, Rome, and Brussels understood their inability to effectively project force far beyond their borders without substantial sacrifices elsewhere, and chose to forego active involvement in China.[205]

MAJOR POWER RIVALRIES AND THE FUNDAMENTS OF FEUDALISATION

This section considers the collective effects stemming from the concurrent foreign intervention efforts examined earlier. It draws out how the different approaches toward securing access in China together affected state form between 1893 and 1922. I look at the collective effects that external intervention into Chinese domestic politics had on political centralisation, territorial exclusivity, and external autonomy. This allows me to highlight how differing foreign approaches toward access competition and the resulting statement amongst external actors fostered the sort of feudalised statehood depicted in the previous chapter.

In this respect, I consider how the behaviour of external actors interacted with each other and their respective local partners to collectively affect state form in China rather than weigh the relative importance of different outside powers. It is clear in retrospect that Britain, Japan, Russia, and the United States were more active in China between the late nineteenth and early twentieth centuries than France, Germany, and others. However, the earlier discussion in this chapter clearly indicates that policymakers in London, Tokyo, St. Petersburg, and Washington at the time seriously considered the influence and reactions – real and potential – of Paris and Berlin when formulating China policy. Hence, analyses of the joint effects of intervention in China from 1893–1922 should include all these players.

Sustaining the balance between the crosscutting integrative and fragmentary pressures that maintained the limited political centralisation behind China's feudalisation were different intervention strategies that various foreign powers adopted. British, American, and, until 1914, Japanese efforts at sustaining non-discriminatory access among external powers within the polity aimed to shore up central government authority, regardless of who controlled Beijing. Russian,

---

[204] China Dept. of Railways and Wang, 1916, 35–78, 285–324, 605–90; McLean, 1973; Nathan, 1976, 196–200; Sun E., 1954, 12–15, 74, 80; AS 03/05/065, "Zhong-Mei, Zhong-Fa, Zhong-Ao tielu shiyi"; AS 03/23/072–080, Foreign Ministry, "Bi yue", 1926.

[205] Kennedy, 1987, 203–19, 49–74.

106 External Intervention and the Politics of State Formation

TABLE 4.1 *Divergent Foreign Expectations about the Opportunity Costs of Intervention in China and Corresponding Approaches to Access Denial, 1893–1922*

Outside Actor	Expected Opportunity Cost	Approach to Access Denial
Britain	High	Nonprivileged Access
United States	High	Nonprivileged Access
Japan	Until 1914, Moderate/High 1914 and after, Moderate	Nonprivileged Access Access Regulation
Russia	Until 1917, Moderate 1917 and after, Prohibitively High	Access Regulation Concede Access
Germany	Until 1914, Moderate 1914 and after, Prohibitively High	Access Regulation Concede Access
France	Moderate	Access Regulation

German, French, and post-1914 Japanese attempts to regulate access over certain regions tended to erode political centralisation and the external autonomy of central governments. Crucially, the needs of imperial defence in addition to the growing security concerns in a Europe hurtling towards the Great War kept the Russian, German, French, and British governments from pursuing their objectives in China more forcefully.[206] Just as vitally, cognizance of relative weakness – and isolationist sentiments in Washington – led the American and Japanese governments to similarly avoid major power war over China in the late nineteenth and early twentieth centuries.[207]

Table 4.1 summarises the opportunity costs expectations for outside actors active in China from 1893 to 1922, and their approaches to competing for access there.

Given their provision of financing, weapons, and equipment to regional regimes, the Russian, French, German, and post-1914 Japanese intervention into Chinese domestic politics were important in eroding political centralisation during the late nineteenth and early twentieth centuries. As long as local political groups were able to help limit access by rival outside actors under agreeable conditions, this group of foreign powers had few qualms about providing various forms of support even if this undermined Beijing's rule.[208] Outside powers gave those running regional regimes the wherewithal to defy the central government.

By persuading outside powers to acquiesce to the Open Door approach, American and British official involvement in China's domestic politics

---

[206] Friedberg, 1988; Kupchan, 1994, 185–213, 385–417; Snyder, 1991, 66–111.
[207] Barnhart, 1995, 16–76; Iriye, 1967, 114–33; Schoonover, 2003.
[208] Chan, 1982, 67–108; Chen, 1983, 78–125; Chi, 1976, 120–23, 56–61; Sheridan, 1975, 83–87; Tang, 2004, 117–46.

External Influence and China's Feudalisation, 1893–1922   107

concurrently helped prevent a partition of the Chinese polity between 1893 and 1922. The Open Door promised sure but limited gains for outside powers in China while hinting at possible confrontations with the United States, Britain, and, for a time, even Japan, should there be violations of this understanding.[209] As seen earlier in this chapter, external actors in China were generally unwilling to risk such a resort to arms.[210] Coupled with a funnelling of funds and military equipment to Beijing that bolstered central government capabilities, the Open Door helped keep a semblance of central rule in China.

So long as the various outside powers avoided military confrontation over China, foreign involvement gave rise to both centralising and fragmentary pressures. For all their interest in maintaining political centralisation to secure non-discriminatory access across China, there is little evidence that the British or U.S. governments provided central authorities with the capacity to bring foreign-aided regional regimes to heel. Except when it appeared that opposition from other major powers was absent, as in the case with Outer Mongolia, governments in Tokyo, Berlin, Paris, and St. Petersburg also tended not to support the outright breakaway of particular regions. Similarly, Japan's takeover of Shandong in 1914 occurred only when fighting World War I in Europe preoccupied Berlin, and action against Germany was unlikely to face resistance from other powers.

The maps shown here illustrate the remarkable stability in the pattern of major power intervention within China between 1893 and 1922.[211] The first shows external spheres of influence in China at the end of the nineteenth century. The second sketches out foreign spheres of influence in China after the Russo-Japanese War and going into the second decade of the twentieth century. Other than the appearance of a Japanese presence first in southern Manchuria in 1905, and then in Shandong after 1914, there was little change to areas that various external powers dominated for most of these two decades.

Foreign unwillingness to take on each other meant that no local group received enough support to defeat its domestic rivals. This was the case whether a local political actor ran a regional regime or controlled the central government. The resulting domestic political stalemate hampered effective indigenous efforts to challenge the outside powers and their influence in China. Further limiting local resistance to outside pressure was the fact that political actors in China derived so much of their economic and coercive capabilities from external support under conditions set by their foreign sponsors.

Furthermore, local actors that cooperated insufficiently faced the prospect of seeing outside assistance severed, if not channelled to an indigenous adversary. As the Duan Qirui government's armed unification efforts and rivalry with the Zhili Clique ran afoul of Tokyo's desire to avoid unsettling other foreign powers,

---

[209] Wang, 1979, 81–82, 100–08, 136–41, 175–97, 220–26.

[210] Cohen, 2000, 41–89; Hunt, 1983, 189–226, 270, 369n23; Iriye, 1967, 80–88, 101–02; Joseph, 1928, 399–422; Tompkins, 1949, 16–29; FHAC 12/4/473, "Yuan Shikai wei Ri E Mei Yi weiding guafen Zhongguo lingtu xinxieyue shi gei Zhao Erfeng de dianbao", 1911.

[211] Map sources: Wu, 1999; Zhang, 1984; Zhongguo ditu and Xinhai geming Wuchang qiyi, 1991.

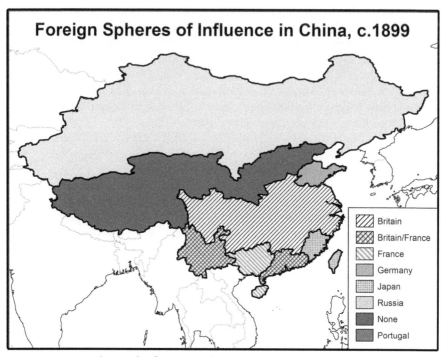

MAP 3 Foreign Spheres of Influence in China, c.1899

Duan and his Anfu allies saw a cut in critical Japanese military, financial, and political backing.[212] As everyone from the Anfu and Fengtian Cliques to the Nationalists discovered, there was little they could do if their external patrons opposed efforts to raise regional autonomy or assert central authority.[213]

Similarly, the relative caution that informed all the relevant external powers' participation in Chinese domestic politics was critical in containing the erosion of China's territorial exclusivity. In a trend that began with the Scramble for Concessions between 1898 and 1900, wariness over conflict in China made efforts to seek the understanding of other outside powers integral to foreign attempts at securing access in China. The Russians and Japanese sought to establish internationally recognised spheres of influence and leaseholds rather than colonies in Manchuria, just as the Germans did the same in Shandong and the French in south and southwest China. Anglo-American efforts to sustain the Open Door rested on acquiring the acquiescence of all the other major powers active in China.[214] Japan's seizure of South Manchuria and Shandong as well as

---

[212] Chan, 1982, 129–31; Pye, 1971, 18–37; Usui and Chen, 1990, 170–90.
[213] Jansen, 1954, 202–22; SHAC 1039/380, "Guanyu Shandong wenti ruhe jiao Guoji Lianhehui ji youguan Shandong wenti zhi shuotie".
[214] Barnhart, 1995, 38–40, 79–86; Hunt, 1983, 196–207, 70, 369n23; Iriye, 1967, 83, 87–88, 101–02; Schoonover, 2003, 110.

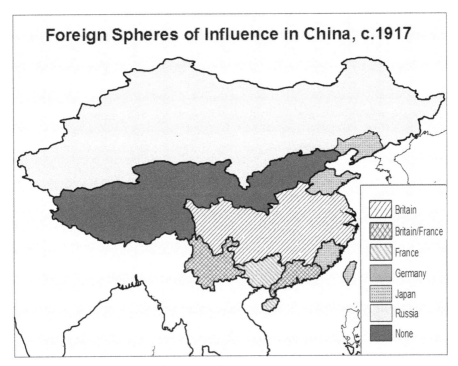

MAP 4 Foreign Spheres of Influence in China, c.1917

Russian absorption of border areas and support for the breakaway of Outer Mongolia after 1911 occurred as the likelihood of extended major power conflict over these regions receded.[215]

Even when foreign powers colluded to increase exclusive access over parts of China by expanding their role in governance, they did so with an eye toward averting conflict with other outside actors. This was evident in the four Russo-Japanese secret agreements between 1907 and 1916 that divided St. Petersburg and Tokyo's influence over Manchuria, Inner Mongolia, Outer Mongolia, Tuva, and Xinjiang.[216] Other examples include Japanese agreements with the British regarding Fujian in 1898 and with other major powers over Shandong and Manchuria in 1919 and 1922, as well as the 1896 Anglo-French understanding on south and southwest China.[217] By cooperating over a limited partitioning of

---

[215] Li, 2000, 367–98.
[216] Barnhart, 1995, 41–54; Li, 2000, 341–65; Tompkins, 1949, 30–43; AS 03/32/517, "E yu Riben dingyue"; AS 03/33/078, "Ri E xieyue".
[217] Barnhart, 1995, 26–37, 76–78; Cohen, 2000, 89–90; Edwards, 1971; Iriye, 1967, 143–45; Joseph, 1928, 150–51, 181–83, 222–414; Platt, 1968, 276–307; Schneider, 1998, 161–82; AS 03/33/165, "Huashengdun huiyi Lu'an yilu", December 1921, AS 03/39/032/05, "Huashengdun huiyi qianding zhi gexiang tiaoyue xieding ji jueyi'an"; AS 03/39/036/04/001–020, "Huashengdun huiyi suoding zhi guanyu Zhongguo shijian tiaoyue shi"; SHAC 1039/375, "Taipingyang huiyi shanhou

China, the major powers restricted the degree that could undermine territorial exclusivity.

The interplay of major power rivalries sustained China's external autonomy as a single entity during the late nineteenth and early twentieth centuries. By accepting the Open Door to avoid domination of Chinese foreign policy by any one outside power, the various foreign actors effectively acquiesced to continued diplomatic recognition of a single, externally autonomous Chinese central government.[218] Deviation from such an approach threatened a potentially costly but inconsequential conflict with other major powers hoping to maintain nondiscriminatory access over the Chinese polity through the central government. Since no outside power wished to chance this outcome, the standoff amongst foreign actors allowed successive central governments to retain singular international representation of China despite chronic military and political weakness.

China could preserve substantial outward autonomy so long as powers such as the United States and Britain backed international recognition of a sole central government and others, like Japan at the end of World War I, limited their opposition to diplomatic protests. These conditions permitted active Chinese participation in major international events such as the Versailles and Washington conferences so long as it was through the internationally recognised central government in Beijing. Continued diplomatic recognition and foreign support also enabled the central government – and those holding sway over it – to access sovereign borrowing. Such dynamics prompted many competing domestic groups in China to follow a common foreign policy to the extent possible, given their desires to take over the central government, its role in external affairs, and, of course, its coffers.[219]

In short, the way foreign rivalries played out into an impasse was key to preserving a high level of external autonomy in China. Outside intervention helped prevent both the takeover of Chinese foreign policy by any single outside power and diplomatic fragmentation. Similarly, external competition over access permitted China to continue enjoying significant freedom of action in international politics and diplomacy.

Key to China's feudalisation were the divergent outside efforts to safeguard access over the polity. Concurrent attempts by different powers to preserve nondiscriminatory access and attain exclusive regulation of access sustained the coexistence of moderate political centralisation and territorial exclusivity alongside high levels of external autonomy. So long as foreign intervention efforts continued to collectively support these core attributes of feudalised statehood, it remained the state form of the Chinese polity.

---

weiyuanhui taolun caibing jiaohui Guangzhouwan, jiejue Shandong xuan'an deng wenti laiwang wenshu ji canyu Huashengdun huiyi wenjian"; SHAC 1039/648, "Waijiaobu wendu: Zhong Ri jiejue Shandong xuan'an linshihuiyilu (xia)", 1923; SHAC 1039/653, "Taipingyang huiyi shanhou weiyuanhui caibing banfa dagang, Shandong wenti shanhou huiyi", 1923.

[218] Joseph, 1928, 399–422; Kirby, 1997, 441–43; Zhang 1991.

[219] Chi, 1976, 190–95; Nathan, 1976, 59–64.

External Influence and China's Feudalisation, 1893–1922

CONCLUSIONS

As centripetal and centrifugal forces simultaneously buffeted China from the 1890s through the early 1920s, this both spurred and limited fragmentation as well as centralisation, contributing to the polity's feudalisation. This stands in contrast to the conventional wisdom that outside intervention was simply a force for division. Behind this dynamic lay the differences in foreign expectations about the opportunity cost of intervening in China, matched by a concurrent desire to avoid a major power war over China. Insofar as such perspectives persisted in informing the major powers and their approaches to competing over China, securing access in conjunction with local partners perpetuated feudalisation. In this regard, the evidence on China from 1893 to 1922 supports the view that efforts by foreign actors to secure access according to their expectations of cost together shaped institutions of governance, authority, and rule in a fragile polity.

I end this chapter with two caveats. First, Japanese attempts to support different groups controlling China's central government in order to buy assistance for its efforts to regulate access in Manchuria and, for a time, Shandong were more robust than initially predicted. Second, my theoretical explanation did not fully anticipate the level of collusion between foreign powers, notably Russo-Japanese cooperation over access regulation in Manchuria, Inner Mongolia, and Xinjiang. Nonetheless, neither development fundamentally contradicts my argument.

CHAPTER 5

The Evolution of Foreign Involvement in China, 1923–1952

Rising Opportunity Costs and Convergent Approaches to Intervention[1]

If the early-twentieth-century feudalisation of the Chinese polity was a collective result of foreign intervention driven by divergent perceptions about the opportunity costs of intervention, changes in those conditions should lead to different outcomes on state form. Convergent beliefs about increasingly high opportunity costs of intervention amongst the powers active in China between 1923 and 1952 should bring substantive changes to institutions of governance in the polity. My argument predicts that such a situation should foster demand for less complete access denial and less direct involvement in domestic politics amongst intervening powers, creating broad external support for the development of sovereign statehood.

I posit that the period from 1923 to 1952 witnessed a convergence in external actor expectations about the high opportunity costs of intervention in China. Given this shift in perspectives, there was growing demand amongst intervening powers for the preservation of nonprivileged access rather than more complete access denial. This brought broad foreign backing for the consolidation of the polity under central government rule. Such dynamics of foreign involvement fostered the emergence of a sovereign Chinese state from the feudalised polity of the previous period. Before turning to the aggregated effects of intervention, I first lay out the opportunity cost expectations and consequent approaches to intervention for the major outside players active in China from 1923 to 1952.

JAPAN AND ITS IMPERIAL EXPERIMENT

From the interwar period until the end of World War II, Japanese leaders expected the opportunity costs of intervention in China to range between moderate and low. Consequently, the choice between complete access denial and expanding the regulation of access dominated debates over China. As elite opinion about intervention coalesced around expectations of low opportunity cost in the 1930s, Tokyo's focus shifted accordingly to fully denying rivals access to large swathes

[1] This chapter and the next builds on Chong, 2010.

112

The Evolution of Foreign Involvement in China, 1923–1952

of the Chinese polity. In comparison, when defeat and occupation by the United States made the anticipated opportunity costs of intervening in China prohibitive, Japanese leaders ceded their claims to access.

Until the early 1930s, Japan's leaders expected intervention costs in China to be moderate, leading to a temporary emphasis on consolidating Tokyo's hold over areas where it already regulated access. Japanese cabinets between 1923 and 1931 generally wished to maintain good relations with the other major powers, especially the United States, whilst focusing on domestic reforms.[2] The European experience with World War I suggested to Japanese elites that the path toward growth and prosperity lay in peaceful economic cooperation rather than confrontation. From 1923 to 1931, these considerations worked to mitigate demands to extend access regulation and even full access denial in China.[3]

Consequently, the attentions and energies of Japan's leaders during the 1920s fixed on economic and political reform as well as the consolidation of Japan's existing overseas possessions. Such reforms ranged from developing Japan's domestic economy and industry to rejoining the gold standard and extending suffrage to all adult male subjects.[4] Kato Takaaki's cabinet even went as far as to reduce the size of the Army and normalise ties with the Soviet Union in order to free up capabilities to attain these goals.[5]

When it came to territories already under Japan's sway, Tokyo sought new ways to subsume the populace under Japanese rule whilst developing the economies of these regions to feed the needs of the metropole, as with Taiwan and Korea.[6] On the mainland, evidence suggests a focus on strengthening access regulation in areas where a robust Japanese presence already existed – whilst largely leaving the rest of the polity alone.[7] This approach had the advantages of limiting the potential for disputes with other major powers whilst intensifying the extraction of benefits from existing holdings. Japan's leaders were looking to invest capabilities into consolidation rather than expansion.

Japanese political elites largely viewed conflict with other major powers as an impediment to economic, political, and social progress. This desire to relieve pressure on Japan's core security interests led Tokyo to accede to the Washington treaties – a move that brought, in the words of historian Michael Barnhart, "nearly

---

[2] This was the case with the Navy-led cabinets of Kato Tomasaburo and Yamamoto Gonnohyoe, the *Kenseikai* cabinet of Kato Takaaki, the *Seiyukai* cabinet of Tanaka Gi'ichi, and the 1929 to 1931 *Minseito* cabinets of Hamaguchi Osachi and Wakatsuki Reijiro in office between 1923 and 1931. Barnhart, 1987, 51–52, 1995, 78–92; Iriye, 1967, 143–72; Shen, 2005, 237–57.

[3] Such calls were particularly prominent within the Imperial Japanese Army, especially the Kwantung Army stationed in Manchuria. Certain businesses with strong interests in the China market also lent their voices to the demand for a greater official Japanese role within the Chinese polity.

[4] Barnhart, 1987, 65, 1995, 18, 78–92.

[5] Barnhart, 1987, 24–29.

[6] Cho, 1973, 377–83; Iriye, 1967, 172–74; Mizuno and Zheng, 1998, 151–54; Schneider, 1998, 185–205; Shen, 2005, 257–64, 278–95, 716–21; Zheng, 2001, 569–71, 643–75.

[7] This came through the "nonintervention policy" initiated by Foreign Minister Shidehara Kijuro and the Kato cabinet, and essentially continued under the Tanaka and Hamaguchi cabinets. Cho, 1973, 377–83; Iriye, 1967, 143–45; Taliaferro, 2004, 99–100; Zheng, 2001, 569–71, 643–75.

114   *External Intervention and the Politics of State Formation*

a decade of stability to Japan's relations with the West".[8] Even hawks like Kato Takaaki of the Twenty-One Demands, Tanaka Gi'ichi, and the Imperial Japanese Army shunned open disputes with other major powers, especially over matters where friction was most likely.[9] Under the premiership of Hamaguchi Osachi, the Japanese government also participated in the London Naval Conference that resulted in a new naval arms control treaty that committed Japan to maintaining a smaller ratio of warships relative to the Americans and British.[10]

However, the collapse of the world economy in the late 1920s convinced many Japanese leaders that survival required access regulation, if not full access denial, over areas that stood outside their empire at the time.[11] Such perspectives were prevalent within the Army, Navy, big businesses, the Diet, and even a sizeable part of the public.[12] This weakened the position of those advocating a continued restriction of access regulation efforts to South Manchuria, Shandong, and, to a lesser degree, Fujian.[13]

The 1930s further witnessed the coming together of an Army-Navy coalition that held a belief in twin mounting threats to Japan. The first was a rapidly industrialising Soviet Russia to the north. Not only was Russia a historical rival, but it now also promulgated a communist ideology that the conservative Japanese military establishment found abhorrent.[14] The second danger was the Anglo-American ability to deny Japan access to vital resources necessary for a long conflict with the Soviet Union, given their colonies in Southeast Asia, naval presence in the Pacific, and perceived influence in China.[15] Growing economic woes from American, British, and European protectionism raised convictions amongst Japan's military leaders about the need to further limit access to China and Asia by other powers.[16]

As the so-called "Army-Navy steamroller" gained the upper hand in Japanese politics, Tokyo began to emphasise the importance of more fully denying other

[8] Barnhart, 1987, 51; Iriye, 1967, 143–45, 163–75.

[9] Barnhart, 1987, 25, 1995, 78–92.

[10] The London Naval Treaty allowed Japan to maintain a 7:10:10 ratio of warships relative to the United States and Britain until 1938, when Japan's proportion of warships would grow to 6:10:10. In the Pacific, the Imperial Navy would enjoy local superiority unless the British and Americans transferred naval assets from elsewhere. Barnhart, 1987, 35–36; Iriye, 1967, 163–75; Kupchan, 1994, 305.

[11] Barnhart, 1987, 22–49, 64–76, 1995, 92–99, 101–21; Cho, 1973, 383–92; Iriye, 1967, 163–64, 76–78; Shen, 2005, 352–67; Snyder, 1991, 115–16.

[12] Chen, 2003, 336–85; Kupchan, 1994, 300–04, 315–28, 350–58; Snyder, 1991, 127–30, 42–50; Zheng, 2001, 603–11.

[13] Those in support of this more restrictive stance included Premiers Hamaguchi, Wakatsuki, Foreign Minister Shidehara, as well as Saionji Kinmochi, then one of the last politically active genros. Barnhart, 1995, 88–139, 200; Cho, 1973, 383–92; Mizuno and Zheng, 1998, 151–54; Schneider, 1998, 161–205.

[14] Barnhart, 1987, 30–46, 100–4, 136–40, 200, 1995, 101–44; Kupchan, 1994, 301–45; Snyder, 1991, 115–16, 120–39; Zheng, 2001, 603–11.

[15] Ienaga, 1978, 80–84, 129–37; Iriye, 1967, 172–78, 207–19; Taliaferro, 2004, 95.

[16] Barnhart, 1987, 148–61, 215–62, 1995, 94–95, 101–39; Ienaga, 1978, 75–84, 129–37; Iriye, 1967, 172–78, 207–19; Kennedy, 1987, 300; Kupchan, 1994, 297–358; Snyder, 1991, 115–30.

The Evolution of Foreign Involvement in China, 1923–1952

major powers access to parts of Asia.[17] For the cabinets in office between 1937 and 1945, failure to exclude rival powers from East Asia and the Pacific threatened to cut Japan off from the raw materials, markets, and strategic locations that seemed vital to its survival. This brought an emphasis on committing capabilities toward denying access to China, Southeast Asia, the Western Pacific, and, eventually, Siberia as fully as possible.[18] The expected gain from successful moves in this direction was the guarantee of long-term survival and prosperity.[19] In contrast, members of the Army-Navy coalition feared that failure on these terms would bring the dissolution of empire, and thrust Japan under the heel of the Soviets or Britain and the United States.[20] These beliefs lowered Tokyo's opportunity cost expectations over intervention to such a degree that the appeal of full access denial across China and the rest of Asia trumped other goals.

In sum, there were two important shifts in Japanese leaders' perspectives between 1923 and 1945. The period from 1923 to the early 1930s saw the expected net gains from completely denying other major powers access across Asia rise significantly. In comparison, the expected net gains of withdrawing from China and the rest of Asia outweighed other options from around 1941 through 1945. Correspondingly, the opportunity costs Tokyo expected from intervening in China between the early 1930s and 1945 moved from moderate to low. Japan's efforts to contend for access in China halted under the post–World War II American occupation.

TOKYO'S ROBUST ACCESS DENIAL EFFORTS

Given that Japanese leaders between the early 1920s and 1930s associated moderated levels of opportunity costs with intervention in China, Tokyo's approach through 1931 focused on firming up access regulation in areas of

---

[17] Prominent Navy proponents of expansion included Togo Heihachiro, the Japanese war hero from the Russo-Japanese War, as well as younger officers such as Kato Kanji, Fushimi Hiroyasu, and Suetsugu Nobumasa. Amongst the Army supporters of expansion were Tojo Hideki, Itagaki Seishiro, Hayashi Senjuro, Ishiwara Kanji, and Araki Sadao. Barnhart, 1987, 136–75, 198–214, 265, 1995, 88–149; Chen, 2003, 335–85; Coble, 1991, 182–282; Ienaga, 1978, 33–46; Ishikawa, 1995, 134–431; Mizuno and Zheng, 1998, 151–54; Sadao, 1973, 225–59; Shen, 2005, 492–516; Snyder, 1991, 142–50; Taliaferro, 2004, 99–100; Zheng, 2001, 603–11; SHAC 18/1513, "Di wei jiyao di 45–46 hao", 1942.

[18] These included three cabinets led by Konoe Fumimaro, one by Abe Nobuyuki, one by Yonai Mitsumasa, one by Tojo Hideki, one by Koiso Kuniaki, and one by Suzuki Kuntaro. Defeats by the Red Army at Changgufeng and Nomonhan in 1938 and 1939 led Tokyo to concentrate on China, Southeast Asia, and the Pacific. Barnhart, 1987, 22–49, 64–114, 136–75, 198–214, 237–73; Borg, 1964, 442–85; Chen, 2003, 335–85; Elleman, 1999, 126–27; Fujiwara, 1973, 189–95; Harkavy, 2007, 90; Kupchan, 1994, 297–358; Shen, 2005, 632–60, 708–16; Taliaferro, 2004, 94–131.

[19] Situations where the Kwantung Army and other Japanese commands in China presented Tokyo with *fait accompli* were common in the 1930s. The Army's influence in politics made it difficult for Japanese leaders to reject such moves. Iriye, 1967, 172–78, 207–19; Shen, 2005, 632–60, 708–16.

[20] Ienaga, 1978, 75–84, 129–37; Taliaferro, 2004, 95–115.

China already under Japanese oversight. This meant providing local partners in southern Manchuria and Jiaozhou Bay the financial and military wherewithal to manage access to markets, raw materials, and communications. To do so, the Japanese government tried to limit the activities of other foreign actors in regions under effective Japanese jurisdiction, whilst bolstering their own influence in adjacent areas. In return, the Japanese government acquired exclusive rights over the construction, operation, and protection of railways, as well as the exploitation of raw materials and markets in and around Japanese-administered territory within China.

Such efforts to sustain access regulation translated into the transfer of arms and monetary assistance to militarists like Manchuria-based Zhang Zuolin, Shandong-based Zhang Zongchang, and Fujian-based Li Houji.[21] Acting on behalf of Tokyo, the Kwantung Army also used bribes to break up opposing militarist coalitions.[22] As a result, Japanese forces and their militarist partners were by the 1930s able to consolidate control over Manchuria and Shandong, and extend their sway into the northern provinces of Suiyuan, Chahar, Shanxi, Rehe, and Hebei.[23] Zhang Zuolin even occupied Beijing and took over the central government between 1924 and 1928.[24] Nevertheless, Japanese leaders remained ready to dispense with wayward local partners who might endanger their interests. Concerns about Zhang Zuolin's growing independence and ambition, especially the potential threat such developments had on Japan's position in Manchuria, led to his assassination by elements of the Kwantung Army and Tokyo's acceptance of the *fait accompli*.[25]

The Japanese policy towards China from 1923 to 1931, therefore, generally followed precedents set during the previous two decades or so. By working with local actors to enhance economic and political privileges, Japanese leaders increased penetration into regions they found to be the most important without overly investing capabilities into administration.[26] Moreover, by concentrating on areas commonly recognised as being under Japanese influence, Tokyo

---

[21] Although the Army was largely responsible for orchestrating aid to friendly regimes in northern China, cabinets in Tokyo generally gave at least tacit agreement to such behaviour. Barnhart 1987, 30, 1995, 82–85, 105; Chen, 1983, 180–208, 1991, 1–206; Ienaga, 1978, 58–59; Mizuno and Zheng, 1998, 151–77.

[22] Ienaga, 1978, 65–74; Usui and Chen, 1990, 365–83; Zheng, 2001, 551–80.

[23] Barnhart, 1987, 78–84; Cho, 1973, 377–92; Coble, 1991, 90–119; Shen, 2005, 257–85; Zheng 2001, 551–80; SHAC 18/375, "Taipingyang Huiyi shanhou weiyuanhui taolun guanyu caibing jiaohui Guangzhouwan, jiejue Shandong xuan'an deng wenti de laiwang wenshu ji canyu Huashengdun huiyi wenjian", 1922; SHAC 1032/653, "Taipingyang Huiyi shanhou weiyuanhui caibing banfa dagang Shandong wenti huiyi shanhou huiyi", 1923.

[24] Mizuno and Zheng, 1998, 97–99, 217–29; Shen, 2005, 257–85.

[25] Barnhart, 1987, 30–31, 1995, 85–86; Ienaga, 1978, 59–79; Mizuno and Zheng, 1998, 174–82; Shen, 2005, 330–39; Zheng, 2001, 567, 580–88.

[26] Barnhart, 1987, 18, 34–39, 1995, 79–139; Cao et al., 2004, 3–151; China, Wai chiao pu. and League of Nations, Commission of Inquiry, 1932, 195–206, 117–52, 187–91, 308–9; Cho, 1973, 377–92; Coble, 1991, 90–119; Snyder, 1991, 133–52; Zheng, 2001, 553–80, 95–675.

The Evolution of Foreign Involvement in China, 1923–1952 117

avoided antagonising other powers.[27] Such actions permitted leaders in Tokyo to manage access opportunities to southern Manchuria, Shandong, and, to some extent, Fujian.[28] As a result, foreign, and even indigenous, attempts to gain access in such regions required at least implicit Japanese acceptance.

With expectations about the costs of intervention falling rapidly in the early 1930s, Tokyo's policy toward China became more aggressive. Rather than just regulating access through local partners, Japanese actions began to focus on fully excluding rivals through immediate territorial control. Beginning with the take-over of Manchuria in autumn 1931, the Japanese military started to occupy large parts of China.[29] By April 1934, the Japan's Foreign Ministry even put forward the Amau Declaration, which declared that all foreign financial and military assistance to actors in China required Japanese government approval.[30] Even before the official outbreak of the Second Sino-Japanese War, Japanese forces conquered much of north China in an undeclared war against the Nationalist government.[31] By the early 1940s, Tokyo held North, East, South, and much of Central China. Seen by leaders in Tokyo as part of its New Order in East Asia, and later the Greater East Asia Co-Prosperity Sphere, Japanese rule aimed to turn these areas into exclusive imperial preserves.[32] Exploitations of the markets, raw materials, and population in these areas were to help fortify Japan and prepare it to face the threats posed by the Soviet Union and Western powers.

As Japanese leaders pursued full denial of access over China, they dropped their wariness about confronting other major powers. In invading and occupying Manchuria, Tokyo ignored protests by the United States, Britain, France, and the League of Nations. When the League-commissioned Lytton Mission investigating the dispute over Manchuria recommended that Japanese forces withdraw, the Tojo cabinet promptly quit the League and established the Manchukuo government in 1932.[33] The Tojo cabinet and its successors likewise disregarded

---

[27] Taliaferro, 2004, 100; Zheng, 2001, 566–73, 643–75.

[28] Iriye, 1967, 143–45, 63–77; Schneider, 1998, 161–82.

[29] Barnhart, 1987, 30–49, 77–161, 1995, 87–112; Chen, 2003, 335–85; China, Wai chiao pu. and League of Nations, Commission of Inquiry, 1932, 2–4, 35–60, 293–96, 319–23, 365–403; Cho, 1973, 383–92; Ienaga, 1978, 57–85; Iriye, 1967, 177–78, 207–11; Kupchan, 1994, 304–15; Shen, 2005, 352–74; Snyder, 1991, 133–52; Zheng, 2001, 603–32; SHAC 18/3043, "Zhong-Ri guanxi wenti zhi beiwanglu", June 1932.

[30] This declaration drew its name from the head of the Intelligence Bureau of the Japanese Foreign Ministry, Amau Eiji, who publicly announced the plan on April 17, 1934. Observers at the time termed the Amau Declaration "Japan's Monroe Doctrine for Asia". Barnhart, 1987, 116, 1995, 103; Borg, 1964, 46–99; Coble, 1991, 153–62; Iriye, 1967, 176, 189; Li, 1999, 232–37; Shen, 2005, 451–57.

[31] Borg, 1964, 138–95; Iriye, 1967, 156–78; Shen, 2005, 285–432; Zheng, 2001, 553–80, 595–632; SHAC 18/3043, "Zhong-Ri guanxi wenti zhi beiwanglu".

[32] Barnhart, 1987, 28–44, 75, 91–114, 137, 151–54; Cao et al., 2004; Chen, 2003, 65–78, 203–323, 366–403; Coble, 1991, 182–282; Hikita, 1988, 101–34; Ienaga, 1978, 153–71; Ishikawa, 1995, 133–354, 434–89; Kirby, 1984, 233–52; Kupchan, 1994, 297–358; Shen, 2005, 517–84, 708–16; Zheng, 2001, 553–80, 595–632, 643–75.

[33] Barnhart, 1987, 33, 57–59, 1995, 97–101; Fei, Li, and Zhang, 1993, 1–32; Ienaga, 1978, 65–67; Iriye, 1967, 179; Shen, 2005, 388–426; SHAC 18/1343, "Chuxi Guolian xingzheng yuan di yibai

External Intervention and the Politics of State Formation

major power opposition as Japanese military forces spread across China in the 1930s and 1940s.[34] The running battles between the Kwantung Army and the Soviet Red Army along Manchuria's Siberian and Mongolian borders in 1938 and 1939 exemplified Tokyo's assertiveness in securing access over China.[35]

In areas under occupation, Japanese military and civilian agencies became responsible for overseeing administration at all levels of government.[36] At the top, Tokyo backed the creation of collaborationist governments. These included various regimes in Inner Mongolia and North China in addition to the better-known examples of Manchukuo and the Nanjing National Government under the Nationalist faction of Wang Jingwei.[37] Even though the Wang regime and other collaborationist governments enjoyed some functional autonomy and the formal abrogation of all unequal treaties, Tokyo directly supervised policy.[38]

ci changwei cong Riben qing Hua baoxing xingzheng yuan de faling he daibiao Gu Weijin de yanshuo", January 24–February 24, 1938; SHAC 18/2920, "Guanyu Ri qinglue Dongbei shi de shoudian", 1931; SHAC 18/2921, "Gu Weijun zhi Zhang Xueliang dian", 1931; SHAC 18/2922, "Zhang Xueliang guanyu Riben qinglue dongbei Waijiaobu dian", November 1937; SHAC 18/2933, "Gu Weijun yu Zhang Xueliang guanyu Riben qinglue Dongbei shi de laiwang dian", November 1931; SHAC 18/3268, Ministry of Foreign Affairs, "Guoji Lianhehui 1938 nian 9 yue suo tongguo guanyu Zhong Ri zhengyi zhijie jueyian ji baogaoshu", October 1938; SHAC 18/3268, "Guoji Lianhehui yu 1939 nian 1 yue suo tongguo Zhong Ri zhengyi zhi jueyian", June 1939; SHAC 18/3426, Ministry of Foreign Affairs of the Republic of China, "Zhong Ri wenti zhi zhenxiang canyu Guolian diaochatuan Zhongguo daibiao tiyi zhi ershijiu zhong shuotie 1932 nian 4 yue zhi 8 yue", March 1933; AH 0700.04/6050.01-01, "Riben fuzhi wei Manzhouguo baogaoshu", April 1932; SHAC 34/629, "Riben zhizao wei Manzhouguo jingguo shiliao zhailu Guowen zhoubao", February 1932—January 1934.

[34] Barnhart, 1987, 33–49, 77–118, 137–57, 1995, 114–43; Borg, 1964, 254–317; Coble, 1991, 182–282; Fei, Li, and Zhang, 1993, 55–165; Ienaga, 1978, 66–79, 129–34; Iriye, 1967, 172–78, 207–11; Kupchan, 1994, 328–50; Shen, 2005, 517–84, 708–16.

[35] Fei, Li, and Zhang, 1993, 169–74; Taliaferro, 2004, 96, 115, 85–200.

[36] Cao et al., 2004; Chen P., 1999; Fei, Li, and Zhang, 1993, 23–50, 80–87, 122–28, 205–10, 272–80; Huang, 1984; Huang and Zhang, 1984, 60–98; Tong et al., 2004, 3–212, 265–418, 487–519, 732–969; Zhongyang dang'anguan (China), 2000; Zhou and Cai, 2003, 219–1024.

[37] The Nanjing National Government differs from the National Government under the mainstream Nationalists of Chiang Kai-shek. Japan and Wang so named their regime to claim the legitimacy of the prewar National Government in Nanjing. Tokyo helped set up the North China government in Beijing – the Provisional Government of the Republic of China, or more commonly, the Huabei Regime. The Huabei Regime and the Nanjing National Government merged in 1940. The Huabei Regime became the North China Political Affairs Committee, which remained highly independent of Nanjing. The Nanjing National Government also included the former Reformed Government of the Republic of China established in Nanjing in 1938. The Inner Mongolian regime was officially the United Mongolian Autonomous Government, or Mengjiang, later rebranded as the Mongolian Autonomous State in 1941. There were other smaller Japanese-sponsored regimes as well. Barnhart, 1995, 120–21, 56–57; Barrett and Shyu, 2001, 21–76, 113–38; Boyle, 1972; Bunker, 1972; Chen, 1991, 239–75; China, Wai chiao pu and League of Nations, Commission of Inquiry, 1932, 3, 158, 301–23, 365–403; Ienaga, 1978, 63–90, 160–71; Iriye, 1967, 173–74, 207–11, 230; Liu, 2002, 1–370; Shen, 2005, 388–426, 47–91, 559–62, 585–631, 680–85, 700–16; Sheridan, 1975, 254; Spector, 2007, 36–37; Wang, 2001, 305–77.

[38] Barrett and Shyu, 2001, 79–132; Cao et al., 2004, 155–852; Chen P., 1999; Hu, 1940; Jiang, 2006; Liu, 2002, 9–254; SHAC 18/3268, Wang Zhaoming (Wang Jingwei), "Guanyu Zhonghua Minguo Ribenguo jian jiben guanxi tiaoyue fushu yidingshu ji fushu yidingshu liaojie shixiang",

The Evolution of Foreign Involvement in China, 1923–1952

Japanese officials maintained oversight of government agencies, whilst Japan's military was charged with security matters until, in the words of the treaty governing Tokyo-Nanjing relations, "all threats to safety are resolved".[39]

The Japanese presence in governance was apparent not only at the top levels. Timothy Brook and others note that locally stationed civilian "pacification teams", supported by the closest Japanese military garrison, watched over local government administration into the county level.[40] Brook notes that Japanese "pacification teams had been the supreme power in occupied counties".[41] Pacification teams, local Japanese garrisons, and resident collaborators together oversaw everything from security and public works, to social services, civil reconstruction, and education, down to individual villages, albeit with varying degrees of success.[42]

Unconditional surrender in August 1945 meant that Japanese leaders could no longer invest capabilities into retaining the positions and arrangements previously set up in China.[43] Without their backer, the various collaborationist regimes collapsed, ending Japanese pretensions to fully exclude other major powers from access.[44] American occupation from 1945 to 1952 saw an abatement of Japanese efforts to compete for access in China.

December 1940; SHAC 18/3268, Wang Zhaoming (Wang Jingwei), "Guanyu shouhui zhujie ji chechu zhiwai faquan'an", April 1943; SHAC 18/2061, "Wang wei zhengfu waijiaobu dangan"; SHAC 18/1714, "33 nian 9 yue 31 ri No. 59 di zi 103 hao", "Di Wei jiyao di 59, 61–67 hao", 1944; SHAC 2061/2134, "Wang wei tiaoyue mulu ji jianbao", 1940–1943; SHAC 18/1714, "Di Wei jiyao No. 59 di zi 103 hao", 31 September 1944; SHAC 2061/2109, "Xingzhengyuan guanyu Huabei, Huazhong tiedao, yunying zhanyou Rijun guanli gei Waijiaobu de xunling", April 1945; SHAC 2061/2115, "Riben zhu Huanan paiqianjun (qinluejun) zhiding Zhongren junlü fa'an de laiwang wenjian", July–August 1945.

[39] Chen, 1996; Lee, 1967; Zhou and Cai, 2003, 219–1024; SHAC 18/3268, "Guanyu Zhonghua Minguo Ribenguo jian jiben guanxi tiaoyue fushu yidingshu ji fushu yidingshu liaojie shixiang"; SHAC 18/3268, Wang Zhaoming, "Zhonghua Minguo dui Ying Mei xuanzhan'an fu Zhong Ri xieli yuanzhu dui Ying Mei zhanzheng zhi gongtong xuanyan", April 1943; SHAC 18/3268, Wang Zhaoming and Zang Shiyi, Foreign Minister of Manchukuo, "Zhong-Ri-Man gongtong xuanyan", December 1940; Second Historical Archive of China 2061/2164, "Zhong-Ri jiben tiaoyue gangyao", November 1938; SHAC 2061/2742, "Waijiao Zhengce", March 13, 1942; SHAC 2061/2745, "Jiaru guoji fangong lianmeng xieding baipishu".

[40] Brook, 2005, 55; Chen P., 1999, 14–35, 116–21, 158–88, 261–68; Shen, 2005, 675–80; Yu, 1985; Liu, 2002; and Cao, 1985; SHAC 18/3268, "Guanyu Zhonghua Minguo Ribenguo jian jiben guanxi tiaoyue fushu yidingshu ji fushu yidingshu liaojie shixiang"; SHAC 2005/581, "Ri wei Huabei Zhi'an Qianghua Zongbenbu de zuzhi dagang he dui Beijing Xishan gongbu zuzhi xilie de xiuding", 1942.

[41] Brook, 2005, 55.

[42] Lee, 1967.

[43] Barnhart, 1995, 145–50; Chen P., 1999, 297–303; Fei, Li, and Zhang, 1993, 338–47; Ienaga, 1973, 229–34; Ishikawa, 1995, 434–88; Liu, 2002, 133–254; *Provisional Verbatim Minutes*, 1951; *Record of Proceedings*, 1951; *Record of Proceedings: Supplement*, 1952; Shen, 2005, 722–54; Wang, 2001, 365–411.

[44] Liu, 2002, 371–254; Zhongyang dang'anguan (China), 2000; Zhou and Cai, 2003, 969–1024.

AN END TO BRITISH PROMINENCE

If the Britannic titan was weary at the turn of the twentieth century, it neared exhaustion by the late 1940s. From 1914 to 1952, the need to fight in and rebuild after two systemic wars, recover from the Great Depression, face an emerging Soviet Cold War threat, and manage relations with a newly preponderant United States beset leaders in London. Consequently, British expectations about the opportunity costs of intervening in the Chinese polity remained high for much of the period 1923 to 1952, and became nearly prohibitive toward the late 1940s. British elites saw the limited aim of pursuing nonprivileged access as the most justifiable use of already stretched capabilities in China, but were open to complete withdrawal if necessary.

British interwar cabinets generally had two primary objectives in China regardless of party affiliation.[45] The first was to ensure nondiscrimination against existing British economic interests by preventing other powers from acquiring exclusive access privileges.[46] Britain was the second largest exporter in China and one of its biggest investors going into the 1920s and 1930s, although its position in the Chinese economy was in relative decline.[47] The second was to preserve access equality through cooperation with other actors, notably China's central government and Japan.

An internal Foreign Office Memorandum by Austen Chamberlain, Foreign Secretary in the Conservative government of Stanley Baldwin, summed up the official British view on China from 1923 to 1937, declaring that:

As regards the principles of British policy in China, these can be stated in a very few words. We have no territorial or imperialistic aims. Our first concern is to maintain our position in the trade of China. . . . Our second concern is to maintain the principle of the "open door" and equal opportunity for all and to see that China does not fall under the tutelage of any single Power. For these reasons we desire to see a united, well-ordered, prosperous and peaceful China, and it is our policy to endeavour to co-operate to that end with the other Great Powers concerned. These are the root principles underlying all our efforts in China.[48]

This view came from the belief that seeking full denial or direct regulation of access in China would distract Britain's already strained capabilities from more important goals elsewhere.[49]

---

[45] These included the Liberal government of Lloyd George, the Conservative governments of Andrew Bonar Law, Stanley Baldwin, and Neville Chamberlain, as well as the Labour government of Ramsay MacDonald. Li, 1999, 1–12, 225–60, 405–12.

[46] Chamberlain, 1946, 1–26; Li, 1999, 1–32, 81–98, 143–53, 225–60, 273, 337, 405–12.

[47] Li, 1999, 407.

[48] Chamberlain, 1946, 4.

[49] Leaders from across party lines including Foreign Secretaries Ramsay MacDonald, John Simon, Samuel Hoare, Anthony Eden, and the Viscount Halifax, as well as Chancellors of the Exchequer Stanley Baldwin, Winston Churchill, and Neville Chamberlain backed this view. Li, 1999, 1–12, 225–60, 405–12.

The Evolution of Foreign Involvement in China, 1923–1952

Voices calling for a more robust British role in China certainly existed. In the early 1920s, British nationals and firms in China lobbied London to suppress the Chinese Nationalists and Chinese nationalism, retain extraterritoriality, and preserve jurisdiction over British-administered areas.[50] Senior diplomats and bureaucrats as well as British businesses active in China called on London to extend technical, political, and financial support for the Nationalist-led central government's monetary reform efforts during the 1930s.[51] They did so to bring China informally into the pound-based sterling bloc and expand British influence over the Chinese financial system.

Given the priorities of interwar British political elites, advocates of a more active British government role in China failed to make headway. Most leaders believed that the greatest returns came from committing capabilities to the metropole's economic revival.[52] This was a result of Britain's economic woes after the Great War and following the rise of a labour movement demanding more attention to working-class needs.

Niall Ferguson observed that, "paying for the [Great] war had led to a tenfold increase in national debt. Just paying interest on that debt consumed close to half of total central government spending by the mid-1920s".[53] Exacerbating conditions were decisions by the Baldwin cabinet and the Chancellor of the Exchequer, Winston Churchill, to return to the gold standard at overvalued 1914 rates. This forced an adoption of deflationary policies that led to rising unemployment, contributing to the 1926 General Strike.[54] Making matters worse, investor confidence flagged because of uncertainty over the will of an indebted British government to support the gold standard, especially as central banks elsewhere undermined that monetary regime.[55] The further deterioration of the British economy following the Great Depression compounded these problems.

As a result, prime ministers from Lloyd George to Neville Chamberlain focused on the creation of a pound-based fixed exchange rate system as well as

---

[50] Behind this stance were the Joint Committee of the British Chamber of Commerce and the Shanghai Branch of the China Association, the British Residents' Association, British and Chinese Corporation, Chartered Bank of India, Australia, and China, Federation of British Industries, the China Association, the China Committee, Butterfield, Swire, and Company, Jardine, Matheson, and Company, the Hong Kong and Shanghai Bank, as well as the Sino-British Trade Council. Chen, 1983, 208–32; Li, 1999, 17–66, 81–127; AH 0645.20/ 2760.01–02, "Zhujie shouhui", November 4, 1930.

[51] Advocating this position were the China Bondholders' Committee, and three former British Ministers and Ambassadors to China – Miles Lampson, Hughe Knatchbull-Hugessen, and Alexander Cadogan, later Permanent Under-Secretary for Foreign Affairs – head of the British Economic Mission to the Far East and chief economic advisor to the British government, Frederick Leith-Ross, as well as officials in the Bank of England and Treasury. Chen, 1983, 208–32; Li, 1999, 273–323; Rothwell, 1975; Young, 1971, 216–38, 378–82, 417–18.

[52] Ferguson, 2004, 271–75; Kupchan, 1994, 131–37, 75–80; Li, 1999, 3, 225, 243.

[53] Ferguson, 2004, 271.

[54] Eichengreen, 1992, 164–67, 210–20, 278–86, 302–25; Industry, 1997, 246–61; Nurkse, 1997, 262–88; War, 1997, 229–45.

[55] Kennedy, 1987, 316–17.

122   *External Intervention and the Politics of State Formation*

a preferential tariff system centred on the British empire.[56] The sterling bloc and imperial preference system aimed to ensure ready access to cheap raw materials and captive markets for British firms by managing access across the empire, effectively creating the world's largest protectionist bloc. Consequently, the share of British exports going to the empire grew from 44 to 48 percent whilst Britain's imports from the empire expanded from 30 to 39 percent.[57] In comparison, China accounted for around 0.5 to 2.5 percent of Britain's trade and about 5 percent of British foreign investment – with the remainder going to the empire and the Americas.[58]

London's single-mindedness over the revival of the British economy made almost all other objectives seem secondary. To spur economic growth, every British cabinet between 1919 and 1932 even reaffirmed the so-called "ten-year rule" that retrenched defence expenditures and channelled savings toward the economy.[59] Implementation of the rule contracted military spending by about a third at a time when similar expenditures by major powers except the United States grew between 55 and 60 percent.[60] If the expected gains from investing in the defence seemed low, perceived returns from intervening in China were nearly negligible – especially if armed confrontation was in the offing.[61] As war cost blood and treasure, and could destroy the very economic potential in dispute, British leaders saw compromise and limited deterrence as the preferred way to address challenges in China.

British leaders rescinded the "ten-year rule" in 1932, but only because of the rise of fascism and Nazism in Europe. Mounting pressure to protect the British Isles spelt a further decline in the importance of securing access in China.[62] Whatever gains were to be had from denying rivals access in China would evaporate should Britain face defeat and the forcible dismantling of its empire. London's long neglect of its military, which left British forces lagging in technology, readiness, and size, only worsened matters. When appeasement failed to prevent Japan from shutting out British access after 1937, London resisted through passive diplomatic and political support for Chiang Kai-shek's government.

Still, British leaders appeared unwilling to cede access over China completely. Withdrawal from China spelt a loss of both current interests and future

---

[56] Kupchan, 1994, 131–38; Li, 1999, 1–12, 242–60, 405–12.

[57] Ferguson, 2004, 272; Great Britain, Board of Trade v., 125–199 (1930—1970); Great Britain, Board of Trade v., 1101–1751 (1918–1930); Li, 1999, 1–12, 242–60, 406–08.

[58] Britain's *Board of Trade Journal* from 1922 to 1952 reveals that trade volume with China was similar to Malaya, putting it behind the United States (18 percent), Canada (6 percent), Australia (6 percent), and India (5 percent). Great Britain, Board of Trade v., 125–199 (1930– 1970); Great Britain, Board of Trade v., 1101–1751 (1918–1930); Li, 1999, 406–8.

[59] The rule assumed that Britain would not be in a major power war within a decade. Ferguson, 2004, 273–75; Li, 1999, 3, 225, 243.

[60] Barnhart, 1987, 62; Kennedy, 1987, 302–20; Kupchan, 1994, 133–44, 160–75.

[61] Chamberlain, 1946, 1–26; Li, 1999, 405–12.

[62] Ferguson, 2004, 279–85; Ienaga, 1978, 78.

The Evolution of Foreign Involvement in China, 1923–1952

opportunities. Moreover, preventing Japan from completely denying access over the Chinese polity could draw Tokyo's attention away from Britain's colonial possessions in Asia, and even promise nondiscrimination against British access in China after the war.[63] Nevertheless, active and direct involvement in the Chinese polity was not something British leaders were willing to stomach whilst fighting raged in Europe, North Africa, and the Atlantic.[64]

The end of World War II did not raise British expectations of gain from securing greater degrees of access in China. Fighting the war left the British government and economy more indebted than before. Demobilisation and the devastation of war drove the British economy into a severe depression matched by massive inflation.[65] Moreover, the postwar Clement Attlee and Winston Churchill cabinets faced the need to address Indian independence and the maintenance of empire.[66] A realisation by Britain's leaders about a looming Communist threat to Europe further convinced British leaders of the need to allocate any remaining capabilities to Western Europe and the empire.[67]

Even if some elites in London desired more access privileges in China at the expense of the other major powers, pursuing such a goal appeared to necessitate the sacrifice of more pressing strategic objectives. Not only was the British economy in shambles, Japan's invasion of China destroyed any access advantages Britain enjoyed. Additionally, London's efforts to sustain the wartime alliance with the Chinese Nationalists meant pressure to relinquish treaty frameworks that undergirded any remaining access privileges.

Consequently, London expected the preservation of nonprivileged access amongst the major powers in China to provide the best return to investment of its limited capabilities between 1923 and 1952. This translated into supporting a largely autonomous central government with a high degree of control over China that was willing and able to preserve nonprivileged access for Britain. London sought to accomplish this through compromises with the central government and the other major powers active in China.

To this end, Britain's policy in China until 1949 combined efforts to back the Nationalist Party–led central government using political concessions with the appeasement of Japanese aggression. The Foreign Office, after all, identified the National Government as having the most viable claim to central government status, although Whitehall acknowledged that Nanjing effectively controlled no more than two to three provinces as late as 1930.[68] This desire to maintain nonprivileged access in China also spelt a willingness to recognise a Communist-led central government once Nationalist rule collapsed.

---

[63] Barnhart, 1995, 121; Li, 1999, 3, 225–60, 337–88; SHAC 18/2954, "Zhong Ying lianhe junshi xingdong tanhua xieding jiyao yu jianyi", July—August 1941.

[64] Ferguson, 2004, 283–94; Hu, 2001f, 2001j, 2001k.

[65] Kennedy, 1987, 367–68; LaFeber, 1993, 52; Leffler, 1992, 143.

[66] Spector, 2007, 73–76.

[67] Ferguson, 2004, 295–301; Roberts, 1993, 33–67.

[68] Chamberlain, 1946, 3–4.

A Strained Defence of the "Open Door"

Economic problems and the rise of new continental threats hemmed in London's willingness to commit capabilities into competition over access in China.[69] Instead of providing financial and material assistance to shore up central governments, British support came in the form of concessions that aimed to entice the central governments in China to help maintain London's interests. It was in this vein that British leaders allowed increased customs tariffs, pledged the eventual relinquishment of control over the use of customs revenues, and promised to progressively remove extraterritorial rights at the 1926 Beijing Tariff Conference.[70] Accepting such conditions could burnish the domestic nationalist credentials of whoever controlled the central government, while promising greater access to a stable source of income. As London believed that such action would shore up a central government supportive of nondiscriminatory British access, Britain's leaders pushed ahead with these policies over protests by British nationals and businesses in China.[71]

For British policymakers, concessions made at the Tariff Conference were a cheap hedge against different possible results of the Nationalists' Northern Expedition, then underway. Since the gains from rolling back extraterritoriality and additional revenues could benefit any party that controlled the central government, such concessions could encourage the eventual victor to avoid discriminating against British access. This was of particular concern given Soviet tutelage of the Nationalists and Feng Yuxiang's Guominjun, as well as Japan's support for Zhang Zuolin and his Fengtian Clique, which was then the force behind the Beijing central government.[72]

Efforts at accommodating China's central government followed into the 1930s and beyond. They included the 1927 and 1928 treaty revisions that saw London hand over a number of concessions and leaseholds across China to the Nationalist-led central government in Nanjing, whilst reducing the British administrative role in other areas.[73] This paved the way for British support of tariff autonomy for Nanjing in 1929, as well as the return of the Boxer Indemnity in 1931.[74] The British government also acquiesced to efforts by the

---

[69] Huang, 2005, 417–569; Kupchan, 1994, 133–75; Lowe, 1981, 126–28.

[70] It was within this context that London released the December Memorandum, also known as the Lampson Policy, laying out the basic structure for an accommodation policy in China. Chamberlain, 1946, 7–9; Iriye, 1967, 154; Li, 1999, 3–4, 17–66, 81–98, 405–07; AH 0645.20/ 2760.01–02, "Zhujie shouhui"; SHAC 18/3466, *Tariff Autonomy Treaty between China and Great Britain*, December 20, 1928.

[71] Atkins, 1995, 13–22; Lowe, 1981, 128–32.

[72] Chamberlain, 1946, 7–10; Liu and Tian, 2004, 116–31; Mizuno and Zheng, 1998, 154–57.

[73] Chamberlain, 1946, 12–22; Chen, 1983, 208–32; Li, 1999, 33–66, 81–127; SHAC 18/3268, Wang Zhengting, Foreign Minister of the Republic of China, "Zhong-Ying jiaoshou Weihaiwei zhuanyue ji xieding", April 14, 1930; SHAC 1032/651, "Beiyang Zhengfu Taipingyang Huiyi Weihaiwei wenti", 1923; SHAC 1032/648, "Beiyang Zhengfu waijiao wendu", 1923.

[74] Brunero, 2006, 86–100; Chen, 1983, 208–32; Lowe, 1981, 132–35.

The Evolution of Foreign Involvement in China, 1923–1952

National Government to exert control over Maritime Customs, beginning with its formal incorporation into the Finance Ministry.[75] London further attempted to win Nanjing's support for British interests by offering technical assistance for monetary and financial reforms through the 1936–1937 Leith-Ross Economic Mission to China.[76]

At the same time, negotiations to progressively end extraterritoriality began in 1928, and brought the abolition of all British special privileges by 1943.[77] In order to secure nonprivileged access in China after World War II, London even considered talks with the National Government over revising the status of Hong Kong between 1944 and 1949.[78] Following the Nationalist disintegration on the mainland in late 1949, Churchill's Conservative cabinet quickly switched recognition to the newly established central government in Beijing by January 1950. Driving this development was the goal of trying to obtain continued nonprivileged access, or in Churchill's words, to "secure a convenience".[79]

The 1927 Nanjing Incident was the only significant departure from official British efforts to accommodate the local actors claiming control over central governments in China. British warships on the Yangzi River shelled the

---

[75] Atkins, 1995, 41–106; Barnhart, 1995, 121; KMTPA *Hankou* 5277, Wang Jingwei, "Haiguan wenti" [The maritime customs issue], January 1924.

[76] Iriye, 1967, 190; Lowe, 1981, 150–54; Young, 1971, 216–38.

[77] Chen, 1991, 155–78; Li, 1999, 279–323; SHAC 18/3268, Foreign Ministry Song Ziwen (T.V. Soong), "Zhong Ying guanyu quxiao Yingguo zai Hua zhiwai faquan qi youguan tequan tiaoyue", November 1943; SHAC 18/3269, Ministry of Foreign Affairs, "Waijiao Baipishu 69 zhi 88 hao", 1946; SHAC 18/3270, Wang Shijie, Foreign Minister of the Republic of China, "Zhong Ying guanyu Zhongguo Haiguan yu Xianggang zhengfu jian guanwu xieding zhi huanwen", January 1948; SHAC 18/3429, Ministry of Foreign Affairs, "Baipishu di 54 zhi 105", 1940–1948; SHAC 18/3285, *Sino-British Treaty for the Abolition of Extraterritoriality and Related Rights in China, signed at Chungking on January 11, 1943, Instruments of Ratification Exchanged at Chungking on May 20, 1945*; AH 0645.20/2760.01–02, "Zhujie shouhui"; AH 0645/8800.01–01, "Chouban shouhui Ying Fa Yi zhujie weiyuanhui huiyi jilu", June 17, 1930; AH 0645.20/7177.01–01, "Xiamen Ying zhujie shouhui"; AH 0645.20/7177.01–02, "Zhenjiang Ying zhujie shouhui"; AH 0645.20/3460.01–01, "Hankou Jiujiang Ying zhujie shouhui", February 19, 1927; AH 0645.20/1035.02–01, "Tianjin Ying zhujie shouhui", January 28–February 23, 1927; AH 0645.20/1035.02–02, "Tianjin Ying zhujie shouhui"; AH 0645.20/1035.02–03, "Tianjin Ying zhujie shouhui", December 17, 1927; AH 0645.30/5338.01–01, "Weihaiwei zhujiedi shouhui'an", 1930; AH 0641.90/5044.01–02, "Zhong-Ying Zhong-Mei tiaoyue ji laiwang zhaohui", May 18, 1943; AH 0641.90/5044.01–01, "Zhong-Ying Zhong-Mei fenbie qianding tiaoyue feichu jiuyue", January 13, 1943; AH 0641.90/2760.01–01, "Geguo zai Hua zhiwai faquan tiaoyue quxiao", December 23, 1942–November 1943.

[78] Chan Lau, 1990, 327; Kirby, 1997, 441; Lane, 1990; Liu, 1994, 191–200; Tucker, 1994, 199; Wang, 1979, 282; SHAC 18/677, "Zhongguo zhi guoji guanxi", 1929; SHAC 18/1927, "Zhixing shouhui faquan geyue xuzhi", 1945; SHAC 18/2545, "Waijiaobu niti Canzhenghui de waijiao baogao", May 9–September 24, 1947; SHAC 18/3270, "Zhong Ying guanyu Zhongguo Haiguan yu Xianggang zhengfu jian guanwu xieding zhi huanwen"; SHAC 18/3429, "Baipishu di 54 zhi 105"; AH 0632/2034.01–01, "Yingguo anshi yuan jiang Xianggang jiang Lianheguo zuowei Yuandong ji Taipingyang qu zhi fensuo an banli qingxing", November 15, 1946; SHAC 18/2951, "Guomindang Zhengfu Waijiaobu guanyu Gang-Jiu wenti de jianbao ziliao", 1945–1946.

[79] Brunero, 2006, 84–86; Lowe, 1997, 85–119; Tucker, 2001, 72; Wolf, 1983.

126   *External Intervention and the Politics of State Formation*

Nationalist Army's positions in Nanjing for three days. This was in response to looting and violence against foreigners by the Nationalist forces after they entered the city as part of the Northern Expedition.[80] This Incident was the last major British military action against Chinese forces inside China, and occurred before the Nationalists secured their hold over the central government.

Alongside trying to demonstrate support for central governments in China to secure nonprivileged access, British leaders were also keen to appease Japan to avert a full-blown Sino-Japanese war.[81] Policymakers in London believed that if the Japanese emerged victorious, they would shut out British interests, as was the case with Manchuria following its absorption into Japan's sphere of influence. Moreover, even if the National Government's forces held out against the Imperial Japanese Army, fighting in Central and South China was likely to force British businesses to withdraw. As a result, British policy elites hoped to broker Sino-Japanese reconciliation, with, if necessary, help from the League of Nations.

Hence, understanding British accommodation of China's central governments requires an appreciation of London's simultaneous concessions to Japan. The most notable of these included British efforts to mediate between Tokyo and Nanjing following the Kwantung Army's seizure of Manchuria in September 1931 and the subsequent Japanese attack on Shanghai in January 1932.[82] In negotiating cease-fires through the League of Nations, London pushed for the unilateral withdrawal of Chinese forces that effectively left demilitarised zones around territory gained by the Japanese, allowing the latter to consolidate its positions.

London only offered symbolic verbal criticism of Tokyo and an ineffectual arms embargo on both belligerents after the League of Nations' Lytton Mission concluded that Japanese claims over Manchuria were weak.[83] Given China's military and industrial limitations, the burdens of the embargo fell disproportionately on Nanjing. Following the Amau Declaration, London even pushed the League to end aid programmes in China.[84]

Concerns over Japanese displeasure were also key in leading London to continually delay a proposed £100 million loan to the National Government recommended by the Leith-Ross Mission and requested by Nanjing for financial and monetary reforms.[85] Likewise, the British government prevented China

---

[80] Chamberlain, 1946, 9–26; Lowe, 1981, 130–31; Shen, 2005, 298–300.

[81] Kupchan, 1994, 156–68; Li, 1999, 18–47, 143–205; Lowe, 1981, 136–76.

[82] The 1933 Tanggu and 1932 Shanghai Ceasefire Agreements paused fighting between Japanese and Chinese forces after the invasion of Manchuria and the attack on Shanghai respectively. Other interim arrangements were the 1935 Chin (Qin)-Doihara Agreement regarding the demilitarisation of Chahar and 1935 Ho (He)-Umezu Accord over the demilitarisation of Hebei. Barnhart, 1995, 103–4, 121; Coble, 1991, 90–119; Li, 1999, 143–205; Shen, 2005, 432–39, 458–69.

[83] The embargo was ineffective, since Japan largely produced its own weapons, whilst enforcement on both sides was virtually nonexistent. Shen, 2005, 408–17; SHAC 18/2920, "Guanyu Ri qinglue Dongbei shi de shoudian"; SHAC 18/2921, "Gu Weijun zhi Zhang Xueliang dian".

[84] Coble, 1991, 156–57; Shen, 2005, 453–54.

[85] Li, 1999, 232–37, 295–323, 410–11; Lowe, 1981, 139–54; Young, 1971, 216–38, 278–82.

The Evolution of Foreign Involvement in China, 1923–1952

from invoking the collective security clause of the League charter following the outbreak of the Sino-Japanese War in 1937, and only gave verbal criticism of Japan.[86] Just as telling of official British attitudes were persistent attempts to reach an understanding with Tokyo between 1931 and 1941. Citing Britain's accommodation in China as a demonstration of goodwill, London aimed to acquire Japanese government guarantees for British interests in China.[87] The rationale behind such moves was to avoid exclusive Japanese access at Britain's expense.

Britain's China policy remained passive even with the start of the Sino-Japanese War. Fear of provoking Japan prompted Chamberlain's cabinet to decline Nanjing's request for arms sales, and restrict assistance to China's central government to two areas. The first was to allow arms from third countries to reach the National Government through Hong Kong by not imposing inspections.[88] The second was to finish the Burma Road that was already near completion, and eventually open Burma and India for the supply of war matériel to Chongqing.[89] British aid to the National Government through 1945 totalled £68.04 million, less than what the Soviets offered the Nationalists between 1937 and 1941.[90] With the end of World War II, the strain of fighting and rebuilding effectively ended active British involvement in China, with the obvious exception of Hong Kong.[91]

DENYING PRIVILEGED ACCESS AND AMERICA'S INVOLVEMENT IN CHINA

China was never of very high priority for leaders in Washington from 1923 to 1952. Congress and presidential administrations from Harding to Truman placed domestic development and security concerns in Europe ahead of issues in the Far East. Behind this general outlook was the expectation that committing capabilities to China would bring much smaller returns than investing those same capacities elsewhere. This fostered an expectation about the high opportunity costs of intervening into the Chinese polity amongst key American elites. Consequently, Washington's approach to China at this time centred on preserving nonprivileged access for American interests.

---

[86] The Chamberlain cabinet used procedural means to prevent the Chinese delegation from invoking collective security clauses in the League's charter. London then referred matters to the Nine Power Treaty Convention, which was unable to move given a Japanese veto. Borg 1964, 399–441; SHAC 18/1311, "Bulujiser huiyi de bao gao", November 24, 1937; AH 0601.41/3120.01–01, "Wei Riben chubing Dongbei San sheng woguo tijiao Guolian Zongcai Zhongguo daibiao Gu Weijun yu Waijiaobu wanglai dianwen", September 21, 1931.

[87] Li, 1999, 143–205, 242–60, 295–323, 337–88, 410–12.

[88] Ministry of Foreign Affairs 1999, 398–99; Tucker, 1994, 198–204.

[89] Lowe, 1981, 157–76; Sun, 1993, 143–44.

[90] Cui, 1995, 242–45, 47.

[91] Chen, 1991, 176–77; Lowe, 1997, 201–08, 1981, 85–161; Wang, 1979, 282–83; SHAC 18/861, "Zhong-Ying youhao tongshang hanghai tiaoyue Zhongwen weiding gao", December 1946.

Between 1923 and 1937, U.S. leaders saw competition for access in China as less important than other objectives. After all, U.S. economic ties with East Asia for the period remained far behind American trade and investment with Europe and Latin America, and paled in importance next to the U.S. domestic market.[92] Within Asia, the value of U.S. trade and investment with China was less than half of that with Japan, America's largest economic partner in the Far East.[93] Trade with Japan often hovered around 10 percent of the U.S. total and never fell below 7 percent through the 1930s, whilst foreign investment in Japan stood at between 7 to 8 percent of total outward American investment.[94]

Hence, most American leaders up until the Pearl Harbour attack saw anything more than diplomatic intervention into the Chinese polity as counterproductive and unnecessarily burdensome. Given Japan's interest in China, U.S. officials believed that active involvement in China could risk confrontation with a well-entrenched Japanese military that America was both unprepared and unwilling to face.[95] Moreover, the need to focus on solving the domestic problems associated with the Great Depression meant that the Hoover and Roosevelt administrations had little time or energy to spare over China.[96] Finally, the domestic chaos that enveloped China through the 1940s suggested to U.S. political leaders that heavy involvement in that polity was a quagmire to avoid.[97] Substantial intervention in China seemed to promise few gains next to other, more pressing concerns.

Yet, Washington policymakers saw total withdrawal from China as untenable. This ironically owed much to the strength of isolationism in the United States. Congress and administrations in office during the interwar period wished to avert a major power war. A large proportion of American leaders believed such an event to be economically disruptive and unnecessarily costly, like the Great War. For interwar U.S. leaders, the key to avoiding such conflict seemed to lie in post–World War I treaties and institutions, which they hoped would restrain major powers from using force on each other.[98]

For American policymakers, forgoing access over China in the face of Japanese aggression threatened to undermine the Washington Naval Treaty and Nine Power Treaty designed to prevent conflict amongst the major powers in China and the Asia-Pacific.[99] Leaders in Washington, including FDR and Secretary of State Henry Stimson, believed that this could contribute to the unravelling of the post–World War I institutional framework.[100] Further, that U.S. economic

---

[92] Cohen, 2000, 93–94, 178; Kennedy, 1987, 281–83.
[93] This was despite the fact that the United States was one of the largest investors in China, next to Japan and Britain. Cohen, 2000, 107–24; Taliaferro, 2004, 102.
[94] Iriye, 1967, 150–65; Memorandum on United States Investments in Japan, 1933; Wilkins, 1982.
[95] Barnhart, 1987, 53–59; Chen, 2003, 360–69; Coble, 1991, 153–62; Cohen, 2000, 106–34; Ienaga, 1978, 65–66, 133; Iriye, 1967, 178–206.
[96] Coble, 1991, 153–62; Kennedy, 1987, 329–30; Tucker, 1994, 9.
[97] Chen, 2003, 360–69; Ienaga, 1978, 133; Zhang, 2004, 417–35, 473–88.
[98] Iriye, 1967, 178–98; Kennedy, 1987, 328.
[99] Ienaga, 1978, 66; Sun, 1993, 131–32.
[100] Borg, 1964, 1–45, 92–120, 176–95; Cohen, 2000, 106–12; Iriye, 1967, 178–98.

The Evolution of Foreign Involvement in China, 1923–1952

interests in China were substantial in absolute terms – even if minor relative to other concerns – meant that Washington did not wish to completely relinquish involvement in China even if it was reluctant to take an active stand.

However, events in Europe between 1938 and 1945 led American leaders to anticipate a slight fall in the cost of intervention in China. This encouraged Washington to become more active in trying to maintain nonprivileged access, even if it still tried to stay away from heavy involvement inside China where possible. Nazi Germany's rise in the late 1930s and early 1940s appeared to point toward the emergence of a world hostile to the United States, a trend that would be complete with the fall of an increasingly beleaguered Britain.[101] In this respect, the Roosevelt administration and Congress became increasingly convinced that the loss of British Empire in the Far East would bring Britain's total defeat.[102] Serious concerns in this regard remained even after Germany turned on the Soviets in 1941.

For American leaders, the key to preventing a British defeat appeared to be bogging down Japanese forces and capabilities in the vast expanse of China, away from British possessions in Southeast Asia and especially India. Planners in the War Department believed that tying down Japanese forces in China could permit the United States to focus on a more pressing German threat.[103] This was the case even after the Japanese strike on Pearl Harbour and the fall of British, Dutch, and American colonies across Southeast Asia in 1942. World War II led American leaders to see greater gains from more involvement in China in terms of its ability to help the United States reap even larger benefits in Europe.

Consequently, Washington strove to secure nonprivileged access over China with as little investment as possible.[104] This translated into assisting actors in China to avoid defeat. As such, any Chinese victory over Japan would be incidental rather than intended. Even after Tokyo's surrender, the United States tried to have Japanese forces and their collaborationist allies turn themselves and their equipment over to Chinese Nationalist forces.[105] This enabled Washington to limit military and financial assistance to the National Government as the latter tried to reclaim formerly occupied territory.

Self-imposed American restrictions on postwar aid to China reflected elite beliefs that returns from securing access in China remained secondary to the gains anticipated from investing in the rebuilding of Europe and constructing an Atlantic alliance system.[106] For Harry Truman and his administration, the

---

[101] Chen, 2003, 369–85; Cohen, 2000, 119–25; Gaddis, 2005, 1–18; Ienaga, 1978, 78–83; Iriye, 1967, 194–226; Kennedy, 1987, 330–33; Tucker, 1994, 11–12.

[102] Barnhart, 1987, 218; Sun, 1993, 143–50.

[103] Cohen, 2000, 123–33; Hu, 2001l; Ienaga, 1978, 132–33.

[104] Cohen, 2001, 105–34; Hu, 2001b, 2001c, 2001f, 2001k; Jespersen, 1996, 108–25; Soong and Hu, 2001, 116–18; Wang, 2003, 201–19.

[105] Cohen, 2000, 153–56; Spector, 2007, 36–65; SHAC 18/3050, "Notes of a Conversation between Dr. Wang (Shijie) and Dr. (Wellington) Koo on one part and Hon. James Bryne, U.S. Secretary of State, 2 p.m., September 11, 1945, at Claridge's Hotel", 11 September 1945.

[106] Gaddis, 2005, 15–18.

130 External Intervention and the Politics of State Formation

reconstruction of a war-torn Europe – and Japan – at the end of World War II could provide the United States with strong partners for the postwar world. This was especially important with the emergence of a Soviet threat, since the ability to build on the preexisting industrial bases in Western Europe and Japan seemed critical to any long-term rivalry.[107] China, with its underdevelopment and internal problems, seemed to have little immediate value except as a foil for mobilising the American public to support a massive rebuilding of Europe and Japan, and perhaps as a buffer against the Soviets in Asia.[108] The potentially catastrophic consequences of war with the Soviet Union, especially with the advent of nuclear weapons, further restrained U.S. leaders from acts that might unnecessarily escalate tensions – such as open intervention in China.[109]

The Truman administration simply saw preventing exclusive Soviet access across China at minimal American expense as sufficient, given other demands on American energies.[110] Postwar policymakers like Dean Acheson, George Kennan, and even Truman himself, continued to hold the perspective that the opportunity costs of intervening in China were high, much like their prewar predecessors.[111] The Korean War and fears of escalating hostilities in East Asia soon raised the perceived cost of involvement on the Chinese mainland even more.[112] However, mobilising for the Korean War and containing Communism in the Far East brought a simultaneous and substantial lowering of the expected costs of intervening in Taiwan to shore up the Chinese Nationalists there.[113]

For all the consistency that U.S. policymakers between 1923 and 1952 demonstrated in their understandings about the high opportunity costs relating to intervention in China, this perspective was in dispute. Chinese leaders like Sun Yat-sen and private American citizens and businesses in China were urging the U.S. government to take a more active role in fostering stability within the Chinese polity since the 1920s.[114] Chiang Kai-shek and the Nationalist Party took matters further by working with allies in Congress and the media to lobby for more extensive and direct support from the U.S. government during the

---

[107] Christensen, 1996, 32–58; Cohen, 2000, 136–76; Gaddis, 2005a, 30–32, 2005b, 18–123; Hawes, 1977, 13–26, 131–33; Ikenberry, 2001, 163–214; Iriye, 1967, 238–49; Jespersen, 1996, 128–31, 63; Kennan, 1993, 17–31; Taliaferro, 2004, 133–40; Tucker, 1983, 19–39, 1994, 22–24.

[108] Schaller, 1979, 119–20; Snyder, 1991, 264–89.

[109] Gaddis, 2005a, 48–68.

[110] Christensen, 1996, 58–133; Gaddis, 2005b, 18–124; Iriye, 1967, 251–84; Kupchan, 1994, 433–82; United States, Dept. of State, and United States, Dept. of State, Bureau of Public Affairs, 1966, No. 31–37 (1949–50).

[111] Gaddis, 2005a, 25–30; Tucker, 1983, 173–94.

[112] Christensen, 1996, 133–93; Gaddis, 2005a, 40–46; Iriye, 1967, 281–300; Kupchan, 1991, 422–23, 458n, 463, 474; Schaller, 1979, 123–44; Snyder, 1991, 289–96; Taliaferro, 2004, 164–72; Tucker, 1983, 195–207; Walt, 1996, 319–23.

[113] Hawes, 1977, 113; Kupchan, 1991, 442, 47n, 72–81; Schaller, 1979, 123–44; Snyder, 1991, 263–64, 289–96; Tucker, 1994, 28–38.

[114] Iriye, 1967, 160; Sun, 1993, 136–43; Tucker, 2001, 38–40, 62–74, 91.

The Evolution of Foreign Involvement in China, 1923–1952

1930s and 1940s.[115] On the other side of the issue, isolationists like Senator Robert Taft, and their associates in Congress worked consistently to encourage greater American disengagement from the world, including from China.[116] Opportunity cost considerations, however, kept U.S. administrations in this period largely unmoved by these calls.

Given their opportunity cost considerations, U.S. leaders from the interwar through postwar eras saw support for a Chinese central government that could maintain a minimum level of stability across the polity as the optimal approach. This was the case so long as the central government did not align too closely with Moscow. Elites in Washington believed that with sufficient political centralisation and external autonomy, such administrations could permit nondiscrimination against American access within China. Anything more was viewed as a waste of capabilities that could go toward economic recovery or securing Western Europe and its large industrial base from first Nazi Germany and then Soviet Russia. This was in keeping with the high opportunity costs American leaders associated with intervention in the Chinese polity at the time.

Inattention and Open Access

Between the conclusion of the Washington Conference until Japan's invasion and the eve of World War II in Europe, American political elites treated China with detachment. So long as there was no discrimination against American access in China, the Harding, Coolidge, and even FDR administrations were happy to maintain a hands-off approach. China policy was to rest on coordination with other foreign powers as well as diplomatic and largely indirect financial assistance for China's central governments, regardless of whether it was in Beijing, Nanjing, or Chongqing.[117]

In this vein, the U.S. government readily backed the remitting of surplus revenues from the Maritime Customs and other foreign-run Chinese official agencies to whomever controlled China's central government, a system reaffirmed by the Washington Treaties.[118] At the 1926 Tariff Conference, Washington even supported the promise of tariff autonomy for China and an upward revision of tariff rates to the Fengtian Clique-led government in Beijing.[119] Not only did such

---

[115] Christensen, 1996, 39–40, 69–76; Cohen, 2000, 115–25, 160–72; Hu, 2001d; Iriye, 1967, 156–67, 211–16, 232–38; Jespersen, 1996, 24–107, 126–71; Tucker, 1983, 12–22, 1994, 80–172.

[116] Hawes, 1977, 17–23; Shao, 1995, 321–42; Snyder, 1991, 263–89.

[117] Barnhart, 1987, 115–35; Borg, 1964, 1–45, 92–99, 176–95; Chen, 2003, 360–69; Cohen, 2000, 82–134; Kennedy, 1987, 302; Zhang, 2004, 417–35, 473–88.

[118] Iriye, 1967, 148–65, 195–98, 216–22.

[119] Cohen, 2000, 93–101; SHAC 1032/650, "1926 nian Beiyang zhengfu jiang guanshui gaiwei zili ji youci er yinqi Zhongguo Beiyang junfa zhengfu ruhe liyong guanshui shouru changhuan geguo zhaiwu wenti waiguo zhengfu dui zhe wenti de yijian", 1926; SHAC 18/3466, *Treaty Regulating Tariff Relations between the Republic of China and the United States of America*, December 20, 1928; AH 0645.20/2760.01–02, "Zhujie shouhui".

132   *External Intervention and the Politics of State Formation*

revenues promise added income, but they also could provide collateral with which central governments in China could secure addition foreign loans.

Likewise, when Nationalist forces established a new National Government in Nanjing in 1928, Washington was quick to switch diplomatic recognition and support from the previous Fengtian-backed central government in Beijing. To the chagrin of some U.S. citizens and businesses in China, leaders in Washington readily entered negotiations with the National Government over the reduction of American extraterritorial rights whilst downplaying differences over the 1927 Nanjing Incident.[120] This last series of moves had the added effect of shoring up popular support for the Nationalist-led central government. These concessions were, of course, to guard against exclusion by winning over those that ostensibly controlled most of China and its external affairs.

Even Japan's invasion of Manchuria in 1931 and subsequent attack on Shanghai the following year did not fundamentally alter the hands-off American approach toward access in China. The primary aim for U.S. leaders remained the avoidance of exclusion from China even if the situation demanded a modification of tactics.[121] Washington now added accommodation of Japan to the provision of limited support to the central government in Nanjing.[122] United States leaders believed that such an approach could encourage both the Japanese and the National Government to refrain from discriminating against U.S. interests in China without a significant commitment of capabilities.[123] This could free the U.S. government to address the problems associated with the Great Depression.

To be sure, many policymakers in Washington joined the chorus condemning Japan's actions both on moral grounds and as a violation of treaty obligations made at the Paris and Washington conferences.[124] Secretary of State Henry Stimson even announced U.S. nonrecognition of the territorial gains Japan made through force in China, whilst the U.S. Navy began to redeploy forces to the American West Coast.[125] At the end of 1935, FDR and Treasury Secretary

---

[120] Chen, 2005, 91–97, 163–70.

[121] Accommodating Japan was not new for the U.S. government. Tokyo's opposition led Washington to scuttle plans for a loan to the central government in Beijing in 1926. What was new in the 1930s was the growing scale and intensity of Japanese aggression in China, and American leaders' decision to ignore these developments. Barnhart, 1987, 115–35; Borg, 1964, 1–45, 92–137, 171–95, 318–441, 504–44; Cohen, 2000, 105–34; Ienaga, 1978, 66–79, 132–33; Schaller, 1979, 40–42; Tucker, 1994, 10.

[122] Following the Japanese government's announcement of the Amau Declaration, a proposed U.S. Government Cotton and Wheat Loan to the National Government underwent a downward revision from US$50 million to US$20 million. Washington also pulled Export-Import Bank representation on a delegation to China put together by the private National Foreign Trade Council for fear of violating the Amau Doctrine. Coble, 1991, 153–62; Shen, 2005, 453–54; Taliaferro, 2004, 102.

[123] Iriye, 1967, 164–98, 216–22.

[124] Chen, 2003, 363–66.

[125] During this time, the U.S. government acquiesced to the formation of private relief organisations dedicated to providing aid to China. These entities consolidated into the United China Relief (UCR) in late 1940. Barnhart, 1987, 116–25, 235; Jespersen, 1996, 45–58.

The Evolution of Foreign Involvement in China, 1923–1952

Henry Morgenthau further agreed to purchase silver from China at a fixed price, helping to provide some respite from the woes that the 1934 U.S. Silver Purchase Act caused for the Chinese economy and the National Government's ability to resist the Japanese.[126] Otherwise, the U.S. government essentially accepted the Japanese *fait accompli*, giving Tokyo a free hand across China.[127]

As the importance of preventing exclusive Japanese access over China grew with the unfolding of World War II in Europe, the Roosevelt administration began to raise support for China's central government. This began in 1939 with the extension of a US$25 million purchase credit to the National Government followed by US$20 million in 1940 and another US$42.5 million in 1941.[128] Washington secured these credits on Chinese tung oil, tin, wolframite, and metals, whilst restricting their use to the appropriation of American manufactured and agricultural products.[129] The Roosevelt administration granted an additional US$95 million in credits in 1941, as well as eligibility for lend-lease, the supply of war material, deployment of military advisors, and a US$500 million loan in 1942.[130]

In 1941, President Roosevelt approved the use of American pilots and aircraft to fly supplies to Chongqing from Burma and India, as well as to assist with air defence on a nonofficial basis. These "volunteer units" – the "Flying Tigers" – would later become a component of official American wartime aid to China. Symbolically, the U.S. government abrogated treaties guaranteeing American extraterritorial rights, relaxed rules on Chinese immigration, maintained diplomatic recognition of Chongqing, and proclaimed China to be one of the "Big Four" postwar powers.[131]

---

[126] Large silver purchases under the Act caused substantial fluctuations in China's silver-based currency, leading to credit contraction and a severe recession that made resisting Japanese incursions all the more difficult. By agreeing to purchase silver from China at a relatively high fixed price, the U.S. government helped stabilise the Chinese currency without offending the Silver Lobby. The Treasury Department restricted the use of revenues from the sale of silver to paying off American creditors or purchasing American goods. Barnhart, 1987, 41, 176–97; Chen, 2003, 369–71; Hu, 2001e; Young, 1971, 211–15, 78–82, 417–18.

[127] Roosevelt, however, decided not to invoke the Neutrality Act following the formal outbreak of Sino-Japanese hostilities in 1937, which would result in a U.S. arms embargo on both China and Japan. Given the underdevelopment of China's arms industry, such an embargo would hurt the National Government more than Japan. Chen, 2003, 363–66; Ienaga, 1978, 78–79; Tucker, 1994, 11.

[128] Chen, 1991, 17–33; Cui, 1995, 240–63; Kimball, 1969, 71, 130; Schaller, 1979, 48–67; Sun, 1993, 134–50; Tucker, 1994, 11–12.

[129] Eastman, 1991, 144–46; Hu, 2001a, 2001b, 2001g, 2001l.

[130] Chen, 1991, 17–58; Eastman, 1991, 114–48; Han, 2003, 100–39.

[131] Chen, 1991, 66–104; Cohen, 2000, 124–47; Gaddis, 2005b, 10–11; Hu, 2001a, 2001h; Iriye, 1967, 251–58; Schaller, 1979, 69–74; Sun, 1993, 150–55; Tsou, 1963, Vol. 1, 33–124; Tucker, 1994, 16; Walt, 1996, 312–14; SHAC 18/155, "Luosifu Zongtong ji Yihui gongshang zhanhou jihua", April 13, 1942; SHAC 18/155, "Guoji zhuzhi yu zhanhou heping xianzai ying taolun de wenti", July 1, 1943; SHAC 18/156, "Kuada de guoji zhuyi yu guli zhuyi yiyang weixian", October 30, 1948; SHAC 18/2987, "Zhongguo daibiaotuan canjia guoji heping jigou huiyi

134   *External Intervention and the Politics of State Formation*

All told, Washington provided approximately US$1.5 billion worth of financial and material assistance to China during World War II, the bulk of which went to the National Government.[132] Conversely, the United States committed US$31 billion in Lend-Lease aid to the British and Commonwealth governments, whilst deploying forces to take part in the active defence of the British Isles and Australia.[133] This suggests that despite its growing importance, China remained subsidiary to America's other concerns. Even the implementation of long-standing plans to use the Chinese coast as a base from which to attack the Japanese Home Islands was to occur only after victory in Europe.

Limited American support for the central government in China is consistent with prevalent perceptions in Washington about the high opportunity costs of intervention in China, given overwhelming strategic concerns in Europe. Warren Cohen observes that even after Pearl Harbour, America's wartime leaders took the position that:

In the defence of the interests of the United States, it was important to give the Chinese [central government] enough aid to keep them fighting, but it was not necessary to give them enough to win. And if they would not fight, Asian affairs could await the settlement of vital issues across the Atlantic. The fight to liberate China was merely a sideshow in the war against the Axis, not an important American priority.[134]

Leaders and policymakers in Washington deemed denying Japan exclusive access over China to be a sufficient wartime goal.

From the final days of World War II until the conclusion of the peace process at San Francisco in 1952, Washington also remained careful to restrict its involvement in China to what was sufficient to prevent discrimination against American access. The deal that Roosevelt struck with Stalin at Yalta secured Soviet assistance in fighting Japan and recognition of the right of a U.S.-assisted National Government to establish centralised control over most of China.[135] This permitted Washington to ensure equality of access over most of the Chinese

---

(Dunbadun huiyi) daibiaotuan baogao", 1944; SHAC 18/2985, "Zhanhou guoji heping jigou ji qita wenti"; SHAC 18/2986, "Guanyu zhanhou shijie heping zhuzhi de gexiang fangan", 1943; SHAC 18/3268, Wei Daoming, Ambassador to the United States, "Zhong-Mei guanyu quxiao zai Hua zhiwai faquan ji chuli youguan wenti tiaoyue", December 1943; SHAC 18/3269, "Waijiao Baipishu 69 zhi 88 hao"; SHAC 18/3429, "Baipishu di 54 zhi 105"; AH 0641.90/5044.01–02, "Zhong-Ying Zhong-Mei tiaoyue ji laiwang zhaohui"; AH 0641.90/5044.01–01, "Zhong-Ying Zhong-Mei fenbie qianding tiaoyue feichu jiuyue"; AH 0641.90/2760.01–01, "Geguo zai Hua zhiwai faquan tiaoyue quxiao".

[132] This includes approximately US$600 million in military aid. Hawes, 1977, 16; Pepper, 1991, 303–05; Sun, 1993, 133–36, 148–50.

[133] Iriye, 1967, 216–22; Kimball, 1969.

[134] Cohen, 2000, 133. Also see Han, 2003, 100–39, 172–207, 132–79; Iriye, 1967, 216–22.

[135] Cohen, 2000, 133, 143–50, 174–75; Iriye, 1967, 243–79; Kuo, 1967; Schaller, 1979, 103–06; Shao, 1995, 142–67; Spector, 2007, 35–36; Tsou, 1963, 237–87; Tucker, 1994, 16–18; SHAC 18/1884, "Wang Shijie rennei yi nian lai zui zhongyao guoji huiyi de baogao", September 1945–September 1946: 4–5.

The Evolution of Foreign Involvement in China, 1923–1952

polity through the National Government without having to sacrifice the capabilities intended for rebuilding Western Europe.[136]

In this regard, Washington kept assistance to the National Government during the late 1940s to a minimum. Insisting that Japanese forces surrender to the Nationalists whilst transferring captured and surplus war material to Nationalist forces gave the National Government territory, equipment, and supplies with little American direct involvement.[137] The U.S. government also provided logistic support and assistance totalling about US$645 million to the National Government from 1945 to 1949.[138]

Aid to the Chinese Nationalist central government was a fraction of the US $17 billion in Marshall Aid for Europe and the US$50 billion in U.S. defence spending for the same period.[139] Additionally, the Truman administration provided US$4.34 billion in postwar loans to Britain, as well as more than US$1.3 billion in military assistance to NATO.[140] In fact, the Truman administration advanced assistance to China's National Government largely to logroll the Isolationists and the Nationalists' "China Lobby" allies in Congress into supporting the massive release of funds for the Marshall Plan and defence build-up.[141]

Moreover, Washington tried to convince the Nationalists to enter into a coalition with the Communists even as it offered support to the National Government, as evidenced by the 1945–1947 Marshall Mission. United States leaders believed that the ensuing peace in China could allow a greater focus of their energies in Europe.[142] The U.S. government was also quick to withdraw

---

[136] Christensen, 1996, 66, 66n–67n; Hawes, 1977, 13–26, 81–133; Kupchan, 1994, 418–76; Tucker, 1994, 21–24.

[137] The United States even encouraged the absorption of surrendered Japanese and collaborationist units by the Nationalist army to bolster their ability to independently fend for themselves. Cohen, 2000, 156–66; Gillin, 1967, 285–88; Iriye, 1967, 251–74; Jespersen, 1996, 132; Schaller, 1979, 106–12; Snyder, 1991, 263–89; SHAC 18/2960, "Junzhengbu jieshou Meifang yijiao wuzi baogao", May 29, 1946; AH 0643/3450.01–01, "Yuandong shoufu diyu xingzheng guanli xieding fangan", June 26, 1944–March 26, 1945.

[138] This figure includes the US$400 million appropriated through the 1948 China Aid Act. In comparison, the regions covered by the Marshall Plan had a combined territory and total population of roughly half of China, and were not in the midst of a civil war. Yet, China only received roughly one-thirteenth of the aid that went to Europe. In the spring of 1947, the Truman administration requested US$400 million in aid just to put down Communist insurgencies in Greece and Turkey. Christensen, 1996, 58–76, 95; Cleveland, 1949; Gaddis, 2005b, 40; Hawes, 1977, 3–26, 35–133; Jespersen, 1996, 132, 54–60; Kupchan, 1991, 442, 456, 463; Shao, 1995, 327–28; United States Dept. of State, 1948, The Far East: China, Vol. VIII; SHAC 18/2960, "Junzhengbu jieshou Meifang yijiao wuzi baogao"; SHAC 18/3541, "Meiguo yuanwai fa'an, Zhong-Mei zhuyao maoyi shangpin tongji", 1947–1948.

[139] Christensen, 1996, 58–76, 95; Cohen, 2000, 150–76; Gaddis, 2005b, 40.

[140] Christensen, 1996, 80–96; Hawes, 1977, 131–33.

[141] Christensen, 1996, 58–96; Kupchan, 1991, 478–82.

[142] Schaller, 1979, 112–21; Shao, 1995, 215–310; Spector, 2007, 67–72; Tsou, 1963, 288–440; Tucker, 2001, 19–39, 57–79, 173–207; Tucker, 1994, 23, 34; Westad, 2003, 35–66, 159–68.

136 *External Intervention and the Politics of State Formation*

American troops from China as the Chinese Civil War reignited.[143] Washington was even ready to abandon the Nationalists following their withdrawal to Taiwan in 1949.[144] Future access in China, after all, appeared possible through cooperation with the new Communist-led central government.[145]

With the eruption of the Korean War, U.S. leaders began to see intervention on the mainland as prohibitively costly given the potential for uncontrolled escalation, and the possibility that Korea was a diversion for a Soviet attempt to seize Europe.[146] Accordingly, Washington was willing to concede access over the mainland. This meant a fall in the opportunity cost of intervening in Taiwan to regulate access. American-backed Nationalist control of the island could provide a strongpoint from which to limit the Communist threat in Asia.[147] Strong American influence over Taiwan had the added benefit of preventing a Nationalist attack on the mainland that could raise tensions unnecessarily. For a defence commitment as well as economic and military aid, then, the Nationalists had to support America's containment strategy and forgo returning to the mainland.[148]

THE SOVIET UNION AND ITS ROLE IN CHINA

For Bolshevik leaders from Lenin to Stalin, Bukharin, and Trotsky, the Soviet Union's security, survival, and future development hinged on its relationship with capitalist societies and bourgeois governments. They believed that capitalist powers would become increasingly hostile as they weakened under the contradictions and war endemic to the capitalist system even as socialism strengthened the Soviet Union.[149] These leaders also expected contradictions amongst capitalist powers to inevitably spur war and revolution, offering the Soviet Union opportunities to forward socialism. Since most major capitalist powers were in Europe and North America, these areas were the focus of Soviet hopes and anxieties. Next to the anticipated returns for investing capabilities in Europe

---

[143] Hawes, 1977, 29–34; Schaller, 1979, 114–21; Shao, 1995, 332–42; Spector, 2007, 67–69; Tsou, 1963, 441–86; Tucker, 1983, 57–79, 173–94.

[144] Christensen, 1996, 105–15; Cohen, 2000, 162–69; Gaddis, 2005b, 45, 101–16; Hawes, 1977, 81–133; Iriye, 1967, 264–85; Jespersen, 1996, 175–78; Kupchan, 1994, 442, 447, 447n, 471–83; Shao, 1995, 332–42; Tsou, 1963, 486–591; Tucker, 1994, 34, 61–92, 2001, 28–32; Walt, 1996, 313–14.

[145] Christensen, 1996, 77–79, 106–37; Gaddis, 2005b, 40–45, 67–68, 83, 100, 140–43; Tucker, 1983, 31–67, 1994, 24–38, 2001, 17, 57–79.

[146] Cohen, 2000, 172; Hawes, 1977, 131–33; Iriye, 1967, 285–300; Kupchan, 1991, 61–85, 422–23; Tucker, 1994, 83–89, 2001, 32–38; Walt, 1996, 319–23.

[147] Schaller, 1979, 132–44; Snyder, 1991, 289–96; Walt, 1996, 316–17.

[148] Christensen, 1996, 115–37; Cohen, 2000, 169–72; Gaddis, 2005b, 112; Iriye, 1967, 285–300; Kupchan, 1994, 461–63, 482–85; Schaller, 1979, 132–44; Snyder, 1991, 289–98; Tsou, 1963, 558–64; Tucker, 1983, 90–91, 1993, 32–38, 2001, 195–207; Zhou, 1997, 292–99.

[149] Kennedy, 1987, 320–24; Kennedy-Pipe, 1998, 18–26; Walt, 1996, 164–75, 199–209; Wohlforth, 1993, 45–46.

The Evolution of Foreign Involvement in China, 1923–1952

between 1923 and 1952, leaders in Moscow expected the opportunity cost of intervening in China to range between moderate and high.

Europe, more so than North America, stood at the centre of Soviet concerns. Even before the October Revolution in 1917, Lenin and other Bolshevik leaders saw Europe – particularly Germany – as hotbeds for proletarian revolution. The attention on Europe was not surprising, given the recent Russian experience of war with Germany, as well as the large French and British role in supporting White Russian forces in the Russian Civil War.[150] As good Marxists, the early Bolsheviks also believed that members of the large working class in industrial European economies would be natural allies against the bourgeois capitalists that held them in subjection.[151] Such views brought the ill-fated Soviet attempt to attack Poland and instigate revolution in 1919, as well as support for the abortive 1921 German Communist Uprising.[152]

Despite a brief respite in the early 1920s, Bolshevik concerns about the European powers soon returned. Entente with the West peaked in 1925 under the influence of Stalin and Bukharin's claims about the "stabilisation" of capitalism, and the need to first build "socialism in one country" as they tried to secure leadership of the Communist Party after Lenin's death in 1923.[153] By 1924, factional infighting within the Soviet Communist Party, as well as the spectre of a resurgent Germany with the 1923 Dawes Plan and the 1925 Locarno Treaty, led to a resurgent belief in imminent attack from capitalist European governments.

This "war scare" presented Stalin with the opportunity to consolidate control over the Soviet leadership, in part by emphasising the need to quickly strengthen the Soviet Union economically and militarily. As such, Stalin purged Bukharin and other backers of the moderate New Economic Policy even as he perpetuated a belief in the need to cow hostile European capitalists through Soviet might. This created a demand for an advantageous "correlation of forces" vis-à-vis capitalist European powers, and later the United States.[154]

Moscow's concern with the "correlation of forces" in Europe continued to inform Soviet strategic thinking into World War II and the Cold War. Even though Stalin and other Soviet leaders expected intracapitalist war to weaken the capitalist powers and pave the way for an eventual Communist victory, they believed that this rested on the ability to deter capitalist aggression for the time being.[155] This depended, in turn, on continued popular mobilisation and the relative Soviet industrial and military strength, especially given the rise of fascism in Europe in the 1930s and 1940s. Soviet leaders even believed that

---

[150] Kennedy-Pipe, 1998, 18–26; Walt, 1996, 133–58.

[151] Kennedy, 1987, 324–27; Kindermann, 1959, 59–72; Uldricks, 1979, 60–63; Walt, 1996, 130–33, 166–88.

[152] Uldricks, 1979, 147–60; Wohlforth, 1993, 36–46.

[153] Entente was evident in the conclusion of the 1919 Anglo-Soviet Trade Agreement, the 1922 Rapallo Treaty with Germany, and the Soviet Union's entry into the League of Nations in 1934. Haigh, Peters, and Morris, 1999, 131–76; Kennedy-Pipe, 1998, 28–32; Uldricks, 1979, 69–95.

[154] Kennedy-Pipe, 1998, 37–42; Wohlforth, 1993, 36–58, 113–15.

[155] Chen, 2003, 336–38; Garver, 1988, 90–128, 182–230, 251–59; Uldricks, 1979, 161–62.

138   *External Intervention and the Politics of State Formation*

the conclusion of the Molotov-Ribbentrop Pact lay with Hitler's appreciation for Soviet might, as demonstrated by strong Soviet economic performance during the Depression.[156]

The Great Patriotic War and its aftermath kept the attentions of leaders in Moscow on denying capitalist access to East and Central Europe.[157] In particular, the German invasion of 1941 suggested that the Soviet Union's existence depended on the ability to resist this specific threat.[158] As such, the demonstration of Soviet military might along the borders of Manchuria between 1938 and 1939 and the 1941 Neutrality Pact with Japan allayed immediate fears of attack and encirclement from the Far East.[159] After the war, the industrial base and resources of Soviet-occupied Europe seemed key to postwar rebuilding.[160] Restricting capitalist access to East and Central Europe could also create a key buffer against the first blows of Western aggression, and avert the devastation of the earlier Nazi advance.

Soviet policymakers from the early 1920s to the early 1950s largely took areas in Central and East Asia as useful, secondary buffer zones. From 1921 and especially after Stalin's ascendancy in 1924, Soviet leaders tried to limit access by the other major powers to areas adjacent the USSR's Central and Northeast Asian boundaries.[161] These regions were, after all, where the British and Japanese governments – supporters of the Bolsheviks' White Russian opponents and perpetrators of intervention during the Civil War – were influential.[162] Denying London and Tokyo free access to neighbouring territories was a way for Soviet leaders to stall potential capitalist aggression in those regions, enabling Moscow to concentrate on more pressing issues.[163]

In comparison, there did not seem to be a clear Soviet approach toward access in China until the 1920s. Previously, the distractions of the civil war, foreign intervention, the Polish campaign, and power struggles within the Soviet Communist Party prevented the formulation of a coherent China policy.[164] Bolshevik leaders only seemed ready to revisit the issue of access in China by 1921, which saw the conceptualisation of northern China as an extension of existing buffers against capitalist-imperialist hostility.[165] Soviet leaders did not see China as central to revolution or the development of socialism.

---

[156] Kennedy-Pipe, 1998, 36–54; Wohlforth, 1993, 46–54.
[157] Gaddis, 2005a, 10–14, 32–34, 99–106; Kennedy-Pipe, 1998, 63–102; Novikov, 1993, 5; Walt, 1996, 129–209.
[158] Kennedy-Pipe, 1998, 57–63.
[159] Hu, 2001g; Ienaga, 1978, 66–67, 81–82.
[160] Bunce, 1985; Kennedy-Pipe, 1998, 58–102; Wohlforth, 1993, 59–87.
[161] Kindermann, 1959, 73–77; Mizuno and Zheng, 1998, 241–79; Walt, 1996, 179–85; Wang, 2003, 432–57.
[162] Haigh, Peters, and Morris, 1999, 41–126.
[163] Mizuno and Zheng, 1998, 241–79.
[164] Kennedy-Pipe, 1998, 31; Uldricks, 1979, 47–95; Whiting, 1954, 24–71.
[165] Walt, 1996, 197–99; Whiting, 1954, 72–154.

The Evolution of Foreign Involvement in China, 1923–1952   139

Bolshevik leaders from the interwar years on wished to avoid having capitalist-imperialist powers completely denying Soviet access to the rest of China. Given China's domestic instability and susceptibility to foreign influence, Moscow policymakers saw the establishment of exclusive foreign access over the polity, or at least part of it, as portending aggression against the Soviet Union.[166] This fear stemmed from the launching of British, French, American, and Japanese incursions into Siberia from China in the early 1920s.[167]

Moscow's Differentiated Approach to Access Denial

Given their concerns, Soviet leaders adopted a multipronged approach to contend for access in China. The first element of this strategy was to prevent any other external power from gaining exclusive access over China south of the Great Wall. A central government possessing sufficient control over most of the polity as well as independence in external affairs could disrupt, distract, or otherwise drain potential aggressors before they significantly endangered the Soviet Union.[168] So long as nonprivileged access opportunities existed, Soviet leaders believed that they could prompt central governments in China to abet Moscow's objectives through offers of material, diplomatic, or political support. By limiting involvement in China to the direct regulation of access in border regions and securing nonprivileged access in the rest of China, Moscow could commit capabilities to Europe where expected returns were higher.[169]

The second component was protecting the USSR's southern approaches by regulating access over regions along the Sino-Soviet border.[170] Policymakers in Moscow believed that this was achievable through cooperation with indigenous regimes and political authorities on the ground, saving them the trouble of day-to-day administration. Along these lines, Moscow even tried to obtain formal major power recognition of its position in areas of China bordering the Soviet Union. Finally, to hedge against the rise of either a strong central government that might seek to eject Soviet influence or one subservient to a foreign rival, Moscow cultivated local actors that it could potentially employ to destabilise an unfriendly Chinese government from the inside.

Turmoil from the Russian Revolution and civil war initially prompted the Bolshevik government to reduce involvement in China, leading to the relinquishment of Tsarist extraterritorial rights and privileges in Outer Mongolia and northern Manchuria.[171] However, Stalin's ascendancy and consolidation of power reinvigorated Soviet involvement in a way that reflected a differentiation

---

[166] Chen, 2003, 336–60; Novikov, 1993, 7–10.
[167] Borisov, 1977, 57–74; Wohlforth, 1993, 36–46.
[168] Garver, 1988, 192–96; Sun, 1993, 112–30; Whiting, 1954, 10–58.
[169] Gaddis, 2005a, 10–14, 32–34, 99–106; Garver, 1988, 99–103, 24; Ienaga, 1978, 66–67, 82–83; Kennedy-Pipe, 1998, 63–78.
[170] Holubnychy, 1979, 126–35; Iriye, 252–53; Novikov, 1993, 9–16; Westad, 2003, 310–20.
[171] Sheridan, 1975, 243; Whiting, 1951, 31–33, 269–75; Zhou, 1997, 24–62.

External Intervention and the Politics of State Formation

in the perceived opportunity costs of intervention across China. This saw Moscow engage in simultaneous efforts to regulate access in areas along the Soviet border whilst preventing major power rivals from acquiring exclusive access over the rest of China going into the early 1950s.

As Japanese military pressure grew alongside the fascist threat in Europe during the 1930s, Stalin extended support to the Nationalist-led government in order to tie down Japanese forces and forestall an outright Japanese victory. Stalin and others believed, for a time, that Japanese success in excluding Soviet access over China could leave the Soviet Union trapped between hostile capitalist-imperialist forces in Europe and the Far East.[172] This made Moscow quick to reestablish diplomatic relations with the Nationalist-led central government in Nanjing by 1932.[173] Ties between the Soviets and Nationalists initially broke down after Chiang Kai-shek's Communist purge in 1927. Following the resumption of relations, the Soviet Union began to equip the Nationalists with money, arms, supplies, and advice that eventually totalled as much as US$556.4 million.[174]

Soviet leaders too were critical in pushing for cooperation between the Communists and Nationalists against Japan over the reservations of Mao Zedong, Chiang Kai-shek, and their followers.[175] Soviet leaders urged Mao and the CCP leadership to seek a Second United Front in 1935, whilst offering aid to the Nationalists to make cooperation with the Communists more palatable after the 1936 Xi'an Incident.[176] In bringing the two together, Moscow aimed to prevent exclusion by bolstering resistance to Japan, consolidating the position of its Chinese Communist allies, and forcing the Nationalists to accept an active Soviet presence. Further, the Second United Front limited Soviet commitment to China, while averting direct confrontation with Japan until Germany's defeat.[177]

Soviet efforts to shore up central government rule to ensure nonprivileged access persisted even after the Chinese Communist victory on the mainland in 1949. Moscow was well aware of the animosity CCP leaders felt towards the

---

[172] Chen, 2003, 354–60; Garver, 1988, 16–52; Ienaga, 1978, 82–83; Wei, 1956, 64–85; Wu, 1950, 213–21, 280–81; Yang, 1997, 312–90.

[173] Barnhart, 1995, 115; Wei, 1956, 111–19; AH 0641.10/5044.01–01/247/1–19, "Zhong Su qianding hubuqinfan tiaoyue zhi zhuyao yuanze" [Primary principles for the signing of a Sino-Soviet non-aggression treaty], April 6, 1933; SHAC 34/624, "1932 nian Zhong Su huifu bangjiao shiliao" [Historical Documents on the 1932 Restoration of Sino-Soviet Diplomatic Recognition], 21 December 1932.

[174] There is some dispute over the amount of Soviet wartime aid to China. The traditional figure is US $250 million. Newer work cites evidence indicating a total between US$306.4 million and US $556.4 million. Cui, 238n1, 38–47, 62–65; Eastman, 144; Garver, 37–48, 104–08, 145–46; Li, 1988, 217; Sun, 1993, 112–30; Wang, 1957, Vol. 3, 1115; Wei, 1956, 129–48; Wu, 1950, 263–71; Young, 1963, 18–26, 54, 125–30; SHAC 18/3222, "Zhong-Su tongshang tiaoyue", 1939; SHAC 18/3283, "Waijiaobu gezhong tiaoyue", 1920–1939; AH 0641.10/5044.01–01/247/1–19, "Zhong Su qianding hubuqingfan tiaoyue zhi zhuyao yuanzhe".

[175] Cohen, 2000, 118, 39–43.

[176] Yang, 1997, 312–90.

[177] Garver, 1988, 80–83, 112–17, 123–48.

The Evolution of Foreign Involvement in China, 1923–1952

other major powers, which together with their fraternal socialist allegiances, seemed to guarantee at least nonprivileged access opportunities for the Soviet Union. To lock in its recently acquired gains, Moscow poured military and technical assistance as well as more than US$400 million in aid to shore up the Communist-led central government in Beijing after 1949.[178] Soviet leaders were also the first to recognise Beijing diplomatically, and even boycotted the United Nations for not admitting the new People's Republic of China government.[179] Nonetheless, Moscow discouraged Beijing from simultaneously trying to take Taiwan during the Korean War, fearing that this could escalate tensions and bring direct conflict with Washington.[180]

As it focused on nonprivileged access elsewhere in China, Moscow aimed to regulate access over Outer Mongolia, Tuva, Manchuria, and, to an extent, Xinjiang. Soviet leaders combined military involvement with political efforts in order to force both other outside powers and China's central government into accepting Soviet dominance in these areas. Choibalsan's Provisional People's Government only managed to seize control over Outer Mongolia in 1921 and establish the Mongolian People's Republic in 1924 with the assistance of Soviet troops.[181] Control over Tuva was likewise established and maintained through the force of Soviet arms. Repelling Japanese and Manchukuo incursions into Outer Mongolia in 1938 were Soviet and Mongolian troops led by Gregorii Zhukov.[182] Moscow's ability to regulate access over parts of Manchuria traversed by the China Eastern and South Manchurian Railways from 1925 to 1935 and from 1945 to 1952 rested in part on a strong Soviet military presence.[183] This was also the case with Liaodong after World War II.

Moscow further pressed China's central leadership between 1923 and 1952 to accept a separate, Soviet-dominated Outer Mongolia, as well as its administration of areas of Manchuria traversed by the China Eastern Railway.[184] This is evident in the 1924 Sino-Soviet Treaty, the 1945 Sino-Soviet Treaty of Friendship and Alliance, and the 1950 Sino-Soviet Treaty of Friendship, Alliance, and Mutual Assistance.[185] These agreements formalised the Soviet Union's direct regulation of

---

[178] Iriye, 1967, 339; Tucker, 2001, 44–45; Westad, 2003, 310–20.

[179] Christensen, 1996, 147–49.

[180] Kim, 1994, 68–78; Yang, 1997, 609–60.

[181] China, Wai chiao pu and League of Nations, Commission of Inquiry, 1932, 301–299; Elleman, 1997, 85–191; Wang, 2003, 419–26; Wei, 1956, 119–24; Wu, 1950, 158–72, 222–33, 272–78.

[182] Borisov, 1977, 57–74; Fei, Li, and Zhang, 1993, 269–71; Kennedy-Pipe, 1998, 53.

[183] China, Wai chiao pu and League of Nations, Commission of Inquiry, 1932, 326–28; Cohen, 2000, 147–49; Garver, 1998, 262; Walt, 1996, 183–84; Wang, 2003, 237–418; Wei, 1956, 178–85, 266–369; Wu, 1950, 151–57, 73–212, 234–47, 286–308, 329–46; AH 0632.97/5011.02–01, "Dongbei jieshou yu dui Su tielu jiaoshe", October 13, 1945; AH 0641.10/5044.01–01, "Zhong Su qianding hubuqinfan tiaoyue zhi zhuyao yuanze".

[184] Yang 2005, 304–26, Zuo 2005, 140–56; AH 0632.97/5011.02–01, "Dongbei jieshou yu dui Su tielu jiaoshe", October 13, 1945; AH 0641.10/5044.01–01, "Zhong Su qianding hubuqinfan tiaoyue zhi zhuyao yuanze".

[185] Garver, 1988, 182–230; Whiting, 1954, 31–33, 208–35, 269–82; Zhou, 1997, 24–41, 117–34; AH 0641.10/5044.01–01, "Zhong-Su youhao tongmeng tiaoyue ji youguan xieding"; AH

access in Outer Mongolia and parts of Manchuria.[186] Worth noting is the fact that Soviet attempts to secure access privileges came after Moscow's official renunciation of extraterritorial rights in China in the 1919 and 1920 Karakhan Manifestos as well as the Sino-Soviet Treaty of 1924.[187]

To establish access regulation over Manchuria after World War II, Moscow encouraged the Chinese Communists to move into and entrench themselves in the region following its occupation by the Soviets in August 1945.[188] This took place even as Stalin publicly promised to return the area to the National Government and cease support for the CCP in the 1945 Sino-Soviet Treaty.[189] Stalin directed Soviet forces to tacitly abet CCP consolidation of the countryside and secondary cities in Manchuria whilst stalling the handover of the territory into 1946.[190] Despite the tension this move precipitated among some Soviet and CCP military commanders, it effectively gave the Chinese Communists almost a year to establish a base with a secure rear area in Siberia, free from the threat of Nationalist encirclement.[191] By prolonging the Nationalists' military deployment around the Northeast, the Soviet Union increased strain on the Nationalists' already weak logistic chain, reducing the combat effectiveness of Nationalist forces.

In return for departing Manchuria militarily, Moscow obtained the withdrawal of the U.S. Marine divisions and other units stationed to support Nationalist efforts to reestablish order and communications in North China.[192] This put the Soviet Union in a position to regulate access over Manchuria virtually unhindered, even if the Nationalists controlled the rest of China. Additionally, the large amounts of captured Japanese arms the Soviet Army quietly channelled to CCP forces in Manchuria featured prominently in the Communists' early battlefield victories against the Nationalists. It is worth noting that Soviet leaders insisted on

---

0641.10/5044.01–01/247/1–19, "Zhong Su qianding hubuqinfan tiaoyue zhi zhuyao yuanze"; PRCFMA 109–000020–01(1), "Zhong-Su youhao tongmeng huzhu tiaoyue, Zhong Su guanyu Zhongguo Changchun tielu, Lushunkou ji Dalian de xieding, Zhong Su guanyu daikuan gei Zhongguo de xieding (Zhong E wenben), yidingshu", 14 February 1950.

[186] Wang, 2003, 265–431; PRCFMA 109–000020–01(1), "Zhong Su youhao tongmeng huzhu tiaoyue".

[187] Cohen, 2000, 90; Elleman, 1997, 23–50, 126–32, 80–81; Ke, 2005, 82–97; Sheridan, 1975, 243; Wei, 1956, 15–38; Wu, 1950, 134–57; Zhou, 1997, 24–62.

[188] Borisov, 1977, 75–252; Garver, 1988, 153–77, 256–57; Wang and He, 2005, 285–328, 380–419; Wei, 1956, 178–208; Wu, 1950, 286–308; Yang, 1997, 519–70.

[189] Atwood, 1999, 137–58; Elleman, 1999, 130–32; Garver, 1988, 214–28, 262–65; Shao, 1995, 150–67; Tucker, 1994, 21–22, 2001, 18; Wang, 2003, 111–215; AH 0641/5044, "Zhong-Su tiaoyue ji zhixing xingyue xuzhi yinzhi", September 3, 1945 – June 11, 1946; AH 0641.10/5044.01–01, "Zhong-Su youhao tongmeng tiaoyue ji youguan xieding", August 14, 1945; SHAC 18/2318, Chinese Embassy in Moscow to the Foreign Ministry, Message No.: 61932, "Guanyu fabiao Su jun chebing Dongbei de gaojian", 8 April 1946.

[190] Levine, 1987; Niu, 1998, 52–61; Shao, 1995, 242–52; Spector, 2007, 27–47, 65–71; Westad, 2003, 35–50, 83–86, 216–17; SHAC 18/2318, "Guanyu fabiao Sujun chebing Dongbei de gaojian"; SHAC 18/3049, "Di yi ci Mosike huiyi", October 19–30, 1945.

[191] Wang, 2003, 374–400; Wei, 1956, 191–205.

[192] Levine, 1987, 45–86; Spector, 2007, 49–70, 224–25.

The Evolution of Foreign Involvement in China, 1923–1952

secrecy when aiding the CCP to avoid confrontation with the United States.[193] Stalin even originally accepted a division of China between the Nationalists and Communists, first in Manchuria and then along the Yangzi, to avoid CCP over-extension and the provocation of direct U.S. military involvement.[194]

To further guarantee its ability to regulate access over Outer Mongolia and Manchuria, Moscow consistently worked to secure acceptance of this position by other major powers. The 1941 Soviet-Japanese Neutrality Pact traded Moscow's acceptance of a Japanese-sponsored Manchukuo in exchange for Tokyo's recognition of a Soviet-dominated Mongolian People's Republic.[195] Similarly, the 1945 Yalta Conference saw Stalin acquire U.S. and British acqui-escence over the resumption of the Tsarist-era privileges in Manchuria and the separation of Outer Mongolia under Soviet tutelage.[196] These concessions, along with acknowledgement of Russian preeminence in Eastern and Central Europe, secured Moscow's declaration of war against Japan and recognition of the Nationalists as China's sole legitimate government.[197]

Attempts to regulate access over areas of China bordering the USSR further saw Moscow provide support to Sheng Shicai, the dominant militarist in Xinjiang, from 1933 to 1942, as well as his predecessor, Qin Shuren.[198] As with other actors Moscow supported in China, Qin and Sheng's commitment to Communism was not entirely clear.[199] Nonetheless, Soviet leaders seemed will-ing enough to provide them with arms, advice, and money as they could help manage access over an area bordering Soviet Central Asia. Sponsorship of Sheng also gave Moscow another point of leverage against the National Government that did not demand much capability investment.[200] After Sheng's defection to the Nationalists in 1942, Moscow tried to continue regulating access in Xinjiang by supporting to Chinese Communists active in the area and cooperative local groups, including proponents of East Turkestan independence.[201] As Xinjiang's importance as a buffer area declined following World War II, so did Soviet interest in maintaining access regulation in the region.

Deserving of some elaboration is the final element of Moscow's efforts to safeguard access over China, namely, maintenance of a potential to disrupt

---

[193] Garver, 1993, 36–39; Wang, 2003, 374–400; Yang, 1997, 519–605.

[194] Niu, 1998, 65–67; Yang, 1997, 607–18.

[195] Garver, 1988, 95–99, 209–28; Wei, 1956, 150–54, 172–75; Wu, 1950, 272–99.

[196] Cohen, 2000, 143–49; Garver, 1988, 114–17, 182–87; Kuo, 1967; Spector, 2007, 35–36; Tucker, 1994, 16–18.

[197] Kennedy-Pipe, 1998, 69–77.

[198] Garver, 1988, 153–77; Li et al., 1997, 445–646; Wei, 1956, 124–29, 156–58; Whiting and Sheng, 1958, 21–97, 163–267; Wu, 1950, 248–62.

[199] Liu and Tian, 2004, 116–31; Sheridan, 1966, 165–69, 97–202; Wang, 2003, 432–38.

[200] Wang, 2003, 432–57; Yang, 1997, 339–90; KMTPA *Zhongzheng hui* 7/3.1, Tian Kunshan *et al*, "Waimeng jun qinru Xinjiang Xizang zhengbian ji woguo dui Yuenan taidu ge weiyuan yijian jilu"; KMTPA *Zhongzheng hui* 7/3.1, Central Political Committee, "Waimeng jun qinru Xinjiang wenti an banli qingxing", July 15, 1947; KMTPA *Zhongzheng hui* 7/3.6, Defence Ministry, "Waimeng jun qin Xin zhi jingguo", June 30, 1947.

[201] Wang, 2003, 438–57, 75–80; Whiting and Sheng, 1958, 98–146.

central government rule. Soviet leaders wished to hedge against a strong, independent, but unfriendly central government as well as one controlled by a rival foreign power, both of which might wish to eradicate Soviet influence from China. To enable the Soviet Union to avoid exclusion without committing too costly occupation and direct military intervention, Moscow cultivated local groups it could use to play off and distract a central government from focusing against Soviet access.[202] This would enable the Soviet Union to maintain its prerogatives over different parts of China.[203] So, even as Soviet diplomats extended diplomatic recognition and support to the Beijing central government under the Zhili and Fengtian cliques between 1920 and 1925, Moscow nurtured the Nationalist and Communist parties in southern China.[204]

The presence of Soviet-supported local rivals to Beijing gave Moscow both bargaining leverage and a means to destabilise the central government should it become too unaccommodating. It was partially in this light that Moscow offered monetary and technical assistance to the fledgling Chinese Communist Party. In fact, the Comintern supplied over 90 percent of the Chinese Communists' operating budget between the latter's founding in 1921 and 1932.[205] Pressure from the Soviet government, including from Lenin, and the Comintern was also responsible for pushing a reluctant CCP leadership under Chen Duxiu to form the First United Front with Sun Yat-sen's Nationalists.[206]

In fact, continued Soviet support to the Chinese Communists between the 1920s and 1940s contributed to the party's persistence and ultimate victory. Admittedly, Comintern-instigated uprisings by the CCP between 1927 and 1934 were brutally put down by Nationalist forces, and led to splits amongst the Chinese Communists as well as the cutting off of regular contact with Moscow.[207] Nevertheless, Soviet assistance sustained the Chinese Communists' viability as a challenger to the Nationalists throughout the 1930s and 1940s. Military, technical, and financial assistance flowing through Outer Mongolia and Soviet-influenced Xinjiang were important in helping the CCP establish and sustain a new base area in Yan'an and Northwest China.[208] Moscow too played a key role in limiting the National

---

[202] Chen, 2003, 336–50; Holubnychy, 1979, 126–245; Kennedy-Pipe, 1998, 36–54.
[203] Walt, 1996, 183–85, 97–99; Whiting, 1954, 10–58.
[204] Chen, 1983, 208–32,2003, 336–50; Elleman, 1997, 23–76, 282–85; Ke, 2005, 105–222, 313–17; Mizuno and Zheng, 1998, 241–48; Schaller, 1979, 38–39; Wei, 1956, 15–63; Whiting, 1954, 72–86, 155–247; Wu, 1950, 134–59, 173–85, 311–16; Yang, 1997, 15–50; Zhou, 1997, 117–46, 202–19, 243–66; SHAC 1039/553, "Zhong-E xieyue E yue yanjiu huiyi jilu ji Zhong E huiyi cankao wenjian", 1919; KMTPA *Han* 13730, "Erquandahui zhi quan E guomin diangao", January 1926; KMTPA *Zheng* 4/4.2–1, "Bao Luoting zhi Jiang Zongsiling dian", 3 February 1927; KMTPA *Zheng* 4/4.2–2, "Zhongzhenghui bishuchu zhi Bao Luoting dian", 9 February 1927; KMTPA *Zheng* 4/4.2–3, "Bao Luoting zhi Zhongzhenghui bishuchu dian"; KMTPA *Han* 17849.12, "E shi yan Guomindang", 19 April 1925.
[205] Elleman, 1997, 55–76, 196–207; Yang, 1997, 9–11.
[206] Li et al., 1997, 7–296; Mizuno and Zheng, 1998, 241–48, 273–76; Yang, 1997, 15–67.
[207] Yang, 1997, 436–65.
[208] Newer scholarship suggests that there is traditionally some underestimation about the importance of Soviet assistance to the Chinese Communists before 1949. Cohen, 2000, 147–53;

The Evolution of Foreign Involvement in China, 1923–1952   145

Government's military push against CCP-held areas in the late 1930s and 1940s by threatening the flow of aid.[209]

When the Nationalists looked like a useful challenger to the Beijing central government, especially during its socialist phase during the early 1920s, Moscow promptly extended a helping hand.[210] By 1923, Soviet leaders were furnishing the Nationalists with weapons, money, organisational expertise, and military training at the price of admitting members of the CCP into its ranks.[211] This aimed to lock in Soviet influence over the Nationalists, which could be especially useful if the latter managed to control the central government.[212] To maintain a working relationship with the Nationalists, Moscow gave way to Chiang Kai-shek after the 1926 Guangzhou Incident despite the ouster of the CCP and its left-wing allies from key posts in the party and the National Revolutionary Army.[213]

Similarly, Moscow directed the Comintern to cultivate Feng Yuxiang and his Guominjun Clique, the preeminent militarist group in Northwest China and Inner Mongolia, as an independent power centre under Soviet influence.[214] This gave Moscow another ally in China with which to check attempts by the Beijing government and others to seal off Soviet access. The partnership with Feng grew even as Soviet officials espoused recognition of the Beijing government and support for the Nationalists and Communists' national unification goals. After the Nationalist ascendancy in 1928, Moscow continued to supply the Guominjun with enough arms, equipment, money, and advice to be a potent military and political force through 1930 – despite its ambiguous ideological leanings.

GERMANY IN CHINA

Following Japan's takeover of Shandong in 1914 and the formal surrender of all German privileges in China during the Paris Peace Conference, there was little German involvement in China until the mid 1920s.[215] Consequently, private initiatives by firms and individuals characterised Sino-German ties from the

---

Garver, 1988, 153–77; Li et al., 1997, 7–138; Shao, 1995, 224–52; Wang, 2003, 432–38; Wei, 1956, 119–29; Whiting and Sheng, 1958, 21–78, 163–254; Yang, 1997, 333–90, 467–518.

[209] Garver, 1988, 128–30, 45–47.

[210] Chen, 1983, 208–32; Cohen, 2000, 88–92; Holubnychy, 1979, 158–78; Zhou, 1997, 11–41, 64–99, 117–266.

[211] Chen, 2003, 336–37; China, Wai chiao pu and League of Nations, Commission of Inquiry, 1932, 326–28; Wilbur, 1969, 224–35, 251–53; KMTPA *Hankou* 17849.12, "E shi yan Guomindang", April 19, 1925.

[212] Holubnychy, 1979, 246–329; Li et al., 1997, 297–646; Yang, 1997, 50–139.

[213] The Zhongshan Warship Incident, the March 20th Incident, and the Guangzhou Incident are different names for the same event.

[214] Chen, 1983, 180–208; Liu and Tian, 2004, 116–31; Mizuno and Zheng, 1998, 129–34; Sheridan, 1966, 165–69, 197–202; Van de Ven, 2003, 96, 108; Whiting and Sheng, 1958, 21–97; AH 0623.20/4412.01–02, "Sulian rao bian", August 26, 1928–October 18, 1928.

[215] Germany's share of investment in China dropped from a high of 20.9 percent at the turn of the century to a low of 2.7 percent in 1921, whilst its share of the China trade fell from 4.7 percent in

146   *External Intervention and the Politics of State Formation*

early to mid 1920s. By the late 1920s, the Weimar government was ready to reinvigorate the German position in China, laying the groundwork for Sino-German cooperation into the late 1930s. In line with German expectations that opportunity cost of intervention in China vacillated between prohibitive and high, Berlin's approach to access shifted between complete withdrawal and the maintenance of nonprivileged access.

The origins of German government interest in nonprivileged access opportunities in China lay with Berlin's efforts to address a seeming hostile European situation. After World War I, the German economy was struggling to recover from devastation whilst trying to meet the financial and other obligations of the Versailles Treaty.[216] French efforts to prevent a German resurgence through the 1920s and 1930s did little to alleviate conditions. These included efforts to maintain a large military presence on the Franco-German border, which came alongside the creation of a system of European alliances and insistence on the repayment of the war indemnity despite severe German economic problems. The Great Depression and British suspicions of Germany in the 1930s compounded matters.

Pressures in Europe created incentives for the Reichswehr and large German industrial concerns to press Berlin for the reconstruction and development of heavy industry, which could pave the way for rearmament.[217] China, the Soviet Union, Latin America, and Southeast Europe appeared to be areas where Germany could at once acquire raw materials, and access markets for investment as well as excess industrial products – including military equipment. This outlook persisted until the beginning of World War II, when the focus of war efforts on Europe, difficulties in long-distance exchange, and the need for a Japanese ally drew Berlin away from competing for access in China.

Of interest to leaders in Berlin was China's potential role in German military and economic recovery. China's large unexploited reserves of high-quality tungsten and the relative absence of restrictions on its trade was a fortuitous opportunity recognised by German military leadership and their domestic allies. Tungsten was a key ingredient in the arms manufacturing that was central to Germany's military resurgence.[218]

Moreover, the relative stability that the National Government seemed to guarantee could open trade and investment opportunities for German firms in the huge China market. As a result, the Weimar cabinet of Gustav Stresemann

---

1914 to 1.3 percent in 1921. This accompanied a corresponding decline in the number of German firms and residents in China. Kirby, 1984, 23–24.

[216] Kennedy, 1987, 304–10; Snyder, 1991, 91–95, 105–09.

[217] German firms pushing for an expansion of Sino-German economic ties included Dornier, A.E.G., Daimler-Benz, Siemens, I.G. Farben, Thyssen, Krupp, Otto Wolff, Stahlunion, Rhinemetall, the Deutsche-Asiatische Bank, and the Handelsgesellschaft für Industrielle Produkt (HAPRO) amongst others. They made some headway into China with the cooperation of the Reichswehr, the China-Studien-Gesellschaft of the Reichsverband der deutschen Industrie, Colonel-General Hans von Seeckt, and, after 1933, economics ministers Hjalmar Schacht and Walter Funk. Chan, 1982, 48–56, 83–84, 116; Chen, 1983, 165–232; Kirby, 1984, 24, 256–57.

[218] Chen, 2003, 78–87; Fox, 1982, 52–78.

The Evolution of Foreign Involvement in China, 1923–1952 147

promoted systematic contact with and support for the newly established National Government in Nanjing starting in 1927.[219] This military and economic reconstruction provided the basis for an expansion in Sino-German ties that continued under the Nazis until Hitler chose to align more closely with Tokyo.[220]

Berlin Tries to Regain Equal Access

To ensure unhindered access to China, both the Weimar and Nazi leaderships until 1938 sought to bolster the military, economic, and political position of the National Government. After all, the Nationalists controlled much of the tungsten mining areas in China – especially as it gained control of Jiangxi in 1934 – and seemed to show promise in bringing the entire polity under its effective jurisdiction.[221] This saw the growing sale of excess German military equipment and arms to the Nanjing government, which came with military advisors and investment in government-linked development projects.[222] German assistance in the 1930s was key in the building of highways, railways, and air links, as well as the new, advanced units of the Nationalist Army that featured prominently in the anticommunist campaigns of the 1930s and the early stages of the Sino-Japanese War. Such interactions saw Sino-German trade grow by more than two-and-a-half times between 1925 and 1938, and German investment in China rising by 750 percent from 1921 to 1938.[223]

Berlin's efforts to retain nonprivileged access in the Chinese polity continued after the initial outbreak of the Second Sino-Japanese War. However, the National Government's apparent inability to hold onto Central and South China seemed to call for an adjustment in German efforts at securing access. Building on growing ties with Japan, Berlin attempted to acquire Japanese approval for nonprivileged access in North China and Manchuria, whilst seeking to reconcile the two sides through the good offices of the German ambassador to China, Oskar Trautmann, and the German military attaché, Eugen Ott.[224]

German leaders hoped to use diplomacy to retain nonprivileged access across the Chinese polity despite ongoing hostilities, and avoid any commitment of

---

[219] Chen, 1983, 180–208; Coble, 1991, 161–62; Fox, 1982, 9–145; Gillin, 1967, 24, 40–41, 166–68, 183; Ma and Qi, 1998, 41–99; Sheridan, 1975, 251; Xue, 2005, 150–61; KMTPA *Zhongzheng Hui* 1/2.2, "Zhong-De tiaoyue", August 17, 1928.

[220] Chen, 2003, 129–334; Fox, 1982, 108–74, 209–331; Kirby, 1984, 233–52.

[221] Fox, 1982, 53–78; Ma and Qi, 1998, 101–470.

[222] Kennedy, 1987, 334; Kirby, 1984, 190–232.

[223] Despite the Great Depression, the total value of Sino-German trade in 1937 reached RM 262.7 million, and German direct investment in China stood at US$300 million. Just four years earlier, Sino-German trade was at a low of RM 116 million while German direct investment in China was also in a trough, at US$40 million. Kirby, 1984, 23–24, 73, 191; Xue, 2005, 139–49.

[224] Chen, 2003, 129–262, 303–18; Eto, 2001, 50–51; Huang and Zhang, 1984, 100–70; Ienaga, 1978, 72; Kirby, 1984, 234–44; Ma and Qi, 1998, 361–87; Shen, 2005, 550–59.

148   *External Intervention and the Politics of State Formation*

capabilities already employed in Europe.[225] Unfortunately for Berlin, the recalcitrance of both Tokyo and Chongqing, as well as Germany's own need for Japan to tie down Allied forces in Asia – particularly the Soviet Red Army – derailed their original plans for China. Accordingly, Nazi government settled for barter agreements and other more limited arrangements with Manchukuo and Wang Jingwei's Nanjing National Government. These lasted, at least in name, until Germany's defeat ended aims to secure access in China.[226]

FRANCE AND ACCESS IN CHINA

The French role in the Chinese polity between 1923 and 1952 was very much on the decline, paling in comparison even next to its relatively passive involvement during the earlier part of the century. Paris's declining attention over access in China had to do with the troubles facing the French government from the interwar period on. Concerns about a resurgent German threat, economic reconstruction, the Great Depression, the German occupation, and post–World War II rebuilding raised the anticipated opportunity costs of intervening in China from high to prohibitive. This moved French leaders away from largely exchange-based relationships with governments in China and toward withdrawal.

Like many other European powers, the primary concern of French leaders after World War I was recovery and preventing the reappearance of a German menace. Despite efforts to invest in its own economy and military throughout the 1920s and 1930s, as well as efforts to create alliances across Europe, it was apparent by the mid 1930s that France was lagging behind Germany economically and militarily. This situation worsened as the full force of the Great Depression hit in 1933, and its continental alliances began to fray.[227] French leaders began to rely on their leading role in the League of Nations, and what they believed was a British ability to hold off any potential German aggression.[228] As a result, French governments had little capacity to spare over access in China.

The French government was similarly preoccupied with developments in Europe and its colonies during and after World War II, and Paris could ill afford to divert valuable capabilities to securing access in China. German occupation and the establishment of the Vichy government of Philippe Pétain in 1940 meant that the government in France was effectively under German domination. Moreover, the focus of Vichy leaders was to keep conditions in France and French colonies under their control amenable to continued German predominance, rather than to worry about China. The more pressing goal of recovering

[225] Barnhart, 1995, 115; Kirby, 1984, 233–52.
[226] Chen, 2003, 263–334; Fox, 1982, 146–331; Ma and Qi, 1998, 465–81; SHAC 18/3268, Wang Zhaoming (Wang Jingwei) and Chu Minyi, "Zhongguo jiaru guoji fanggong xieding'an", October 1942.
[227] Kennedy, 1987, 277–84, 310–16, 334–40; Kupchan, 1994, 213–67.
[228] Christensen and Snyder, 1990.

The Evolution of Foreign Involvement in China, 1923–1952   149

France likewise kept the Free French government-in-exile from worrying about access in China. With the defeat of Germany and the return of the Free French government in 1945, the attentions of Paris switched to postwar reconstruction and the reestablishment of control over colonies in Africa and Indochina.

French Nonchalance

From the 1920s into the early 1950s, French elites and policymakers paid scant attention to China and the Far East. Between early 1938 and the defeat of the Third Republic in mid 1940, French assistance to the National Government was a paltry 660 million French francs with an additional £160,000 – approximately £26.5 million all told.[229] There was also little attention paid to the French colonies in Indochina, where the porous border with the southern Chinese provinces of Guangdong, Guangxi, and Yunnan became an important transit area for Allied war matériel going to the National Government.[230] Paris was similarly hands-off in overseeing – much less developing – the French leasehold in Guangzhou Bay, despite the supposedly close relationship that the Vichy government responsible for Indochina shared with the Axis powers. This situation persisted until Japan effectively took control over French Indochina and most of Guangdong by 1941.

World War II also saw France end the formal, legal access privileges it held in China. To help gain goodwill, the Vichy regime had relinquished all remaining special privileges France enjoyed on paper to the Wang Jingwei-led Nanjing National Government in 1941.[231] When London and Washington gave up their extraterritorial and other special rights in 1943, the London-based Free French government followed suit.[232] Except for the maintenance of border trade with Indochina, this effectively ended French involvement in securing access in China.[233] The need to quell the Viet Minh after World War II even drove Paris to attempt to seal access to China from the mid 1940s on.[234]

---

[229] Cui, 1995, 245–47; Eastman, 1991, 144.

[230] Barnhart, 1995, 123; Chan, 1982, 54–63, 102–05; Spector, 2007, 117–21; Taliaferro, 2004, 102–04; AH 641/5034.04-01, "Zhong-Fa guiding Yuenan yu Zhongguo biansheng guanxi tiaoyue", 16 May 1930–4 May 1935.

[231] SHAC 18/3268, "Guanyu shouhui zhujie ji chechu zhiwai faquan'an"; SHAC 18/1917, "Zhonghua Minguo Guomin Zhengfu guanyu feichu bupingdeng tiaoyue yu Ying Mei Rui deng guo qianding xin tiaoyue ji fujian", 1943–1946.

[232] SHAC 18/1927, "Zhixing shouhui faquan geyue xuzhi"; SHAC 18/2545, "Waijiaobu niti Canzhenghui de waijiao baogao"; SHAC 18/3269, Ministry of Foreign Affairs, "Waijiao Baipishu 69 zhi 88 hao"; SHAC 18/3429, "Baipishu di 54 zhi 105"; SHAC 18/877, "Zhonghua Minguo Guomin Zhengfu yu Faguo Linshi Zhengfu jiaoshou Guangzhou Wan zhujie zhuanyue", December 1946; SHAC 18/879, "Zhong-Fa guanyu Faguo 'fangqi' zai Hua zhiwai faquan ji qita youguan tequan tiaoyue", February 1946.

[233] Colbert, 1977, 62–63; Garver, 1993, 44; Kupchan, 1994, 267–96; Westad, 2003, 316–18; SHAC 18/3269, "Zhong Fa yu bianjie wenti jiejue", 1946; SHAC 18/3429, "Baipishu di 54 zhi 105".

[234] Cohen, 2000, 169; Kennedy, 1987, 381–83; Yang, 1997, 621–22.

CONCLUSION

What this chapter makes clear are the convergent outside actor expectations about the high opportunity costs of intervening in China between 1923 and 1952. Insofar as this confluence in opportunity cost expectations created a common focus on nonprivileged access, the various foreign powers turned to support central government rule in order to safeguard nonprivileged access opportunities across China. However, opportunity cost expectations and policies alone tell only part of the story. To support the view that external pressures fostered sovereign statehood, such changes in the collective pattern of intervention should bring the high levels of political centralisation, territorial exclusivity, and external autonomy that ultimately emerged in China. The next chapter traces these developments.

However, exceptions to the trend of rising perceptions about the opportunity costs of intervention going into the early 1950s did exist. These were Soviet views toward access in Outer Mongolia, and, to some extent, Manchuria, post-1950 American perspectives about Taiwan, and Japanese understandings of access in China during the Sino-Japanese War. Corresponding with their leaders' perceptions about the moderate opportunity costs of involvement in such areas at various times, Washington, Moscow, and Tokyo tried to regulate access in these regions. However, such gradations in opportunity cost perceptions over different parts of China do not contradict my argument; they simply reflect its sheer size and diversity. Such variation, particularly along China's frontiers, is not surprising.

CHAPTER 6

How Intervention Remade the Chinese State, 1923–1952

Foreign Sponsorship and the Building of Sovereign China

That state organisation in the Chinese polity approached sovereign statehood by the early 1950s is in little dispute. This development was, however, a significant shift away from the feudalised trajectory that China was on from the late nineteenth century until the end of World War II. The swing toward sovereign statehood resulted from changes to external intervention patterns given the broad realignment of opportunity costs expectations for foreign actors by the mid 1940s. As seen previously, this position stands in tension with conventional wisdoms that see popular nationalism as the primary force behind the rise of state sovereignty in China. However, the discussion here suggests that explanations which underemphasise the effects of changing external intervention patterns risk providing an incomplete view of state formation.

This chapter argues that convergent expectations among outside powers about the high opportunity costs of intervention described earlier brought a common focus on ensuring nonprivileged access in China through support for state sovereignty. These conditions contrast with the late nineteenth and early twentieth centuries, where divergent foreign expectations about the opportunity costs of intervention perpetuated the crosscutting fragmentary and integrative pressures that sustained China's feudalisation. Such developments are consistent with my claim that when intervention seemed expensive, outside actors fostered the development of sovereign statehood in China as the next best alternative to their greatest fear, its domination by rivals.

CONVERGING PERCEPTIONS ABOUT THE HIGH OPPORTUNITY COSTS OF INTERVENTION

External powers active in and around China until the end of World War II fell into two broad categories. Until the immediate postwar era, one group expected the net gains from investing capabilities toward substantial access denial in China to significantly outweigh the likely net gains of committing those same capabilities toward other objectives. Through the mid 1940s, those leading this set of powers saw robust intervention efforts to manage access into China as

151

External Intervention and the Politics of State Formation

promising both security and prosperity. However, systemic changes leading up to the post–World War II period meant that greater relative net benefits seemed attainable by placing capabilities elsewhere, and access denial over China no longer appeared as attractive to this group of actors.

Before the end of World War II, further denying access over China to rivals appeared to permit the accrual of significant returns, ranging from the creation of strategic buffer zones to advantages in exploiting markets and raw materials. Given that policymakers in this first set of powers believed these advantages to be difficult to obtain elsewhere, they associated low to moderate opportunity costs with intervening in the Chinese polity. As such, this first group of powers committed considerable capabilities toward regulating, if not fully denying, rivals' access to China until the perceived costs of doing so turned prohibitive. This change owed much to the demands of post–World War II recovery and the Cold War.

Among the first set of powers were Japan and the Soviet Union. Despite their aversion to major power conflict, Japanese leaders of the 1920s saw a need to consolidate an ability to regulate access to those parts of China already under Tokyo's sway.[1] This covered much of Manchuria as well as Shandong, Fujian, and Taiwan. Such a move promised to secure the markets and resources Japanese leaders felt their country lacked. These policies provided the basis for efforts to invade China in the 1930s and 1940s when the military ascendancy and fears of encirclement made autarky seem ever more attractive. Defeat, occupation, and the needs of domestic rebuilding between the outbreak of World War II and its aftermath, however, drove Tokyo to end intervention in China during the postwar era as the costs of doing so became unacceptably high.

Soviet leaders, on the other hand, saw managing exclusive access in northern and northwest China as a means to defend the Soviet Far East and Soviet Central Asia from capitalist aggression and secure a strategic presence in East Asia.[2] After all, northern China was a staging area for foreign intervention against the Bolsheviks following the Russian Revolution. Mongolia and Manchuria offered an easier route to Siberia, an ability to project power into China, and additional raw materials.[3] For much of the interwar period, Stalin's Soviet Union was willing to invest in access regulation over Tuva, Xinjiang, as well as Inner and Outer Mongolia to obtain these advantages.[4] Beginning in the late 1930s, however, the increasingly acute threat posed by Nazi Germany followed by the needs of rebuilding and facing off against the United States in the Cold War spelt more pressing demands for limited Soviet capabilities. This drove Stalin to restrict active access denial efforts to Tuva, Outer Mongolia, and, to a lesser degree, Manchuria.

[1] Barnhart, 1987, 27–29; Iriye, 1967, 172–74; Shen, 2005, 257–95, 716–21.
[2] Walt, 1996, 129–209; Wang, 2003, 432–57; Wohlforth, 1993, 36–58, 113–15.
[3] Haigh, Peters, and Morris, 1999, 41–126.
[4] Kennedy-Pipe, 1998, 31; Uldricks, 1979; Whiting, 1954.

How Intervention Remade the Chinese State, 1923–1952 153

To pursue their goals on access denial, elites leading this first set of powers sought to sponsor local groups willing to take on subordinate roles in support of at least access regulation. In return, they received backing against local adversaries and a cut of the polity's surpluses. Such arrangements manifested themselves in Tokyo's sponsorship of Zhang Zuolin's Manchuria-based Fengtian Clique, and various wartime collaborationist regimes across China.[5] These included Manchukuo, Mengjiang, the North China Political Affairs Commission, and the Nanjing National Government under Chinese Nationalist Party stalwart Wang Jingwei. They respectively oversaw Manchuria, Inner Mongolia, North China, and Central and South China.[6]

Likewise, Moscow extended support to the Mongolian revolutionary forces of Khorloogiin Choibalsan, Feng Yuxiang's Inner Mongolia-based Guominjun, as well as the dominant warlord in Xinjiang, Sheng Shicai, in order to manage access to these areas.[7] To ensure its hold over areas of interest, Moscow further supported first the Nationalists and then the Communists to distract China's successive central governments and their foreign supporters from effectively challenging the Soviet presence in the north and northwest.[8] Critically, efforts to sponsor local proxies cut across ideological lines – Tokyo worked with elements of the Chinese Nationalists to set up the collaborationist Nanjing regime, just as Moscow cooperated with Feng and Sheng despite their dubious revolutionary credentials.

It is worth highlighting the change in Soviet behaviour once Moscow began to associate high opportunity costs with intervention in China. As Germany's resurgence under Nazism became a serious security concern for the Soviets, Stalin scaled back access regulation efforts outside of Tuva and Outer Mongolia and turned toward supporting nonprivileged access across the rest of China.[9] This was despite an understanding that a Japanese victory in China could mean total exclusion for the Soviet Union. Hence, Moscow's roughly US $556.4 million in economic and military aid to the Nationalist-led central government was what Soviet leaders deemed as just enough to help the Nationalists avoid capitulation.[10] For Soviet leaders from the late 1930s on, China was a secondary theatre they had to prevent from becoming a distraction.

Accordingly, postwar reconstruction and meeting the U.S. Cold War challenge in Europe led Stalin to focus on shoring up a sovereign China to prevent

---

[5] Barnhart, 1995, 82–85; Mizuno and Zheng, 1998, 151–57; Shen, 2005, 257–85.

[6] China, Wai chiao pu and League of Nations, Commission of Inquiry, 1932, 3, 158, 301–403; Fei, Li, and Zhang, 1993; Liu, 2002; Mitter, 2000; Tong et al., 2004; Wang, 2001, 305–64; Zhongyang dang'anguan (China) 2000.

[7] China, Wai chiao pu and League of Nations, Commission of Inquiry, 1932, 326–28; Sheridan, 1966, 165–69, 97–202; Whiting and Sheng, 1958; AH 0623.20/4412.01-02, "Sulian rao bian".

[8] Elleman, 1997, 55–76; Li et al., 1997; Yang, 1997, 15–67.

[9] Kennedy-Pipe, 1998, 63–78; Westad, 2003, 310–20.

[10] Eastman, 1991, 144; Garver, 1988, 37–48, 104–46; Li, 1988, 217; Yang, 1997, 312–90; SHAC 18/3222, "Zhong Su tongshang tiaoyue"; SHAC 18/3283, "Waijiaobu gezhong tiaoyue"; AH 0641.10/5044.01-01/247/1–19, "Zhong Su qianding hubuqinfan tiaoyue zhi zhuyao yuanze".

154 *External Intervention and the Politics of State Formation*

access discrimination beyond Outer Mongolia, Tuva, and Manchuria with limited Soviet commitment. Both the 1945 and 1950 Sino-Soviet Treaties aimed to foster a territorially exclusive and externally autonomous China with highly centralised political rule, regardless of whether this was under the Nationalists or the Communists.[11] In fact, Moscow openly supported the Chinese Communist effort to seize the central government only when Nationalist defeat was evident and direct U.S. participation in the Chinese Civil War seemed remote.[12] This was despite the fact that Soviet postwar efforts to retain limited access regulation over Manchuria by backing CCP control of the region had laid the foundations for the latter's civil war victory.[13] Likewise, Moscow shaped assistance to the Chinese Communists during the Korean War to help consolidate Beijing's domestic and international position at an arm's length while avoiding actions that could invite direct U.S. intervention.[14]

A second set of outside actors from the 1920s through the early 1950s consistently saw limited net returns from committing capabilities to substantial access denial in China vis-à-vis pursuing alternative goals. The positive albeit small net gains to be had from preventing adversaries from seizing markets, resources, or strategic advantage suggested that there was some value to competing over access, even if this did not warrant heavy investment. For the leaders of these intervening powers, it seemed sufficient to prevent rivals from acquiring access advantages with as small a commitment of capabilities as necessary. This meant backing a local actor that could ensure nonprivileged access for all outside powers across the polity without being overly dependent on external help.

British, American, and German leaders from the interwar years through the early postwar era associated intervention into the Chinese polity with such high expectations of opportunity cost. Regardless of their political leanings, British cabinets throughout this period saw access denial in China as secondary to a multiplicity of other goals. Those goals included defending the British Isles from first Germany and then the Soviet Union, rebuilding from the Great Depression and the devastation of two World Wars, as well as holding onto what they could of the empire.[15] Maintaining Britain's declining, but still leading, economic position in China was a good thing to do, but the 3 percent of total British trade and outward investment represented by the China market hardly called for substantial commitments of capabilities.[16] Elites in London generally felt that it was sufficient to lock in British interest in China by ensuring that no other power could acquire privileged access.

---

[11] Elleman, 1999, 130–32; Garver, 1988, 182–230; Wang, 2003, 265–431.
[12] Westad, 2003, 49–50, 216–19; Yang, 1997, 607–18.
[13] Levine, 1987; Wang and He, 2005; Westad, 2003, 83–86; Yang, 1997, 519–70.
[14] Kennedy-Pipe, 1998, 98–100; Kim, 1994; Yang, 1997, 607–60.
[15] Ferguson, 2004, 273–85.
[16] Maddison and Organisation for Economic Co-operation and Development Centre, 2001, 99; Mitchell, 1962, 315–27.

How Intervention Remade the Chinese State, 1923–1952

United States administrations from Harding to Truman anticipated the returns from investing capabilities toward furthering access denial in China as persistently falling short of the expected benefits from committing to other goals. These included domestic economic development and recovery in the 1920s and 1930s, facing off against Germany and Japan during the early to mid 1940s, and subsequently competing with the Soviet Union over Europe.[17] These issues appeared to have direct bearing on American prosperity and security in ways that fuller access denial over China could not, especially if such action portended U.S. participation in a major power conflict. Despite the possibilities it offered for access to markets and resources, most U.S. policymakers in this period saw political involvement in China as a means to avoid upsetting other more important objectives.[18]

Just as the FDR administration designed wartime aid to the Nationalist-led central government to prevent its defeat, the Truman administration limited U.S. commitments to what was necessary to logroll Congress into backing the Marshall Plan and a peacetime defence build-up.[19] Contrary to traditional perceptions about American support, total U.S. assistance to China during World War II was less than 5 percent of Lend-Lease to Britain and the Commonwealth.[20] Despite Washington's anticommunist rhetoric and the China Lobby's supposed influence, U.S. aid to the Nationalists from 1945 to 1950 was less than 1 percent of commitments toward the reconstruction and defence of Western Europe and Japan.[21] This was in spite of Nationalist efforts to control an area and population larger than Western Europe and Japan even as it engaged in an active civil war. Indeed, the Truman administration was by early 1949 tacitly ready to accept a Communist-run central government in China that the U.S. government could work with to acquire nonprivileged access in future.[22]

Likewise, policymakers in the Weimar and Nazi regimes saw China's expansive markets and raw materials as a key to Germany's economic and military development. This remained the case until the outbreak of the European War and Germany's eventual defeat forestalled Berlin's ability to compete for access in China. German leaders saw Chinese tungsten as key to circumventing post–World War I restrictions on Germany's rearmament, while Chinese demand for heavy machinery and weapons provided opportunities to boost the redevelopment of German industry.[23] However, more pressing needs in Europe and physical distance eroded the anticipated net gains of investing more extensively

---

[17] Cohen, 2000, 105–34; Iriye, 1967, 178–207.
[18] Iriye, 1967, 201–26; Jespersen, 1996, 108–25; Wang, 2003, 201–19.
[19] Christensen, 1996, 58–96; Cohen, 2000, 117–66.
[20] Hawes, 1977, 16; Kimball, 1969; Tsou, 1963.
[21] United States aid to the Nationalists between 1945 and 1949 totalled US$645 million, while Marshall Aid stood at US$17 billion and the defence budget during this period topped US$50 billion. Christensen, 1996, 58–96; Cleveland, 1949; Hawes, 1977; Tsou, 1963; Tucker, 1983; SHAC 18/2960, "Junzhengbu jieshou Meifang yijiao wuzi baogao"; SHAC 18/3541, "Meiguo yuanwai fa'an, Zhong Mei zhuyao maoyi shangpin tongji".
[22] Christensen, 1996, 77–79, 106–09, 128–31; Tucker, 1983, 17, 57–79.
[23] Chen, 2003, 78–87; Kirby, 1984.

156   *External Intervention and the Politics of State Formation*

efforts in access denial over China. As a result, both Weimar and Nazi leaders concentrated on acquiring nondisadvantaged access to China's markets and raw materials vis-à-vis other external powers.[24]

For this second set of powers, ensuring nonprivileged access across the entire polity with minimal investment meant backing the local actor that seemed most able to establish centralised rule, territorial exclusivity, and external autonomy with limited support. To this end, the British and Americans were quick to transfer diplomatic, economic, and military support from the Fengtian Clique to the Chinese Nationalists once the latter seemed likely to succeed in establishing a centralised, exclusive, and autonomous China in 1928.[25] Just as the desire to secure nonprivileged access spurred British and U.S. support for the Nationalist government during World War II, it also led them toward the Communists once the Nationalists appeared unable to guarantee nonprivileged access over China.[26] Elites in Washington were ready to abandon the Nationalists in the hope of being able to work with a Communist central government later on, while Winston Churchill led London to become the first Western power to recognise the new People's Republic in 1950. Nazi Germany was similarly willing to switch its alliance with the Nationalist-led central government to various Japanese-sponsored collaborationist regimes in order to safeguard continued nonprivileged access in China.[27]

Tables 6.1 and 6.2 summarise changes to the perceived opportunity costs of intervention for the various outside actors and their approaches to access denial in China.

BEHIND FEUDALISED "SEMI-COLONISATION"

As Chapters 3 and 4 detail, China remained a feudalised state with limited centralisation and exclusivity matched with substantial autonomy so long as various external powers diverged on their expectations about the returns from denying access over that polity. Acting on their different perceptions of gain, policy elites led their respective governments to seek a broad spectrum of objectives within the Chinese polity. These included establishing full access denial through annexation to imposing direct access regulation by way of colonisation and fostering equal, nonprivileged access by promoting sovereign statehood. That several powers anticipating dissimilar gains were contending over China until the mid 1940s implied that no one actor could prevail and all had to settle for less than their preferred goals. Consequently, external intervention efforts sustained external autonomy and political centralisation as well

---

[24] Fox, 1982; Ma and Qi, 1998, 41–99.
[25] Borg, 1964; Chamberlain, 1946, 12–22; Iriye, 1967, 178–98; Lowe, 1981, 132–35; SHAC 18/3268, "Guanyu shouhui zhujie ji chechu zhiwai faquan'an"; SHAC 1032/648, "Beiyang Zhengfu waijiao wendu"; SHAC 1032/651, "Beiyang Zhengfu Taipingyang Huiyi Weihaiwei wenti".
[26] Wolf, 1983.
[27] Chen, 2003; Fox, 1982; Kirby, 1984, 233–52.

How Intervention Remade the Chinese State, 1923–1952

TABLE 6.1 *Divergent Foreign Expectations about the Opportunity Costs of Intervention in China and Corresponding Approaches to Access Denial, 1923–1945*

Outside Actor	Expected Opportunity Cost	Approach to Access Denial
Britain	High	Nonprivileged Access
United States	High	Nonprivileged Access
Japan	Until 1931, Moderate 1931–1945, Low/ Moderate	Access Regulation Complete Access Denial
Soviet Union	High Bordering USSR, Moderate	Nonprivileged Access Access Regulation
Germany	High	Nonprivileged Access
France	High	Nonprivileged Access

TABLE 6.2 *Convergent Foreign Expectations about the High Opportunity Costs of Intervention in China and Corresponding Approaches to Access Denial, 1945–1952*

Outside Actor	Expected Opportunity Cost	Approach to Access Denial
Britain	High	Nonprivileged Access
United States	High	Nonprivileged Access
Japan	Prohibitively High	Concede Access
Soviet Union	High Bordering USSR, Moderate	Nonprivileged Access Access Regulation
Germany	Prohibitively High	Concede Access
France	High	Nonprivileged Access

as regional fractionalisation and limited territorial exclusivity simultaneously, resulting in a feudalisation of the state.[28]

Political Centralisation

By consistently channelling political, economic, and military support to successive Chinese central governments, external attempts to ensure nonprivileged access buttressed political centralisation in China going into the 1940s. This remained the case when the central government came under the Fengtian militarist clique in the

---

[28] Chong, 2009.

158   *External Intervention and the Politics of State Formation*

mid 1920s, and when the Chinese Nationalists took charge from the late 1920s through the late 1940s.[29] Simultaneous efforts by foreign actors trying to entrench either full access denial or direct access regulation in conjunction with cooperative local proxies, however, generated fragmentary forces.[30] As long as infusions of foreign military and financial assistance persisted, local actors holding various regions could resist central government efforts to cow them into submission.

Such sharp divisions persisted in China even after the Nationalists proclaimed their successful "unification" of the country after the Northern Expedition in 1928. The National Government in Nanjing faced repeated threats from supposedly subordinate regional administrations and breaks within Nationalist ranks that it was at pains to put down, including the 1929 Jiang-Gui War, the 1930 Central Plains War, the 1933–1934 Fujian Mutiny, the 1936 Guangdong-Guangxi Incident, and the 1936 Xi'an Incident, to name a few.[31] Even the National Government's relocation to Southwest China after 1937 required efforts to simultaneously accommodate and coerce regional militarists there.[32] These events came on top of efforts to suppress Communist Soviet areas (*suwei'ai/suqü*) around China and the Communist regional government (*bianqü zhengfu*) eventually set up at Yan'an.

Eroding political centralisation also were various regimes created by foreign intrusion into China. After expanding into Manchuria, parts of northern China, and Inner Mongolia, Tokyo established Manchukuo in 1932 and the Mongolian Region Autonomous Political Affairs Committee in Inner Mongolia in 1934 in conjunction with various local groups.[33] Late 1937 saw the Japanese military establish the United Mongolian Autonomous Government in southern Suiyuan, the Northern Shanxi Autonomous Government, and the Southern Chahar Autonomous Government, which in 1939 combined into the Mengjiang United League/Inner Mongolia Autonomous Government.[34] Japan subsequently backed the creation of the Provisional Government of Republic of China to oversee north China as well as the Nanjing-based Reformed Government of the Republic of China in 1937 and early 1938 respectively.[35] Tokyo later merged these into a new

---

[29] Chi, 1976; Pye, 1971; Sheridan, 1966; Waldron, 1995.

[30] Gillin, 1967, 30–58, 79–117; Wilbur, 1969, 204–21.

[31] Casualty estimates for the Jiang-Gui War and Central Plains War stand at between 250,000 and 300,000. Coble, 1991, 334–74; Eastman, 1990, 85–143, 175–76, 251–52, 268–70; Eastman, 1991, 1–32; Gillin, 1967, 110–17; Mizuno and Zheng, 1998, 341–44; Sheridan, 1975, 184–97; Sheridan, 1966, 263–67; Shi, 1992; Wang, 2001, 185–218; Xu, 1999, 225–371; Zhongyang yanjiuyuan, Jindaishi yanjiusuo, "Koushulishi" bianji, 1996; SHAC 18/2921, "Gu Weijun zhi Zhang Xueliang dian", 1931; SHAC 18/2922, "Zhang Xueliang yu Riben qinglue Dongbei Waijiaobu dian", November 1931; SHAC 18/2933, "Gu Weijun yu Zhang Xueliang guanyu Rijun qinglue Dongbei shi de laiwang dian", November 1931.

[32] Chi, 1982, 87–88, 113–17; Eastman, 1984, 10–44, 130–71; Strauss, 1997; Yi, 1978, 354–82.

[33] Fei, Li, and Zhang, 1993, 1–32, 75–92, 132–65; SHAC 34/629, "Riben zhizao wei Manzhouguo jingguo shiliao zhailu Guowen zhoubao", February 1932—January 1934.

[34] Fei, Li, and Zhang, 1993, 75–92, 141–46.

[35] Barrett and Shyu, 2001; Brook, 2005; Fei, Li, and Zhang, 1993, 55–74, 93–114; Tong et al., 2004; KMTPA *Zheng* 6/60, "Guofu wei Beiping wei zuzhi xuanyan'an", December 1937; KMTPA *Zheng* 6/60.1, "Guofu wei Beiping wei zuzhi xuany'an".

How Intervention Remade the Chinese State, 1923–1952 159

National Government under the Re-Organisationist faction of one-time Nationalist premier and party chairman, Wang Jingwei, in 1940, although North China retained substantial autonomy under the North China Political Affairs Committee.[36]

The various Soviet-sponsored local regimes likewise cut against political centralisation. From 1924, Moscow-backed indigenous actors managed regimes in both Outer Mongolia and Tuva that stood outside the purview of central governments in China.[37] The Soviet Union even pressed successive Chinese governments, including the Nationalist regime, to effectively sanction the continued separation of these territories.[38]

Territorial Exclusivity

Alongside circumscribed political centralisation, divergent outside approaches over access denial in China gave rise to limited territorial exclusivity. As part of efforts to ensure nonprivileged access over China, those foreign powers expecting lower returns tried to limit direct participation in administering government agencies and encouraged other external actors to do the same.[39] Cases in point were the official British and American support for tariff autonomy and the drawdown of foreign management of the Chinese Maritime Customs and other extraterritorial privileges from the mid 1920s.[40]

---

[36] Barrett and Shyu, 2001; Brook, 2005, 32–61, 229–30; Chen, 1999; Fei, Li, and Zhang, 1993, 175–232; Huang, 1984; Huang and Zhang, 1984; Tong et al., 2004, 213–64, 732–811; Twitchett and Fairbank, 1978, 120–22; Wang, 2001, 276–363; Zhou, 2003.

[37] Elleman, 2001, 177–91; Elleman, 1999, 124–26; Tong et al., 2004; Wei, 1956, 30, 120–29, 85–86, 242; Whiting, 1958; Whiting, 1954, 208–35; Wu, 1950, 170, 222–23; AS 03/32/201, "Shouhui Kucha yu chetui zhu Meng Hongjun zhi jiaoshe", 1923; AS 03/32/485, "Zhong E huiyi gexiang wenjian", 1924; AS 03/32/204, "Waimeng wenti", 1925.

[38] Atwood, 1999, 137–58; Elleman, 1999, 177–91; Elleman, 1997, 124–31; Garver, 1988, 209–28, 63–65; Liang, 1978, 404–22; Niu, 1998, 69–74; Tsou, 1963, 46, 70–83, 242–52, 327–38, 526–34; United States, Dept. of State, and United States, Dept. of State, Bureau of Public Affairs., No. 30, 116–27; Wang, 2003; Yang, 1997, 609–18, 67–69; AS 03/32/201, "Shouhui Kucha yu chetui zhu Meng Hongjun zhi jiaoshe", 1923; AS 03/32/485, "Zhong E huiyi gexiang wenjian", 1924; AS 03/32/204, "Waimeng wenti", 1925; AS 03/32/205/02, "Zhu Meng Hongjun chetui shi jiaoshe an (Waimeng baogao)", 1925; SHAC 18/3268, "Zhong Su youhao tongmeng tiaoyue ji qita youguan wenjian", November 1945; SHAC 18/3428, "Baipishu di 54 zhi 105", 1940 – 1948; AH 0641/5044.01-01/123, "Zhong Su tiaoyue ji zhixing xinyue xuzhi yinzhi", September 1945–June 1946; AH 0632.97/5011.02-01, "Dongbei jieshou yu dui Su tielu jiaoshe", 13 October 1945–3 February 1947; AH 0641.10/5044.01-01, "Zhong Su youhao tongmeng tiaoyue ji youguan xieding", 14 August 1945; FMPRC 109/000020/01(1), "Zhong Su youhao tongmeng huzhu tiaoyue, Zhong Su guanyu Zhongguo Changchun tielu, Lushunkou ji Dalian de xieding, Zhong Su guanyu daikuan gei Zhongguo de xieding (Zhong E wenben), yidingshu", 14 February 1950.

[39] Wright, 1980; AS 03/02/050/01, "Baozai Diangzheng jiekuan'an", November–December 1922.

[40] *The China Monthly Review ... Special Tariff Conference Issue.* Issued as a Supplement of the *China Weekly Review* for November 1, 1925; Finch, 1926; M. H., 1927; SHAC 18/1927, "Zhixing shouhui faquan geyue xuzhi"; SHAC 1039/648, "Beiyang waijiao wendu", 1923; SHAC 1039/650, "1926 nian Beiyang zhengfu jiang guanshui gaiwei zhili ji youci yinqi de

External Intervention and the Politics of State Formation

Conversely, outside powers hoping to fully deny or regulate access, attempted to maintain direct vetoes over large areas of domestic governance through intrusive intervention efforts. Just as Japanese forces maintained highly active supervisory roles in the collaborationist administrations of Manchukuo, Mengjiang, and the wartime Nanjing Regime, Moscow kept a direct hand in the running of Outer Mongolia and Tuva from the 1920s.[41] Japan and France too asserted the continuation of extraterritorial rights, which included maintaining leasehold territories and consular jurisdiction over their own nationals.

External Autonomy

Contemporaneous outside attempts to assert different degrees of access denial over China through partnerships with local political actors until the end of World War II fostered significant external autonomy for the polity. In extending diplomatic recognition and support to the Chinese central government, external powers trying to promote nonprivileged access prevented other powers from exercising a veto over China's external relations. Accordingly, China's central government participated actively in the international diplomatic system even though it did not mean that Chinese foreign policy was obstacle-free.[42] This came in spite of Japanese efforts to determine the nature and extent of China's interactions with other foreign governments from the mid 1930s to the mid 1940s.[43] It was under this formula that Tokyo permitted client regimes in China to have foreign relations.

Zhongguo Beiyang junfa zhengfu ruhe liyong guanshui shouru changhuan geguo zhaiwi de wenti waiguo zhengfu dui zhe wenti de yijian", 1926; SHAC 1039/653, "Taipingyang huiyi shanhou weiyuanhui caibing banfa dagang; Shandong wenti huiyi shanhou weiyuanhui", 1923; KMTPA *Han* 4960, Wang Jingwei, "Wang Jingwei zhi zhangzhi baogao", January 1926; KMTPA *Han* 5148, "Guomin Zhengfu Caizhengbuzhang Song Ziwen shang zhongyang zhengzhi huiyi cheng", 16 June 1927; KMTPA *Han* 5276, "Liao Zhongkai ti'an", January 1924; KMTPA *Zheng* 1/2.3, "Zhong Ying guanshui tiaoyue"; KMTPA *Zheng* 1/ 2.4, "Zhong Fa guanshui tiaoyue", 22 December 1928; KMTPA *Zheng* 1/8.3, "Jieshou zujie, Rijun qinhua, Zhong Ri jiaoshe"; AH 0645.20/2760.01–01/40, "Zujie shouhui", December 1930; AH 0645.30/4460.01–04, "Guling wairen bishu zujiedi shouhui"; AH 0645.20/8431.01–01, "Xiamen Ying zujie shouhui"; AH 0645.20/8431.01–02, "Zhenjiang Ying zujie shouhui"; AH 0645.20/3460.01–01/165/1401–1429, "Shouhui Hankou Jiujiang Ying zujie Zhong Ying xieding (Chen-Ou xieding)", 19 February 1927; AH 0645.20/1035.02–02/165, "Tianjin Ying zujie shouhui", 14–16 April 1927; AH 0645/8800.01–01/157, "Chouban shouhui Ying Fa Yi zujie weiyuanhui huiyi jilu", 1930; AS 03/20/079, "Qianhuan yangkuan", 1924.

[41] Barrett and Shyu, 2001; Brook, 2005; Elleman, 1999; Fei, Li, and Zhang, 1993; Mitter, 2000; Wang, 2001; KMTPA *Zheng* 6/60, "Guofu wei Beiping wei zuzhi xuanyan an", December 1937; KMTPA *Zheng* 6/60.1, "Guofu wei Beiping wei zuzhi xuanyan"; AS 03/32/485, "Zhong E huiyi gexiang wenjian", 1924; AS 03/32/204, "Waimeng wenti", 1925.

[42] Garver, 1988; Wang, 2003; Zhou, 1999; SHAC 1039/650, "1926 nian Beiyang zhengfu jiang guanshui gaiwei zili ji youci'er yinqi Zhongguo Beiyang junfa zhengfu ruhe liyong guanshui shouru changhuan geguo zhaiwu de wenti waiguo zhengfu dui zhe wenti de yijian", 1926; SHAC 18/2318, "Guanyu fabiao Sujun chebing Dongbei de gaojian"; SHAC 18/3049, "Di yi ci Mosike huiyi".

[43] Li, 1999, 232–37; Shen, 2005, 451–57.

MARCH TO SOVEREIGN STATEHOOD

In comparison, the postwar convergence in foreign expectations about the high costs of intervening in China brought concurrent external efforts to secure nonprivileged access. This pushed China away from feudalisation and toward sovereign statehood. Much lower anticipated gains from full access denial toward the end of World War II meant that external actors in large part no longer actively sought full access denial or direct access regulation over much of China. Consequently, foreign support coalesced around domestic groups that seemed most able to deliver on the cheaper goal of preventing other external powers from acquiring exclusive access privileges. This is evident from the consistency of the 1945 Yalta agreement with the 1945 and 1950 Sino-Soviet Treaties and the superpower restraint toward direct intervention in the Chinese Civil War and Korean War.[44] Such dynamics nurtured the high levels of political centralisation, territorial exclusivity, and external autonomy characteristic of sovereign statehood.

Political Centralisation

Expectations of limited gain from full access denial meant that foreign powers were almost uniformly for a high degree of centralised rule over China by an indigenous political actor. Outside powers could minimise their capability investments in China by having a local partner bear the burden of governance and maintaining nonprivileged access amongst external actors. Which domestic group won the civil war was not critical to the external powers still contending over China so long as the victorious side did not grant other foreign powers advantages in access. Moscow was ready to accept a Nationalist-run central government in most of China immediately after World War II under such terms, just as Washington and London were willing to settle for a Communist-led one by the late 1940s.[45] That Soviet assistance to the Chinese Communists eventually proved more strategically effective than U.S. aid to the Nationalists was

---

[44] Weathersby, 1998; Westad, 2003, 35–50; Yang, 1997, 520–669; SHAC 18/1923, "1945 nian Su Mei Ying suo qianding de Ya'erda xieding", 1945; SHAC 18/3268 "Zhong Su youhao tongmeng tiaoyue ji qita youguan wenjian", November 1945; SHAC 18/3428, "Baipishu di 54 zhi 105", 1940–1948; PRCFMA 109–000020–01(1), "Zhong Su youhao tongmeng huzhu tiaoyue", AH 0641/5044.01–01/123, "Zhong Su tiaoyue ji zhixing xinyue xuzhi yinzhi", September 1945–June 1946; AH 0632.97/5011.02–01, "Dongbei jieshou yu dui Su tielu jiaoshe", 13 October 1945–3 February 1947; AH 0641.10/5044.01–01, "Zhong Su youhao tongmeng tiaoyue ji youguan xieding", 14 August 1945.

[45] Christensen, 1997, 97–133; Wang, 2003; SHAC 18/1923, "1945 nian Su Mei Ying suo qianding de Ya'erda xieding"; SHAC 18/3268, "Zhong Su youhao tongmeng tiaoyue ji qita youguan wenjian"; SHAC 18/3428, "Baipishu di 54 zhi 105"; 0641/5044.01–01/123, "Zhong Su tiaoyue ji zhixing xinyue xuzhi yinzhi"; AH 0632.97/5011.02–01, "Dongbei jieshou yu dui Su tielu jiaoshe"; AH 0641.10/5044.01–01, "Zhong Su youhao tongmeng tiaoyue ji youguan xieding".

162   *External Intervention and the Politics of State Formation*

incidental, since both superpowers sought to limit investment toward access competition in China.[46]

With the Soviet invasion of Manchukuo toward the end of World War II, Moscow pushed the Chinese Communists to acquire a secure staging area in Manchuria by 1945.[47] Under directions from Stalin, the Soviet Army delayed a handover of the territory to the Nationalists for about a year.[48] During this time, the Soviets transferred the large amounts of captured Japanese weapons to the Chinese Communists and promoted the consolidation of Communist rule over the territory.[49] This raised Communist warfighting capabilities while straining already stretched Nationalist logistic capacities in ways that discounted advantages Nationalist forces enjoyed from infusions of American arms and money as well as limited U.S. airlift support. It was from Manchuria that the Communists launched their successful bid to establish central government control over China.

The postwar focus among foreign powers on pursuing nonprivileged access through political centralisation also implied a general drying up of foreign political, military, and economic assistance for regional warlords and collaborationist regimes. This forced the capitulation of regional regimes to efforts by first the Nationalists and ultimately the Communists to exert oversight from the centre.

Territorial Exclusivity

Changing approaches to intervention based on external powers' convergent expectations about the limited utility of full access denial also created high levels of territorial exclusivity. As the various external powers began to expect higher returns from investing in other strategic goals, they became increasingly unwilling to devote capabilities toward maintaining direct oversight of governance in China. By the end of World War II, the external powers active in the Chinese polity renounced most of their roles in managing governance in a slew of new treaties with the Nationalist-led central government.[50] These included all foreign responsibility in managing the Chinese Maritime Customs, the right to possess most leasehold territories, as well as consular jurisdiction.

---

[46] Goncharenko, 1998, 142–45; Levine, 1987; Westad, 2003, 35–64, 175.

[47] AH 0632.97/5011.01–02/400, "Dongbei jieshou yu dui Su'E jiaoshe", 10 August 1945–6 June 1946.

[48] Wang and He, 2005, 285–328, 80–419; Yang, 1997, 519–70; SHAC 18/2318, "Guanyu fabiao Su jun chebing Dongbei de gaojian"; SHAC 18/3049, "Di yi ci Mosike huiyi".

[49] Levine, 1987; Tucker, 2001, 21–22; Westad, 2003, 83–86.

[50] Chen, 2003, 155–78; Fishel, 1952; Wang, 2003, 104–30; SHAC 18/877, "Zhonghua Minguo Guomin Zhengfu yu Faguo Linshi Zhengfu jiaoshou Guangzhou Wan zhujie zhuanyue"; SHAC 18/879, "Zhong Fa guanyu Faguo 'fangqi' zai Hua zhiwai faquan ji qita youguan tequan tiaoyue"; SHAC 18/1927, "Zhixing shouhui faquan geyue xuzhi"; SHAC 18/3033, "Zhong Mei shangye tanpan guocheng wenjian", 1948; SHAC 18/3247, "Zhong Mei youhao tongshang hanghai tiaoyue", 1945; AH 0641.90/1010.01–04/54, "Bupingdeng tiaoyue feichu hou yingying cuoshi'an", 1943–1945.

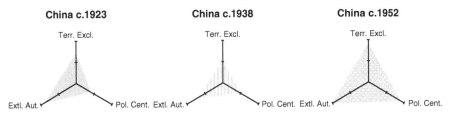

FIGURE 6.1 Shifts in State Form for China, 1923–1952

External Autonomy

Attempts by various external actors to attain nonprivileged access across China reinforced the high degrees of external autonomy that already characterised that polity. Given that leaders of the relevant outside powers believed the returns from complete access denial in the Chinese polity to be small, there were no realistic attempts to oversee and direct China's outward relations with foreign actors after World War II. Even post-1949 American nonrecognition of the Communist government and efforts to exclude it from the United Nations merely constrained the polity's outward autonomy without imposing a veto.

Shifts in the patterns of intervention based on a growing coalescence of beliefs among foreign leaders about the diminishing returns of full access denial ushered in sovereign statehood for China by the early 1950s. Rising demands on the limited capabilities of intervening powers, particularly by the end of World War II, undercut the anticipated returns from securing fuller access denial over the Chinese polity. Accordingly, policymakers in various major power capitals concluded that it was generally no longer cost effective to pursue anything more than nonprivileged access in China. This change brought external pressure to bear uniformly on raising levels of political centralisation and territorial exclusivity across the polity, while sustaining already high levels of external autonomy. As Figure 6.1 and the illustrations here indicate, such adjustments in foreign competition moved China away from its feudalised path and toward sovereign statehood.[51]

Still, the maps also indicate several previously centrally ruled regions that remained separate from the sovereign Chinese state post-1952. These were areas where various outside powers retained relatively high expectations of net gain from access denial and did not face external opposition to efforts at asserting themselves. This dynamic lay behind continued Soviet and British efforts to regulate access respectively over Outer Mongolia and Hong Kong after World War II, as well as limited American oversight of access over Taiwan after the outbreak of Korean War.[52] Unchallenged moves by Moscow to maintain full access denial over Tuva saw the absorption of the territory into the Soviet Union,

---

[51] Map sources: Spence, 1999, 427; Wu, 1995, 1999; Zhang, 1984; Zhongguo Ditu and Xinhai Geming Wuchang Qiyi, 1991.
[52] Chan Lau, 1990, 327; Christensen, 1996, 133–76; Elleman, 1999, 130–32.

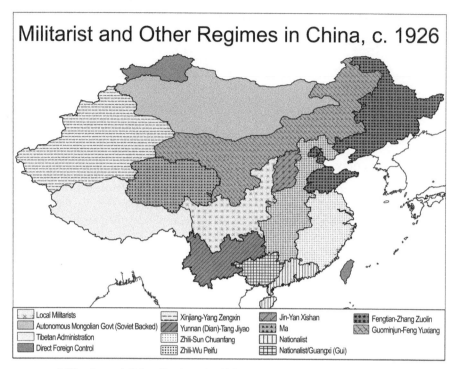

MAP 5. Militarist and Other Regimes in China, c.1926

while formal U.S. and British acquiescence gave Moscow oversight of communications in Manchuria into the 1950s.[53] Alongside separation from the rest of China, continued external domination reinforced foreign votes over internal governance and external affairs in these regions.

ALTERNATIVE TAKES ON CHINA'S MOVEMENT TO SOVEREIGN STATEHOOD

So far, it appears that the interventionist position presents a plausible case for the Chinese polity's movement from feudalised to sovereign statehood between 1923 and 1952. However, the persuasiveness of my main argument also rests, in part, on how it fares next to the other perspectives put forward to explain the change in China's state organisation during this period. From a review of available evidence, it seems that the ideational, institutional commitment, and bellicist positions each provides a piece of the puzzle. As such, attempts to understand dynamics behind the development of the sovereign Chinese state

---

[53] Wang, 2003, 419–505; Yang, 1997, 609–69; PRCFMA 109–000020–01(1) "Zhong Su youhao tongmeng huzhu tiaoyue".

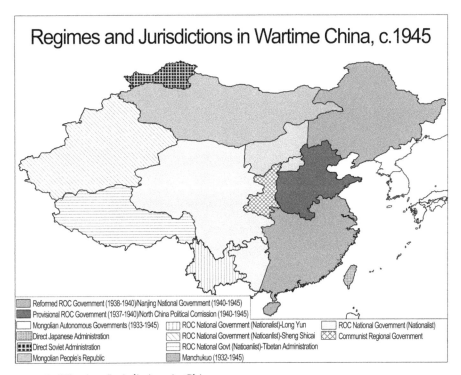

MAP 6. Wartime Jurisdictions in China, c.1945

during the twentieth century need to take the interventionist claim seriously. Nonetheless, it is important here to explicitly consider the various alternative accounts about the Chinese polity's shift toward sovereign statehood during the mid twentieth century.

Nationalism and Self-Determination Norms

The strength of the ideational and normative claims lay in their account of popular mobilisation and widespread demands for the realignment of state organisation along the lines of sovereign statehood. Many claim that nationalist ideology is especially important when trying to understand the popular support garnered by the Chinese Communists and by the Nationalists in the face of mounting Japanese aggression in China during the 1930s and 1940s.[54] Fused

[54] Benton, 1995, 124–41; Bianco, 1995, 175–85; Ch'en, 1991, 105–14; Cohen, 2000, 117–18, 39–40; DeVido, 2000, 173–85; Eastman, 1991a, 245–70; Eastman, 1991b, 45–48; Eastman, 1991c, 125–34; Esherick, 2000, 59–82; Feng, 2000, 155–69; Goodman, 2000, 131–49; Hartford, 1995, 144–69; Iriye, 1965, 254–77; Iriye, 1987, 1992, 69–70; Johnson, 1962, 1–70; Keating, 2000, 25–51; Mao, 1979, 169–75; Nathan and Ross, 1997, 32–34; Pepper, 1991,

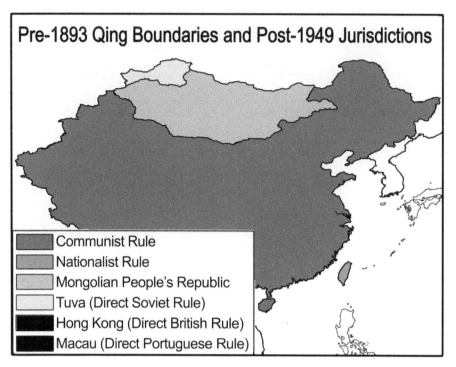

MAP 7. Pre-1893 Qing Boundaries and Post-1949 Jurisdictions

with the rising global appeal of self-determination norms, nationalism in China became synonymous with popular demands for high degrees of political centralisation, territorial exclusivity, and external autonomy.[55] Indeed, promises to meet such pleas formed a critical component of both Nationalist and Chinese Communist attempts to rally China's population behind their respective causes from the 1920s on.[56]

Here, it is important to remember that popular aspirations for nationalism and self-determination in the form of modern sovereign statehood were an important political force within China since the late nineteenth century. As observed in Chapter 4, this is a fact clearly apparent in the declared objectives of political groups from the Communists and Nationalists going back to the Tongmenghui and the Wuxu Reformers of

319–26; Selden, 1971, 79–276, 1995, 230–36; Teng, 1969, 441; Tian, 2000, 115–29; Tucker, 1994, 9–16; van Slyke, 1991, 194–99; Waldron, 1995, 241–62; Wei, 2000, 93–111; SHAC 18/ 1343, "Wang Shijie yu Zhongguo qingnian de lixiang Zhongguo yu lixiang shijie de yanshuo", 3 May 1941.
[55] Creek, 1995, 235–56; Eastman, 1984, 89–108, 72–215; Iriye, 1967, 198–99, 245–49, 271–78, 1987, 1992, 69–70; Johnson, 1962, 176–87; Mao, 1979, 175–78; Selden, 1971, 208–78; Wang, 2003, 1–23.
[56] Benton, 2000, 189–215; Bianco, 1971, 148–66; The Common Program for the People's Republic of China, 1979, 186–93; Eastman, 1984, 89–108, 172–215; Johnson, 1962, 176–87.

1898.[57] International norms supporting national self-determination had likewise been popular since the late nineteenth century, and even institutionalised after World War I – before the formalisation of the United Nations system at the 1952 San Francisco Conference.[58] Further, proponents of the nationalist and self-determinationist positions admit that foreign pressure helped prevent sovereign state creation in China, indicating that these norms and ideas were by themselves unable to foster significant changes to state organisation.[59] In the end, the link between the popularity of beliefs about national self-determination and the rise of a sovereign Chinese state after World War II seems empirically weak.

Arguments emphasising the force of ideas and norms do less well in establishing a direct connection between popular mobilisation behind nationalism and self-determination, and the evidence about change in state organisation. The rallying of popular support behind these beliefs undoubtedly contributed to the National Government and Communists' prolonged resistance against Japan, as well as the Communists' victory on the mainland. However, the mobilisational qualities of nationalism and self-determination norms did not end the fragmentation of the polity that came with Japanese efforts to impose its Greater East Asian Co-Prosperity Sphere in China.[60] That took the American atomic bombing of Hiroshima and Nagasaki, as well as the Soviet invasion of Manchuria, Sakhalin, and the Kurils, which rapidly – and exponentially – raised Tokyo's expectations about the opportunity costs of intervening in China.[61] Similarly, nationalist fervour did not bring central government rule over Taiwan, Outer Mongolia, Tuva, or, in some respects, Manchuria and Tibet between the end of World War II and the Korean War.[62]

---

[57] Chiang and Jaffe, 1947; Chiang and Wang, 1947; Garver, 1988, 3–7; Iriye, 1992, 41–88; Lei, 1968; Liang and Liang, 1990; Lin and Lei, 1971; Mao, 1948a , 1948b, 1951, 1952a, 1952b, 1954; Snow, 1937; Snow and Mao, 1979; Sun, Sun, 1926, Sun, 1954, Sun, 1927.

[58] SHAC 18/2987, "Zhongguo daibiaotuan canjia guoji heping jigou huiyi (Dunbadun huiyi) daibiaotuan baogao"; SHAC 18/2986, "Guanyu zhanhou shijie heping zuzhi de gexiang fang'an"; AH 0631/6077.01–02(403), "Guoji heping jigou", 18 August 1944–20 February 1945; AH 0631.30/4480.02–01(403), "Jiujinshan Lianheguo huiyi youguan dianwen", 28 February 1945–24 June 1945.

[59] Chiang and Jaffe, 1947; Chiang and Wang, 1947; Garver, 1988, 182–270; Lei, 1968; Liang and Liang, 1990; Lin and Lei, 1971; Mao, 1948a, 1948b, 1951, 1952a, 1952b, 1954; Snow, 1937; Snow and Mao, 1979; Sun K., 1945, Sun Y., 1926, Sun Y., 1954, Sun Y., 1927.

[60] Chi, 1982, 40–181; Eastman, 1984, 148–51; Iriye, 1967, 198–99, 245–49, 271–78, 1987; Tong et al., 2004, 3–37, 126–210, 213–418, 487–535, 551–60, 625–41, 642–79, 732–863; Tsou, 1963, 48–56; van Slyke, 1991, 273–79; Yu, 2006, 186–89.

[61] Barnhart, 1995, 149–50; Ienaga, 1978, 126, 150, 200–2, 231; Iriye, 1967, 238–43, 1997; Wang and He, 2005, 207–84, 329–79.

[62] Atwood, 1999, 137–58; Copper, 1999, 29–39; Elleman, 1997, 177–91, 1999, 124–31; Garver, 1988, 209–28, 263–65; Niu, 1998, 69–74; Roy, 2003, 108–19; Tsou, 1963, 242–52, 270–83, 327–38, 526–46; Wang, 2003, 111–216, 312–72, 500–05; Wei, 1956, 120–29, 242, 266–80; Whiting, 1954, 208–35; Wu, 1950, 170, 222–33; Yang, 1997, 609–18, 667–69; AH 0601.16/ 2234.01–01/143/2308–2374, "Zhaohui Riben kangyi gai guo zhanzhu Dongsansheng duli bing

168 *External Intervention and the Politics of State Formation*

Finally, nationalism and self-determination also do not quite account for the continued and politically significant, albeit less extensive, limitations on China's political centralisation, territorial exclusivity, and external autonomy that continued past 1952. For all China's popular nationalism and demands for self-determination, there was acceptance of the persistent separation of Outer Mongolia, Taiwan, Hong Kong, Macau, and Tuva from the fatherland, as well as Soviet extraterritoriality in Manchuria. If the clamour for national self-determination and unity was truly behind the defeat of the Japanese and the ouster of the Nationalists, it is curious why such motivations fell short when faced with seemingly less arduous tasks. After all, despite claiming to represent Chinese nationalism, the Communists likewise did little to seriously resolve these issues until later, if at all.

Institutional Commitments and Rising Peasant Prominence

The most convincing institutional commitment account for China's development of sovereign statehood is one that highlights formalised collaboration between a centralising, autonomy-seeking Communist Party and a newly prominent peasant class. From this perspective, the Chinese polity's transformation in state organisation between 1923 and 1952 came about as natural disasters, economic turmoil, and incessant warfare substantially increased peasant disaffection with prevailing political institutions.[63] Such exogenous shocks weakened the bourgeois and capitalist segments of society that could conceivably form countervailing organisational coalitions with other political actors in China, such as the Nationalists, militarists, and Japanese proxies.[64]

Seizing the opportunities opened by such shifts in the social milieu, the Communists sought to create new organisations of governance that guaranteed the peasantry larger and more stable redistribution of the state's surpluses in return for peasant support.[65] This allowed for the suppression of other actors and social classes, leaving a Chinese polity under Communist rule that had substantial political centralisation, territorial exclusivity, and external autonomy.[66] In fact, widespread peasant dissatisfaction going into the 1940s and the success of CCP land reform in garnering popular support lend credence to this view.[67]

Where the institutional commitment position leaves doubt, however, is in the difficulty it has in fully explaining the timing and nature of the Chinese polity's

---

xuanshi Zhongguo lichang ji Riben zhaofuwen", 9 October 1931; AH 0632.97/5011.01–02/400, "Dongbei jieshou yu dui Su'E jiaoshe".

[63] Billingsley, 1981; Eastman, 1990, 181–243, 1991, 152–76; Feng, 2004, 191–232; Pepper, 1991, 305–19; Sha, 2005, 307–24, 385–99.

[64] Eastman, 1984, 45–88, 172–202; Rawski, 1980, 6–48, 1989, 168–79.

[65] Benton, 1995, 124–41; Bianco, 1995, 175–85; Hartford, 1995, 144–69; Johnson, 1969, 397–437; Mao, 1948a, 1948b, 1951; Selden, 1971, 79–120, 77–276; Snow and Mao, 1979; Westad, 2003, 107–46, 259–93.

[66] Chen, 2006, 227–94, 434–45; Johnson, 1962, 1–70, 92–122, 149–55, 176–87.

[67] Selden, 1995, 1–165.

How Intervention Remade the Chinese State, 1923–1952 169

movement towards sovereign statehood. Many observers note that the natural and man-made calamities facing China's peasants were not unique to the mid twentieth century.[68] Such events were quite severe in the eighteenth and nineteenth centuries, and contributed to several large-scale peasant revolts and numerous smaller ones.[69] Likewise, groups aiming to reorganise the governance institutions of the Chinese polity along the lines of sovereign state were also present since the nineteenth century. Yet, such conditions were somehow insufficient to foster sovereign statehood until after World War II.

Even accounting for a long gestation period, the institutional commitment position does not fully explain why the alliance between a centralising domestic actor and a disgruntled peasantry took place only in the mid twentieth century. After all, centralising local political groups and an unhappy peasant class, for all their importance, were unable to actually defeat occupying Japanese forces and their indigenous proxies. It is also curious that the Chinese Communists most successfully exploited peasant frustration in areas that experienced limited foreign access denial. The institutional commitment perspective, in addition, does not quite establish why peasants in Outer Mongolia, Tuva, Taiwan, Hong Kong, and, to some extent, Manchuria and Tibet did not readily sign up to the Chinese Communist-led sovereign state formation project.[70] This is despite having undergone similar experiences as peasants elsewhere in China, albeit in varying degrees.[71]

Whither Capitalised Coercion

Bellicist approaches show some promise in explaining the development of sovereign statehood in the Chinese polity from 1923 to 1952. Indeed, the ability of militarist cliques, collaborationist groups, and others to both resist central governments and engage external actors rose and fell with their capacity to hold both sources of wealth and the tools of coercion.[72] Corruption, economic mismanagement, hyperinflation, and damage to its primary economic base in East China, on the other hand, helped cripple the Nationalists' ability to accumulate and concentrate capital after World War II. As a result, the Nationalists could not muster the coercive capacities necessary to extend and preserve their

---

[68] Kuhn, 2002, 1–26, 80–113; Kuhn, 1980, 189–211.

[69] Chesneaux, 1973, 7–78; Kuhn, 1980, 105–225; Naquin, 1976, 1981; Wakeman, 1975, 163–224.

[70] The New Territories contained large agricultural areas until the 1970s. Boikova, 1999, 107–19; Chan Lau, 1990; Chen, 1972, 2006, 227–94, 434–45; Cohen, 2000, 180–85; Copper, 1999, 29–39; Elleman, 1999, 123–31; Endicott, 1999, 63–64; Lane, 1990; Roy, 2003, 32–119; Tucker, 1994, 29–36; Wang, 2003, 421–58, 475–80; Wang, 1979, 278–89; Wei, 1956, 30, 120–29, 185–86, 242; Westad, 2003, 259–93; Wu, 1950, 170, 222–33.

[71] Brook, 2005, 62–220; Ching, 2001; Copper, 1999, 29–36; Ka, 2003; Katz, 2005; Lamley, 1999, 213–19; Lo, 2001, 116–32; Phillips, 1999, 276–303; Schoppa, 2001, 156–79; Seybolt, 2001, 201–25; Tucker, 1994, 31–38; Wang, 1979, 251–89, 1999, 321–26.

[72] Barrett, 2001, 102–15; Brook, 2005, 1–62, 221–48; Chan, 1982, 109–26; Remick, 2004, 41–138; Sheridan, 1975, 59–96, 164–206, 256–83.

reach as a central government, which could have allowed for the establishment of a sovereign Chinese state by the early postwar years.[73]

Conversely, the Chinese Communists' ability to secure and enlarge areas from where it could acquire and sustain the stable concentration and accumulation of wealth helped pave the way for their success in seizing control of the state. [74] Monopolisation over the control of capital in areas under their jurisdiction both contributed to and benefitted from the battlefield prowess and proficiency in internal security that characterised the Communists' success over domestic rivals.[75] This dynamic ultimately gave rise to the high levels of political central-isation, external autonomy, and territorial exclusivity under central Chinese government control in areas other than Outer Mongolia, Taiwan, Tuva, Hong Kong, Macau, and, to a smaller degree, Manchuria and Tibet by the early 1950s.[76]

Bellicist arguments, however, do not fully address the role external powers played in the concentration and accumulation of both capital and coercion by different domestic actors. Major power support gave militarist cliques and other political actors a jumpstart in acquiring the financial and coercive wherewithal to keep regional powerbases. For political actors receiving outside help, this injection of capital and coercion translated into the creation and sustenance of indigenous, regional administrations with a capacity for autonomous action outside the reach of China's central governments.[77] This enabled the limitation, even outright destruction, of central government capacities.[78] Such effects of foreign influence were most readily apparent up to the end of World War II, but are also responsible for the continued political separation of the aforementioned regions from the rest of China beyond the mid twentieth century.

Outside interference too relates to the Chinese Communists' ability to acquire the level of concentration and accumulation of both capital and coercive instruments to attain victory over internal adversaries, notably the Nationalists. The

[73] Bianco, 1971, 140–66; Chi, 1982, 132–240; Eastman, 1984, 45–88, 130–202, 1991, 152–60; Pepper, 1999, 7–41, 95–195; Rawski, 1989, 168–69; Remick, 2004, 133–38; Richardson, 1999, 93–97; Spector, 2007, 36–38, 62–63; Westad, 2003, 181–211.

[74] Benton, 1995, 124–41; Bianco, 1971, 175–85; Chen, 1995, 263–94; Gao, 2000, 440–644; Hartford, 1995, 144–69; Johnson, 1962, 92–122, 149–55, 176–87; Selden, 1995, 152–65, 169–213; Selden, 1971, 79–276; Sheridan, 1975, 245–83; Westad, 2003, 17–32, 107–43, 181–293; Yang, 1997, 519–70.

[75] Gao, 2000, xi–xiii, 605–44, 647–57; Mao and Li, 1995; Pepper, 1991, 229–422.

[76] Boikova, 1999, 107–19; Brook, 2005, 108, 214–16, 238–39; Chan Lau, 1990; Christensen, 1996, 127–37, 174–76; Copper, 1999, 34–39; Elleman, 1999, 123–31; Endicott, 1999, 63–64; Iriye, 1967, 207–11; Lane, 1990; Nathan and Ross, 1997, 29–40, 197–206; Roy, 2003, 108–19; Tucker, 1994, 31–38, 197–204; Wang, 1979, 251–89; Wang, 2003, 373–480; Wei, 1956, 30, 120–29, 185–86, 242, 281–309; Wu, 1950, 170, 222–33; Yang, 1997, 519–70, 667–68.

[77] Barrett, 2001, 102–15; Brook, 2005, 31–62, 221–39; Chan, 1982, 1–43, 109–37; Chi, 1969, 90–97; Sheridan, 1975, 59–96, 164–70, 187–206, 256–83; Spector, 2007, 46–47, 63–70; Westad, 2003, 235, 289–93, 310–25.

[78] Coble, 2001, 135–55; Huang and Yang, 2001, 56–76; Iriye, 1965, 160–91; Schoppa, 2001, 156–79; Seybolt, 2001, 201–25; Tucker, 1994, 9–15.

How Intervention Remade the Chinese State, 1923–1952

Soviet provision of surrendered Japanese arms and a secure rear area in Manchuria from which to extract wealth clearly boosted postwar Communist capabilities, further enhancing the effectiveness of Communist military mobilisation.[79] In early 1949, Mao Zedong even admitted to Soviet envoy Anastas Mikoyan that:

> If there had not been any help from the Soviet Union, we would hardly have been able to gain today's victories. This does not mean that we should not rely on our own forces. Nevertheless, it is necessary to take into account that the military aid of the Soviet Union in Manchuria, that amounts to one fourth of your total aid, plays quite a substantial role.[80]

This admission is revealing about the role of external intervention in shaping a domestic political actor's ability to concentrate and accumulate both capital and coercion.

Likewise, the Chinese Communists' ability to consolidate their hold over much of China from 1949 to 1952 benefitted heavily from the substantial amounts of technical, military, and economic assistance the Beijing government secured from Moscow.[81] The Communists also gained from the limitation of American aid to their Nationalist adversaries, as well as active U.S. efforts to limit the Nationalists' ability to attack the mainland from Taiwan after mid 1950.[82] Moreover, what drove the patterns of external involvement discussed here were expectations about the opportunity costs of intervention in China prevalent in the various major power capitals.

CONCLUSION

Available evidence indicates that the case for the interventionist claim about the establishment of sovereign statehood in the Chinese polity between 1923 and 1952 seems much stronger than the alternatives. External involvement, coloured by convergent postwar expectations about the high opportunity costs of intervention, allowed for the rise of sovereign statehood in what constitutes today's People's Republic of China. Informed by expectations about the high opportunity costs of intervening in China by the mid twentieth century, the major powers turned to securing nondisadvantaged positions when competing for access over

---

[79] Borisov, 1999, 140–252; Borisov and Koloskov, 1975, 47–62; Chen, 2006, 418–24; Garver, 1993, 37–39; Goldstein, 1994, 232–35; Levine, 1987, 23–28; Liu, 2002, 444–53; Spector, 2007, 46–47, 63–70; Tsou, 1963, 300–05, 327–45; United States, Dept. of State, and United States, Dept. of State, Bureau of Public Affairs, No. 30, 145–72; Wang, 2003, 373–418, 460–75; Wang and He, 2005, 285–328, 80–419; Westad, 2003, 30–48, 61–64, 175; Yang, 1997, 519–70; AH 0632.97/5011.01–02/400, "Dongbei jieshou yu dui Su'E jiaoshe".

[80] Quoted in Goncharenko, 1998, 144.

[81] Goldstein, 1994, 232–36; Goncharenko, 1998, 142–45; Kaple, 1998, 117–30; Wang, 2003, 500–5; Yang, 1997, 609–46; Zhang, 1998, 189–200.

[82] Christensen, 1996, 74–76, 133–37; Copper, 1999, 37–39; Goldstein, 1994; Iriye, 1967, 295; Nathan and Ross, 1997, 57–62; Roy, 2003, 108–19; Tsou, 1963, 494–551; Tucker, 1994, 31–38; Wang, 1999, 321–36; Westad, 2003, 31–61, 159–62, 185–88, 291–93.

the polity. This perspective adds to accounts of sovereign state formation in China provided by explanations focusing on nationalism, self-determination norms, institutional commitments, and the effects of war on extractive and coercive capacities.

Only where major power expectations about the opportunity costs of intervention remained low to moderate along China's fringes did efforts to pursue the full denial of access to rivals or direct regulation of access continue. In areas where major powers still anticipated low to moderate opportunity costs to intervention within the pre-1894 Chinese state, outside pressure brought lower levels of territorial exclusivity, external autonomy, and political centralisation. By fostering the persistence of foreign satellites, annexed territory, colonies, *de facto* protectorates, and extraterritoriality along China's periphery, external intervention too was responsible for residual feudalisation past 1952. That foreign powers in effect sponsored the creation of the sovereign Chinese state contrasts understandings that pit the Chinese nation against outside forces and see external involvement as a driver of division. The Chinese people may have stood up in October 1949, but the rise of China's sovereign statehood rested on the props of external intervention.

CHAPTER 7

Creating Indonesia, 1893–1952

Major Power Rivalry and the Making of Sovereign Statehood

As a general theoretical framework, my argument about state formation needs to explain more than China. It needs to account for cases like the East Indies' movement from a Dutch colonial state to the sovereign Republic of Indonesia too. I contend that the intervention logic bears out when examining the relationships between the development of governance and shifts in the aggregated patterns of outside intervention in the East Indies. This was in spite of the geographic, ethnic, and religious differences between Indonesia and China, as well as the archipelago's long history under a colonial yoke. Convergent external expectations about the significant opportunity costs of intervention, in particular, fostered the development of sovereign statehood in the East Indies after World War II. Conversely, perceptions about the moderate opportunity costs in first The Hague and then Tokyo coupled with the belief by other foreign actors about the excessive costs of intervention sustained colonial statehood in the archipelago until the mid twentieth century.

Considering the East Indies is useful for this project as it presents another less likely case for my argument. Many accounts tie the persistence of Dutch colonialism, Japanese occupation, and the polity's eventual move toward sovereign statehood to the development of Indonesian nationalism. In this respect, it is possible to be more confident of my claims if they hold for the East Indies in addition to China and Siam. Still, the dynamics surrounding external intervention are more straightforward and less disputed in Indonesia than in China. This permits me to discuss the East Indies as a more condensed supporting case.

By applying structured, focused comparisons of the East Indies from 1893 to 1922 and from 1923 to 1952, I can examine my theory against alternative accounts of state formation. These include the diffusion of global self-determination norms, nationalism, institutional commitment, and capitalised coercion. In evaluating the state formation experience of the East Indies against China and Siam, I can control for preexisting cultural conditions, the nature of intervening powers, geography, and regional peculiarities.

173

CONTINUITY AND THE DUTCH COLONIAL STATE IN THE EAST INDIES, 1893–1922

The persistence of the Dutch colonial state in the Indonesia from 1893 to 1922 represents a situation where an external power that anticipated moderate opportunity costs to intervention prevailed in the competition for access. The Hague was able to regulate access over the East Indies between the late nineteenth and early twentieth centuries as other powers largely conceded access over that polity. Dutch efforts to manage access led the Netherlands Indies to demonstrate low external autonomy and high territorial exclusivity whilst political centralisation grew. The Hague controlled the external affairs of its colony and oversaw the policies of the Batavia-based Dutch East Indies colonial administration, which could in turn veto political developments across the archipelago.

Opportunity Cost Expectations and Patterns in External Involvement

Between 1893 and 1922, Dutch leaders anticipated the opportunity costs of intervening in the East Indies to be moderate. The Hague expected a continuation of efforts to regulate access across the archipelago to promise high net returns to an investment of limited capabilities. Other powers active around Southeast Asia expected the costs of intervening into the East Indies to be prohibitively high, and were unwilling to seek more than nonprivileged access. Such a configuration of approaches toward intervention in the East Indies left Holland as the only power able to shape governance in the archipelago between the end of the nineteenth century and the second decade of the twentieth.

Dutch Opportunity Costs Perceptions and Rule in the Late Colonial East Indies

From the perspective of Dutch elites in late nineteenth and early twentieth centuries, an ability to control access to the East Indies was key to prosperity. Official sponsorship of cash crop production and export in Java as well as other parts of the Indonesian archipelago was key to Dutch economic development since the initiation of the *cultuurstelsel*, or cultivation system, in the 1830s.[1] By the 1850s, remittances from the Netherlands Indies accounted for more than 30 percent of Dutch state revenues whilst the livelihoods of about one-in-five Dutchmen rested directly or indirectly on the East Indies economy.[2] Making the East Indies seem even more attractive by the late nineteenth and mid twentieth centuries was the discovery of oil in the Outer Islands and the suitability of these regions for large-scale rubber planting.[3] A near simultaneous rise in world

---

[1] The "Culture System" is a more popular, but less accurate, name for the Cultivation System. Drakeley, 2005, 39–42; Ricklefs, 1993, 119–28, 153–54; van den Bosch, 1977, 5–15; van Niel, 1990, 67–89; Vlekke, 1943, 269–78, 1945, 151–61; Wiarda, 2007, 128–29.

[2] Kahin and Kahin, 1995, 20; Vandenbosch, 1941, 223–24, 351–52; Vlekke, 1943, 291–93.

[3] Barlow and Drabble, 1990, 187–208; Furnivall, 1939, 303–45; Owen, 2005, 184–86; Vlekke, 1943, 295–97, 1945, 164–68.

Creating Indonesia, 1893–1952

demand for these commodities and the abundance of cheap labour further augmented the appeal of exclusive access over the East Indies for Dutch business and political leaders.

Dutch leaders, however, faced significant capability limitations when it came to securing access over Indonesia. The sheer social diversity and size of the archipelago – which included more than 17,000 islands with a land area roughly that of Australia and a population of about 30 million around 1900 – required substantial administrative capacities.[4] Being halfway around the world and with an estimated population of around 5 million at the turn of the century, ruling the East Indies was a challenge for Dutch elites.[5] Compounding matters were the European rivalries of the late nineteenth century that unfolded into World War I. Though Holland managed stay out of the complications of great power politics through armed neutrality, this policy rested on maintaining pricey military forces.[6]

Given the potential for substantial gains from access denial and the significant investment in capabilities needed to accrue such benefits, Dutch policymakers between 1893 and 1922 saw moderate opportunity costs to intervening in the East Indies. Fully denying rivals access to the archipelago was a goal beyond reach of the Netherlands government given its physical and fiscal constraints, especially next to security concerns in Europe. Allowing other major powers complete equality in access to its Southeast Asian colony was not something leaders in The Hague were ready to accept given the rents they desired to accrue by maintaining exclusionary access. The most feasible option seemed to be regulating access by cultivating of indigenous elites and promoting the subservience of the local population. This could minimise capability commitments whilst enabling Dutch interests to capture many of the gains from access denial.

Colonialism as Access Regulation

The economic liberal and commercial interests prominent in the Dutch parliament, the States-General, along with their political allies were willing to forego full access denial in the East Indies.[7] Working with humanitarians like Conrad Théodoor van Deventer, who wished to improve the lot of indigenous peoples under Dutch colonial rule, economic liberals and capitalists pushed the Ethical Policy (*Ethische Politiek*) for the Netherlands Indies through the States-General in 1901.[8] This policy continued at least in name until the early 1940s. Here, the Dutch government used cooperative indigenous elites in various regions and localities to govern the East Indies whilst offering order, development, technical

---

[4] Preger, 1944, 21, 39.
[5] Vandenbosch, 1941, 380–96.
[6] Ricklefs, 1993, 160–61, 72–76.
[7] Furnivall, 1939, 225–36; Ricklefs, 1993, 151–53.
[8] Brooshooft, 1977, 65–77; Drakeley, 2005, 45–46; Kat Angelino and Renier, 1931, 71–129, 205–57, 354–426; Vlekke, 1943, 317–20, 1945, 162–64, 175.

176 *External Intervention and the Politics of State Formation*

education, and healthcare to help consolidate Dutch rule over the populace.[9] The Ethical Policy represented an effort to maximise the gains from access regulation with a minimal commitment of capabilities by an intervening power perceiving moderate costs.

To impose rule from Batavia, the Dutch colonial administration sponsored cooperative groups from Javanese *bupati* to Minangkabau *penghulus* and Acehnese *uleëbalangs*.[10] In return, these local nobles received substantial financial and military assistance from Batavia, support for the maintenance of their social standing, and opportunities to profit from the colonial economy and, in some cases, limited administrative autonomy.[11] The colonial government nurtured indigenous people to serve as civil administrators, or *priyayi*, and soldiers by offering economic and social advancement – in fact, Indonesians outnumbered Europeans almost two-to-one in the 42,000 strong colonial army.[12] To acquire local support, the Dutch also allowed for some indigenous tempering of colonial policies by bringing local elites into advisory and consultative assemblies in the centre, regions, and villages.[13]

Under the shadow of World War I, The Hague and Batavia further established a colony-wide assembly, the Volksraad or People's Council, in 1918. This arrangement allowed a degree of indigenous representation in exchange for local participation in a part-time militia raised to defend the colony.[14] Known as the *Indië weerbaar*, this policy used local militia to offset the expenditures associated with defending the Netherlands Indies by avoiding an expansion of the professional armed forces.

For their support, representatives of the indigenous population, along with Dutch colonists and Chinese business people, could offer counsel to the colonial government, even if the Governor-General formally did not have to heed this advice. By the mid 1920s, the *priyayi* took up about 40 percent of the Volksraad, even if conservative, Dutch-dominated local councils controlled voting.[15] Such

---

[9] This approach was perhaps most evident under Alexander W.F. Idenburg in his long, almost unbroken tenure as Minister of Colonies and Governor-General of the Netherlands Indies between 1902 and 1919. Kahin, 1952, 21–22; Ma, 1957, 20–24; Preger, 1944, 13–20, 38–42, 57–61, 84–113; Robertson and Spruyt, 1967, 207–09; Surjomihardjo, 1978, 277–306; Tarling, 2001, 337–40; Taylor, 2003, 283–93; Van der Veur, 2006; Vandenbosch, 1941, 63–73, 147–57, 200–22.

[10] Abdullah, 1978, 216; Benda, 1972, 236–52; Ma, 1957, 4–7.

[11] Kahin, 1993, 14–17, 32–42; Ricklefs, 1939, 119–76.

[12] In 1905, the Royal Dutch East Indies Army, or the Koninklijk Nederlands Indisch Leger (KNIL), was 68 percent Javanese and 21 percent Ambonese, with the rest being Sundanese, Madurese, Bugis, Timorese, and Malay. Anderson, 1991, 115n–16n; Frederick, 1989, 34–80; Furnivall, 1939, 284–301; Mrázek, 1978, 15–19; Tagliacozzo, 2005, 54–58; Van den Bosch, 1941, 166–73, 343–50.

[13] Furnivall, 1939, 257–95; Kahin, 1952, 14–17; Kat Angelino and Renier, 1931, 80–97, 324–426; Robertson and Spruyt, 1967, 205–07; Tagliacozzo, 2005, 58–70; Vandenbosch, 147–57.

[14] Robertson and Spruyt, 1967, 205–07; Spruyt, 2005, 169; Vlekke, 185.

[15] The colonial government set up most of these regional and village councils between 1905 and 1930. An electorate of a little more than two thousand Dutch leaders, *priyayi* elites, and influential Chinese selected members for the Volksraad. Benda, 1958, 64–66; Dahm, 1971, 45–51, 70–71; Frederick, 1989, 1–28; Vandenbosch, 1941, 114–17, 343–44; Vlekke, 1943, 296–97, 348–49.

Creating Indonesia, 1893–1952 177

co-optation of cooperative local elites enabled The Hague to regulate access over the East Indies.

So long as Dutch interests received most of the gains from the regulation of access, The Hague was open to non-Dutch capital in certain sectors of the economy, particularly if done in conjunction with Dutch businesses. This was most evident in the oil industry, where the major player was the Anglo-Dutch concern, Royal Dutch Shell, but also included the California Texas Oil Corporation, the Standard Vacuum Oil Company, and the Japanese-owned Borneo Oil Company.[16] Nonetheless, the ability of the Dutch government to regulate access in the East Indies enabled Dutch businesses to dominate the lucrative rubber, sugar, coffee, and tea sectors to the exclusion of other powers.[17]

Britain and Access Denial in the East Indies

Key to The Hague's success in pursuing its preferences on access denial in the East Indies was the way that the other external powers active in the Far East anticipated the opportunity costs of intervention in the Indonesian archipelago. British leaders viewed the opportunity costs of intervention into Dutch-controlled areas to be high even though Britain's territories in North Borneo, Malaya, Burma, India, Australia, and New Guinea surrounded the Netherlands Indies.[18] The strategic preoccupation of leaders in London from 1893 to 1922 was the management of relative decline next to the rise of Germany, the United States, and Japan.[19] This meant that British leaders saw far greater returns from investing their limited capabilities into securing the British Isles and maintaining the empire than expanding access denial elsewhere, especially if it meant armed confrontation.

Moreover, policymakers in London did not see much advantage from actively reducing Dutch access to the East Indies. Holland was an entrenched presence in the archipelago, which London incidentally recognised in a series of Anglo-Dutch agreements.[20] Rolling back Dutch rule seemed likely to involve a significant capability investment that the British government could ill afford between the late nineteenth and early twentieth centuries. It might even throw doubt over the credibility of similar arrangements that Britain made with France and other imperial powers to stabilise mutually shared colonial frontiers.[21] Overassertiveness toward the East Indies could then turn Holland and other

---

[16] Gouda and Zaalberg, 2002, 66–82; Ricklefs, 1993, 152–53; Vlekke, 1945, 166–68.
[17] Caldwell and Utrecht, 1979, 37–51; Vlekke, 1943, 291–92.
[18] Tarling, 1993, 26–32; Vandenbosch, 1941, 378–79.
[19] Brendon, 2007, 214–88; Ferguson, 2004, 185–245; Friedberg, 1988.
[20] Fasseur, 2007, 50–66; Ricklefs, 1993, 138–47; Tagliacozzo, 2005; Tarling, 1975, 19–25.
[21] Anderson, 1991, 99; Crosby, 1945, 60–61; Crosby and Great Britain, Foreign Office, Historical Section, 1920, 3–12; Grenville, 1964; Hargreaves, 1953; Kupchan, 1994, 105–13, 210–11; Tagliacozzo, 2005; Terwiel, 2005, 211–12, 226; Wyatt, 1984, 183–89, 204–31.

178 *External Intervention and the Politics of State Formation*

major powers against Britain at a time when it did not need additional challenges to its strategic situation.

Consequently, British leaders did not challenge Dutch access regulation efforts in the East Indies. London believed that the needs of defending its empire and managing the rise of new rivals were already stretching its capabilities. Coupled with expectations about the high costs of intervention into the Indonesian archipelago, London was happy to accept the nondenial of access and even the granting of some access to British commercial interests by the Dutch.[22] This allowed British investment in the East Indies and encouraged the British government's openness toward bilateral trade between the Netherlands Indies and adjacent areas of the British Empire.[23]

Japan and the United States

Japanese and American policymakers were likewise too preoccupied with other concerns to seriously contemplate access denial in the East Indies during the late nineteenth and early twentieth centuries. Tokyo's efforts at access denial efforts between 1893 and 1922 focused on Korea, Manchuria, Taiwan, to some degree Fujian, and, by the mid 1910s, Shandong.[24] Washington committed American attentions first toward the incorporation of the Philippines and then preventing German denial of access over Europe during the Great War.[25] Both the U.S. and Imperial Japanese governments saw little gain from investing their already stretched financial, military, and political capabilities into intervention in the Netherlands Indies. Like the British, Washington and Tokyo nonetheless welcomed nonexclusion from the East Indies where possible, as seen in investments in the oil industry and efforts to develop trade with Indonesia.[26]

France, Germany, and Russia

Other powers active in the Far East from 1893 to 1922 forwent competing for access in the Netherlands Indies as such an exercise promised to draw significant capabilities away from other more pressing objectives. When not concerned with security in Europe, the French Third Republic appeared happy to concentrate its military and financial capabilities in Africa, Indochina, and, to a more limited extent, South and Southwest China. Despite its postunification and pre–Great War imperial ambitions, Wilhelmine Germany wanted to focus its energies on Europe, Africa, Shandong, and existing holdings in the Pacific instead of competing with the Netherlands over the East Indies. Russia's leaders, both Tsarist and Bolshevik, prioritised the need to safeguard against threats in Europe and then competition for access over Siberia, Manchuria, and Mongolia when it

---

[22] Vandenbosch, 1941, 352–53.
[23] Field and Institute of Pacific Relations, 1934, 448–50; Ricklefs, 1993, 152–53; Tagliacozzo, 2005.
[24] Barnhart, 1995, 21–78.
[25] Kennan, 1984, 3–73; Schoonover, 2003, 65–122.
[26] Ricklefs, 1993, 87, 152; Tagliacozzo, 2005, 139–46; Vandenbosch, 1941, 397–98.

Creating Indonesia, 1893–1952

TABLE 7.1 *Foreign Expectations about the Opportunity Costs of Intervention in Indonesia and Corresponding Approaches to Access Denial, 1893–1922*

Outside Actor	Expected Opportunity Cost	Approach to Access Denial
Holland	Moderate	Access Regulation
Britain	Prohibitively High	Concede Access
United States	Prohibitively High	Concede Access
Japan	Prohibitively High	Concede Access

came to investing capabilities. By ignoring the East Indies from the 1890s to the early 1920s, these powers effectively conceded access to Holland.

Table 7.1 summarises the pattern of foreign expectations about the opportunity costs of intervention and approaches toward access denial in Indonesia.

That other powers conceded Dutch access regulation over the East Indies meant *de facto* acceptance of the The Hague's efforts to continue and enhance colonial rule over the polity.

State Form in the Netherlands Indies under Late Colonial Rule

Absent effective challenges from other outside powers, the Dutch government was able to work through its local allies to regulate access over the East Indies from 1893 to 1922. On the ground, this spelt the persistence of a colonial state where The Hague directly oversaw foreign relations and domestic administration through the colonial government in Batavia. Dutch attempts to exert greater control through its local elites brought a rise in the Batavia government's ability to veto political developments across the East Indies.

Political Centralisation

As Dutch leaders strove to consolidate their hold over the Indonesian archipelago between the late nineteenth and early twentieth centuries, political centralisation grew markedly despite an official call for devolving government.[27] On Java, the colonial government increasingly curtailed the role of the aristocracy as Batavia-appointed Residents and Controleurs to each regional court took on greater administrative responsibilities.[28] Dutch attempts to assert a more active role in governance all but relegated traditional Javanese rulers to largely ceremonial roles by the turn of the twentieth century. Following the first decade of the twentieth century, Dutch oversight grew even in the Outer Islands, in locales such as Kalimantan, Bali, Lombok, and Aceh, which had until then experienced

[27] Benda, 1958, 34–38, 64–66; Kat Angelino and Renier, 1931, 365–426; Ong, 1978, 112–57; Vandenbosch, 1941, 74–109, 26–57.
[28] Benda, 1972, 236–52; Furnivall, 1939, 255–60; Kahin, 1952, 41–42; Kat Angelino and Renier, 1931, 71–129, 354–426; Ricklefs, 1993, 128–30.

180   *External Intervention and the Politics of State Formation*

limited foreign involvement in internal governance.[29] Concerted Dutch efforts to regulate access systematically across the Netherlands Indies ultimately brought Batavia's direct political supervision to the entire polity.[30]

Dutch dominance meant that The Hague could proscribe political developments within the Indonesian archipelago through the Batavia government and the latter's indigenous proxies. The central colonial government in Batavia was especially effective in diluting political activities that could erode Dutch rule. Moderate groups advancing greater indigenous rights, such as Budi Utomo and Sarekat Islam, saw the absorption of many of their leaders into the colonial administration.[31] Using existing political divisions, the Batavia government and its local allies too were able to encourage groups to turn on each other and isolate the more radical elements, as exemplified by the Dutch-backed expulsion of radical leftists within Sarekat Islam.[32] Moreover, with its large, locally staffed police and military, Batavia could suppress the most troublesome local groups – like the Indische Partij as well as the radical leftists in Afdeeling B (Section B) of Sarekat Islam, and the Partai Komunis Indonesia (PKI).[33]

Batavia was likewise able to override local opposition to the social and economic programmes of the Ethical Policy between 1893 and 1922. Just as the colonial government extended infrastructure, some basic education, and rudimentary healthcare across Indonesia, sometimes in face of local resistance, it also pushed emigration from Java to the Outer Islands and forcible village amalgamation.[34] In the process, the colonial government extended direct oversight into the village level through the appointment of local Residents and Controleurs to more areas whilst increasing the incomes – and loyalties – of village headmen.[35] This was despite the growth in corruption, poverty, and crime resulting from the rapid social displacement associated with these

[29] Abdullah, 1978, 211–20; Owen, 2005, 130–36; Reid, 1969; Ricklefs, 1993, 131–47; Tagliacozzo, 2005, 27–106; van den Doel, 1994, 62–68.
[30] Houben, 1994, 191–210; Spruyt, 2005, 168–69; Taylor, 2003, 238–78; Vlekke, 1943, 348, 1945, 168–74.
[31] Dahm, 1971, 45–51; Nagazumi, 1972, 51–150; Report of the Meeting of the Partij Sarekat Islam Held on 26 January 1928, to Commemorate Its Fifteen Years of Existence, 1977, 257–61; Ricklefs, 1993, 163–73; Tjokroaminoto, 1977, 255–57; Vandenbosch, 1941, 315–23.
[32] Sarekat Islam began as a diffuse organisation that contained a central Sarekat Islam associated with other regional organisations functioning under the same name. It was only after infighting in the late 1910s and early 1920s, particularly with leftist elements in the organisation, that sustained attempts to establish "party discipline" and greater centralisation emerged. Benda and Castles, 1972, 269–301; Benda, 1958, 70–71; McVey, 1965, 76–154; Shiraishi, 1990, 216–48; van Dijk, 1994.
[33] Benda and Castles, 1972, 269–301; Douwes Dekker, 1977, 228–27; Frederick, 1989, 5–6; Kahin, 1952, 60–77; Mangoenkoesoemo, 1977, 234–35; Poeze, 1994, 229–32; Robertson and Spruyt, 1967, 209–10; Shiraishi, 1990, 113–16, 203–15, 309–38; Soerjaningrat, 1977, 232–34; Van der Veur, 2006, 183–236, 379–438.
[34] Field and Institute of Pacific Relations, 1934, 34–35; Preger, 1944, 38–42, 57–61, 80–113; Surjomihardjo, 1978, 277–306; Tarling, 2001, 337–40.
[35] Furnivall, 1939, 257–95; Kahin, 1952, 14–17; Kartodirdjo, 1978, 237–46; Kat Angelino and Renier, 1931, 258–644; Ricklefs, 1993, 156.

Creating Indonesia, 1893–1952　　　　　　　　　　　　　　　　　181

policies.[36] The Dutch ability to overcome dissent fuelled the rise of resource extraction industries and plantation agriculture along with food shortages and the rise of a colonial economy prone to commodity price fluctuations.[37]

Territorial Exclusivity

Dutch attempts to regulate access during the late nineteenth and early twentieth centuries brought a high degree of territorial exclusivity to the Netherlands Indies. As part of their access regulation efforts, Dutch leaders in The Hague had delegated oversight of the Netherlands Indies to the colonial government in Batavia since the early nineteenth century.[38] Together with The Hague, the Batavia administration ensured that no other foreign actor would be responsible for governance within the East Indies. This translated into efforts to take charge of government administration, work with reliable local partners, and seal formal arrangements with potential foreign rivals, as in the instances of the 1824 and 1871 Anglo-Dutch Treaties.[39] Consequently, Holland largely succeeded in relegating the role of other governments to facilitating commercial investment and trade for their own nationals and corporations under Dutch colonial auspices.[40]

External Autonomy

External relations for the Netherlands Indies also remained under the sole purview of The Hague, through the Ministry of Colonies and the colonial government in Batavia. Dutch officials reporting to The Hague were responsible for all negotiations with other foreign powers relating to the Netherlands Indies, whilst policies, treaties, agreements, and wars entered into by The Hague applied to the Dutch East Indies.[41] Indonesia, for instance, underwent increased taxation and mobilisation to help sustain Holland's high-priced armed neutrality during World War I at the expense of welfare, economic development, and personal incomes.[42] Acehnese efforts to acquire American, Italian, and Japanese support between 1873 and 1905 was the last time an indigenous government in the East Indies attempted to exercise an independent foreign policy until 1945. Not only

---

[36] Ma, 1957, 20–24; Preger, 1944, 84–113; Ricklefs, 1993, 156.

[37] Notably, the Netherlands Indies produced about half the world's rubber supply by 1930. Ma, 1957, 20–24; Owen, 2005, 184–86; Ricklefs, 1993, 152–55.

[38] Benda, 1972, 83–92; Benda, 1958, 9–99; Fasseur, 2007, 50–66; Kat Angelino and Renier, 1931, 130–93; Spruyt, 2005, 167–68; Vandenbosch, 1941, 26–46, 76–97, 74–109; Vlekke, 1943, 348; Wolters, 1994, 173–87.

[39] In addition to settling a number of outstanding issues in Anglo-Dutch relations in Europe, Africa, and Asia, the 1824 London Treaty, 1871 Treaty of Sumatra, as well as associated agreements fixed the boundaries of jurisdiction between the Netherlands Indies and British holdings in Malaya and North Borneo. The treaties also permitted trade between Dutch- and British-dominated territories in Southeast Asia. Fasseur, 2007, 50–66; Ricklefs, 1993, 138–47; Tagliacozzo, 2005, 1–181; Tarling, 1975, 19–25.

[40] Field and Institute of Pacific Relations, 1934, 448–50; Ricklefs, 1993, 152–53; Tagliacozzo, 2005.

[41] Vandenbosch, 1941, 74–109, 293–301; Vlekke, 1943, 298–301, 348.

[42] Booth, 1990, 217–29.

182 *External Intervention and the Politics of State Formation*

did the other powers ignore Aceh, these attempts at diplomacy invigorated Dutch suppression efforts, leading to full Dutch dominance over the foreign relations until World War II.[43]

Clearly, Dutch leaders managed to consolidate the colonial state in the Netherlands Indies between 1893 and 1922. In conjunction with cooperative local elites, The Hague and the colonial government in Batavia managed to sustain high levels of political centralisation and territorial exclusivity alongside a low degree of external autonomy. Dutch success in this regard came from the ineffectiveness of resistance by indigenous groups. This in turn rested on the fact that neither major power challenges to Dutch authority nor serious outside support for domestic opponents of Dutch rule existed during this period. As a result, Dutch leaders experienced few restraints when shaping the institutions of governance, rule, and political authority in the East Indies in accordance with their cost considerations.

RISING OPPORTUNITY COSTS AND A SOVEREIGN INDONESIA, 1923–1952

State form in the East Indies between 1923 and 1952 continued to approximate the colonial state until the end of World War II. It was only during the mid 1940s that the Indonesian polity began to move definitively toward sovereign statehood, adding a high level of external autonomy to already significant territorial exclusivity and political centralisation. Behind this shift were the increasingly high opportunity cost expectations that those external powers with an interest in access denial over the East Indies associated with intervention. This drove the relevant outside actors to support a takeover of the polity by a local political actor that could guarantee nonprivileged access to all foreign powers.

External Intervention under Rising Cost Expectations

The period from the early 1920s to the early 1950s saw a rise in the perceived opportunity costs of intervention into the Indonesian archipelago amongst the relevant foreign powers. From the Great Depression and World War II to postwar rebuilding and the strains of the early Cold War, there were growing demands on the capacities of the outside actors most able to compete for access in the East Indies. Most of the alternative options for committing capabilities even seemed to offer greater net returns than competing for full access denial in what was to become Indonesia. As a result, these foreign powers were unwilling to sink more capabilities into the East Indies than were adequate to safeguard equal opportunities for access relative to other outside actors.

[43] Owen, 2005, 132; Reid, 2005, 2006.

Creating Indonesia, 1893–1952   183

The Growth of Opportunity Costs and Dutch Acceptance of Nonprivileged Access

From 1923 to 1952, Dutch leaders continued to foresee substantial benefits from sustained securing of access over the East Indies. A reason for the persistence of this view despite the difficulties associated with intervention was the expectation that the wealth of the Indies could help bail the metropole out of its financial troubles. Despite the fall in trade levies and taxes that led to a revenue crisis for the Batavia colonial government during the Depression, preferential trading arrangements allowed the East Indies to absorb exports from Holland.[44] As a proportion of Netherlands Indies imports from 1934 to 1938, Dutch products grew from 13 percent to 22 percent, or from less than 8 percent of Holland's exports to just below 12 percent.[45]

Even in the wake of World War II, the expected gains from denying access to rivals over the East Indies relative to other objectives remained high for Dutch leaders. Between the German occupation of Holland in May 1940 and Japan's takeover of the East Indies in March 1942, the Netherlands Indies became the only substantial territory controlled by the Dutch exile government in London. Continuing to secure the archipelago could signal solidarity with the Allies as well as a contribution to the Allied defence of the Far East, especially in terms of denying vital war material, notably oil and rubber, to an increasingly bellicose Japan.[46] In the postwar era, The Hague saw securing access in the archipelago as an economic foundation for rebuilding Holland, as was the case after the Napoleonic Wars.[47] What ended Dutch involvement was American conditioning of Marshall Aid – crucial for Dutch reconstruction – on The Hague's acceptance of Indonesian independence, which evaporated expected net gains from securing access.[48]

For their part, Dutch officials and policymakers recognised the heavy investment in capabilities necessary to safeguard access across the Netherlands Indies from 1923 on, given Holland's broader economic and security concerns. The structural problems of a fairly small metropole ruling over a vast population and territory became more acute as the East Indies populace grew, rising from 48.3 million in 1920 to 59.1 million in 1930 and 70 million in 1939.[49] Lording over

---

[44] Booth, 1990a, 228–29, 1990b, 279–93; Den Baker and Huitker, 1990, 190–93; Furnivall, 1939, 428–45; Vandenbosch, 1941, 293–309; Vlekke, 1943, 363–67.

[45] Den Baker and Huitker, 1990, 18; Field and Institute of Pacific Relations, 1934, 448–51; Ricklefs, 1993, 187; Vandenbosch, 1941, 235–43.

[46] Barnhart, 1987, 166, 207–24; Ford, 1996, 16–27; Taylor, 2003, 213–313.

[47] Booth, 1990, 210–17; Ricklefs, 1993, 119–24, 212–13; Spruyt, 2005, 148–66; van Niel, 1990, 67–89; Vandenbosch, 1941, 293–309.

[48] From the end of World War II to the end of Dutch efforts to recolonialise the East Indies, the U.S. government provided Holland with about US$979 million in aid. This included US$298 million in Marshall Plan aid to the Netherlands, US$61 million in Marshall Plan aid for the East Indies, US $130 million for the acquisition of U.S. war surpluses, US$190 million in supplies, and US$300 million in Export-Import Bank credits. Dahm, 1971, 136–42; Gouda and Zaalberg, 2002, 290–92; Kahin, 1977, 355–58; Ricklefs, 1993, 230–32; Spruyt, 2005, 173–75.

[49] Colbert, 1977, 92; Kahin and Kahin, 1995, 20; Ricklefs, 1993, 155, 161; Vandenbosch, 1941, 223–24.

184   *External Intervention and the Politics of State Formation*

Indonesia were roughly 240,000 Dutch and Dutch Eurasians in the East Indies and 7.5 million or so Dutchmen in the Netherlands.[50] Further dampening The Hague's expected ability to commit capabilities to secure access in the East Indies were the economic strain of the Great Depression and the Nazi threat that culminated in the German occupation of Holland in May 1940.[51] Anticipated burdens on Dutch government capabilities continued to expand after World War II given the demands of reconstruction.

Still, the promise of large gains made a seemingly hefty commitment of capabilities to secure access seem worthwhile for The Hague until the late 1940s. This suggests that Dutch leaders' expected costs of intervention in the East Indies remained moderate to that point. Even as anticipated gains from securing access across the Netherlands Indies rose under the pressures of the Great Depression, the outbreak of World War II, and postwar rebuilding, The Hague was unwilling to seek complete access denial.[52] Dutch leaders understood that a highly extensive and intrusive role in Indonesia would likely erase the gains from access denial given the capability limitations they faced. Nevertheless, in raising the expected returns from access denial in the East Indies, events between 1923 and the end of the 1940s temporarily reduced official views on the costs of intervention in the territory.[53] That was until the American linking of Dutch withdrawal from Indonesia to Marshall Plan aid in 1949 made any net returns from intervention look unattainable.[54]

Access Regulation under Pressure

Following from the lowered but still moderate expected opportunity costs of intervention between 1923 and 1942, The Hague continued to pursue regulation of access over the Indonesian archipelago. Even as attempts to foster active indigenous collaboration and raise Batavia's oversight in access occurred, there was a simultaneous and systematic reduction of local voice opportunities in administrative affairs.[55] Up until the Japanese occupation, The Hague curtailed the activities of the Volksraad and local councils and increasingly repressed those agitating against Batavia.[56] The expected gains from committing capabilities into securing access outweighed the burdens of pursuing such action amidst the Great Depression and rising tensions in Europe.

Indicative of Dutch views about the moderate opportunity costs of intervention in the Indonesian archipelago after World War II was The Hague's resolve in trying to preserve access regulation despite the burdens of postwar rebuilding.

---

[50] Maddison, 1990, 322–25; Ricklefs, 1993, 155.
[51] Vandenbosch, 1941, 380–90.
[52] Kahin, 1952, 99–100, 345–50, 405–06, 432; Wiarda, 2007, 130–31.
[53] Caldwell and Utrecht, 1979, 81–82; Colbert, 1977, 39–41, 92; Ford, 1996, 13–25; Kahin and Kahin, 1995, 20; Spruyt, 2005, 11–38, 146–75.
[54] Such net returns can include ideological commitments to imperialism, although they are hard to measure. Gouda and Zaalberg, 2002, 290–92; Kahin, 1997, 355–58; Ricklefs, 1993, 230–32.
[55] Benda, 1972e, 236–52; Ricklefs, 1993, 181–95.
[56] Ricklefs, 1993, 188–95.

Creating Indonesia, 1893–1952

So long as it seemed that the East Indies could help fuel Holland's reconstruction, Dutch leaders worked with pliant indigenous groups to forcibly reinstitute access regulation over Republican resistance between 1945 and 1949.[57] Dutch efforts in this respect remained constant despite the substantial problems Republican guerrilla and scorched earth tactics created for Holland's reconquest. Until the threat of losing Marshall Plan aid raised the opportunity costs of intervention over most of the archipelago to high levels in 1949, Dutch attempts to regulate access generally stayed consistent whether liberals or conservatives ran East Indies policy.[58] In places where concerted American-led opposition was absent, The Hague's expected costs of intervention remained moderate and Dutch access regulation persisted past 1952, as was the case with continued colonial rule over West New Guinea.[59]

Dutch government efforts to regulate access to the Netherlands Indies based on expectations about the moderate costs of intervention extended also to the management of the territory's external affairs. Increased Indonesian absorption of Dutch products during the Depression was a result of increased protectionist measures that reduced imports from elsewhere. Japan, the top exporter to the East Indies in the 1930s, saw its exports fall from a high of 32.5 percent of imports into the Netherlands Indies in 1934 to 25.4 percent in 1936 and 14.4 percent in 1938.[60] Even after Holland's fall to the Nazis, the government-in-exile continued access regulation over the archipelago to the extent of reducing oil, rubber, and tin exports to Japan in July 1941 despite Tokyo's efforts to acquire Dutch collaboration.[61] In not accommodating Tokyo, the exiled Dutch leadership helped precipitate the confrontation between Japan and Netherlands forces

---

[57] To engage in its "police actions" against the Republican forces, the Dutch government raised and maintained a 100,000-strong army in spite of trying postwar conditions in Holland. Gouda and Zaalberg, 2002, 287–91; Kahin, 1952, 142–46, 213–55, 332–445, 2003, 27–28; Ricklefs, 1993, 215–31; Spruyt, 2005, 148–66.

[58] Between 1926 and 1949, liberal supporters of the Ethical Policy like Governor-General Andries C.D. de Graeff as well as conservative leaders such as Governors-General Bonifacius C. de Jonge, Alidius W.L. Tjarda van Starkenborgh Stachouwer, Hubertus J. van Mook, and Minister of Colonies Hendrikus Colijn were all staunchly behind efforts to make Dutch regulation of access in the East Indies more robust. Kahin 1952, 99–100, 142–46, 213–19, 235–54, 332–445, 1977, 355–58, 2003, 23–25; Ricklefs, 1993, 185–91, 216–32; Spruyt, 2005, 148–75.

[59] Colbert, 1997, 72, 186–91; Kahin and Kahin, 1995, 34–45; Ricklefs, 1993, 232–43; Tarling, 2005, 26–44, 131–48; Taylor, 2003, 312–14, 350–52.

[60] Japan's imports to the Dutch East Indies exceeded Dutch imports between 1931 and 1938. Aziz, 1955, 99–120; Booth, 1990, 279; Field and Institute of Pacific Relations, 1934, 448–51; Indonesia, and Netherlands, Regeeringsvoorlichtingsdienst, 1942, 36–45; Sato, 1994, 4–5; Vandenbosch, 1941, 235–43, 398–411; Vlekke, 1943, 363–65.

[61] By 1940, Tokyo was pressuring Dutch leaders first in The Hague and later Batavia to open bases to Japanese forces, as was the case in Vichy French-held Indochina, and to free the exports of raw materials, especially oil and rubber, to Japan. Tokyo sent a high-level mission led by former Foreign Minister Yoshizawa Kenkichi in early 1941 to secure Dutch cooperation on these issues in exchange for Japanese support for continued Netherlands rule over the Indonesian archipelago. Furnivall, 1939, 333–34; Ricklefs, 1993, 194–200; Van der Veur, 2006, 539–43; Wilkins, 1973, 366–67.

186   *External Intervention and the Politics of State Formation*

in the only major territory they controlled.[62] Unlike during the Indonesian Revolution, however, defeat to Japan represented Dutch capability constraints and failures in ability more than shifts in opportunity cost considerations.

Tokyo's Imperial Gamble and Changing Japanese Opportunity Cost Expectations

Japanese leaders from 1923 to 1945 saw their expected opportunity costs of intervention in the East Indies fall from prohibitively high to moderate levels. This variation lay in part with relatively constant perceptions about the substantial capability investments necessary to compete for access over the Netherlands Indies, which was likely to take away from efforts to safeguard access in China. After all, leaders in Tokyo recognised the structural problems associated with the vastness of the Indonesian archipelago, its sizeable population, and distance from the Home Islands.[63] This was despite the fact Japan possessed greater military, financial, administrative, and manpower capabilities than the Netherlands, and was substantially closer to the East Indies.

What changed for leaders in Tokyo toward the mid twentieth century were expectations of gain from the East Indies. Until the mid 1930s, Japan's leaders seemed satisfied with the gains from investing in and trading with the Netherlands Indies.[64] As the war in China unfolded and fears of the Soviets as well as Western powers grew with the militarist ascendancy in Tokyo, Japanese leaders began to see the East Indies, along with the rest of Southeast Asia, as offering crucial war material and a forward strategic position vital to averting defeat.[65] Such beliefs intensified with the imposition of the U.S. trade embargo on Japan in 1941. With defeat in 1945 and U.S. occupation through 1952, however, Tokyo was no longer in a position to compete for access over the Dutch East Indies.

As its expectations about the opportunity costs of intervention in the East Indies fluctuated between prohibitive, moderate, and high levels, the Japanese government accordingly ceded access, pursued access regulation, and sought nonprivileged access. Tokyo, for example, did not challenge protectionist measures put in place over the East Indies by the Dutch during the 1930s, even though they led to significant declines in Japanese exports to the archipelago.[66] As the anticipated opportunity costs of intervention fell to moderate levels in the early 1940s, Tokyo offered political, organisational, and military support to local political groups willing to support Japanese access regulation efforts over the

---

[62] Declaration of the Netherlands Government in Exile in London, 27 January 1942, 149, Ford, 1996, 13–25; Robertson and Spruyt, 1967, 211; Tarling, 2001, 66–68; Vlekke, 1945, 193–201.

[63] Barnhart, 1987, 19, 44–45, 146–75, 191–224, 245, 1995, 127–65.

[64] Schneider, 1998, 161–82; Toru, 1977, 321–26; Vlekke, 1945, 189–202.

[65] Benda, 1972; Benda, Irikura, and Kishi, 1965, 1–52; Goto, 1986; Iriye, 1967, 201, 308, 372; Ishikawa, 1995, 406–530; Kinhide, 1973, 597–98; Kupchan, 1994, 334–55; Sadao, 1973, 244–54; Sato, 1994, 5–80; Snyder, 1991, 112–52; Tarling, 2001, 39–83, 125–46, 174–92, 219–31; Vickers, 2005, 88–90; Vlekke, 1943, 363–65, 375–76; Wilkins, 1973, 366–67.

[66] Field and Institute of Pacific Relations, 1934, 448–51; Vandenbosch, 1941, 398–411.

Creating Indonesia, 1893–1952 187

East Indies.[67] Between its defeat in 1945 and 1952, Japan was under American occupation and unable to seek access denial over the East Indies.

America's Search for Nonprivileged Access and Washington's Anticipation of Rising Net Gains

For the U.S. government, the perceived opportunity costs of intervention in the East Indies fell from prohibitively high levels to high between 1923 and 1952. Until the late 1940s, the strength of isolationist sentiments and then the strain of the Great Depression, fighting World War II, and rebuilding Europe made the diversion of capabilities toward securing access in the East Indies seem unnecessary.[68] Given the perceived unimportance of the East Indies next to the need for a strong, noncommunist Holland, the Truman administration, for all its anticolonial rhetoric, began the postwar era complicit in Dutch recolonisation efforts.[69] It was only with the intensification of the early Cold War in the late 1940s that expectations about the potential gains from increased involvement in the Indonesian archipelago grew. At this time, a perceived need in Washington to prevent rising communist influence in Southeast Asia increased the importance of access denial in the East Indies, even if this goal remained secondary next to objectives in Europe.[70]

Prioritising the rebuilding of allies and industrial bases in Europe and Japan in the face of domestic opposition meant that Washington would commit only limited capabilities toward securing access in the East Indies. Undoubtedly a perceived rise in communist threats across Asia, growing Soviet assertiveness in Europe, and the consolidation of noncommunist Holland in the late 1940s raised the value of securing access over the East Indies in Washington.[71]

---

[67] Benda, 1958, 103–94; Benda and Larkin, 1967, 219–24; Iwatake, 1989, 254–74; Toru, 1977, 324–26; Vlekke, 1945, 194–95.

[68] Cohen, 1973, 457; Colbert, 1977, 27–51, 86–92; Ford, 1996, 18–49; Gouda and Zaalberg, 2002, 66–118; Graebner, 1973, 44–51; Iriye, 1967, 201; Kahin, 345–49, 51–52; Kahin and Kahin, 1995, 25, 29–31; Kennan, 1993, 74–90; Lowe, 1997, 173–76; Mrázek, 1978, 61–62; Weigley, 1973, 181–87.

[69] Early U.S. and U.S.-backed United Nations efforts at brokering a Dutch-Indonesian truce led to the 1948 Renville Agreement. The agreement favoured the Dutch in calling for the withdrawal of Republican forces from Dutch-held territory and a lifting of the Dutch blockade on Republican-held areas, after which there would be a plebiscite in Dutch-controlled areas on whether to be under Dutch or Republican rule. The plebiscite in never took place, and Washington did not press The Hague. The United Nations Security Council then established the Committee of Good Offices to mediate between the Dutch and Indonesian Republican governments, as well as to oversee any agreements that ensued from negotiations. Colbert, 1977, 27–53, 70–71, 86–92; Kahin, 1952, 146, 213–29, 254–55, 1977, 355–58, 2003, 19–32; Kahin and Kahin, 1995, 29–31; Ma, 1957, 237–47; Mrázek, 1978, 62–75; Ricklefs, 1993, 225–31; Roadnight, 2002, 26–77; Tarling, 1998, 160–73, 211–36, 280–95.

[70] Colbert, 1977, 137–43; Gouda and Zaalberg, 2002, 25–65, 131–64, 190–236, 266–304; Iriye, 1977, 378–405; LaFeber, 1977, 43–62; McMahon, 2006, 77–78; Nagai, 1977, 15–38; Tadashi, 1977, 66–85; Thayer, 1953; Toru, 1977, 329–30; Yamamoto, 1977, 408–24.

[71] 1948 and 1949 brought the Berlin Blockade, the Soviet-instigated communist coup in Czechoslovakia, the Communist victory in China, as well as Communist insurrections in

188 External Intervention and the Politics of State Formation

However, the Truman administration's focus on Western Europe and Japan after World War II and in the early Cold War meant that it was willing to commit only to the more limited goal of denying privileged access to the communist Soviets and Chinese elsewhere.[72] This increased the attractiveness of creating a sovereign state in Indonesia that could help limit communist influence in the archipelago without substantially diverting American capabilities destined for other places.

Following from the shifts in their expected opportunity costs of intervention in the East Indies from prohibitively high to high, U.S. leaders moved from minimal involvement to supporting a centralised, autonomous, and territorially exclusive Indonesian state. Rather than just permitting U.S. corporations to invest in and trade with the archipelago, as was the situation before World War II, Washington began to throw diplomatic and political weight behind the Republican cause in the late 1940s.[73] In particular, U.S. assistance spiked after the Indonesian Republicans suppressed the 1948 Communist uprising within their ranks.[74] Washington even attempted to broker settlements between the Dutch and Indonesians, finally threatening cut off Marshall Plan aid to The Hague in 1949 if it did not accept Republican rule over most of the archipelago.[75] To further ensure the denial of privileged access to the East Indies by the communists without committing capabilities meant for Europe and Japan, Washington provided the fledgling Indonesian Republic with limited economic and military assistance after 1949.[76]

Britain and the East Indies

British leaders also perceived a fall in the costs of intervention in the East Indies from prohibitively high levels to high 1923 and 1952. The growing need to invest capabilities into the defence of Britain and the empire as well as to deal with the effects of the Great Depression meant that British leaders consistently

---

Malaya, Burma, and the Philippines. These events put pressure on the U.S. government to resist communism whilst concentrating its capabilities on the rebuilding of Europe and Japan. Kahin 1977, 349–50, 2003, 122–25; Kahin and Kahin, 1995, 29–31; Mrázek, 1978, 91–103; Prados, 2006, 40–41; Roadnight, 2002, 1–77.

[72] Colbert, 1977, 81–90, 144–51; Vickers, 2005, 109.

[73] Colbert, 1977, 72, 89–92, 137–74, 186–91; Gouda and Zaalberg, 2002, 25–65, 394–404; McMahon, 2006, 77–78; Ricklefs, 1993, 225–31; Spector, 2007, 274; Wilkins, 1973, 374.

[74] The Madiun Rebellion is another name for this event. Gouda and Zaalberg, 2002, 266–99; Kahin, 1977, 256–331, 2003, 19–32, 54–62; Kahin and Kahin, 1995, 31–33; Ma, 1957, 251–78; Mrázek, 1978, 64–68, 91–122; Reid, 1974, 59–102, 121–47; Roadnight, 2002, 55–102; Robertson and Spruyt, 1967, 232–34; Swift, 1989; Yahuda, 1996, 32.

[75] The exception in U.S. calls for the incorporation of the Netherlands Indies into the Indonesian Republic was West New Guinea, which remained the Dutch colony of Netherlands New Guinea until 1962. Drakeley, 2005, 80–81, 99; Kahin, 1977, 355–58; Spruyt, 2005, 173–75; Tarling, 2005, 26–44, 131–48; Taylor, 2003, 336, 350–52.

[76] Caldwell and Utrecht, 1979, 79–80; Ricklefs, 1993, 225–31.

Creating Indonesia, 1893–1952   189

saw little net gain from trying to secure access over the East Indies until the mid 1940s.[77] Even with the mounting Japanese threat to Southeast Asia, London committed only a minimum of military forces to defend Malaya and the holdings of its Dutch ally in the Indonesian archipelago.[78] Nevertheless, the need for at least nonprivileged access in less-developed parts of the world given rising communist threats and British imperial retreat in the late 1940s brought a limited willingness in London to invest some capabilities in the East Indies.[79] After engaging in a brief, limited military operation to recover and stabilise the archipelago following the Japanese surrender, the Attlee cabinet ultimately pushed Holland to accommodate the Indonesian Republicans.[80]

The Soviet Union and Limited Role in the East Indies

Soviet involvement in the East Indies from 1923 to 1952 was highly limited as Moscow saw the opportunity costs of intervention in the archipelago to be prohibitively high. Given Soviet leaders' primary focus on threats in Europe and their secondary concerns with Japanese expansion in Manchuria and China through the mid 1940s, securing access in the far-off Indonesian archipelago did not feature highly in Moscow.[81] The priority of facing down the American-led threat in Europe immediately after World War II again placed peripheral areas like the East Indies on the strategic backburner.[82] Despite calls for global revolution, the Soviet Union restricted access denial efforts in the archipelago, with Moscow only committing capabilities to train small numbers of revolutionaries from the East Indies and giving refuge to exiled leftist leaders.

Table 7.2 highlights the opportunity cost expectations and the approaches taken to securing access by the most active foreign actors in Indonesia between 1923 and 1952. The fact that external powers in a position to intervene either sought nonprivileged access actively or conceded over access denial by the late

---

[77] Brendon, 2007, 289–480; Ferguson, 2004, 245–302; Kennedy, 2002; Kimball, 1969, 80–81; Ricklefs, 1993, 195–200, 228–31; Tarling, 1998, 40–43.

[78] Bayly and Harper, 2007, 158–89; Colbert, 1977, 63–67; Ford, 1996, 18–49; Kahin, 1952, 101; Kahin and Kahin, 1995, 25–27; Lowe, 1981, 173–80; Tarling, 1993, 108–10, 130–58.

[79] The British government had to deal with a communist insurgency in its colonies in Malaya and Singapore starting in 1948. Malayan rubber and tin were key to earning the foreign exchange that helped keep the British postwar economy afloat, while Singapore allowed the British to extend its trade and naval presence in the Far East. A communist Indonesia could seriously complicate London's efforts to maintain its position in Malaya and Singapore. Anderson, 1972, 131–39; Dennis, 1987; Kahin, 19, 39–40; Toru, 1977, 326–36; Watt, 1977, 89–118.

[80] Postwar British military operations in the East Indies included several large-scale skirmishes with Indonesian Republican forces. The Battle of Surabaya led to more than 6,000 Indonesian civilian casualties. The British were also responsible for the 1946 Linggajati Agreement, the first internationally backed attempt at a settlement between the Dutch and Indonesian Republicans. Kahin, 1952, 141–46, 1977, 338–40; McMillan, 2005; Ricklefs, 1993, 216–26; Spector, 2007, 169–214; Tarling, 1998, 87–105, 160–73; Tarling, 1993, 192–93.

[81] McVey, 1965, 34–104, 155–256, 336–46; Tanigawa, 1977, 362–76.

[82] Colbert, 1977, 81–86, 192–96; Kahin, 1977, 342–45, 2003, 39–40.

190 *External Intervention and the Politics of State Formation*

TABLE 7.2 *Convergent Foreign Expectations about the High Opportunity Costs of Intervention in Indonesia and Corresponding Approaches to Access Denial, 1923–1952*

Outside Actor	Expected Opportunity Cost	Approach to Access Denial
Holland	Until 1949, Moderate 1949 and after, High	Access Regulation Nonprivileged Access
Britain	Until 1945, Prohibitively High 1945 and after, High	Concede Access Nonprivileged Access
United States	Until 1945, Prohibitively High 1945 and after, High	Concede Access Nonprivileged Access
Japan	Until 1941, Prohibitively High 1941–1945, Moderate 1945–1952, under Occupation	Concede Access Access Regulation Concede Access
Soviet Union	Prohibitively High	Concede Access

1940s spelt, in effect, convergent outside support for the establishment of sovereign statehood in the East Indies.

External Intervention and the Rise of the Indonesian Republic

Successful Dutch and Japanese efforts to regulate access over the East Indies with cooperative local actors gave rise to high degrees of territorial exclusivity and political centralisation coupled with low external autonomy until 1945. Subsequent shared perceptions amongst outside actors about the high opportunity costs of intervention in the Indonesian archipelago led to wide support for high external autonomy to go along with already substantial political centralisation and territorial exclusivity. Consequently, the archipelago moved away from colonial statehood and toward sovereignty.

State Form in the Interwar Years

POLITICAL CENTRALISATION   Without serious external opposition to Dutch access regulation efforts, the Netherlands Indies continued as a colonial state between 1923 and 1942. During this time, the East Indies saw growing political centralisation matched with a substantial degree of territorial exclusivity and low external autonomy. Growing Dutch restrictions on the Volksraad and efforts to extend direct administration to villages spelt a rise in Batavia's ability to veto developments across the East Indies, a trend underscored by increasing control over political activity.[83]

[83] Frederick, 1989, 1–28; Owen, 2005, 127–36; Ricklefs, 1993, 188–95; Spruyt, 2005, 168–69; Vickers, 2005, 80.

Creating Indonesia, 1893–1952 191

Faced with growing suppression, all local groups – from the nationalist Partai Nasional Indonesia (PNI) and Partindo, to the left-leaning Pendidikan Nasional Indonesia and Partai Sosialis, PKI, the Islamic-oriented Partai Sarekat Islam Indonesia, and local nobles – saw their ability to shape politics decline.[84] When the PKI attempted to launch a colony-wide revolt in 1926, the Dutch effectively suppressed resistance within weeks. Colonial authorities arrested more than 13,000 people following that abortive rebellion, including most of the PKI's top leadership.[85] Enforcing political centralisation was the sizeable number of Javanese, Madurese, Ambonese, and other locals absorbed into the colonial administration, intelligence services, police, and military.

EXTERNAL AUTONOMY AND TERRITORIAL EXCLUSIVITY   The lack of external resistance to The Hague's access regulation efforts further permitted the Dutch government to impress a low degree of external autonomy and high levels of territorial exclusivity over the East Indies until the 1942 Japanese takeover.[86] Under direction from The Hague, the Dutch East Indies substituted cheaper Japanese imports for dearer Dutch imports during the Depression.[87] Even after its exile to London in 1940, the Dutch government was able to work with Batavia to reject Japanese demands for the use of military bases in the Netherlands Indies and even attempt to resist invasion from much stronger Japanese forces.[88] With its local partners, the colonial government in Batavia continued to be responsible for domestic governance in the Netherlands Indies, limiting any foreign relationship with the archipelago, however substantial, to commercial activity.[89]

Institutions of Governance and the Japanese Interregnum

Japanese attempts to regulate access over the East Indies – often following earlier Dutch efforts – brought the continued rise of political centralisation whilst territorial exclusivity and external autonomy respectively remained at high and low levels. Still, Tokyo's ability to perpetuate the colonial state in the East Indies resulted from the ultimate ineffectiveness of Dutch and Allied resistance to Japanese expansion.[90] To occupy and administer Indonesia, the Japanese

---

[84] The Dutch either disbanded these groups or placed significant restrictions on their activities. Often, the Batavia government arrested and exiled the leaders of these movements, including Sukarno, Mohammad Hatta, Sutan Sjahrir, and Amir Sjarifuddin. Benda, 1977, 61–99; Kediri, 1977, 288–91; McVey, 1965, 343–46; Poeze, 1994, 232–42.

[85] Benda, 1958, 23–36; Benda and McVey, 1977, 284–87; Caldwell and Utrecht, 1979, 54–60; Kahin, 1995, 60–63, 77–100; McVey, 1965, 343–46; Poeze, 1994, 232–42.

[86] van Asbeck, 1940, 252–70; Vandenbosch, 1941, 76–109, 150–68, 341–42, 405–11.

[87] Aziz, 1955, 106–40; Ricklefs, 1993, 187; Vlekke, 1943, 190–222.

[88] Indonesia, 1985, 149; Iwatake, 1989, 19–21; Kahin and Kahin, 1995, 22; Ma, 1957, 73–76; Ricklefs, 1993, 194–95; Vlekke, 1943, 381–92.

[89] Batavia even succeeded in raising taxes in the East Indies to help fund the London-based Dutch government-in-exile between 1940 and 1941. Frederick, 1989, 81–88; Vandenbosch, 1941, 86–109; Vlekke, 197.

[90] Bastin and Benda, 1968, 124; Ford, 1996, 13–49; Ricklefs, 1993, 195–201; Tarling, 2001, 85–95, 174–92, 226–31; Vlekke, 1943, 393–408, 1945, 211–22.

192   *External Intervention and the Politics of State Formation*

military sponsored indigenous groups dissatisfied or marginalised under Dutch colonial rule, such as Minangkabau and Acehnese *ulamas* as well as political parties like Gerindo.[91] The Japanese military also attempted to co-opt indigenous groups previously aligned with the Dutch, including Javanese *priyayi*, East Sumatran *rajas*, Minangkabau *penghulus*, and Acehnese *uleëbalangs*.[92] Through these local allies, the Japanese administration tried to extend and consolidate its reach into the villages in order to reshape the economy and mobilise the populace in support of Japan's war effort.[93]

POLITICAL CENTRALISATION   To centralise rule over the East Indies, Tokyo attempted to actively harness Indonesian nationalism. This included recruiting nationalist figures like Sukarno and Hatta as well as traditional and Islamic leaders like Ki Hadjar Dewantara and Kyai Haji Mas Mansur, respectively.[94] Like the Dutch before them, Japanese leaders tried to mobilise and penetrate the populace through mass organisations.

Japanese-sponsored organisations included the Islamic-oriented Majlis Syuro Muslimin Indonesia (Consultative Council of Indonesian Muslims, Masyumi) as well as the secular nationalist Pusat Tenaga Rakyat (Centre of People's Power, Putera) and its successor, the Jawa Hokokai (Java Service Association) amongst others.[95] The Japanese military also helped to establish and train local armed forces, including a regular military, the Pembela Tanah Air (Protectors of the Fatherland, PETA), and a semimilitary youth corps.[96] Japan's military too sponsored the creation and maintenance of vigilante corps and guerrilla groups under Masyumi and Jawa Hokokai, as well as an indigenous auxiliary force attached to the Imperial Army and Navy, the Heiho.

EXTERNAL AUTONOMY AND TERRITORIAL EXCLUSIVITY   In terms of territorial exclusivity and external autonomy, Japanese rule retained many

---

[91] In the initial phases of its occupation of the East Indies, the Japanese even co-opted remaining Dutch administrators to manage local governance in parts of the archipelago. Aziz, 1955, 142–66, 182–245; Benda, 1958, 103–94, 1972, 37–49; Benda, Irikura, and Kishi, 1965, 1–100, 133–234, 37–79; Benda and Larkin, 1967, 219–24; Indonesia, and Netherlands, Regeeringsvoorlichtingsdienst, 1942, 57–63; Reid, 2005.

[92] Colbert, 1977, 57–58; Frederick, 1989, 89–105, 33–71; Ismail, 1994, 79–87; Owen, 2005, 305–6; Reid, 2005; Ricklefs, 1993; Sato, 2005, 10–12, 22–200.

[93] Aziz, 1955, 152–66, 82–93, 222–26; Frederick, 1989, 89–118, 33–71; Iwatake, 1989, 18–54, 95–110, 159–214, 254–74; Poeze, 2005, 152–78; Raben, 2005, 197–212; Sato, 2005, 129–51; Taylor, 2003, 310–39.

[94] Benda, 1958, 103–49; Benda, Irikura, and Kishi, 1965, 59–279; Kahin, 1952, 104–06; Legge, 1988, 3–4, 42–66; Robertson and Spruyt, 1967, 213–15; Spruyt, 2005, 171; Tarling, 2001, 125–46, 174–92, 226–31; Vickers, 2005, 93–95.

[95] Estimates put the total strength of these organisations to be more than 2 million by the end of World War II, with about 60 percent in the vigilante corps, the Keibodan. Aziz, 1955, 200–45; Benda, 1958, 150–68, 1972, 37–49; Sato, 1994, 53–59, 71–75.

[96] Anderson, 1972, 16–39, 237; Bastin and Benda, 1968, 145–46; Maekawa, 2005, 179–96; Mrázek, 1978, 22–34; Taylor, 2003, 319–20; Vickers, 2005, 94.

Creating Indonesia, 1893–1952   193

features of the Dutch colonial state in the East Indies. Governance and official agencies across the archipelago lay under the purview of an administration under a Military Governor located in the former capital of the Dutch Indies, now referred to by its precolonial name, Jakarta, instead of Batavia.[97] As in the case of the Netherlands Indies, the metropole delegated the domestic management of territory to the Military Government with the aid of indigenous advisory councils. Like the Dutch colonial government, the Japanese administration in the East Indies similarly took charge of taxation, monetary and fiscal matters, and development.[98] Tokyo further enjoyed a veto over the external relations of the East Indies very much like the Dutch, even toying with the idea of a quasi-autonomous Indonesia within its Greater East Asia Co-Prosperity Sphere.[99]

Revolution and Beyond

From Japanese defeat in 1945 through the end of the Indonesian Revolution in 1949, the East Indies displayed declining political centralisation coupled with rising external autonomy, and levels of territorial exclusivity moving from moderate and high. These shifts in state form demonstrated the resilience of Dutch access regulation efforts and the importance of the aggregated effects of external intervention on state formation. In the chaotic transition between the end of Japanese rule and the start of the British-led receivership of the East Indies, the nationalists, with Sukarno as President and Hatta as Vice-President, declared the independence of the Indonesian Republic.[100] Here, the nationalists attempted to establish sovereign statehood by appropriating the politically centralised and territorially exclusive institutions of rule set up by the Japanese – including the various military and paramilitary organisations.[101] To these, they tried to add substantive external autonomy and, in doing so, set the stage for conflict as the British-led Allies and Dutch tried to revive the prewar *status quo*.[102]

POLITICAL CENTRALISATION   By the time British troops under South-East Asia Command handed jurisdiction of the East Indies to the Dutch government in 1946, the Dutch and Republicans effectively divided the archipelago given the separate areas they controlled. The postwar British-led Military Administration

---

[97] Benda and Larkin, 1967, 219–24; Ricklefs, 1993, 201–8; Sato, 1994, 10–12, 61–71.
[98] Benda, Irikura, and Kishi, 1965, 59–279; Benda and Larkin, 1967, 219–24; Iwatake, 1989, 18–54, 201–40, 292–30; Sato, 1994, 10–12, 60–80.
[99] Aziz, 1955, 244–58; Benda, 1958, 169–94; Iwatake, 1989, 95–110; Kahin, 1952, 120–27; Spruyt, 2005, 171–72; Taylor, 2003, 319–27.
[100] Sukarno and Hatta declared independence as the leaders of the Komité Nasional Indonesia Pusat (KNIP, or the Central Indonesian National Committee). Anderson, 1972, 61–124; Caldwell and Utrecht, 1979, 67–68; Kahin, 1952, 134–212; Kahin and Kahin, 1995, 25–26; Reid, 1974, 19–39.
[101] Drakeley, 2005, 75–77; Kahin, 1952, 141–212, 230–47; Mrázek, 1978, 34–49; Robertson and Spruyt, 1967, 213–20; Taylor, 2003, 324–27.
[102] Ford, 1996, 229–69, 281–331, 343–411; Frederick, 1989, 193–97, 230–67; Gouda and Zaalberg, 2002, 173–90; Kahin, 1977, 338–40; Tarling, 1993, 192, 1998, 87–95.

194   *External Intervention and the Politics of State Formation*

permitted Dutch military forces and civil administrators to take over areas in East Indonesia, Sulawesi, eastern Sumatra, and most of Java.[103] British troops even engaged in the suppression of Indonesian nationalists, notably in Surabaya, where the battle between British and Republican forces devastated the latter's manpower and equipment, even if the incident became a rallying event for the Republicans.[104] In formerly British-held areas, the Dutch Lieutenant-Governor's office began to work with local aristocrats and leaders to reestablish the old colonial state, with an eye to retaking the entire archipelago.[105] From Republican-dominated areas in Central Java, Madura, and Sumatra, the Indonesian nationalists took pains to assert greater centralisation, territorial exclusivity, and outward autonomy across Indonesia through armed resistance and mass mobilisation.

Dutch efforts to reimpose colonial rule over the Indonesian archipelago met with surprisingly considerable, albeit costly, successes for a time. This brought a fragmentation of the polity until late 1949. Negotiations between the belligerents from 1946 to 1948 led to arrangements for a federal Indonesia within a Dutch-Indonesian union, with The Hague controlling areas outside Java, Sumatra, and Madura.[106]

However, The Hague unilaterally attempted to establish this federal Indonesia under complete and direct Dutch rule. Soon after the announcement of the union, colonial forces under Lieutenant-Governor Hubertus van Mook tried to forcefully install cooperative local elites. Following two major "police actions", Dutch forces reduced Republican-held areas to Aceh and the interior of Central Java by early 1948 and occupied all major towns, including the Republican capital of Jogjakarta, late that year.[107] These developments

---

[103] Bayly and Harper, 2007, 158–89; Kahin, 2003, 19; Kahin and Kahin, 1995, 27; McMillan, 2005, 10–12, 85–106, 131–37; Reid, 1974, 42–57, 104–19; Spector, 2007, 178–214.

[104] Anderson, 1972, 139–66, 296–97; Colbert, 1977, 63–67; McMillan, 2005, 31–84.

[105] Chauvel, 1985, 237–61; Cribb, 1985, 179–201; Harvey, 1985, 207–28.

[106] These include a secret agreement between Sjahrir and van Mook in March 1946, as well as the British-brokered Linggajati ceasefire arrangement in November of that year. After United Nations ceasefire calls in July 1947, the Dutch and Indonesian governments reached the Renville Agreement. This effectively recognised Dutch control over territory behind lines of advance achieved under the first police action. Cribb, 1985, 199–200; Kahin, 1952, 99–100, 146, 235–47, 345–90, 406–8; Ma, 1957, 191–205, 234–47, 297–304; Tarling, 1998, 160–73, 211–36, 280–95.

[107] When moving into Jogjakarta, Dutch forces captured Sukarno, Hatta, Foreign Minister Agus Salim, Sjahrir, and most of the Republican cabinet. Facing a strong Dutch offensive, Republican leaders gave themselves up in the hope that unilateral Dutch actions would incense the rest of the world, particularly the United States, leading to pressure for a Dutch withdrawal. With the loss of most areas under Republican control and the arrest of its leaders, Republican forces increased guerrilla warfare efforts from the interior and behind Dutch lines. Adrian Vickers notes that Dutch casualties from the fighting between 1945 and 1949 were remarkably light, with less than 700 soldiers killed in action. Estimates of Indonesian casualties stand at between 45,000 and 100,000, with another 7 million people displaced on Java and Sumatra alone. Kahin, 1952, 213–47, 332–469; Reid, 1974, 112–14, 49–53; Vickers, 2005, 99–111.

Creating Indonesia, 1893–1952

deepened the divides between areas in Republican control and those under reinstituted Dutch rule.[108]

What allowed for initial postwar Dutch recolonisation – and hence greater fragmentation – and the subsequent emergence of sovereign statehood in the East Indies, were U.S.-led efforts to ensure nonprivileged access across most of the archipelago. Cessation of American aid that could be directed to the Dutch war effort in Indonesia during December 1948 made recolonisation increasingly difficult, and eventually impossible, to sustain.[109] Making withdrawal even more compelling were American threats to cease economic aid, which could spell the evaporation of all postwar reconstruction funding since U.S.-led pressure at the United Nations made alternative sources of assistance difficult to come by. In the end, in return for guarantees for Dutch investments in the East Indies, Indonesian responsibility for Netherlands Indies debt, and continued Dutch control over West New Guinea, The Hague accepted the formation of a sovereign Indonesian state by mid 1950.[110] This enabled political centralisation, territorial exclusivity, and external autonomy across much of the archipelago to become substantial by the early 1950s, with foreign roles relegated to trade, investment, commercial services, and some advisory roles.[111]

After the collapse of Dutch efforts to reconquer the East Indies, the Indonesian Republicans moved to assert their external independence and consolidate their rule over most of the archipelago.[112] Whilst many of the federal regions created during the postwar Dutch colonial administration underwent rapid absorption into Indonesia, several areas attempted to assert a degree of autonomy from the new central government in Jakarta.[113] These included regional authorities in West Kalimantan, South Sulawesi, Ambon, East Sumatra, and Aceh as well as religious-inspired militants such as groups in West Java.[114] Given their lack of sustained international support, these efforts to establish much higher degrees of regional autonomy soon saw either capitulation or political marginalisation.[115] This enabled the

[108] Dahm, 1971, 127–29; Ricklefs, 1993, 230–31; Spruyt, 2005, 172–73.

[109] Kahin and Kahin, 1952, 30–45; Roadnight, 2002, 55–77; Spector, 2007, 274.

[110] To support the new Indonesian government and encourage the acceptance of the terms of the Dutch withdrawal, the Truman administration offered the Republicans a low-interest US$100 million loan from the Export-Import Bank. United States plans for having the Indonesian Republic shoulder the debt of the Netherlands Indies government was in part to avoid undermining the newly achieved political and economic stability of the noncommunist government in The Hague. Kahin, 1977, 352–55, 2003, 19–22, 86–125; Tarling, 1998, 357–73, 2005, 26–44, 131–48.

[111] Shell, Standard Oil, and Caltex remained prominent in the oil industry, while Dutch, British, and ethnic Chinese firms dominated banking. Dutch commercial concerns also continued their heavy involvement in inter-island shipping. Ma, 1957, 307–50; Ricklefs, 1993, 239.

[112] Anderson, 1998, 278–80; Colbert, 1977, 185–91; Elson, 2008, 149–98; Liddle, 1970; Mrázek, 1978, 83–122; Vickers, 2005, 113–41.

[113] Tarling, 2001, 490–92; Taylor, 2003, 336–48; Wiarda, 2007, 131.

[114] Feith, 1962; Harvey, 1985; Kahin and Kahin, 1995, 37–40, 54; Ricklefs, 1993, 227–47.

[115] Caldwell and Utrecht, 1979, 86–88; Feith, 1962; Harvey, 1985; Reid, 1979, 162–68; Roadnight, 2002, 78–102.

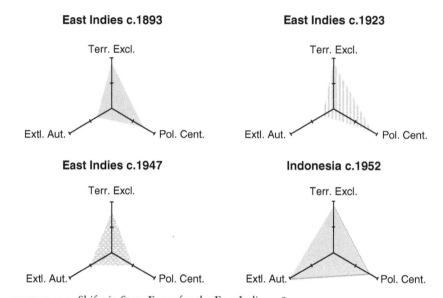

FIGURE 7.1 Shifts in State Form for the East Indies, 1893–1952

Indonesian state to add increasingly high levels of political centralisation to the high degrees of external autonomy and territorial exclusivity present from independence.

Shifts in the aggregated effects of external intervention, conditioned by perceptions about the opportunity costs of intervention, drove shifts in state form for the East Indies from 1923 to 1952. So long as an external actor expecting moderate opportunity costs of intervention prevailed over other interested powers, the archipelago remained a colonial state. In fact, the Dutch colonial state was able to persist in West New Guinea past 1952, as The Hague's efforts to act on its moderate expectations of opportunity costs there went unchallenged. Otherwise, state form in the East Indies shifted towards sovereign statehood once all the competing powers access began to act on anticipated high opportunity costs. Political fragmentation between 1945 and 1949 is consistent with my expectations of developments when rival external actors are still working out differences over access.

As Figure 7.1 above illustrates, 1893 to 1922 brought a consolidation of the colonial state in the East Indies, whilst state form shifted toward sovereign statehood in the years between 1923 and 1952, albeit with a brief fragmentary phase from 1945 to 1949.

ALTERNATIVE EXPLANATIONS

I now turn to the main competing positions also purporting to account for the East Indies' movement from colonial to sovereign statehood between 1893 and

Creating Indonesia, 1893–1952 197

1952. As in the other cases in this study, I examine competing claims from the nationalist, normative, institutional commitment, and capitalised coercion perspectives. I argue that these positions do not fully consider how interactions between external and domestic forces inform Indonesia's state formation process. This does not take away from the fact that these arguments illustrate important details about Indonesia's state formation.

Nationalism and Self-Determination

By far the most popular explanation for the persistence of the colonial state in the East Indies from 1893 to 1922 and the movement toward sovereign statehood between 1923 and 1952 is the rise of nationalism. According to this view, the rise of Malay as a *lingua franca* through the development of mass media and standardised education, alongside commonalities in religion and culture, enabled the emergence of a common consciousness across the archipelago.[116] Seizing this opportunity, nationalist groups and leaders – like Sukarno, Hatta, Sjahrir, and others – mobilised this awareness into an anticolonial political force that came of age during the middle of the twentieth century.[117]

What the nationalist position does not fully account for is the fact that external forces, Dutch or Japanese, were quite adept at manipulating, dividing, and suppressing nationalist-inspired groups. Also, Japanese and, subsequently, American backing were key to the success of the nationalist Republicans in building a sovereign Indonesian state after World War II. Nationalism seemed insufficient for creating sovereign statehood in the East Indies even if it was necessary.

Another perspective on the establishment of the sovereign Indonesian state takes the role of self-determination norms as vital. According to this view, broad international support for national self-determination and disdain for colonialism after World War II pressured The Hague into the decolonisation whilst bolstering indigenous efforts to create sovereign statehood in the East Indies. Evidence for this comes from the diplomatic support for the Republican cause at the United Nations, which included demonstrations of sympathy from the United States, Soviet Union, and, eventually, Britain.[118]

However, it was when support for a Republic of Indonesia separate from Dutch rule became politically expedient for achieving larger Cold War aims in both Europe and Asia, that Washington threw its weight behind the creation of sovereign statehood in the East Indies. Until then, the U.S. government did not

---

[116] The term for the official version of Malay spoken in Indonesia is "Bahasa Indonesia", or the Indonesian Language. Abdulgani, 1978, 257–75; Anderson, 1991, 9–82, 119–54, 176–82; Kahin, 1952, 41, 108–33; Leifer, 2000, 159–60; Mrázek, 2002, 31–42; Oemarjati, 1978, 307–28.

[117] Anderson, 1998, 77–130, 278–80; Benda and Larkin, 1967, 189–96; Elson, 2008, 44–148.

[118] Kahin 1952, 146, 213–29, 254–55, 1977, 355–58, 2003, 19–32; Kahin and Kahin, 1995, 29–31; Ma, 1957, 234–47, 307–14; Roadnight, 2002, 26–77.

oppose The Hague's use of American postwar aid for its efforts to reestablish colonial rule in the archipelago. Similarly, expectations of high and prohibitively high opportunity costs were respectively behind British support for and Soviet absence from the sovereign state creation process in Indonesia.

Bellicism and State Formation

Bellicist accounts provide quite a compelling approach to understanding the shift from colonial to sovereign state over much of the Indonesian archipelago. Changes in the relative ability of the Republican forces to amass arms and access wealth alongside the Dutch may account for both the continuation of the colonial state and the establishment of a sovereign Indonesia. Key to the indigenous capacity to both accumulate and concentrate capital as well as the tools of coercion, however, were the roles played by intervening external actors not included in standard capitalised coercion logic. Japanese rule reinforced the local role in governance already extant under the Dutch, whilst providing the training and equipment that expanded the ability of indigenous groups to manipulate the levers of coercion. Conversely, American limitation of aid curtailed Dutch attempts to redevelop centralised, extractive institutions and to defeat the Republicans militarily.

Institutional Commitments and Institutions of Governance

The institutional commitment perspective gives a final competing assessment about the rise of sovereign statehood in the Indonesian archipelago from 1893 to 1952. Just as co-opting traditional local elites and professionals permitted the persistence of colonial statehood, the Republicans' ability to win over many of these groups during Japanese rule strengthened the nationalist cause before the Indonesian Revolution. Yet, the building of the nationalist coalition was set in motion by the wartime Japanese military administration of the East Indies as a means of first expelling Dutch and Allied opposition and then ruling the archipelago. Further, the wider inclusion of different social groups into the Republican cause alone did not establish the sovereign Indonesian state. Critical to the creation of sovereign statehood in the East Indies were Dutch, American, Japanese, and, to a lesser extent, British actions based on their leaders' changing expectations about the opportunity costs of interceding into Indonesian domestic politics.

CONCLUSION

Shifts in the aggregated pattern of foreign intervention in the East Indies, dependent on changes in external expectations about opportunity costs, lay behind this variation in state form. The consolidation of the colonial state under both the Dutch and Japanese resulted from the prevailing of outside actors that anticipated moderate opportunity costs of intervention in the archipelago.

Creating Indonesia, 1893–1952 199

Sovereign statehood in the polity came about when all external powers desiring to secure access began to foresee intervention into the archipelago as expensive and turned to support this outcome.

The robustness of the interventionist approach is evident from its ability to account for the Indonesian polity's movement from colonial to sovereign state between 1893 and 1952. Not only is my argument able to address the development of sovereign statehood in the East Indies, it provides an explanation for the persistence of the colonial state in that polity. This makes it more comprehensive than most normative arguments that take either nationalist or self-determinationist understandings. By adding a dimension of foreign competition, the interventionist claim helps overcome key gaps in the capitalised coercion and institutional commitment views of state formation. The particular strength of the interventionist perspective lies in taking seriously the power asymmetry between actors in the target polity and other international actors, which suggests that future studies may gain by considering such conditions alongside systemic pressures.

CHAPTER 8

Siam Stands Apart, 1893–1952

External Intervention and Rise of a Sovereign Thai State

Since the late nineteenth century, the major actors active in East Asia perceived the opportunity costs of intervention over most of Thailand to be high, especially given the seemingly substantial capability investments needed to deny rivals access completely.[1] External powers focused on minimising capabilities commitments to Siam whilst preventing rival foreign actors from acquiring access advantages that they could not enjoy. These foreign powers collectively enabled Siam to develop high degrees of external autonomy, territorial exclusivity, and political centralisation much earlier than most of its neighbours.

I argue that Thailand between 1893 and 1922 demonstrated a movement from feudalised to sovereign statehood, and subsequently the stabilisation of the sovereign state from 1923 to 1952. In looking at these two periods, I also consider the main alternative explanations about changes in state form for Siam. Together with my other cases, Siam permits me to highlight the effects of external intervention on state formation by controlling for cultural, geographic, regional, and other factors that may affect state form.

Similar to the Indonesia case, I apply a set of structured, focused comparisons to examine Thailand from 1893 to 1952. Thailand likewise presents a least likely instance for my argument, albeit for different reasons from the popular nationalist resistance attributed to China and the East Indies. Popular opinion credits Siamese diplomacy, particularly the ability to play foreign powers against each other, and domestic modernisation for staving off foreign domination and developing sovereign statehood. If my argument applies to Thailand in addition to Indonesia and China, I will be more confident in its robustness and generalisability. Like Indonesia, intervention dynamics in Thailand at this time are less complicated than for China, so I can treat this case in a more straightforward manner.

---

[1] The name Thailand only came into official usage after 1939. This chapter uses Siam, Thai, and Thailand interchangeably unless specifically noted.

200

Siam Stands Apart, 1893–1952

OUTSIDE PRESSURE AND SIAM'S PATH TOWARD SOVEREIGN STATEHOOD, 1893–1922

Siam's early movement toward sovereign statehood between 1893 and 1922 was a consequence of the high opportunity costs of intervention perceived by the two external powers most active around the polity, Britain and France. In comparison to potential capability investments elsewhere, London and Paris saw limited returns from committing capabilities into access regulation, much less full access denial, across most of the Thai polity. The British and French governments concentrated on denying privileged access to one another and to other foreign actors. Such dynamics nurtured the development of a Thai state with high political centralisation, territorial exclusivity, and external autonomy.

Expectations of High Opportunity Cost and the Limits to Intervention

By the end of the nineteenth century, both the British and French governments perceived the opportunity costs of intervention into much of Siam to be high. As a result, leaders in London and Paris sought to deny rival external actors, especially each other, access privileges in the Thai polity that they did not enjoy themselves. Behind this reasoning lay the belief that more robust efforts to intervene in Siam were likely to increase the potential for an Anglo-French war in Southeast Asia. British and French leaders generally expected such an event to erase gains from access in Siam, resulting in very low returns to any substantial investment in capabilities, especially given other more pressing strategic concerns. The limited goal of ensuring nondisadvantaged access appeared more commensurate with British and French perceptions about the returns from interceding in Thai politics.

High Opportunity Cost Expectations, Nonprivileged Access, and the Fringes of the British Empire

Leaders in London viewed growing strategic demands from the early 1890s to the early 1920s as further straining already stretched British capabilities, meaning that there was little spare capacity to devote to securing more complete access denial in Siam. Unlike its imperial heyday, the end of the nineteenth century saw Britain increasingly mired with financial and economic woes as well as the need to deal with the challenges posed by the rise of Germany, the United States, and Japan.[2] Making a commitment of capabilities toward securing access in Siam even more trying were successive British efforts to absorb neighbouring Burma, fight the Boer War, and resist the Central Powers in the Great War.[3]

British leaders also believed that efforts to deny access over Siam more completely would likely threaten French interests in Indochina immediately to

---

[2] Friedberg, 1988; Kupchan, 1994, 105–30.
[3] Brendon, 2007, 214–349; Ferguson, 1994, 185–245; Howard, 1991, 31–41.

202   *External Intervention and the Politics of State Formation*

the east, which might unnecessarily intensify Anglo-French rivalries. London believed that this could derail efforts to manage Germany's rise in Europe, especially through cooperation with Paris. In fact, Anglo-French rivalry over Siam even threatened to spill over into war as late as 1893.[4] Ultimately, the freezing of Britain and France's Far Eastern colonial expansion around Siam was part of the 1894 Salisbury-Courcel Agreement that helped to lay the groundwork for the later Entente Cordiale, Anglo-French Alliance, and Triple Alliance of World War I.[5]

At the same time, British cabinets from 1893 to 1922 did not see increased penetration into the Thai polity in the late nineteenth and early twentieth centuries as promising returns much greater than what they already enjoyed. Between the conclusion of the 1855 Bowring Treaty and the post–World War I treaty revisions, British firms enjoyed low, fixed *ad valorem* taxes and could enter almost all areas of the Siamese economy whilst British subjects could reside and own land within the polity.[6] London also exercised extraterritorial jurisdiction over British subjects in Siam until the early 1930s.[7] The 1909 Anglo-Siamese Treaty further granted British firms the right to construct the Bangkok-Singapore railway, and transferred the northern Malay sultanates of Kelantan, Trengganu, Kedah, and Perlis from Siamese vassalage to British jurisdiction.[8] Even without access regulation, British interests controlled about 90 percent of Siam's trade by the turn of the century, whilst colonies elsewhere in Southeast Asia gave Britain extensive and exclusive access to the kinds of resources Siam had to offer.[9]

Given perceptions about the relatively spare gains and heavy burdens associated with heavier access denial in Siam, British leaders from 1893 to 1922 associated high opportunity costs with intervention in Siam. From London's perspective, complete access denial over the Thai polity would entail a significant commitment of already limited capabilities to address both the immediate task of securing access and the broader consequences following such action.[10] Even

---

[4] Baker and Phongpaichit, 2005, 61; Crosby, 1945, 45–61; Deignan, 1943, 16–17; Lowe, 1981, 50–51; Morant, Pritsadang and Brailey, 1989, 1–11.

[5] The Salisbury-Courcel agreement also covered accommodation over French and British interests in Southwest China, Africa, and the Middle East. Anderson, 1991, 99; Crosby, 1945, 60–61; Crosby and Great Britain, Foreign Office, Historical Section, 1920, 3–12; Grenville, 1964; Hargreaves, 1953; Kupchan, 1994, 105–13, 210–11; Terwiel, 2005, 211–12, 26; Wyatt, 1984, 183–89, 204–31.

[6] The Anglo-Siamese Treaty abolished all official monopolies with the exception of opium. This allowed British firms to freely invest and engage in commercial activity for the most part. The Treaty set import taxes at 3 percent *ad valorem* and export taxes at 5 percent *ad valorem*. Mead, 2004, 32–37.

[7] Crosby and Great Britain, Foreign Office, Historical Section, 1920, 3–10; Wyatt, 1984, 184–87, 206, 31, 51.

[8] Crosby, 1945, 54–58; Terwiel, 2005, 223–24; Wilson, 1962, 8.

[9] Timber, rice, tin, and, later, rubber produced in Siam were available from Britain's other Southeast Asian possessions. Total foreign investment in Malaya in 1914, which was largely British, was more than three times that of Siam. Anderson, 1991, 100; Baker and Phongpaichit, 2005, 19; Field and Institute of Pacific Relations, 1934, 462–65.

[10] This was a continuation of British policy toward Siam since the mid nineteenth century. Morant, Pritsadang, and Brailey, 1989, 36–41; Tarling, 1975, 174–229.

Siam Stands Apart, 1893–1952

then, success in competition over access in Siam seemed to promise little in the way of gains for British interests. Cabinets in office from 1893 generally held the view that investing capabilities into preparing for potential threats to the metropole or keeping the empire whole would offer better returns than seeking full access denial over the Siamese polity.[11] London deemed investing just enough capabilities to maintain nonprivileged access over the Thai state as appropriate for its purposes of sustaining Britain's hold over Burma and Malaya, as well as its economic position in Siam.

EQUAL ACCESS FOR ALL   Stemming from its high opportunity cost expectations regarding intervention into Siam, London looked toward the Thai central government to prevent rivals from gaining privileged access in that polity. The British government was open to an active role for rival external powers in the Siamese economy and even Siamese politics so long as they ensured equal treatment of British interests without necessitating active involvement by London. British leaders preferred the emergence of a strong, stable, and independent Siamese central government that would honour Britain's most-favoured-nation status and extend the privileges acquired by rival foreign actors.

British efforts to guarantee nonprivileged access in Siam translated into diplomatic and political backing for authorities in Bangkok in the form of training for its leadership and assistance in bureaucratic reforms.[12] Just as importantly, London simultaneously withheld support from local actors that could challenge Bangkok, helping to bolster the central administration's position. In return, Britain enjoyed the access privileges Bangkok granted any other foreign actor, as well as official Siamese guarantees to prevent third powers access to Peninsular Thailand, which bordered British-held Malaya.[13] To further ensure nonprivileged access, the British agreed with France to jointly guarantee the independence of, and nonexclusive access over, a centralised Thai state in the Chao Phraya watershed.[14]

Ensuring Nonprivileged Access and the Limits to French Colonial Expansion

Like London, Paris perceived committing significant capabilities into denying rivals access in the Siamese polity from the late nineteenth to early twentieth centuries as diverting its energies away from more urgent undertakings. Given France's long land border with Germany and memories of the Franco-Prussian

---

[11] Mead, 2004, 46–64, 111–12; Terwiel, 2005, 212–13; Wyatt, 1984, 210–35.

[12] Baker and Phongpaichit, 2005, 68; Crosby, 1945, 54–61, 95.

[13] Crosby and Great Britain, Foreign Office, Historical Section, 1920, 6–12; Lowe, 1981, 47–48; Wyatt, 1984, 204–06.

[14] This understanding meant that Paris accepted British positions in Malaya and Burma, whilst London would not challenge French claims over Siamese vassals east of the Mekong in Laos, Cambodia, and along the Southeast coast of the Gulf of Siam. Baker and Phongpaichit, 2005, 61; Grenville, 1964; Hargreaves, 1953; Lowe, 1981, 50–51; Terwiel, 2005, 211–12, 26; Wilson, 1962, 7.

204 *External Intervention and the Politics of State Formation*

War, the pressure successive French governments from late nineteenth to early twentieth centuries felt in the face of Germany's rise was palpable.[15] French leaders expected to endure the most from any major conflict with Germany – a fear to be borne out during World War I.

Consequently, Paris prioritised the commitment of capabilities first into the defence of the metropole against a potential German threat and later the task of rebuilding after the Great War. Such a commitment seemed to offer a better return to investment than risking conflict with a potential ally over an area in its periphery. The 1880s to early 1920s also saw the Third Republic try to consolidate its hold over Indochina, North, West, and Central Africa, and, after the Great War, former Ottoman territories in the Middle East.

During this time, the French government invested whatever capabilities were left over from safeguarding security in Europe into accruing the expected gains from regulating regions already under its imperial purview. Even then, Paris was careful to limit its late-nineteenth and early-twentieth-century colonial pursuits in a way that avoided unnecessary tensions and conflict with potential allies such as Britain.[16] As French actions could cause alarm in London, French leaders treated Siam with caution even though it could impose access regulation over much of the polity from Indochina. Siam, after all, shared long land boundaries with British possessions in Burma and Malaya, whereas Laos only bordered Burma in the difficult-to-reach upper northeast reaches of the Mekong River and Cambodia was not contiguous with any British holding.

Leaders of the Third Republic also recognised limited potential gains from greater access denial over much of Siam between 1893 and 1922. Like London, Paris secured most-favoured-nation status in Siam by the mid nineteenth century. This accorded nonprivileged access, low, fixed tariffs, and extraterritorial concessions guaranteed by the Siamese government in Bangkok.[17] Active expansion, three successive Franco-Siamese treaties between 1886 and 1907, and settlements with London also afforded Paris access regulation over most of Indochina – including the former Siamese vassals, Laos and Cambodia.[18]

France's position in Indochina further promised exclusive French access in exploiting the then-untapped markets, mineral and forest resources in the area, and a "backdoor" to China, which was highly similar to what securing further access in Siam could provide. Since much of the gains from further access in Siam were already available, committing capabilities to ensure the success of alternative objectives seemed a more worthwhile investment to many French leaders.[19]

---

[15] Kupchan, 1994, 185–214.

[16] Grenville, 1964; Hargreaves, 1953; Wyatt, 1984, 195–206.

[17] By 1914, such capital inflows were predominantly French. Baker and Phongpaichit, 2005, 91; Crosby, 1945, 59–61; Wyatt, 1984, 184–87.

[18] Baker and Phongpaichit, 2005, 59–61; Crosby, 1945, 59–61; Crosby and Great Britain, Foreign Office, Historical Section, 1920, 4–11; Deignan, 1943, 17; Kupchan, 1994, 194; Wilson, 1962, 8; Wyatt, 1984, 184–206.

[19] Baker and Phongpaichit, 2005, 59–61; Grenville, 1964; Hargreaves, 1953.

Siam Stands Apart, 1893–1952

Consequently, French leaders from the last decade of the nineteenth century until the beginning of the second decade of the twentieth viewed the opportunity costs of intervention over most of the Thai state as high. Except for temporary incursions to secure access regulation over Cambodia and Laos, leaders of the Third Republic tended to see anything more than ensuring nonprivileged access in Siam as providing less-than-adequate returns.[20] Attempting to regulate access over Siam proper would be likely to divert capabilities away from addressing the growing German threat and consolidating empire.[21]

AVOIDING DISADVANTAGE IN THAILAND   Expectations about the high opportunity costs of intervention over most of Siam from 1893 to 1922 led the French government to limit direct involvement in Siam by concentrating on the maintenance of nondisadvantaged access. This meant cooperation with the British over ensuring the existence of a Bangkok-centred Siamese state along the Chao Phraya watershed, in which no foreign power could come to acquire exclusive access.[22] This spelt shoring up the Thai government in Bangkok, especially in terms of training for leaders and officials, assistance in administrative reforms, eventual acceptance of diplomatic equality, and not supporting challengers to central authority.[23] French help came at the price of maintaining its most-favoured-nation status, which ensured that France would have the same access as other external actors. Notably, French leaders tried to extend their colonial reach into Siamese vassals when they did not expect the same high opportunity costs to intervention, seen in Paris's attempts to impose its writ over Laos and Cambodia.[24]

Other Powers

Other major powers active in Asia generally refrained from competing for access over Siam from the end of the nineteenth century to the early 1920s, since their governments and leaders generally perceived prohibitively high opportunity costs to intervention. Aside from the fact that concerns elsewhere were more pressing for the other major powers, the entrenched positions of the French and British on mainland Southeast Asia made it difficult for rivals to compete for access over Siam. At most, other outside actors would try to seek nonprivileged access in the Thai polity by demanding most-favoured-nation treatment where

[20] Deignan, 1943, 17; Morant, Pritsadang, and Brailey, 1989, 1–11; Wilson, 1962, 7–8.
[21] Kupchan, 1994, 185–214; Wyatt, 1984, 201–06.
[22] Anderson, 1991, 99; Baker and Phongpaichit, 2005, 61–68; Crosby and Great Britain, Foreign Office, Historical Section, 1920, 11–12; Grenville, 1964; Hargreaves, 1953; Kupchan, 1994, 194, 210–11; Terwiel, 2005, 206–26.
[23] Crosby, 1945, 54; Crosby and Great Britain, Foreign Office, Historical Section, 1920, 3–6; Wyatt, 1984, 210, 30–38.
[24] To compel Siamese renouncement of suzerainty and acceptance of French overlordship over Luang Prabang and Champassak in Laos as well as Battambang, Siem Reap, and Sisophon in Cambodia, French forces occupied the southeast Thai provinces of Trat and Chanthaburi from 1893 to 1907. Terwiel, 2005, 219–20; Wilson, 1962, 8.

206　　External Intervention and the Politics of State Formation

TABLE 8.1 *Convergent Foreign Expectations about the High Opportunity Costs of Intervention in Thailand and Corresponding Approaches to Access Denial, 1893–1922*

Outside Actor	Expected Opportunity Cost	Approach to Access Denial
France	High	Nonprivileged Access
Britain	High	Nonprivileged Access
United States	Prohibitively High	Concede Access
Japan	Prohibitively High	Concede Access

possible, though most were open to accepting limited access.[25] Such expectations of prohibitively high opportunity costs to intervention drove the other major powers toward passivity over access competition in Siam.

Table 8.1 lists the opportunity costs perceptions of the major external actors most active in Siam from 1893–1922 and their approaches to competing for access denial.

External Forces and Sovereign State Formation, 1893–1922

State form in Siam moved definitively toward sovereign statehood in the years from 1893 to 1922, well before other weak polities in Asia and elsewhere. Integral to this transformation was external support for the central Thai government in both domestic politics and foreign affairs. This stemmed from broad foreign reticence about directly managing access in Siam. Specifically, attempts by Britain and France to prevent discriminatory access by the other, coupled with the absence of outside opposition gave rise to substantial political centralisation, territorial exclusivity, and external autonomy.

Political Centralisation
Foreign backing for the Bangkok central government prompted a significant rise in political centralisation between 1893 and 1922. From 1892 on, the new, functional ministries established by King Chulalongkorn's (Rama V, r.1868–1910) wide-ranging administrative reforms began to exert greater central control across the Thai polity.[26] A key change was the gradual incorporation of semiautonomous regional and provincial administrations into the Interior Ministry between 1892 and 1902. This placed taxation, commerce, law, communications, education, police powers, and religious affairs in various regions and provinces under the oversight of central government ministries run by

---

[25] Crosby and Great Britain, Foreign Office, Historical Section, 1920, 4; Wyatt, 1984, 184, 231.
[26] Brown, 1992; Bunnag, 1977; Peleggi, 2007, 61–64; Riggs, 1966, 117–21; Steinberg, 1985, 324–25; Wilson, 1962, 102–08; Wyatt, 1984, 194–200, 21.

Siam Stands Apart, 1893–1952

professional bureaucrats.[27] Just as critical to restructuring efforts was the consolidation of control over previously decentralised government finances – particularly official expenditures – under the British-influenced Finance Ministry.[28]

Under a British- and French-advised Department of the Military, the Siamese government in Bangkok created a modern, central military that superseded the decentralised, regionally based traditional military forces.[29] Military reforms included universal conscription into the central Siamese military, giving Bangkok the ability to monopolise the coercive force across the Thai polity more firmly.[30] Another important bureaucratic change was a systematic revision and centralisation of Siamese legal codes along the Napoleonic model by the French- and Belgian-advised Justice Ministry.[31] These legal changes helped Bangkok end extraterritorial jurisdiction in the 1920s based on possession of a "modern", "civilised", and "nonbarbaric" justice system.[32]

With the momentum for centralisation provided by external forces, the reign of Chulalongkorn's successor, Vajiravudh (Rama VI, r.1910–1925), saw an initiation of state-sponsored popular nationalism. Vajiravudh actively promoted the sense of a common Thai identity amongst the populace through the mass media and education system. Core to this new "Thai-ness" was a sense of loyalty to, and willingness to sacrifice for, the trinity of "nation-religion-king", as well as widespread adoption of the Bangkok Thai in literature, writing, and speech.[33] To create a common Thai nation, Vajiravudh's government also pushed the public to clamour for equal international treatment, popular participation in national defence, and economic liberation from the alleged domination of non-Thais, especially the ethnic Chinese.[34] This new feeling of nationhood allowed popular mobilisation behind military modernisation efforts that bolstered Bangkok's domestic political position.[35]

---

[27] Until the late nineteenth century, provincial governorships were semihereditary, whilst the northern area of Chiang Mai had a ruling noble house separate from the royal line in Bangkok. As Interior Minister from 1892 to 1915, Prince Damrong Rajanubhan, a half-brother of King Chulalongkorn, was responsible for the centralising initiatives carried out by his ministry. Another royal, Prince Wachirayan, was responsible for reforms in education and religious life. Rising central control in these areas saw Bangkok Thai to supersede regional scripts and dialects, whilst the royally supported Thammayutika sect of Siamese Buddhism was institutionalised as the state religion. Arsa, 1962, 96–124; Baker and Phongpaichit, 2005, 53–71; Crosby and Great Britain, Foreign Office, Historical Section, 1920, 13–14; Mead, 2004, 43–92; Peleggi, 2007, 104–12; Phongpaichit and Baker, 2002, 244–55; Riggs, 1966, 121–47; Siffin, 1966, 42–136; Terwiel, 2005, 203–23; Wyatt, 1969, 1984, 200–20.

[28] Terwiel, 2005, 197–230.

[29] Anderson, 1991, 99; Arsa, 1962, 1–95; Mead, 2004, 93–111; Terwiel, 2005, 203.

[30] Baker and Phongpaichit, 2002, 61–62; Phongpaichit and Baker, 2005, 244–45.

[31] Baker and Phongpaichit, 2002, 56, 68; Wyatt, 1984, 210, 38.

[32] Terwiel, 2005, 225–26; Wilson, 1962, 8–9; Wyatt 1984, 210.

[33] Baker and Phongpaichit, 2005, 62–65, 106–09; Phongpaichit and Baker, 2002, 249–50.

[34] Mead, 2004, 126–53; Owen, 2005, 351–52; Terwiel, 2005, 232–34; Wilson, 1962, 110–11; Wyatt, 1984, 225–30.

[35] Peleggi, 2007, 63, 119–20.

208 *External Intervention and the Politics of State Formation*

Bangkok's attempts to raise political centralisation understandably prompted regional opposition. Several western provinces resisted the construction of telegraph lines under Bangkok's control by drawing on the patronage of Chulalongkorn's former regent, Si Suriyawong.[36] Early 1902 first saw a revolt in the southern Malay region of Pattani against growing central government control over revenues and the appointment of key local officials, which included an appeal for British assistance against Bangkok.[37] Almost concurrently, the old nobility in the northeast threw their weight behind a religious-inspired uprising against what they viewed as new encroachments by the central government.[38] Later that year, old local elites in northern Siam, chafing under the Bangkok's rising control of taxation, abetted a major rebellion by immigrant Shans from Burma.[39]

Strong outside backing for the Bangkok government doomed these efforts to challenge the imposition of governance, authority, and rule from the centre. Opponents of centralisation lacked the infusions of money, arms, expertise, and political support that the central government could draw on. Such foreign backing helped Bangkok rapidly expand the scale and efficiency of its ability to extract wealth and wield force.[40]

Consequently, Bangkok promptly crushed challenges to its centralisation efforts militarily – none of the aforementioned uprisings lasted more than several weeks. When domestic opponents were too politically influential to cross directly, Bangkok leaders simply waited for the death or retirement of key individuals, as in the case of Si Suriyawong.[41] Following from these developments, there was little dispute over the central government's ability to effectively veto political developments within the Thai polity. This reality was especially apparent by the second decade of the twentieth century.

Territorial Exclusivity

Foreign expectations about the high opportunity costs of intervention brought the transfer of all external roles in domestic governance to the central Bangkok government. Undoubtedly, foreign penetration into government administration undercut territorial exclusivity into the 1920s. Beginning with the 1855 Anglo-Siamese Treaty and running through the nineteenth century, major foreign powers secured agreements with Bangkok guaranteeing extraterritorial jurisdiction in Siam alongside the ability to set tariffs for the polity's external trade.[42] The foisting of most-favoured-nation clauses on the Siamese government by these treaties also restricted Bangkok's ability to differentiate amongst foreign

---

[36] Wyatt, 1984, 198.
[37] Ibrahim, 1985, 60–62; Tarling, 2001, 483–84; Wyatt, 1984, 213–14.
[38] Phongpaichit and Baker, 2002, 241–43; Terwiel, 2005, 218–20.
[39] Wyatt, 1984, 213–14.
[40] Mead, 2004, 62–64.
[41] Wyatt, 1994, 194–220.
[42] Mead, 2004, 32–37; Wyatt, 1984, 183–87, 204–12, 30–31.

Siam Stands Apart, 1893–1952

actors over commercial and legal issues. Moreover, the setting of boundaries for colonial expansion along the Chao Phraya Valley by London and Paris at the end of the nineteenth century effectively established the borders of the modern Thai state.[43]

That French and British leaders agreed to ensure Siam's continued independence and nonexclusive access in the polity, given expectations about the high opportunity costs of intervention, clearly restricted foreign participation in Thailand's domestic administration. Since other outside actors were reluctant to test Anglo-French resolve following from their own expectations about prohibitively high intervention costs, they implicitly supported the restriction of active external participation in Siam's domestic governance. In view of Bangkok's growing ability to independently safeguard nonprivileged access amongst foreign powers by the early 1920s, London and Paris saw little need to maintain direct involvement in administrative matters within the Thai state.[44] Britain and France even agreed to relinquish extraterritorial jurisdiction and the regulation of commerce after World War I, which led to an end of official foreign involvement in governance within Siam.

External Autonomy

British and French efforts to guarantee Siam's independence beginning in the last decade of the nineteenth century also spelt the preservation of high degrees of external autonomy for the Thai state going into 1922. By committing to the upkeep of an independent Siamese central government, French and British leaders backed Bangkok's ability to exercise its external relations free from outside sources of authority. With *de facto* Anglo-French acquiescence, the Siamese government could enter into, modify, and break relationships based on its own calculations of interest. This saw Bangkok continue a policy of trying to balance foreign influence by giving a range of outside powers a stake in Siam even if this meant making concessions.[45] Under the leadership of Prince Devawongse, Siam's Foreign Ministry became quite deft in employing Siam's autonomy to defend and forward certain limited prerogatives with Paris and London.[46]

Indicative of Siam's high degree of external autonomy were the Thai government's efforts to remove foreign extraterritorial privileges and reclaim tariff autonomy. Sensing the opportunity to end foreign privileges and to avoid dominance by a victorious Britain, the Siamese government declared war on the Central Powers soon after the United States entered the Great War on the Allied side.[47] Bangkok even sent a small Siamese Expedition Force to France in 1918.

---

[43] Anderson, 1991, 99, 171–75; Baker and Phongpaichit, 2005, 45–61; Owen, 2005, 102–05; Thongchai, 1994, 1996, 67–91; Wilson, 1962, 7.

[44] Mead, 2004, 62–64.

[45] Owen, 2005, 103–05.

[46] Wyatt, 1984, 184–206.

[47] Crosby and Great Britain, Foreign Office, Historical Section, 1920, 8; Terwiel, 2005, 223–24, 241–44.

Through the seat at the Paris Peace Conference secured by its Allied status, Bangkok launched a concerted effort to renegotiate extraterritoriality and tariff autonomy with all the foreign powers active in the Thai state.[48] Between 1920 and 1930, Thai efforts led to the conclusion of new treaties revoking almost all externally imposed conditions Bangkok found objectionable.

Siam's final discarding of feudalised statehood in favour of the modern sovereign state form rested on collective major power behaviour based on expectations of high to prohibitively high opportunity costs to intervention. Expectations that intervening directly to deny rivals access was highly costly led the major powers most active in Siam's vicinity, France and Britain, to act in support of political centralisation, territorial exclusivity, and external autonomy. Acceptance of Anglo-French terms by other actors due to expectations of prohibitively high costs, alongside Bangkok's receipt of foreign assistance for state reorganisation, created conditions ripe for the development of sovereign statehood. The fact that French and British colonial expansion stripped Siam of autonomous vassals also enabled Bangkok to avoid the potentially problematic processes of integrating these areas. The central government could concentrate on undercutting regional prerogatives, upping territorial exclusivity, and preserving extant external autonomy, ultimately replacing a feudalised Thai state with a sovereign alternative.

SUSTAINING THE SOVEREIGN THAI STATE, 1922–1952

Persistent major power expectations about the significant opportunity costs of intervening in the Thai polity enabled state form in Siam to stabilise around sovereign statehood going into the mid twentieth century. Foreign powers with an interest in competing over access in Siam between 1923 and 1952 had few incentives to commit capabilities into anything beyond preventing rivals from gaining access advantages. This was as true of prewar British and French efforts to secure access in Siam as it was with wartime Japanese and postwar American attempts to contend over access denial. Other outside actors with less of a stake were happy to avoid rocking the boat, as was the case from 1893 to 1922. Such a configuration in the approaches that external powers adopted when vying for access enabled the sovereign Thai state to weather World War II and its aftermath, despite the wartime alliance with Japan and the Axis Powers.

The Major Powers and Expectations of Rising Opportunity Costs

Together with already prevalent major power beliefs about the high opportunity costs of intervention into Siam going into the middle of the twentieth century were the cumulative effects of the Great Depression, World War II, and the early Cold War. These conditions entrenched the view amongst the leadership of the

---

[48] American advisors to the Siamese Foreign Ministry played a particularly big role in helping to hone and implement the campaign to end extraterritoriality after World War I. Wyatt, 1984, 230–31.

Siam Stands Apart, 1893–1952

major powers that limited capabilities could be better spent accruing greater returns elsewhere than from completely denying or directly regulating access over the Thai polity. Even the governments of the ascendant Japan and the United States came to share the British and French view that the maintenance of nonprivileged access in the Siamese state was sufficient. Such circumstances prompted continued outside support for an independent Thai central government fully responsible for managing the entire polity going into the early 1950s.

The Evolution of Anglo-French Opportunity Costs Expectations and Access Competition

British and French expectations about the opportunity costs of intervention into the Thai polity remained high until the start of World War II, after which they trended toward prohibitively high levels. Through the 1920s and much of the 1930s, leaders in both Paris and London saw the maintenance of equal opportunities as the preferable approach for competing over access in the Thai state. Behind this view lay the greater imperative of investing capabilities to manage post–World War I reconstruction, the effects of the Great Depression, and the reemergence of a German threat in Europe.[49] Like their predecessors from the 1893 to 1922 period, British and French leaders expected the returns from even full access denial over Siam to remain limited.

From the late 1930s on, however, the British and French governments began to recognise that they had to largely concede efforts to secure access in that polity. This stemmed from the needs of ensuring their own survival with the outbreak of war in Europe. With the French surrender in mid 1940, there was also little the Free French or Vichy governments could commit into securing access over Siam. After the war, the demands of rebuilding, addressing East-West tensions in Europe, and coping with the end of empire took further precedence over access denial in Thailand in the eyes of British and French leaders.[50] Since competing for access in the Thai polity promised very little, the governments in London and Paris decided to largely forgo demands for exclusivity in access.

A LESS-ACTIVE APPROACH TO ACCESS   Anglo-French attempts to safeguard access within the Thai state tracked shifts in perspectives on the opportunity costs of intervention held by leaders in London and Paris. Reflective of expectations about the high opportunity costs of intervention, the French and British governments sought to ensure nonprivileged access through the central government in Bangkok in return for limited diplomatic, political, and technical support until the late 1930s.[51] So long as the Thai government did not discriminate against British and French access vis-à-vis other powers, London and Paris

---

[49] Brendon, 2007, 289–480; Cohen, 1991, 43–67; Ferguson, 2004, 185–302; Kupchan, 1994, 130–84, 214–67; Lowe, 1981, 175–76; Stowe, 1991, 205–06.

[50] Colbert, 1977, 98–101; Crosby, 1945, 65, 122–25; Kupchan, 1994, 267–96; Stowe, 1991, 125–29, 65; Tarling, 1998, 2–9, 2005, 1–5.

[51] Crosby, 1945, 54–65, 93–94.

External Intervention and the Politics of State Formation

even acceded to Bangkok's demands for the relinquishment of extraterritoriality. This paved the way for post–World War I British and French agreements to return tariff autonomy to the Thai government and end extraterritorial jurisdiction.

When the leaders in London and Paris began to see the opportunity costs of intervention as prohibitively high with start of World War II, efforts to secure even nonprivileged access receded. Accordingly, French attempts to safeguard access largely ceased. The British restricted activities in Thailand to small-scale support for the anti-Japanese Free Thai meant to disrupt the Japanese rear and the pro-Japanese Bangkok government of Phibun Songkhram.[52] These operations were, however, afterthoughts that came late in the war.[53] Upon victory, Britain's Attlee cabinet attempted to impose punitive demands on Bangkok that would establish access regulation over Thailand.[54] Such calls came alongside the retrocession to British control of areas in northern Malaya and Burma that Siam annexed with Japanese support during World War II.

However, London was unwilling to commit anything more than diplomatic pressure to obtain these goals and, in the face of American opposition, substantially rolled back these claims.[55] France, on the other hand, demanded and, in 1947, received the retrocession of areas administered by French-run Cambodia and Laos before the war in return for not vetoing Thailand's United Nations admission.[56] Even as their Southeast Asian colonies came under increasing nationalist and communist pressure by the late 1940s, neither London nor Paris sought more than the guarantee of nonprivileged access into Thailand.[57]

---

[52] Baker and Phongpaichit, 2005, 142–43; Brailey, 1986, 103–13; Haseman, 2002; Reynolds, 2005; Tarling, 1998, 22–26; Terwiel, 2005, 277; Wilson, 1962, 20–22; Wyatt, 1984, 259.

[53] Stowe, 1991, 258–332.

[54] Demands included preferential economic treatment, the indefinite positioning of British troops in Thailand, and the provision of 1.5 million tons of free rice in addition to full compensation for losses to British property during the war. These demands aimed to keep the Thai military in check as well as to punish the Thai government for its earlier alliance with Japan, acquiescence of Japan's use of Thai territory to stage invasions into Malaya and Burma, and Bangkok's annexation of northern Malaya and the Shan states in Burma. The northern Malay states and Shan areas that the Thai government took over during the war were regions under Thai suzerainty as late as 1909. Brailey, 1986, 114–27; Colbert, 1977, 96–97; Ibrahim, 1985, 67; Muscat, 1990, 19; Stowe, 1991, 337–59; Tarling, 1998, 26–50, 108–28; Terwiel, 2005, 275–80; Wyatt, 1984, 262; Yahuda, 1996, 34.

[55] The final settlement between the Thai and British governments involved the sale of the 1.5 million tons of rice below market prices. Brailey, 1986, 114, 27–28; Colbert, 1977, 96–101; Kahin, 1953, 37; Muscat, 1990, 19; Terwiel, 2005, 279–80; Wyatt 1984, 259.

[56] Like the aforementioned areas in Burma and Malaya, regions in Cambodia and Laos that came under Thai control during World War II were under Siamese suzerainty until 1907. Wyatt, 1984, 262.

[57] With the beginning of the communist insurgency in Malaya and rising tensions with the Eastern Bloc in Europe in 1948, the British government extended quick diplomatic recognition to the military cabinet Phibun Songkhram led after his successful *coup d'etat*. London did so in hope of acquiring Thai help in controlling Thai-Malayan border where the Malayan Communist Party operated rather than to compete over access denial within Thailand. Colbert, 1977, 94–97; Kahin, 1953, 37; Lowe, 1997, 3–4; Tarling, 1998, 108–28, 151–60, 180–83, 236–54, 270–72, 295–309, 373–402, 2005, 55–70, 122–26, 206–10; Wyatt, 1984, 267–68.

Siam Stands Apart, 1893–1952

Opportunity Cost Expectations and the Tempering of Japanese Imperialism

From 1923 to 1952, Japanese leaders' expectations about the opportunity costs of intervention declined from prohibitive to high before returning to prewar levels. Until the early 1940s, Japan's government was happy to forgo serious attempts to secure access in Thailand in order to concentrate capabilities on expanding access denial efforts in China. This represented the predominant view in Tokyo at the time, which understood access denial in China to promise greater returns than similar goals elsewhere.

With the militarist ascendancy in Tokyo in the mid 1930s and the subsequent curtailing of war material made available to Japan by America, Britain, and Holland, access denial over Southeast Asia grew in prominence for Japan's leaders.[58] The Japanese military saw Thailand as a staging area for Japanese military operations into Burma to the west and into Malaya and the East Indies to the south, piquing Japanese interest in ensuring at least nonprivileged access through the backing of cooperative indigenous groups.[59] Tokyo's concern with directly competing for access in Thailand ended with Japan's defeat and occupation.

JAPAN'S RESTRAINT TOWARD THAILAND   In line with the shifts in the Japanese governments' perceptions about the opportunity costs of intervention in Siam, Tokyo sought to ensure nonprivileged access over Thailand only between 1942 and 1945. Bangkok's initial reluctance to grant the Japanese military the right of passage through Thailand led to a brief Japanese attack on the morning of December 8, 1941, but this ceased when Prime Minister Phibun Songkhram acceded to Japanese demands several hours later.[60] Notably, the Japanese did not attempt to occupy Thailand or directly manage and regulate access over the polity once assured of Bangkok's cooperation. Rather, Tokyo welcomed the Phibun Songkhram government as an independent partner of Japan, even handing over control of former Siamese vassal territories in Malaya, Cambodia, and Laos to Bangkok whilst abetting a Thai invasion of the Shan states in Burma.[61] As was the case elsewhere in Asia, Tokyo was unable to contend for access in Thailand between defeat in the Pacific War and the end of the U.S. occupation in 1952.

---

[58] Barnhart, 1987, 19, 44, 63, 146–75, 191–224, 245–46, 1995, 127–42; Crosby, 1945, 63–65; Ishikawa, 1995, 406–89; Iwatake, 1989; Kinhide, 1973, 597–98; Kupchan, 1994, 334–55; Sadao, 1973, 244–54; Sato, 1994, 5–14; Snyder, 1991, 112–52; Tarling, 2001, 39–83, 125–46; Toru, 1977, 322–26; Wilkins, 1973, 366–67.

[59] Baker and Phongpaichit, 2005, 135–37; Barnhart, 1987, 159n–60n, 206–20; Bastin and Benda, 1968, 124–26; Bayly and Harper, 2004, 108–15, 57, 218; Crosby, 1945, 64–67, 108, 25; Haseman, 2002, 11–13; Ibrahim, 1985, 67; Katsuro, 1973, 299–301; Stowe, 1991, 179–223; Tarling, 2001, 61–66, 83–85, 125–46, 204–10, 246–49; Terwiel, 2005, 275.

[60] Baker and Phongpaichit, 2005, 135–37; Brailey, 1986, 84–86; Crosby, 1945, 128–30; Haseman, 2002, 4–11; Lowe, 1981, 178; Stowe, 1991, 218–26; Wyatt, 1984, 256–58.

[61] Barnhart, 1987, 213–20; Crosby, 1945, 64–67; Haseman, 2002, 11–13; Katsuro, 1973, 299–301; Terwiel, 2005, 275–76; Wilson, 1962, 19–20.

AN AMERICAN APPROACH TO ACCESS COMPETITION AMIDST GLOBAL CONCERNS   American leaders saw the opportunity costs of intervention in the Thai state decline from prohibitively high levels to high between 1923 and 1952. Up through the outbreak of the Pacific War in late 1941, a mixture of isolationist sentiments and pressure from the Great Depression convinced Washington that serious competition for access on the Asian mainland was a waste of precious capabilities. Securing access in Siam – as in other Southeast Asian locales outside the Philippines – could potentially tie down capabilities with little to show for in return.[62] This remained the case during World War II, where Washington policymakers saw Siam as an opportunity to disrupt the Japanese rear.[63]

The end of World War II and the inklings of a global Cold War, however, raised the value of access denial in the eyes of the U.S. government. United States policymakers thought it important to keep nonprivileged access over the Thai state in order to maintain a noncommunist ally.[64] Trying to directly regulate access or fully deny access to the Siamese polity would distract from greater concerns in Europe and elsewhere, but less than nonprivileged access for American interests could erode the U.S. position in Southeast Asia.[65] This remained the case after 1948, with tensions rising in Europe, the start of the Malayan Emergency, Communist victory in China, and the outbreak of the Korean War, even if increased commitments were necessary just to sustain nonprivileged access.[66]

Corresponding with prohibitively high U.S. expectations about the opportunity costs of intervention from 1923 to around 1945, Washington retained a limited presence in Thailand before World War II. Since the early twentieth century, the American government permitted citizens affiliated with U.S. officialdom to provide advice to the central Thai government, especially in foreign policy, but the American role in Siam paled in comparison to Britain and France.[67] Probably because of the perceived limited importance of Siam, Washington was also the first major Western power to end its claims to extraterritorial privileges in Siam following the Versailles Conference. In anticipation of the Pacific War and as a response to Siam's annexation of parts of Indochina after France's fall, however, Washington seized Thai arms purchases and conditioned petroleum sales on guarantees of Thai tin and rubber from late 1940 to

[62] Kennan, 1984, 3–90; Lowe, 1981, 126–222.
[63] Haseman, 2002; Wyatt, 1984, 260–68.
[64] Brailey, 1986, 111–17, 71–79; Colbert, 1977, 27–51, 86–100, 137–43, 163–64, 197–217; Tarling, 1998, 108–28; Toru, 1977, 331–32; Yahuda, 1996, 34–35.
[65] Barnhart, 1987, 183, 96, 217; Cohen, 1973, 457; Darling, 1962, 96–100; Graebner, 1973, 44–51; Kahin, 1977, 345–52; Kupchan, 1994, 472; Lowe, 1981, 173–76; Weigley, 1973, 181–87; Wyatt, 1984, 267–72.
[66] Baker and Phongpaichit, 2005, 140, 144; Fineman, 1997, 89–125; Gaddis, 2005, 87–124; Lowe, 1997, 126–222; Muscat, 1990, 18–19; Thayer, 1953; Toru, 1977, 229–333.
[67] Francis B. Sayre, later Ambassador to Siam, High Commissioner of the Philippines, and an Assistant Secretary of State under Franklin D. Roosevelt, for instance, was instrumental in helping Bangkok renegotiate treaties with the foreign powers after the Great War. Sayre was also a son-in-law of Woodrow Wilson. Darling, 1962, 93–96; Eldon, 1922; Wyatt, 1984, 178, 231.

Siam Stands Apart, 1893–1952 215

mid 1941.[68] As the Pacific War got underway, Washington merely saw access in Thailand as a means to disturb Japanese lines, evidenced by the small-scale joint operations with the British and the Free Thai from 1944 on.[69]

Given the drop of the anticipated opportunity costs of intervention to high levels after World War II, U.S. leaders began to invest capabilities into sustaining an independent and centralised Thai government that would not discriminate against American access. Washington defused British pressure for the punitive treatment of Thailand for its wartime government's siding with Japan, while helping Bangkok reestablish relations with Britain and France as well as to enter the United Nations.[70] At the same time, U.S. leaders extended US$10 million in loans for rebuilding whilst purchasing large amounts of Thai commodities to help give Bangkok much-needed foreign exchange.[71]

With American fears about a growing global communist threat by the late 1940s, including in neighbouring Indochina, Washington evinced even more support for the central Thai government in Bangkok. Supportive actions included backing a new Phibun Songkhram military cabinet that came to power through a *coup d'etat*. Such assistance came in spite of the cabinet's nonliberal proclivities and the fact Phibun was heavily responsible for pushing Thailand into its wartime alliance with Japan.[72] Bangkok further received substantial U.S military as well as developmental training and advice.[73]

In addition, the Thai government received about US$500 million in military and economic aid from Washington between 1951 and 1957.[74] American assistance amounted to 26 percent of the central government budget at the time, whilst U.S. military aid alone stood at almost two-and-a-half times the Thai defence budget. Further, the sourcing of commodities from Thailand by the United States

---

[68] The U.S. government redirected aircraft purchased by Phibun Songkhram's government to the Philippines, and stopped petroleum shipments from November 1940. Barnhart, 1987, 213, 220; Stowe, 1991, 166–67, 188; Wyatt, 1984, 244–45, 256.

[69] The Phibun government joined the Axis on January 25, 1942, even declaring war on the United States and Britain. Acting on his own authority, the Thai ambassador to Washington, Seni Pramoj, refused to deliver the declaration of war. Many claim that this created U.S. goodwill toward Thailand, which brought American support in the face of French and British postwar demands for punitive action. B.J. Terwiel, however, cites Josef Goebbels's diary in noting that the Japanese government actually advised Bangkok against declaring war on Britain and the United States. Baker and Phongpaichit, 2005, 137; Brailey, 1986, 103–28; Darling, 1962, 95–98; Haseman, 2002; Reynolds, 2005; Stowe, 1991, 258–332; Terwiel, 2005, 275, 75n, 77–80; Wilson, 1962, 20–22.

[70] Colbert, 1977, 94–101, 37–43; Kahin, 1953, 37; Muscat, 1990, 18–21; Tarling, 1998, 108–28; Wyatt, 1984, 261–62.

[71] Baker and Phongpaichit, 2005, 144; Darling, 1962, 97; Koyle, 1953, 117–18; Muscat, 1990, 32–41; Yahuda, 1996, 34–35.

[72] Baker and Phongpaichit, 2005, 144–47; Bastin and Benda, 1968, 168–69; Brailey, 1986, 146–55; Fineman, 1997, 11–125, 147–68; Peleggi, 2007, 17; Terwiel, 2005, 281–82.

[73] Anderson, 1998, 142–46; Colbert, 1977, 154–64, 209–10; Darling, 1962, 99–100; Fineman, 1997, 69–125, 147–68; Muscat, 1990, 20–145; Terwiel, 2005, 282–83.

[74] Anderson, 1998, 142–46; Brailey, 1986, 179–86; Fineman, 1997, 131–99; Muscat, 1990, 20–70; Terwiel, 2005, 282–83; Wyatt, 1984, 271–72.

216 *External Intervention and the Politics of State Formation*

TABLE 8.2 *Convergent Foreign Expectations about the High Opportunity Costs of Intervention in Thailand and Corresponding Approaches to Access Denial, 1923–1952*

Outside Actor	Expected Opportunity Cost	Approach to Access Denial
France	High	Nonprivileged Access
Britain	High	Nonprivileged Access
United States	Until 1945, Prohibitively High 1945 and after, High	Concede Access Nonprivileged Access
Japan	Until 1941, Prohibitively High 1941–1945, High 1945 and after, Prohibitively High	Concede Access Nonprivileged Access Concede Access

during the Korean War fuelled a war boom in the Thai economy.[75] For the Truman administration, such assistance aimed to help consolidate the position of Thai leaders who could guarantee nonprivileged access and free up U.S. capabilities for more urgent uses.[76]

Table 8.2 depicts the opportunity cost expectations and approaches to safeguarding access denial for external governments most active in and around Thailand.

External Involvement in Consolidating Sovereign Statehood

Persistent, shared major power perceptions about the high opportunity costs of intervening within the Thai polity created conditions conducive to the entrenchment of sovereign statehood between 1923 and 1952. Foreign actors with an interest in competing for access over the Thai state placed consistent support behind a highly centralised government in Bangkok that exercised substantial external autonomy and territorial exclusivity. This provided an environment where state form in Siam could solidify in the direction of sovereign statehood going from the 1920s into the mid twentieth century.

EXTERNAL AUTONOMY

That external actors tended to extend outright support for Thai independence fostered substantial external autonomy even as colonisation and wartime occupation embroiled the rest of East Asia. Persistent expectations about the high opportunity costs of intervention amongst the major powers involved in competition over access in and around Siam meant that no external actor was ready to impose its authority over Bangkok's foreign relations. The prewar

[75] Baker and Phongpaichit, 2005, 144–52; Bastin and Benda, 1968, 168–69.
[76] Colbert, 1977, 96–100, 137–43, 163–64, 197–217; Wyatt, 1984, 267–68.

Siam Stands Apart, 1893–1952

Anglo-French guarantee of Siamese independence and the Japanese and Allied reluctance to take over Thailand during and after World War II gave the Thai government the freedom to consistently manage its external affairs without an outside veto.

What was effectively major power backing for a high level of external autonomy for the Siamese state gave the Thai government the leeway to manage its foreign affairs based on its own calculations of interest, free from external oversight. Based on its desire to restore tariff autonomy and end extraterritorial jurisdiction, Bangkok could unreservedly engage in efforts to renegotiate its treaty relations with foreign governments throughout the 1920s.[77] In 1941, under the direction of the Phibun cabinet and with Japanese political support, the Thai military moved successfully against French forces in Indochina to take over territories along the Thai-Cambodian border ceded to France in 1893.[78] The Thai government was likewise able to ally with Japan early in the Pacific War and then quickly switch allegiances as the tide of war changed.[79] The post–World War II Bangkok government also found that it could move to the anticommunist camp for guarantees of American diplomatic, military, economic aid as the Cold War escalated the late 1940s.[80]

TERRITORIAL EXCLUSIVITY

By refraining from direct involvement in governance within the Siamese polity, foreign powers fostered the development and continuation of a high degree of territorial exclusivity in Thailand between 1923 and 1952. Reassurance that rivals would not receive advantages in access coupled with expectations about the high opportunity costs of intervention enabled all external actors to accede to Siamese demands to rescind extraterritorial privileges by the late 1920s.[81] This ended direct foreign participation in governance within the Thai state, which was at any rate confined to the management of tariffs and legal jurisdiction over foreign nationals.

Subsequently, all matters pertaining to government administration fell completely to indigenous actors inside the Thai state. Most obvious were language standardisation using Bangkok Thai, implementation of anti-Chinese policies, and transitions in regime type from absolute to constitutional monarchy by 1932 and toward military rule from 1938 to 1944 and again after 1948.[82] Foreign

---

[77] Wyatt, 1984, 230–31.

[78] Barnhart, 1987, 213, 220; Crosby, 1945, 117–21; Terwiel, 2005, 272–76; Wilson, 1962, 19–20; Wyatt, 1984, 244–72.

[79] Baker and Phongpaichit, 2005, 116–41; Brailey, 1968, 94–105; Haseman, 2002, 11–13, 122–29; Muscat, 1990, 18–19; Stowe, 1991, 143–251, 80–359; Tarling, 2001, 61–85, 204–10, 246–49; Terwiel, 2005, 275–79; Wyatt, 1984, 256–61.

[80] Bastin and Benda, 1968, 124–37, 168–69; Muscat, 1990, 18.

[81] Wyatt, 1984, 230–31.

[82] Bastin and Benda, 1968, 168–69; Batson, 1984; Benda and Larkin, 1967, 185–89; Brailey, 1986, 25–78, 143–64; Chaianan, 1982, 6–18; Crosby, 1945, 72–91; Lissak, 1976, 73–107; Mokrapong,

218 *External Intervention and the Politics of State Formation*

governments also avoided intrigue in the events leading to and following King Prajadhipok's (Rama VII, r.1925–1935) abdication from the constitutional monarchy in 1935.[83] Outside powers remained similarly aloof from Thai domestic politics following the mysterious death of Prajadhipok's successor, King Ananda Mahidol (Rama VIII, r.1935–1946), in 1946.[84] This was in spite of the substantial British military presence in and around Thailand at the time, deployed to oversee the de-mobilisation of Japanese forces in mainland Southeast Asia.

POLITICAL CENTRALISATION

Major power efforts to secure nonexclusionary access across Siam by shoring up the central government fostered the entrenchment of high levels of political centralisation going into the early 1950s. Continued expectations about the high opportunity costs of intervention in Thailand amongst relevant major powers brought the extension of indirect efforts to ensure nonprivileged access through a central government. By not supporting regional challengers to central political authority, outside attempts to deny rivals privileged access in Siam gave Bangkok increasing wherewithal to veto political developments inside the polity.[85] Simultaneous economic, military, political, and other forms of assistance further bolstered the strength of the Bangkok central government.[86]

Going toward the 1950s, the central government in Bangkok was more able to impose its influence and will across the territory and population of Thailand. Bangkok was able to capitalise on its predominant domestic position as well as foreign support to further extend central government control across the Thai state.[87] This was despite frequent periods of economic and political uncertainty. In particular, the Bangkok government used Siam's already highly centralised institutions of governance to mobilise popular support. Both civilian and military cabinets in the period of leading up to World War II continued Vajiravudh's practice of promoting popular participation in paramilitary groups, such as the *Yuwachon* or "Angry Youth" movement, as a means of fostering national identity.[88] Together with the regular military and reserves, these paramilitary groups accounted for roughly 1 million people in arms and under central government control from a total population of approximately 14 million.[89]

1976, 73–96; Phongpaichit and Baker, 2002, 258–307; Suehiro, 1989, 106–34; Wilson, 1962, 11–30, 54–57, 69–70, 112–42.

[83] Owen, 2005, 35; Peleggi, 2007, 96–97; Phongpaichit and Baker, 2002, 268–72; Stowe, 1991, 9–120; Terwiel, 2005, 253–81.

[84] On June 9, 1946, attendants discovered Ananda Mahidol dead in his bed with gunshot wounds. The exact events remain unclear. Phongpaichit and Baker, 2002, 286; Terwiel, 2005, 280–81; Wyatt, 1984, 263–64.

[85] Riggs, 1966, 128–31, 148–207, 311–66; Wyatt, 1984, 230–72.

[86] Arsa, 1962, 120–349; Phongpaichit and Baker, 2002, 151–254.

[87] Riggs, 1976, 406–24; Siffin, 1976, 387–405; Wilson, 1962, 19, 54–57, 69–70, 150–163.

[88] Stowe, 1991, 85, 100, 112, 153.

[89] Wyatt, 1984, 249–59, 268.

Siam Stands Apart, 1893–1952 219

Bangkok's efforts to cultivate Thai nationalism also brought the suppression of non-Thai groups, especially the ethnic Chinese and Malay minorities.[90] Nationalist-driven programmes shut the Chinese out from particular business sectors, barred them from certain occupations, increased taxes on the Chinese-dominated commercial class, and established an alien registration tax for non-citizens.[91] Policies to promote the national Thai language restricted public instruction and publication in regional dialects as well as in Chinese and Malay.[92] Under the rubric of nationalism, Bangkok placed restrictions that suppressed organisation by Malays in the south, which brought about the arrest of a number of Malay leaders.[93] A change in the country's official title from "Siam" to "Thailand" in 1939 by the military-backed government of Phibun Songkhram too formed part of this attempt to foster nationalism. The significance of the new nomenclature lay in its suggestions of a link amongst all Tai-speaking peoples inside the Siamese state and out, as well as the belief that the whole polity belonged solely to Thai peoples.

The resulting primacy of the central government led political struggles to move away from differences between Bangkok and Siam's various regions and toward control of the centre. Whether they were supporters of absolute monarchy, promoters of constitutional monarchy, civilian politicians, or militarists, the prime political prize Thai politicians aspired to between 1923 and 1952 was to hold Bangkok.[94] An ability to manage government institutions at the centre spelt dominion over the entire polity. Prominence in a particular region was no longer as attractive, since the various parts of the Thai polity were increasingly subject to the central government.[95]

Evidence from 1923 to 1952 indicates that the aggregated pattern of external intervention based on continued common major power expectations of high and prohibitively high opportunity costs helped confirm Siamese sovereign statehood. Common conceptions about the high opportunity costs of intervention in Thailand led interested major powers to focus on preventing rivals from acquiring privileged access in the polity through support for a strong central government. Those with less verve simply stayed out of the way. Collectively,

---

[90] Ibrahim, 1985, 63–77; Terwiel, 2005, 281.

[91] Baker and Phongpaichit, 2005, 129–33; Brailey, 1986, 74–78; Peleggi, 2007, 201–02; Stowe, 1991, 118–20; Suehiro, 1989, 106–34.

[92] Crosby, 1945, 72–74; Peleggi, 2007, 121–23.

[93] Ibrahim, 1985, 63–77; Wyatt, 1984, 237, 253–68.

[94] The first major coup attempt in modern Thai history looked to take over the central government rather than the separation of a particular region as well. Behind this failed 1912 putsch were dissatisfied ethnic Chinese within the Thai military establishment. Chaianan, 1982, 6–18; Lissak, 1976, 73–107, 207–19; Neher, 1976, 367–86; Riggs, 1966, 211–41, 1976, 242–310, 406–24; Scott, 1976, 344–66; Siffin, 1976, 387–405; Terwiel, 2005, 253–72; Wilson, 1962, 67–69, 116–273, 1976, 331–43.

[95] Arsa, 1962, 120–349; Peleggi, 2007, 15–16, 232–52; Suehiro, 1989, 135–77; Thongchai, 1996, 67–91; Thongchai, 1994; Wyatt, 1984, 237, 267–68.

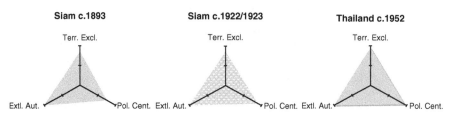

FIGURE 8.1 Shifts in State Form for Siam, 1893–1952

such actions had helped lock in the high levels of external autonomy, territorial exclusivity, and political centralisation already evident from 1893 to 1922. Acting on their expected opportunity costs, foreign actors jointly secured the sovereign Thai state.

Figure 8.1 here provides an outline of shifts in Thailand's state form between 1893 and 1922.

ALTERNATIVE PERSPECTIVES

Bellicism and State Form

Bellicist arguments provide a persuasive alternative explanation of the development and consolidation of Siamese sovereign statehood from 1893 to 1952 on some level. Evidence suggests that the shift from moderate to high levels of political centralisation and territorial exclusivity in the Thai state resulted from the central government's superior accumulation and concentration of capital as well as coercion relative to its domestic adversaries. The further strengthening of territorial exclusivity and political centralisation going into the mid twentieth century also rested on Bangkok's sustained edge in both concentrating and accumulating capital and the tools of coercion over its internal opponents. Coupled with Siam's existing high degree of external autonomy, this capital- and coercion-driven rise in political centralisation along with territorial exclusivity represented the polity's development from a feudalised state to a sovereign one.

However, the central Thai government's ability to concentrate and accumulate coercive abilities and capital more effectively than other domestic actors did not result from pressure to go to war. The aggregated actions of outside actors, notably France, Britain, Japan, and the United States, empowered the central government and abetted the latter's efforts to rule the entire Thai polity. Outside assistance enabled the central government to acquire increasing financial and coercive wherewithal. Further, Bangkok's acceptance of foreign assistance in developing its capacity to acquire and employ both force and wealth across the polity originated from a desire to mollify rather than openly resist external

Siam Stands Apart, 1893–1952 221

threats.[96] Bangkok's demonstration of Siam's value as a stable buffer and ally gave foreign actors incentives to maintain an independent Thai polity under central government jurisdiction and refrain from abetting fragmentary forces.[97]

Institutional Commitment and State Formation

The institutional commitment perspective carries some initial weight in explaining the emergence and persistence of sovereign statehood in the Thai polity, but remains unable to discount the critical role of foreign intervention. Rising relative levels of administrative and bureaucratic effectiveness were important in helping Bangkok to commit more credibly to providing public goods and protecting commercial activity than regional authorities, such as the Chiang Mai and Pattani nobility.[98] In return, the central government could then demand more regular support and extract revenues more consistently from the population compared to domestic rivals from the late nineteenth century on.[99] Yet, the revamping of governance was a process heavily supported by external powers planning to maintain a relatively strong Thai central government able to independently ensure nonprivileged access across the entire polity on the cheap.[100] Such a central government may also provide an interlocutor that could credibly commit to maintaining foreign interests.

Self-Determination and Nationalism

Self-determinationist arguments about Thailand's departure from feudalised statehood and the subsequent entrenchment of sovereign statehood in the 1893 to 1922 and 1923 to 1952 periods appear weaker. Siam's movement toward sovereign statehood in the late nineteenth century coincided with the cresting of the last great wave of colonial expansion, and predated the early rise in global self-determination norms in the 1910s by about two decades.[101] Admittedly, foreign powers enjoyed extraterritorial privileges in the Thai polity into the late 1920s, but major powers imposed a host of similarly demanding conditions on many weaker sovereign European states after both World Wars.[102]

---

[96] Williams, 1976, 188–89, 234–37.

[97] Wyatt, 1984, 201–10, 230–31, 256–72.

[98] Brown, 1988; Hewison, 1989, 41–91; Mead, 2004.

[99] Brown, 1988, 151–81; Phongpaichit and Baker, 2002, 256.

[100] Wyatt, 1984, 208–31, 256–72.

[101] This challenges claims that the post–World War I and post–World War II emergence of self-determinationist, anticolonial norms around the world largely spurred sovereign state creation. See, for example, Barnett and Finnemore, 1999, 713; Fazal, 2007.

[102] Stephen Krasner argues that demands on the new European states included acceptance of minority rights and particular regime types. He claims that external demands that erode territorial exclusivity are common to polities that approximated sovereign statehood in the nineteenth to twentieth centuries. Krasner, 1999.

Nationalism too seems to have its limits as an explanation for the development of sovereign statehood in the Thai polity. Mobilisation under a nationalist banner in Siam only began in earnest during the 1910s, by which time sovereign statehood was already a fixture. Central government bureaucracies like the Interior, Finance, and Education ministries, as well as the military, were the major conduits for promoting common beliefs and language, which proponents of nationalism deem so critical, amongst the population.[103] This suggests that sovereign statehood gave rise to modern nationalism in the Siamese polity rather than the other way around.[104] Nationalist mobilisation, however, did seem to help consolidate sovereign statehood by motivating mass support behind Bangkok's efforts to firm up already high levels of political centralisation.[105] Even then, nationalist mobilisation seemed more geared toward forwarding the positions of particular groups, regimes, and agendas than directly advancing sovereign statehood.[106]

CONCLUSION

Common major power perspectives about the high to prohibitively high intervention costs in Siam led efforts at securing access to have the collective effect of promoting sovereign statehood. Such pressures enabled state form in Siam to shift from feudalised toward sovereign statehood by the early twentieth century, well before many other weak polities along the global periphery. Constant major power expectations regarding the high opportunity costs of intervening in the Thai state between the early 1920s and early 1950s further bolstered already high levels of political centralisation, external autonomy, and territorial exclusivity. That the aggregated effects of major power efforts to secure access – as shaped by consistent expectations about the high opportunity costs of intervention – drove the emergence and consolidation of a sovereign Siamese state supports my intervention-based perspective.

Aside from highlighting my theoretical claims, among the more interesting aspects of state formation in Thailand from 1893 to 1952 are the implications for understanding nationalism. Nationalist mobilisation played a limited role in Siam's initial movement away from feudalised statehood. Rather, successful sovereign state creation actually reinforced nationalism and nationalist mobilisation. Insofar as it pertained to particular political agendas, nationalism may

---

[103] Baker and Phongpaichit, 2005, 105–39; Barmé, 1993; Crosby, 1945, 50–51, 111–16; Phongpaichit and Baker, 2002, 259–78; Wyatt, 1969, 376–85, 1984, 225–39, 252–59, 272.

[104] For arguments about the centrality of a common language and set of beliefs as a cause of sovereign state formation, see Anderson, 1991; Smith, 1983; Tarling, 2001, 343–94, 2004.

[105] Barmé, 1993; Crosby, 1945, 50–51, 72–74, 97–98, 107–16; Phongpaichit and Baker, 2002, 259–78; Wyatt, 1969, 376–85, 1984, 227–30, 252–68.

[106] Brailey, 1986, 74–78; Ibrahim, 1985, 63–77; Stowe, 1991, 118–20; Suehiro, 1989, 106–34; Terwiel, 2005, 281; Wilson, 1962, 54–57, 69–70.

Siam Stands Apart, 1893–1952

demonstrate its greatest effect as an instrument through which Thai leaders consolidated and extended sovereign statehood, especially political centralisation. This suggests that nationalism may have varying political and social effects depending on how it interacts with other factors in the broader environment. In this respect, it may be worthwhile to further probe the dynamics surrounding nationalism and nationalist mobilisation.

CHAPTER 9

Domesticating International Relations, Externalising Comparative Politics

Foreign Intervention and the State in World Politics

Outside intervention into the domestic politics of weak states is a prominent part in world politics, and one that has far-reaching consequences for the nature of governance and political authority in fragile polities. This is as true for places like Afghanistan, Iraq, Somalia, and Timor Leste today as it was for China, Siam, and the Netherlands Indies from the late nineteenth to the mid twentieth centuries. My project is an attempt to add to systematic efforts at examining the effects of external intervention on institutions of governance, rule, and political authority. In particular, I elaborate on the broader influences that outside forces can have on the establishment and maintenance of order over populations and territory.

Through a focus on East Asia, this study addresses these issues by examining the effects of external involvement on state formation – particularly the establishment of sovereign statehood – in the global periphery. I posited that the state form a weak polity adopts results from changes in the pattern of major power competition, conditional on major power perceptions about the opportunity costs of intervention in the area. Sovereign statehood developed when major powers settled on promoting nonprivileged access in a fragile state when expected intervention costs were high. Foreign governments saw this outcome as the next best alternative to their greatest fear, domination of the area by adversaries.

I evaluated this claim by paying special attention to China, the Netherlands Indies/Indonesia, and Siam/Thailand between the end of the nineteenth century and the middle of the twentieth. These polities – particularly China – during this period presented "least likely" cases for my position that also embodied the features of weak states both in East Asia and elsewhere. Since my argument applies to these instances, I have greater confidence in its robustness and generalisability. By expanding on existing work on external intervention as well as state formation in weak states, this project is an effort to expand on existing insights about these subjects.

One key finding is that foreign competition over and outside intervention into a polity can have the counter-intuitive effect of bolstering the development of

224

sovereign statehood under the right conditions. A common claim is that foreign involvement in the domestic politics of fragile polity fuels either domination or fragmentation. However, in looking to participate in the internal affairs of a state, foreign actors may at times have an incentive to shore up local order and governance. When all outside interveners share this outlook, the resulting policies of supporting stability through indigenous partners can help a weak state establish greater political centralisation, local territorial control, and outward autonomy. By highlighting how various external intervention efforts interact with each other and affect relations amongst local actors within a fragile polity, I provide another perspective through which to view intervention and its associated dynamics.

With a fuller appreciation for the relationship between foreign intervention and state formation, it may be possible to consider the possibilities and challenges facing externally supported attempts to establish order in weak states more fully. As recent examples in Iraq, Afghanistan, as well as Egypt and Libya during the 2011 Arab Spring attest, external efforts at reshaping domestic politics can have real, immediate, and serious consequences for the lives of people in a targeted polity. The nature of a state's institutions of governance – or lack of thereof – that result from outside interference can also affect the security of neighbouring populations. Understanding changes in the basic unit of the contemporary international system also may further efforts to appreciate how the contours of world politics can shift. Looking at external intervention and state formation too can help spur rethinking over the scope of bellicist, nationalist, self-determinationist, and institutional commitment accounts about state formation.

EXTERNAL POWERS, LOCAL ACTORS, AND THE MARKET FOR INTERVENTION

When outside intervention efforts converge on denying privileged access to rivals, a targeted polity tends to demonstrate the high levels of territorial exclusivity, political centralisation, and external autonomy associated with sovereign statehood. Motivating approaches to intervention into a particular polity are the expectations policymakers in an intervening power hold about the opportunity costs of intervention in the targeted area. Such considerations inform the strategy an external power adopts when trying to influence the domestic politics of a targeted state, notably the types of partnerships to strike with local political groups. The institutional configuration of governance and political authority that define state form in a target polity results from the aggregation of attempts by various foreign powers to shape domestic politics in conjunction with indigenous interlocutors.

The Supply and Demand of External Intervention

Behind the supply of external efforts to shape the domestic politics of a target state are elite expectations about the opportunity costs of intervention in that state. Leaders of intervening powers are fundamentally interested in denying access to rivals when it comes to competition over a targeted polity. Variations in approach rest on differences in how elites of an intervening power anticipate the opportunity costs of intervention in that state. The higher the expected net returns of committing limited capabilities toward denying access over a target state relative to those of investing in the next best alternative, the lower the anticipated opportunity costs of intervening in that polity. With low expectations of opportunity cost, outside powers seek to more completely and directly deny rivals access through greater control over local partners.

Foreign involvement in China, the East Indies, and Siam from the late nineteenth through the mid twentieth centuries illustrates ways in which opportunity cost expectations inform external approaches toward access denial and intervention in weak states. Japanese elite beliefs about the necessity of denying rivals access to China and the East Indies given increasingly severe systemic competition drove Tokyo's highly intrusive access regulation efforts over these two areas in the 1930s and 1940s. Elite perceptions about the importance of access denial over the East Indies to Holland's prosperity brought attempts by The Hague to sustain the Dutch colonial project in the Indonesia. Therefore, both Tokyo and The Hague cultivated local actors willing to subordinate themselves to foreign direction in return for control over a share of the state's surpluses whilst suppressing indigenous groups unsupportive of their goals.

In comparison, where elite views about systemic pressure reduced the expected net gains from access denial in a polity, external powers readily scaled back intervention efforts. General American, British, and, to some degree, Russian restraint toward the Chinese polity from the end of the nineteenth century to the middle of the twentieth stemmed from the focus of leaders in Washington, London, St. Petersburg, and Moscow on issues elsewhere. These ranged from heightened security concerns in Europe to imperial management and addressing systemic power transitions. Consequently, these external powers sought to minimise capability commitments in China whilst preventing other foreign actors from acquiring privileged access. This meant helping to put local actors in a position to independently manage and defend the polity.

Expected high intervention costs likewise led to Japanese, British, and French efforts to secure nondiscriminatory access in Siam, as well as London and Washington's promotion of equal access in Indonesia by the mid twentieth century. Limited foreign involvement in Siam throughout this time testifies to the consistency of foreign expectations about the high opportunity cost of intervening in that polity.

On the demand side, outside sponsorship provided various local actors in fragile states with valuable infusions of financial, military, and political assistance. This buttressed attempts by various indigenous groups to prevail over domestic competitors. Outside assistance may prove critical to indigenous political groups vying for control over at least parts of the state and its distribution of surpluses, whether militarist cliques, political parties, or criminal gangs.

Domesticating International Relations, Externalising Comparative Politics 227

The normally large number of domestic groups contending over a peripheral polity relative to the number of intervening powers pressures local groups to be price-takers rather than price-makers when setting conditions for external assistance. Indigenous political actors have an incentive to toe the line set by real and prospective foreign partners lest these external actors shift support toward rival domestic groups that promise to be more pliant. Local groups are more passive than outside powers in shaping state form precisely because of their larger numbers and power asymmetries next to outside actors.

This propensity of local groups to compromise with foreign sponsors plays out in the domestic politics in China, Siam, and the East Indies from the late nineteenth to mid twentieth centuries. Under the right conditions, groups from the Chinese Nationalists and Communists to the Indonesian Republicans and Thai militarists were ready to cede the same interests and concessions to foreign powers they accused opponents of betraying. Payoffs surrounding such deals often included foreign provision of military, financial, and political backing. For such support, the Chinese Nationalists were ready to give the Japanese exclusive privileges over railway and mining rights in Guangdong, just as Chinese Communists restored lapsed Tsarist concessions over Northeast China to the Soviet Union. By doing so, the behaviour of the standard-bearers of Chinese nationalism looked remarkably similar to the actions of the militarist cliques they vehemently opposed.

Domestic political actors appeared to experience the most success when they received greater and more consistent outside sponsorship than their adversaries. The militarist regimes of Duan Qirui's Anfu Clique and Zhang Zuolin's Fengtian Clique reached the height of their power when constant Japanese military and financial support gave them the edge to dominate or eliminate rivals. Aristocrats in the East Indies fared best when simultaneous strong Dutch backing and suppression of other domestic groups made their domestic prominence unassailable. Both the Chakri monarchy and the various post-1932 regimes in Siam were able to flourish under first Anglo-French, then Japanese, and subsequently American tutelage. The political fortunes of the Chinese Nationalists and Communists as well as the Indonesian Republicans likewise waxed and waned with the degree of foreign assistance they received relative to their rivals.

Foreign Intervention, Local Collaboration, and State Form

Attempts to impose different degrees of access denial gave rise to the development of dissimilar state forms. Higher levels of access denial favour institutions of governance that guarantee an intervening power a more substantial and exclusive veto over a polity's external affairs and internal administration. Annexation permits a foreign power to attain full denial of access over a polity. Colonisation enables access regulation, whilst sovereign statehood forestalls privileged access amongst external actors more or less equally. These are just some more common state forms. There are clearly other variations that fall

228 *External Intervention and the Politics of State Formation*

between or outside the list I present in terms of the degree of access denial they present to foreign actors.

Nevertheless, state form in a peripheral state ultimately results from the aggregation of efforts by various intervening powers to compete over access denial in conjunction with local partners. The institutional configuration of governance that develops within a peripheral state comes from the pressures and compromises that collectively result from the jostling between different external actors and their local partners. If a particular outside power and its domestic allies prevail, a target polity's state form may acquire characteristics most conducive to the dominant intervening actor's preferences for access denial.

If the contending external parties reach an impasse, each outside power would work with its indigenous partner to establish the desired degree of access denial over parts of the polity they control, fracturing of the state. If fragmentation is sufficiently severe, such stalemate may prompt disintegration of the polity, with each broken off area demonstrating state form consistent with the access denial demands of the dominant outside power there. This seems evident when considering patterns of foreign domination and independence in areas formerly within the Ottoman Empire from the late nineteenth century on.[1]

The cases examined in this study demonstrate the collective effects of external intervention on the shaping of state form in weak states. China's feudalisation until the mid twentieth century, where limited central authority and high external autonomy remained atop growing regional autonomy and external management of domestic governance, resulted from deadlocked external competition over access. This standoff came about from the fact that powers contending for access over China had divergent opportunity cost expectations about intervention, but generally did not wish to risk war to attain their preferred outcomes. The existence of the Dutch and Japanese colonial states in the East Indies followed from successful external attempts to impose access regulation over the polity, given that other powers were unwilling or unable to oppose. Siam's late-nineteenth-century shift toward sovereign statehood as well as later analogous developments in China and the East Indies reflect combined foreign attempts to promote nonprivileged access, as driven by beliefs about high opportunity costs.[2]

---

[1] Fromkin, 2009; Kayaoğlu, 2010.

[2] Some observers claim that the risk of malaria presented a direct cost that led both Britain and France to abstain from intervening more directly and robustly in Siam. Indeed, the reasoning here follows the logic presented by Daron Acemoglu, Simon Johnson, and James Robinson, among others, that mortality rates affected European colonisation and institution-building attempts. I contend that if the expected gains were sufficient, there still would have been attempts to regulate access. Malaria and other tropical diseases were no less prevalent in British colonies in Burma and Malaya, as well as French Indochina. For a discussion on mortality rates, colonisation, and institution formation, see Acemoglu, Johnson, and Robinson, 2001.

INTERVENTION AND STATE FORMATION TODAY

Foreign intervention in domestic politics remains integral to state formation processes in fragile polities today. A cursory glance at the world between the end of the twentieth century and the beginning of the twenty-first centuries reveals ample examples of heavy external participation in the domestic politics of state creation. These include the ongoing U.S.-led international efforts in Afghanistan and Iraq. Foreign roles in state formation are also clear in African Union attempts to instil order in Somalia and Southern Sudan, United Nations efforts in East Timor and Namibia, as well as the Euro-American project to help create a sovereign Kosovo. American and Israeli support for the Palestinian Liberation Organisation too may represent outside involvement in the internal dynamics of state formation. Foreign support and aid also proved helpful in the creation of the various sovereign polities that emerged from the Soviet Union.

The actions of outside powers continue to have a role in stunting the development of sovereign statehood in many instances as well. Pressures of external opposition and limited foreign support helped prevent the fuller development of sovereign statehood in Somaliland, Taiwan, Abkhazia, and South Ossetia, for example. Similarly, insufficiently strong foreign backing given forceful Russian opposition consigned the sovereign state creation project in Chechnya to failure. Divergent external efforts to shape domestic politics may similarly constrain the development of sovereign statehood in places like Lebanon, just like lack of sustained outside interest may consign Somalia to continued anarchy. Foreign involvement in state formation processes seems unlikely to abate in the twenty-first century, making a study of this relationship particularly salient for understanding world politics today.

Conversely, success in contemporary foreign-led endeavours to raise autonomy, centralisation, and territoriality in weak states seems to be tied to effective external convergence in commitment, sponsorship of local actors, and restrictions on foreign "spoilers". American progress in stabilising Iraq after 2007 appears to rest on substantial military and financial investment, incorporating the Sunni "Awakening", and limiting Iranian influence.[3] Devoting overwhelming military, financial, and logistic capacities, backing cooperative local actors, and curtailing unwanted outside forces too were key in advancing United Nations state-making attempts from Cambodia to Timor Leste, Sierra Leone, Namibia, Kosovo and South Sudan.[4] Similarly, there broad is recognition that the U.S.-led effort to foster a centralised, autonomous, and territorially exclusive Afghanistan may depend on such dynamics.[5] This may explain the Obama administration's willingness to increase military involvement, support for the regime in Kabul, coordination with international partners, and pressure on the

---

[3] To Receive Testimony on the Situation in Iraq and Progress Made by the Government of Iraq in Meeting Benchmarks and Achieving Reconciliation, 2008.

[4] Berdal and Economides, 2007; Caplan, 2005; Clark, 2001, 325–416; Ferguson, 2006, 310.

[5] Christia and Semple, 2009; Hearing to Receive Testimony on the Situation in Afghanistan, 2010.

Islamabad to deal with the Taliban and their supporters in neighbouring Pakistan. That said, building an orderly and stable polity with all the attributes of a sovereign state says little about domestic civil and political liberties, justice, and equality.

Looking at foreign attempts to intervene in the domestic politics of state formation both in aggregation and in interaction with local forces is clearly useful in understanding and even advising on how the institutionalisation of governance can develop in a polity. The organisation of political authority, government administration, and rule in a state tends to be a consequence of the playing out of multiple contending and complementary forces. By taking seriously the collective effects of competition and compromise amongst external powers and indigenous actors, my argument offers a precise and comprehensive account of why a state comes to take on the organisational form that it does. Such a perspective may be informative for scholars and policymakers with an interest in understanding and addressing issues relating to governance and order in fragile states.

In looking at different external approaches to intervention in weak polities, I also highlight the variegated characteristics of outside participation in domestic politics. Competition over access is a fundamental motivation for the intervening powers, but different understandings of opportunity cost can lead outside powers to adopt divergent strategies even when interceding in the same target polity. Based on dissimilar expectations about the net gains of investing in access denial over a state relative to an alternative goal, foreign powers may intervene in the state to subjugate, fragment, destabilise, or even bolster governance, rule, and political authority. My study highlights how intervention can go beyond the conquest, mediation, reconstruction, or extension of loans often associated with outside involvement in domestic politics.[6]

Apart from adding a consideration of outside intervention to the literature on state formation, this book speaks to a wider discussion on the potential for change in the units that constitute the international system. My second image-reversed perspective extends the claim that membership in the international system rests on external, great power recognition. Specifically, it highlights the influence of major powers on the nature of governance and political authority in a weak polity, especially as they respond to shifting systemic pressures.[7]

Accounting for external intervention may also present a way to understand the effects of anticolonial and self-determinationist norms on the propagation of sovereign statehood around the mid twentieth century.[8] After all, these norms predated World War II. The majority of anticolonial and self-determination

---

[6] See Centeno, 1997, 2002; Centeno and López-Alves, 2001; Herbst, 2000; Hui, 2004, 185–94, 2005, 50–108; Taylor and Botea, 2008.

[7] For examples of work on the roles of external powers on international system membership, see Coggins, 2006; Fazal, 2004, 2007.

[8] For a discussion on the roles that anticolonial and self-determination norms played in promoting sovereign statehood after World War II, see Fazal, 2004, 2007.

Domesticating International Relations, Externalising Comparative Politics 231

movements also did not attain their avowed goals of independence during World War II, when major colonial powers faced significant economic, political, and strategic stress. Self-determination and anticolonial movements instead seemed most successful when receiving support from one of the competing Cold War sides even as reconstruction or other concerns absorbed the coloniser.

Considering the dynamics of intervention also may help generate insights into the directions in which the current international system may develop. If ongoing power transitions and nonstate security threats alter elite perceptions about the opportunity costs of intervention sufficiently, especially amongst the major powers, this may portend changes in the nature of systemic competition. Such shifts may imply a new acceptability of external intervention efforts in weak states that cut against sovereign statehood. Perhaps U.S.-led efforts to reformulate the state in Afghanistan and Iraq reflect the playing out of such forces. If nothing else, the logic of intervention provides another perspective with which to think about the possibilities for change in world politics.

NATIONALISM MAY BE OVERSTATED

Worth some elaboration is the finding that nationalist groups may sometimes have a far smaller role in state formation than commonly supposed and that they have survived domestic and foreign pressures through external sponsorship. This finding suggests a need to better appreciate the limits as well as the many diverse effects of nationalist ideologies. Groups with nationalist agendas existed in China and Indonesia well before the appearance of sovereign statehood, sometimes by several decades or more. For much of this time, colonial authorities and rival domestic actors were able to effectively curtail, or even suppress, nationalist groups, rendering them unable to muster the support necessary to effect substantial political change. In Siam, nationalism even seemed to follow the establishment of sovereign statehood rather than the other way around.

Instead of some wellspring of popular backing, what gave nationalist groups the financial, military, and political wherewithal to persist against the challenges they faced was often patronage by foreign powers. When accepting outside help, nationalist groups often accepted provisions that restricted the state's territorial exclusivity and external autonomy. Such infusions of outside aid enabled nationalist groups to resist political centralisation efforts by other domestic actors. This suggests that nationalist groups may be willing to sacrifice their goals of promoting sovereign statehood for a degree of control over the polity and the distribution of its surpluses.

Nationalist success at establishing sovereign statehood in fragile polities too tended to follow the effects of foreign intervention rather than just cultivation and consolidation of popular support. Groups propounding nationalism in weak states often prevailed domestically when they consistently received more effective external backing than their local opponents, or when external intervention rendered rivals unable to compete. Local groups tended not to enjoy

232   *External Intervention and the Politics of State Formation*

distinct advantages when vying for power through efforts to mobilise the population behind a nationalist agenda alone.

The wave of post–World War II nationalist successes came as the cumulative effects of the Depression, World War II, reconstruction, and the Cold War diminished major power expectations about the net gains of access regulation across much of the world. Elites in most major powers found it more cost-effective to concentrate capabilities on more pressing strategic matters relating to rebuilding and the Cold War standoff. In the periphery, they accepted more limited goals of denying rivals privileged access through the backing of appropriate local groups. This meant supporting nationalists to seek sovereign statehood.

The more limited role of nationalist mobilisation during state formation does not imply a lack of significance, however. Nationalism was especially important for state-building after the creation of sovereign statehood. Nationalism may be a little bit overrated, but it is consequential. This nonlinearity between the processes of state formation and state-building in fact suggests that factors important in establishing a particular organisational form may differ from those that sustain its existence. Nationalism may come to the fore as a tool for mobilising a population behind efforts to institutionalise political authority and rule by a group once it is able to shape and direct the content as well as meaning of patriotism.

Such manipulation of nationalism for state consolidation purposes informed the Chinese Communists' decision to participate in the Korean War, initiate the 1954 and 1958 Taiwan Strait crises, and launch various mass campaigns following 1949.[9] This logic similarly guided the Sukarno government's efforts to mobilise the Indonesian populace behind its Guided Democracy and the *Konfrontasi* policies in the 1950s and 1960s. Elite-led popular nationalism too emerged as a major instrument for state-building in Siam after modernising Thai leaders effectively seized control of the state from the 1910s onward.

Popular impressions about the overarching importance of nationalism in both state formation and state-building may originate from *post hoc* attempts to remake the nationalist narrative. As part of efforts to mobilise public support after victory, it is understandable that nationalist groups emphasised their contributions and successes whilst playing down factors that undercut such claims.[10] This task was easier when a particular group in effect monopolised the interpretation and recounting of events. Even as forceful a proponent of the nationalist position as Benedict Anderson notes that:

[I]n the "nation-building" policies of the new states one sees both a genuine, popular nationalist enthusiasm and a systematic, even Machiavellian, instilling of nationalist ideology through the mass media, the educational system, administrative regulations, and so forth.[11]

---

[9] Chen, 1994, 220–23; Christensen, 1996, 194–241.
[10] Anderson, 1991, 159.
[11] Anderson, 1991, 114–15.

Domesticating International Relations, Externalising Comparative Politics 233

Avoiding unintended biases arising from such interpretations of events was a major challenge in my efforts to understand the processes behind state formation. Understanding states, institutions, and political processes may require distinguishing the nation from other phenomena as well as consideration of alternative accounts alongside nationalist narratives.[12]

PATHS FOR FURTHER ENQUIRY

A crude survey of commonly available datasets suggests that a large number of armed conflicts involve military participation by outside third parties. If the bellicist perspective is correct in identifying an association between war and state formation, then the data suggest that external intervention may be part of this process. Even then, available large-n data generally do not provide sufficiently fine-grained information to allow for a further investigation of the relationship between external intervention and state creation. Available data also restrict observations to foreign participation in armed conflict and crises, and exclude outside external intervention in domestic politics short of such situations. Close examination of the approaches to and consequences of foreign involvement in domestic politics can help further understandings of state formation and state-building.

According to the Correlates of War Project (COW) data, for instance, 24.3 percent of intra- and extrastate wars between 1816 and 1997 included armed third-party involvement.[13] Data on Armed Conflict from the Uppsala Conflict Data Project and International Peace Research Institute listed third-party military involvement in 12.7 percent of conflict years and 12.8 percent of inter-, intra-, and extrastate conflicts from 1946 to 2006.[14] Of the international crises between 1918 and 2005 in the International Crisis Behaviour Project (ICB) dataset, 15 percent contained some form of great power participation and 37.8 percent elicited third-party mediation.[15] With the exception of the ICB dataset – which excludes internal conflicts – information about intervention in the other datasets does not go beyond whether external intervention occurred and the number as well as identity of the intervening governments.

In focusing on intervention, this project can help refine and extend current work on state formation. Specifically, it can offer another means with which to evaluate the effects of external intervention on state formation in weak states for both qualitative and quantitative research. If nothing else, it suggests additional variables to consider and test. To begin, these may include the amounts, types, and

---

[12] Dikötter, 2008; Duara, 1995, 2009.
[13] The datasets list extrastate wars as conflicts between state governments and nonstate actors that are not contenders in a civil war. This distinction is not entirely clear, as explanations of the data list nonstate actors in extrastate wars as having an interest in control over populations and territory. The COW interstate data do not include information on external intervention. Sarkees, 2000, 123–44; Singer and Small, 1994.
[14] Uppsala Conflict Data Programme and International Peace Research Institute, 2007; Gleditsch et al., 2002, 615–37.
[15] Brecher and Wilkenfeld, 2007.

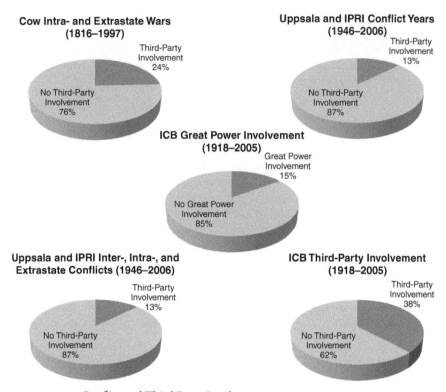

FIGURE 9.1 Conflict and Third-Party Involvement
Sources: Brecher and Wilkenfeld, 2007; Gleditsch et al., 2002; Uppsala Conflict Data Programme and International Peace Research Institute, 2008; Sarkees, 2000; Singer and Small, 1994.

conditionality of assistance competing local actors received from outside sources, or the number and aims of external and domestic actors contending over a polity. Highlighting the critical but oft overlooked role external actors play in domestic politics also may allow for a more thorough and accurate appreciation of state formation processes than existing approaches permit. This can pave the way for improvements in the understanding of changes in state form. Figure 9.1 above provides a snapshot of the role of outside intervention according to several popular datasets.

A consideration of foreign involvement in domestic politics may prove useful for attempts to consider state-building as well. After all, outside intervention may continue even after a particular institutional configuration of governance takes shape.[16] As in the experiences of so many colonies, client states, and even Western European states after World War II indicate, outside powers can persist in consolidating, bolstering, and undermining particular state forms after their initial emergence. As in the case of state formation, highlighting the effects of

[16] Fearon and Laitin, 2004.

external intervention may foster greater knowledge about the dynamics of state-building. Such a perspective can help efforts to understand developments in areas like Afghanistan, Cambodia, Iraq, Kosovo, Sierra Leone, Somalia, and Timor Leste between the end of the twentieth century and the beginning of the twenty-first as more information becomes publicly available.

PARTING BLOWS

Incorporating the study of foreign intervention in domestic politics brings together the strengths of international relations and comparative politics to understanding how political institutions develop and attain particular character-istics. This process enabled my project to explore and speak to broader efforts at understanding governance, rule, and political authority. Using a second image-reversed perspective to examine evidence drawn from the historical experiences of East Asian states proved particularly helpful for underscoring state formation dynamics in fragile polities. This approach permitted a fuller account of the roles international systemic pressures and foreign powers played in what many have assumed to be largely domestic political processes, and a rethinking of popular views on state formation.

As witnessed through the many cases of weak and failing states today, outside intervention and state formation processes can have profound and far-reaching consequences for both domestic and international politics. Institutional config-urations of governance can determine order and stability within a polity, whilst also affecting security outside the state's borders.[17] The approach foreign actors take toward politics inside a state may affect how such dynamics play out. Attempts to address issues of governance and rule in fragile polities may do well to consider the complexities of external involvement in domestic politics more systematically and with more sensitivity to historical context.

[17] Miller, 2007.

Appendix
Questions for Focused, Structured Comparisons

1. What was the perceived opportunity cost of intervention in a target polity for an external actor? How did this affect the external actor's approach toward securing access in the target polity, if at all?
2. Did the external actor work with any local group if it intervened in the target polity?
3. What were the nature and goals of the local partner(s), and why did the external actor work with this (these) particular group(s)? If no groups were involved, why did the external actor not seek a local partner?
4. What were the conditions underlying partnerships between external actors and local groups where they existed?
5. When local groups worked with an intervening actor, what was the effect of the partnership on changes in state form for a target polity, if any? If an intervening actor did not have a local partner, how did that affect state form in a target polity, if at all?
6. Did simultaneous external intervention efforts collectively affect state form in a target polity? If so, how? If not, why not?

References

Abdulgani, Roeslan. 1978. Nationalism, Pancasila, Soekarno. In *Dynamics of Indonesian History*, edited by Haryati Soebadio-Noto and Carinne A. du Marchie Sarvaas. Amsterdam; New York: North-Holland Pub. Co.; distributors for the U.S. A. and Canada Elsevier/North-Holland.

Abdullah, Taufik. 1978. Impacts of Colonial Policy on Sumatra. In *Dynamics of Indonesian History*, edited by Haryati Soebadio-Noto and Carinne A. du Marchie Sarvaas. Amsterdam; New York: North-Holland Pub. Co.; distributors for the U.S. A. and Canada Elsevier/North-Holland.

Acemoglu, Daron, Simon Johnson, and James A. Robinson. 2001. The Colonial Origins of Comparative Development: An Empirical Investigation. *The American Economic Review* 91(5): 1369–69.

Acharya, Amitav. 2009. *Whose Ideas Matter? Agency and Power in Asian Regionalism, Cornell Studies in Political Economy*. Ithaca, N.Y.: Cornell University Press.

2004. Will Asia's Past Be Its Future? *International Security* 28(3): 149–64.

Adams, Julia. 2005. *The Familial State: Ruling Families and Merchant Capitalism in Early Modern Europe*. Ithaca, N.Y.: Cornell University Press.

Ali, Fachry. 1994. Masses without Citizenship: Islamic Protest Movements in Nineteenth-Century Java. In *The Late Colonial State in Indonesia: Political and Economic Foundations of the Netherlands Indies, 1880–1942*, edited by R. B. Cribb, 247–83. Leiden: KITLV Press.

Anderson, Benedict R. O'G. 1998. *The Spectre of Comparisons: Nationalism, Southeast Asia, and the World*. London; New York: Verso.

1991. *Imagined Communities: Reflections on the Origin and Spread of Nationalism*. Rev. and extended ed. London; New York: Verso.

1972. *Java in a Time of Revolution: Occupation and Resistance, 1944–1946*. Ithaca, N.Y.: Cornell University Press.

Anderson, Perry. 1974a. *Lineages of the Absolutist State*. London: N.L.B.

1974b. *Passages from Antiquity to Feudalism*. London: N.L.B.

Arendt, Hannah. 1970. *On Violence*. New York: Harcourt.

Arsa, Meksawan. 1961, 1962. The Role of the Provincial Governor in Thailand. Thesis, [Institute of Public Administration, Thammasat University] Indiana University.

Atkins, Martyn. 1995. *Informal Empire in Crisis: British Diplomacy and the Chinese Customs Succession, 1927–1929, Cornell East Asia Series, 74*. Ithaca, N.Y.: East Asia Program, Cornell University.

References

Atwood, Christopher P. 1999. Sino-Soviet Diplomacy and the Second Partition of Mongolia, 1945–1946. In *Mongolia in the Twentieth Century: Landlocked Cosmopolitan*, edited by Stephen Kotkin and Bruce A. Elleman, xx, 313 p. Armonk, N.Y.; London: M.E. Sharpe.

Audi, Robert. 1999. *The Cambridge Dictionary of Philosophy*. 2nd ed. Cambridge, U.K.; New York: Cambridge University Press.

Aziz, Muhammed Abdul. 1955. Japan's Colonialism and Indonesia. Issued also as thesis, Leyden, M. Nijhoff.

Baker, Christopher John, and Pasuk Phongpaichit. 2005. *A History of Thailand*. New York: Cambridge University Press.

Barlow, Colin, and John Drabble. 1990. Government and the Emerging Rubber Industries in Indonesia and Malaya 1900–1940. In *Indonesian Economic History in the Dutch Colonial Era*, edited by Anne Booth, W.J. O'Malley, and Anna Weidemann. New Haven, Conn.: Yale University Southeast Asia Studies.

Barlow, Jeffrey G. 1979. *Sun Yat-Sen and the French, 1900–1908*. Berkeley: Center for Chinese Studies, Institute of East Asian Studies, University of California.

Barmé, Scot. 1993. *Luang Wichit Wathakan and the Creation of a Thai Identity, Social Issues in Southeast Asia*. Singapore: ISEAS.

Barnett, Michael N. 2002. *Eyewitness to a Genocide: The United Nations and Rwanda*. Ithaca, N.Y.: Cornell University Press.

Barnett, Michael N., and Martha Finnemore. 1999. The Politics, Power, and Pathologies of International Organizations. *International Organization* 53(4): 699–732.

Barnhart, Michael A. 1995. *Japan and the World since 1868, International Relations and the Great Powers*. London; New York: Edward Arnold; distributed exclusively in the U.S.A. by St. Martin's Press.

——— 1987. *Japan Prepares for Total War: The Search for Economic Security, 1919–1941, Cornell Studies in Security Affairs*. Ithaca, N.Y.: Cornell University Press.

Barrett, David P. 2001. The Wang Jingwei Regime. In *Chinese Collaboration with Japan, 1932–1945: The Limits of Accommodation*, edited by David P. Barrett and Lawrence N. Shyu. Stanford, Calif.: Stanford University Press.

Barrett, David P., and Lawrence N. Shyu. 2001. *Chinese Collaboration with Japan, 1932–1945: The Limits of Accommodation*. Stanford, Calif.: Stanford University Press.

Bartelson, Jens. 2001. *The Critique of the State*. Cambridge, U.K.; New York: Cambridge University Press.

——— 1995. *A Genealogy of Sovereignty, Cambridge Studies in International Relations*. Cambridge, U.K.; New York: Cambridge University Press.

Bastin, John Sturgus, and Harry Jindrich Benda. 1968. *A History of Modern Southeast Asia: Colonialism, Nationalism, and Decolonization*. Englewood Cliffs, N.J.: Prentice-Hall.

Batson, Benjamin A. 1984. *The End of the Absolute Monarchy in Siam, Southeast Asia Publications Series*. Singapore; New York: Oxford University Press.

Bayly, C. A., and T. N. Harper. 2007. *Forgotten Wars: Freedom and Revolution in Southeast Asia*. Cambridge, Mass.: Belknap Press of Harvard University Press.

Bayly, Christopher, and Tim Harper. 2004. *Forgotten Armies: The Fall of British Asia, 1941–1945*. London: Allen Lane.

Beissinger, Mark R., and Crawford Young. 2002. *Beyond State Crisis? Postcolonial Africa and Post-Soviet Eurasia in Comparative Perspective*. Washington, D.C.,

References 241

Baltimore: Woodrow Wilson Center Press; distributed by Johns Hopkins University Press.

Benda, H. J., and R. T. McVey. 1977. Communist Uprisings, 1926–1927. In *Indonesia: Selected Documents on Colonialism and Nationalism, 1830–1942*, edited by C. L. M. Penders. St. Lucia: University of Queensland Press.

Benda, Harry J., and Lance Castles. 1972. The Samin Movement. In *Continuity and Change in Southeast Asia*, edited by Harry Jindrich Benda. New Haven, Conn.: Yale University Southeast Asia Studies.

Benda, Harry Jindrich. 1972a. Christiaan Snouck Hurgronje and the Foundations of Dutch Islamic Policy in Indonesia. In *Continuity and Change in Southeast Asia*, edited by Harry Jindrich Benda. New Haven, Conn.: Yale University Southeast Asia Studies.

1972b. The Communist Rebellions of 1926–1927 in Indonesia. In *Continuity and Change in Southeast Asia*, edited by Harry Jindrich Benda. New Haven, Conn.: Yale University Press.

1972c. *Continuity and Change in Southeast Asia*. New Haven, Conn.: Yale University Southeast Asia Studies.

1972d. Indonesian Islam under the Japanese Occupation, 1942–1945. In *Continuity and Change in Southeast Asia*, edited by Harry Jindrich Benda, xii, 307 p. New Haven, Conn.: Yale University Press.

1972e. The Patterns of Administrative Reforms in the Closing Years of Dutch Rule in Indonesia. In *Continuity and Change in Southeast Asia*, edited by Harry Jindrich Benda, xii, 307 p. New Haven, Conn.: Yale University Press.

1958. *The Crescent and the Rising Sun: Indonesian Islam under the Japanese Occupation, 1942–1945*. The Hague; New York: W. van Hoeve; distributed in the U.S.A. by the Institute of Pacific Relations.

Benda, Harry Jindrich, James K. Irikura, and Koichi Kishi. 1965. *Japanese Military Administration in Indonesia: Selected Documents*. New Haven, Conn.: Yale University Southeast Studies.

Benda, Harry Jindrich, and John A. Larkin. 1967. *The World of Southeast Asia: Selected Historical Readings*. New York: Harper & Row.

Bendix, Reinhard. 1977. *Max Weber: An Intellectual Portrait*. Berkeley: University of California Press.

Benton, Gregor. 2000. Comparative Perspectives: North and Central China in the Anti-Japanese Resistance. In *North China at War: The Social Ecology of Revolution, 1937–1945*, edited by Chongyi Feng and David S. G. Goodman. Lanham, MD: Rowman & LIttlefield Publishers.

1995. Under Arms and Umbrellas: Perspectives on Chinese Communism in Defeat. In *New Perspectives on the Chinese Communist Revolution*, edited by Tony Saich and Hans J. van de Ven. Armonk, N.Y.: M.E. Sharpe.

Berdal, Mats R., and Spyros Economides. 2007. *United Nations Interventionism, 1991–2004*. Rev. and updated ed., *Lse Monographs in International Studies*. Cambridge, U.K.; New York: Cambridge University Press.

Bianco, Lucien. 1995. Peasant Responses to CCP Mobilisation Policies, 1937–1945. In *New Perspectives on the Chinese Communist Revolution*, edited by Tony Saich and Hans J. van de Ven. Armonk, N.Y.: M.E. Sharpe.

1971. *Origins of the Chinese Revolution, 1915–1949*. Stanford, Calif.: Stanford University Press.

Bickers, Robert A. 1999. *Britain in China: Community Culture and Colonialism, 1900–1949*. Manchester; New York: Manchester University Press; distributed exclusively in the U.S.A. by St. Martin's Press.

Billingsley, Phil. 1981. Bandits, Bosses, and Bare Sticks: Beneath the Surface of Local Control in Early Republican China. *Modern China* 7(3): 235–88.

Boikova, Elena. 1999. Aspects of Soviet-Mongolian Relations, 1929–1939. In *Mongolia in the Twentieth Century: Landlocked Cosmopolitan*, edited by Stephen Kotkin and Bruce A. Elleman. Armonk, N.Y.: M.E. Sharpe.

Boli, John, and George M. Thomas. 1997. World Culture in the World Polity: A Century of International Non-Governmental Organization. *American Sociological Review* 62(2): 171–71.

Booth, Anne. 1990a. The Evolution of Fiscal Policy and the Role of Government in the Colonial Economy. In *Indonesian Economic History in the Dutch Colonial Era*, edited by Anne Booth, W. J. O'Malley, and Anna Weidemann. New Haven, Conn.: Yale University Southeast Asia Studies.

1990b. Foreign Trade and Domestic Development in the Colonial Economy. In *Indonesian Economic History in the Dutch Colonial Era*, edited by Anne Booth, W. J. O'Malley, and Anna Weidemann, 369 p. New Haven, Conn.: Yale University Southeast Asia Studies.

Borg, Dorothy. 1964. *The United States and the Far Eastern Crisis of 1933–1938; from the Manchurian Incident through the Initial Stage of the Undeclared Sino-Japanese War, Harvard East Asian Series, 14*. Cambridge, Mass.: Harvard University Press.

Borisov, Oleg Borisovich. 1977. *The Soviet Union and the Manchurian Revolutionary Base: (1945–1949)*. Moscow: Progress Publishers.

Borisov, Oleg Borisovich, and B. T. Koloskov. 1975. *Soviet-Chinese Relations, 1945–1970*. Bloomington: Indiana University Press.

Boyle, John Hunter. 1972. *China and Japan at War, 1937–1945; the Politics of Collaboration*. Stanford, Calif.: Stanford University Press.

Brailey, Nigel J. 1986. *Thailand and the Fall of Singapore: A Frustrated Asian Revolution, Westview Special Studies on South and Southeast Asia*. Boulder, Colo.: Westview Press.

Braisted, William R. 1968. China, the United States Navy, and the Bethlehem Steel Company, 1909–1929. *The Business History Review* 42(1): 50–50.

Brautigam, Deborah, Odd-Helge Fjeldstad, and Mick Moore. 2008. *Taxation and State-Building in Developing Countries: Capacity and Consent*. Cambridge, U.K.; New York: Cambridge University Press.

Brautigam, Deborah A., and Stephen Knack. 2004. Foreign Aid, Institutions, and Governance in Sub-Saharan Africa. *Economic Development and Cultural Change* 52(2): 255–85.

Brecher, Michael, and Jonathan Wilkenfeld. 2007. International Crisis Behaviour Project, 1918–2004. *(ICPSR 9286, 2007)*.

Brendon, Piers. 2007. *The Decline and Fall of the British Empire, 1781–1997*. London: Jonathan Cape.

Brook, Timothy. 2005. *Collaboration: Japanese Agents and Local Elites in Wartime China*. Cambridge, Mass.: Harvard University Press.

Brooshooft, P. 1977. The Ethical Direction in Colonial Policy, 1901. In *Indonesia: Selected Documents on Colonialism and Nationalism, 1830–1942*, edited by C. L. M. Penders. St. Lucia: University of Queensland Press.

Brown, Ian. 1992. *The Creation of the Modern Ministry of Finance in Siam, 1885–1910, Studies in the Economics of East and South-East Asia*. London: Macmillan.

References

1988. *The Élite and the Economy in Siam, C. 1890–1920, East Asian Historical Monographs*. Singapore; New York: Oxford University Press.

Brunero, Donna. 2006. *Britain's Imperial Cornerstone in China: The Chinese Maritime Customs Service, 1854–1949, Routledge Studies in the Modern History of Asia, 36*. London; New York: Routledge.

Bukovansky, Mlada. 2002. *Legitimacy and Power Politics: The American and French Revolutions in International Political Culture, Princeton Studies in International History and Politics*. Princeton, N.J.: Princeton University Press.

Bull, Hedley. 1977. *The Anarchical Society: A Study of Order in World Politics*. New York: Columbia University Press.

Bunce, Valerie. 1985. The Empire Strikes Back: The Evolution of the Eastern Bloc from a Soviet Asset to a Soviet Liability. *International Organization* 39(1): 1–1.

Bunker, Gerald E. 1972. *The Peace Conspiracy: Wang Ching-Wei and the China War, 1937–1941, Harvard East Asian Series*. Cambridge, Mass.: Harvard University Press.

Bunnag, Tej. 1977. *The Provincial Administration of Siam, 1892–1915: The Ministry of the Interior under Prince Damrong Rajanubhab*. London; New York: Oxford University Press.

Buzan, Barry, Charles A. Jones, and Richard Little. 1993. *The Logic of Anarchy: Neorealism to Structural Realism, New Directions in World Politics*. New York: Columbia University Press.

Caldwell, Malcolm, and Ernst Utrecht. 1979. *Indonesia, an Alternative History*. Sydney, Australia: Alternative Pub. Co-operative.

Cao, Bihong, Huiru Pang, Zhongyang dang'anguan (China), Zhongguo di 2 lishi dang'anguan., and Jilin Sheng shehui kexueyuan. 2004. *Huabei Jingji Lüeduo. Di 1 ban. ed., Riben Diguo Zhuyi Qin Hua Dang'anziliao Xuanbian*. Beijing Shi: Zhonghua shuju.

Caplan, Richard. 2005. *International Governance of War-Torn Territories: Rule and Reconstruction*. Oxford; New York: Oxford University Press.

Carlson, Allen. 2005. *Unifying China, Integrating with the World: Securing Chinese Sovereignty in the Reform Era, Studies in Asian Security*. Stanford, Calif.: Stanford University Press.

Castex, Raoul, and Eugenia C. Kiesling. 1994. *Strategic Theories, Classics of Sea Power*. Annapolis, Md.: Naval Institute Press.

Centeno, Miguel Angel. 2002. *Blood and Debt: War and the Nation-State in Latin America*. University Park: Pennsylvania State University Press.

1997. Blood and Debt: War and Taxation in Nineteenth-Century Latin America. *The American Journal of Sociology* 102(6): 1565–605.

Centeno, Miguel Angel, and Fernando López-Alves. 2001. *The Other Mirror: Grand Theory through the Lens of Latin America*. Princeton, N.J.: Princeton University Press.

Chaianan, Samutwanit. 1982. *The Thai Young Turks*. Singapore: Institute of Southeast Asian Studies.

Chamberlain, Austen. 1946. Foreign Office Memorandum of January 8, 1930, on British Policy in China [F 6720/3/10]. In *Documents on British Foreign Policy, 1919–1939*, edited by Great Britain. Foreign and Commonwealth Office., E. L. Woodward, and Rohan d'Olier Butler. London: H. M. Stationery Office.

Chan, Anthony B. 1982. *Arming the Chinese: The Western Armaments Trade in Warlord China, 1920–1928, Asian Studies Monographs; 4*. Vancouver: University of British Columbia Press.

Chan, K. C. 1971. British Policy in the Reorganization Loan to China 1912–13. *Modern Asian Studies* 5(4): 355–72.

Chan Lau, Kit-ching. 1990. *China, Britain and Hong Kong, 1895–1945*. Hong Kong: The Chinese University Press.

Chauvel, Richard. 1985. Ambon: Not a Revolution but a Counter-Revolution. In *Regional Dynamics of the Indonesian Revolution: Unity from Diversity*, edited by Audrey Kahin. Honolulu: University of Hawaii Press.

Cheek, Timothy. 1995. The Honourable Vocation: Intellectual Service in Ccp Propaganda Institutions in Jin-Cha-Ji, 1937–1945. In *New Perspectives on the Chinese Communist Revolution*, edited by Tony Saich and Hans J. van de Ven. Armonk, N.Y.: M.E. Sharpe.

Chen, Cun'gong. 1983. *Lieqiang Dui Zhongguo Di Junhuojinyun: Minguo 8 Nian –18 Nian*. Chu ban. ed., *Zhongyang Yanjiuyuan Jindaishi Yanjiusuo Zhuankan; 47*. Taipei: Zhongyang yanjiuyuan jindaishi yanjiusuo.

Chen, Edward I Te. 1972. Formosan Political Movements under Japanese Colonial Rule, 1914–1937. *The Journal of Asian Studies* 31(3): 477–97.

Ch'en, Jerome. 1991. The Communist Movement, 1927–1937. In *The Nationalist Era in China, 1927–1949*, edited by Lloyd E. Eastman. Cambridge: Cambridge University Press.

———. 1968. Defining Chinese Warlords and Their Factions. *Bulletin of the School of Oriental and African Studies, University of London* 31(3): 563–600.

Chen, Jian. 1994. *China's Road to the Korean War: The Making of the Sino-American Confrontation, U.S. And Pacific Asia – Studies in Social, Economic, and Political Interaction*. New York: Columbia University Press.

Chen, Jian-Yue. 2004. American Studies of Wang Jingwei: Defining Nationalism. *World History Review* 2(1): 2–34.

Chen, Jung-fa. 1995. The Blooming Poppy under the Red Sun: The Yan'an Way and the Opium Trade. In *New Perspectives on the Chinese Communist Revolution*, edited by Tony Saich and Hans J. van de Ven. Armonk, N.Y.: M.E. Sharpe.

Chen, Leslie H. Dingyan. 1999. *Chen Jiongming and the Federalist Movement: Regional Leadership and Nation Building in Early Republican China, Michigan Monographs in Chinese Studies; 86*. Ann Arbor: Center for Chinese Studies, University of Michigan.

Chen, Liwen. 1991. *Song Ziwen yu Zhanshi Waijiao*. Chu ban. ed. Taipei: Guoshiguan.

Chen, Mushan. 1996. *Cong Handian Shiliao Guan Kangzhan Shiqi Wang Jingwei Jituan Zhi Yue Genggai*. Chu ban. ed. Taipei: Taiwan xuesheng shuju.

Chen, Pengren. 1999. *Wang Jingwei Xiang Ri Midang*. Chu ban. ed. Taipei: Lianjing chuban shiye gongsi.

———. 1991. *Riren Bixia di Jiu Yi Ba Shibian*. Chu ban. ed. Taipei: Shuiniu chubanshe.

Chen, Renxia. 2003. *Zhong De Ri Sanjiao Guanxi Yanjiu, 1936–1938*. Beijing di 1 ban. ed. Beijing Shi: Shenghuo, dushu, xinzhi sanlian shudian.

Chen, Sanjing. 2005. *Zhongshan Xiansheng yu Meiguo*. Edited by Zhongshan xueshu wenhua jijin dongshihui. *Zhongshan Xueshu Wenhua Jijinhui Jushu*. Taipei: Taiwan xuesheng shuju.

Chen, Xueping. 1941. Wei Woguan de Pouxi. *Zhanguoce* 15–16: 7–19.

Chen, Yongfa. 2006. *Zhongguo Gongchan Geming Qi Shi Nian*. Xiuding ban ed. 2 vols. Vol. 1, *Zuijin Liang Bai Nian Zhongguo Shi*. Taipei: Linking Books.

Chesneaux, Jean. 1973. *Peasant Revolts in China, 1840–1949*. London: Thames & Hudson.

References 245

Chi, Hsi-sheng. 1982. *Nationalist China at War: Military Defeats and Political Collapse, 1937–45, Michigan Studies on China*. Ann Arbor: University of Michigan Press.

———. 1976. *Warlord Politics in China, 1916–1928*. Stanford, Calif.: Stanford University Press.

Chi, Hsi-sheng. 1969. *The Chinese Warlord System: 1916 to 1928*. Washington: U.S. Dept. of Commerce National Technical Information Service.

Chiang, Kai-shek. 1943. *Zhongguo zhi Mingyun*. Chongqing: Zhengzhong shuju.

Chiang, Kai-shek, and Philip J. Jaffe. 1947. *China's Destiny & Chinese Economic Theory*. New York: Roy Publishers.

Chiang, Kai-shek, and Ch'ung-hui Wang. 1947. *China's Destiny*. New York: The Macmillan Company.

China. Dept. of Railways and Ching-ch un Wang. 1916. *Railway Loan Agreements of China*. Peking: Railway Association.

The China Monthly Review. 1925. *Special Tariff Conference Issue*. Issued as a Supplement of the *China Weekly Review* for November 1, 1925. Shanghai, China.

The China Weekly Review. 1923. Shanghai, China: Millard Publishing House.

China. Wai chiao pu., and League of Nations. Commission of Inquiry. 1932. *Memoranda Submitted by the Chinese Assessor to the Commission of Enquiry of the League of Nations, April–August L932*. Bilingual ed. [S.l.]: The Commercial Press.

Ching, Leo T. S. 2001. *Becoming "Japanese": Colonial Taiwan and the Politics of Identity Formation*. Berkeley: University of California Press.

Cho, Yukio. 1973. An Inquiry into the Problem of Importing American Capital into Manchuria: A Note on Japanese American Relations, 1931–1941. In *Pearl Harbor as History: Japanese-American Relations, 1931–1941*, edited by Dorothy Borg and Shumpei Okamoto. New York: Columbia University Press.

Chong, Ja Ian. 2010. How Intervention Made the Sovereign State: Foreign Actors, Local Complicity, and State Formation in Weak Polities. *Security Studies* 19(4): 623–55.

———. 2009. Breaking up Is Hard to Do: Foreign Intervention and the Limiting of Fragmentation in the Late Qing and Early Republic, 1893–1922. *Twentieth Century China* 35(1): 75–98.

Christensen, Thomas J. 1996. *Useful Adversaries: Grand Strategy, Domestic Mobilization, and Sino-American Conflict, 1947–1958, Princeton Studies in International History and Politics*. Princeton, N.J.: Princeton University Press.

Christensen, Thomas J., and Jack Snyder. 1990. Chain Gangs and Passed Bucks: Predicting Alliance Patterns in Multipolarity. *International Organization* 44(2): 137–37.

Christia, Fotini, and Michael Semple. 2009. Flipping the Taleban: How to Win in Afghanistan. *Foreign Affairs* 88(4): 34–46.

Clark, Wesley K. 2001. *Waging Modern War: Bosnia, Kosovo, and the Future of Combat*. 1st ed. New York: Public Affairs.

Cleveland, Harlan. 1949. Economic Aid to China. *Far Eastern Survey* 18(1): 1–6.

Cloete, Pieter G. 2000. *The Anglo-Boer War: A Chronology*. Pretoria: J.P. van der Walt.

Coble, Parks M. 2001. Japan's New Order and the Shanghai Capitalists: Conflict and Collaboration, 1937–1945. In *Chinese Collaboration with Japan, 1932–1945: The Limits of Accommodation*, edited by David P. Barrett and Lawrence N. Shyu. Stanford: Stanford University Press.

———. 1991. *Facing Japan: Chinese Politics and Japanese Imperialism, 1931–1937, Harvard East Asian Monographs*. Cambridge, Mass.: Council on East Asian Studies; distributed by Harvard University Press.

246   *References*

Coggins, Bridget L. *Secession, Recognition and the International Politics of Statehood.* Ohio State University, 2006.

Cohen, Eliot A. 1991. Churchill and Coalition Grand Strategy in World War II. In *Grand Strategies in War and Peace*, edited by Paul M. Kennedy. New Haven, Conn.: Yale University Press.

Cohen, Warren I. 2000. *America's Response to China: A History of Sino-American Relations.* 4th ed. New York: Columbia University Press.

     1973. The Role of Private Groups in the United States. In *Pearl Harbor as History: Japanese-American Relations, 1931–1941*, edited by Dorothy Borg and Shumpei Okamoto. New York: Columbia University Press.

Colbert, Evelyn S. 1977. *Southeast Asia in International Politics, 1941–1956.* Ithaca, N.Y.: Cornell University Press.

Collins, Randall. 1986. *Weberian Sociological Theory.* Cambridge, U.K.; New York: Cambridge University Press.

Common Program for the People's Republic of China. 1979. In *The People's Republic of China: A Documentary History of Revolutionary Change*, edited by Mark Selden and Patti Eggleston. New York: Monthly Review Press.

Copper, John Franklin. 1999. *Taiwan: Nation-State or Province?* 3rd ed. *Nations of the Modern World Asia.* Boulder, Colo.: Westview Press.

Corbett, Julian Stafford. 1972. *Some Principles of Maritime Strategy.* Annapolis, Md.: Naval Institute Press.

     1917. *England in the Mediterranean; a Study of the Rise and Influence of British Power within the Straits, 1603–1713.* 2nd ed. London, New York, Bombay: Longmans Green.

Cribb, Robert. 1985. Jakarta: Cooperation and Resistance in an Occupied City. In *Regional Dynamics of the Indonesian Revolution: Unity from Diversity*, edited by Audrey Kahin. Honolulu: University of Hawaii Press.

Crosby, Josiah. 1945. *Siam: The Crossroads.* London: Hollis & Carter ltd.

Crosby, Josiah, and Great Britain. Foreign Office. Historical Section. 1920. *Siam.* London: H.M. Stationery Office.

Cui, Guohua. 1995. *Kang Ri Zhanzheng Shiqi Guomin Zhengfu Caizheng Jinrong Zhengce.* Di 1 ban. ed. Chengdu: Xinan caijing daxue chuban she: Sichuan Sheng xinhua shudian jingxiao.

Cunliff Committee on Currency and Foreign Exchanges after the War. 1997. First Interim Report. In *The Gold Standard in Theory and History*, edited by Barry J. Eichengreen and Marc Flandreau. London: Routledge.

Dahm, Bernhard. 1971. *History of Indonesia in the Twentieth Century.* London, New York: Praeger.

Darling, Frank C. 1962. American Policy in Thailand. *The Western Political Quarterly* 15(1): 93–110.

Davis, Clarence B. 1982. Financing Imperialism: British and American Bankers as Vectors of Imperial Expansion in China, 1908–1920. *The Business History Review* 56(2): 236–64.

Declaration of the Netherlands Government in Exile in London, 27 January 1942. 1977. In *Indonesia: Selected Documents on Colonialism and Nationalism, 1830–1942*, edited by C. L. M. Penders. St. Lucia: University of Queensland Press.

Deignan, H. G. 1943. *Siam Land of Free Men.* Washington, D.C.: The Smithsonian Institution.

Den Baker, Gert P., and Theo A. Huitker. 1990. The Dutch Economy 1921–39: Revised Macroeconomic Data for the Interwar Period. *Review of Income & Wealth* 36(2): 187–206.

References

Dennis, Peter. 1987. *Troubled Days of Peace: Mountbatten and South East Asia Command, 1945–46, War, Armed Forces, and Society*. New York: St. Martin's Press.

DeVido, Elise A. 2000. The Survival of the Shandong Base Area, 1937–1943: External Influences and Internal Conflicts. In *North China at War: The Social Ecology of Revolution, 1937–1945*, edited by Chongyi Feng and David S. G. Goodman. Lanham, Md.: Rowman & Littlefield Publishers.

Dikötter, Frank. 2008. *The Age of Openness: China before Mao, Understanding China: New Viewpoints on History and Culture*. Hong Kong: Hong Kong University Press.

Douwes Dekker, E. F. E. 1977. The Indies Party, Its Nature and Objectives, 1913. In *Indonesia: Selected Documents on Colonialism and Nationalism, 1830–1942*, edited by C. L. M. Penders. St. Lucia: University of Queensland Press.

Doyle, Michael W. 1986. *Empires, Cornell Studies in Comparative History*. Ithaca, N.Y.: Cornell University Press.

Drakeley, Steven. 2005. *The History of Indonesia, The Greenwood Histories of the Modern Nations*. Westport, Conn.: Greenwood Press.

Du, Chunmei. 2009. *Gu Hongming and the Re-Invention of Chinese Civilization. Ph.D*, Princeton University.

Duara, Prasenjit. 2003. Sovereignty and Authenticity: Manchukuo and the East Asian Modern. *Lanham, Md.*: Oxford: Rowman & Littlefield Publishers.

    1995. *Rescuing History from the Nation: Questioning Narratives of Modern China*. Chicago: University of Chicago Press.

    1987. State Involution: A Study of Local Finances in North China, 1911–1935. *Comparative Studies in Society and History* 29(1): 132–61.

Eastman, Lloyd E. 1991a. Nationalist China During the Nanking Decade, 1927–1937. In *The Nationalist Era in China, 1927–1949*, edited by Lloyd E. Eastman. Cambridge: Cambridge University Press.

    1991b. Nationalist China During the Sino-Japanese War, 1937–1945. In *The Nationalist Era in China, 1927–1949*, edited by Lloyd E. Eastman, x, 406 p. Cambridge, U.K.; New York: Cambridge University Press.

    1990. *The Abortive Revolution: China under Nationalist Rule, 1927–1937, Harvard East Asian Monographs; 153*. Cambridge, Mass.: Council on East Asian Studies Distributed by Harvard University Press.

    1984. *Seeds of Destruction: Nationalist China in War and Revolution, 1937–1949*. Stanford, Calif.: Stanford University Press.

Edwards, E. W. 1971. The Origins of British Financial Co-Operation with France in China, 1903–6. *The English Historical Review* 86(339): 285–317.

    1966. Great Britain and the Manchurian Railways Question, 1909–1910. *The English Historical Review* 81(321): 740–69.

Eichengreen, Barry J. 1992. *Golden Fetters: The Gold Standard and the Great Depression, 1919–1939, Nber Series on Long-Term Factors in Economic Development*. New York: Oxford University Press.

Eldon, R. James. 1922. Jurisdiction over Foreigners in Siam. *The American Journal of International Law* 16(4): 585–603.

Elleman, Bruce A. 1999. The Final Consolidation of the USSR's Sphere of Interest in Outer Mongolia. In *Mongolia in the Twentieth Century: Landlocked Cosmopolitan*, edited by Stephen Kotkin and Bruce A. Elleman, xx, 313 p. Armonk, N.Y.; London: M.E. Sharpe.

    1997. *Diplomacy and Deception: The Secret History of Sino-Soviet Diplomatic Relations, 1917–1927*. Armonk, N.Y.: M.E. Sharpe.

Elson, R.E. 2008. *The Idea of Indonesia: A History*. Cambridge, U.K.; New York: Cambridge University Press.

Endicott, Elizabeth. 1999. Russian Merchants in Mongolia: The 1910 Moscow Trade Expedition. In *Mongolia in the Twentieth Century: Landlocked Cosmopolitan*, edited by Stephen Kotkin and Bruce A. Elleman. Armonk, N.Y.: M.E. Sharpe.

Engels, Friedrich. 1978. The Origin of the Family, Private Property, and the State. In *The Marx-Engels Reader*, edited by Karl Marx, Friedrich Engels, and Robert C. Tucker. New York: Norton.

Ertman, Thomas. 1997. *Birth of the Leviathan: Building States and Regimes in Medieval and Early Modern Europe*. Cambridge, U.K.; New York: Cambridge University Press.

Esherick, Joseph W. 2000. Revolution in a "Feudal Fortress": Yangjiagou, Mizhi County, Shaanxi, 1937–1948. In *North China at War: The Social Ecology of Revolution, 1937–1945*, edited by Chongyi Feng and David S.G. Goodman. Lanham, Md.: Rowman & Littlefield Publishers.

Eto, Shinkichi. 2001. Japanese Manoevures for Peace with China, 1937–1940. In *China in the Anti-Japanese War, 1937–1945: Politics, Culture and Society*, edited by David P. Barrett and Lawrence N. Shyu. New York: Peter Lang.

Fairbank, John King. 1964. *Trade and Diplomacy on the China Coast the Opening of Treaty Ports, 1842–1854, Harvard Historical Studies; V.62–63*. Cambridge, Mass.: Harvard University Press.

Fasseur, C. 2007. Colonial Dilemma: Van Vollenhoven and the Struggle between Adat Law and Western Law in Indonesia. In *The Revival of Tradition in Indonesian Politics: The Deployment of Adat from Colonialism to Indigenism*, edited by Jamie Seth Davidson and David Henley. London; New York: Routledge.

Fazal, Tanisha M. 2007. *State Death: The Politics and Geography of Conquest, Occupation, and Annexation*. Princeton: Princeton University Press.

2004. State Death in the International System. *International Organization* 58(2): 311–44.

Fearon, James D. 1995. Rationalist Explanations for War. *International Organization* 49(3): 379–79.

Fearon, James D., and David D. Laitin. 2004. Neotrusteeship and the Problem of Weak States. *International Security* 28(4): 5–43.

Fei, Zheng, Zuomin Li, and Jiaji Zhang. 1993. *Kangzhan Shiqi di Weizhengquan*. Di 1 ban. ed. Zhengzhou: Henan renmin chubanshe.

Feith, Herbert. 1962. *The Decline of Constitutional Democracy in Indonesia, The Modern Indonesia Project, Southeast Asia Program, Cornell Univesity*. Ithaca, N.Y.: Cornell University Press.

Feng, Chongyi. 2000. The Making of the Jin-Sui Base Area: Peasants, Intellectuals, and Democratisaton. In *North China at War: The Social Ecology of Revolution, 1945–1937*, edited by Chongyi Feng and David S.G. Goodman. Lanham, Md.: Rowman & LIttlefield Publishers.

Feng, Xiaocai. 2004. *Beifa Qianhou de Shangmin Yundong, Yi Jiu Er Si-Yi Jiu San Ling*. Chu ban. ed. Taipei: Taiwan shangwu yinshuguan.

Ferguson, Niall. 2004. *Empire: The Rise and Demise of the British World Order and the Lessons for Global Power*. 1st U.S. pbk. ed. New York: Basic Books.

Feuerwerker, Albert. 1958. *China's Early Industrialization: Sheng Hsuan-Huai (1844–1916) and Mandarin Enterprise, Harvard East Asian Studies*. Cambridge, Mass.: Harvard University Press.

References 249

Field, Frederick Vanderbilt, and Institute of Pacific Relations. 1934. *Economic Handbook of the Pacific Area.* 1st ed. Garden City, N.Y.: Doubleday, Doran.

Finch, George A. 1926. The Chinese Customs Tariff Conference. *The American Journal of International Law* 20(1): 124–27.

Fineman, Daniel. 1997. *A Special Relationship: The United States and Military Government in Thailand, 1947–1958.* Honolulu: University of Hawaii Press.

Fishel, Wesley R. 1952. *The End of Extraterritoriality in China.* Berkeley, Los Angeles: University of California Press.

Fisher, Roger, William Ury, and Bruce Patton. 1983. *Getting to Yes: Negotiating Agreement without Giving In.* New York, N.Y.: Penguin Books.

Ford, Jack M. 1996. *Allies in a Bind: Australia and Netherlands East Indies in the Second World War.* 2nd ed. Loganholme, Qld.: Australian Netherlands Ex-Servicemen and Women's Association.

Fox, Grace Estelle. 1940. *British Admirals and Chinese Pirates, 1832–1869.* London: K. Paul, Trench, Trubner & Co.

Fox, John P. 1982. *Germany and the Far Eastern Crisis, 1931–1938: A Study in Diplomacy and Ideology.* Oxford New York: Clarendon Press; Oxford University Press.

Fravel, M. Taylor. 2005. Regime Insecurity and International Cooperation: Explaining China's Compromises in Territorial Disputes. *International Security* 30(2): 46–83.

Frederick, William H. 1989. *Visions and Heat: The Making of the Indonesian Revolution.* Athens: Ohio University Press.

Friedberg, Aaron L. 1988. *The Weary Titan: Britain and the Experience of Relative Decline, 1895–1905.* Princeton, N.J.: Princeton University Press.

Fromkin, David. 2009. *A Peace to End All Peace: The Fall of the Ottoman Empire and the Creation of the Modern Middle East.* 2nd Holt pbk. ed. New York, N.Y.: Henry Holt and Co.

Fudan daxue (Shanghai China). "Sha E Qin Hua Shi" bianxie zu. 1986. *Sha E Qin Hua Shi.* Di 1 ban. ed. Shanghai: Shanghai renmin chubanshe: Xinhua shudian Shanghai faxingsuo faxing.

Fujiwara, Akira. 1973. The Role of the Japanese Army. In *Pearl Harbor as History: Japanese-American Relations, 1931–1941,* edited by Dorothy Borg and Shumpei Okamoto. New York: Columbia University Press.

Fuller, William C. 1992. *Strategy and Power in Russia, 1600–1914.* New York: Free Press.

Furnivall, J. S. 1939. *Netherlands India; a Study of Plural Economy.* Cambridge: Cambridge University Press.

Gaddis, John Lewis. 2005a. *The Cold War: A New History.* New York: Penguin Press.

2005b. *Strategies of Containment: A Critical Appraisal of American National Security Policy During the Cold War.* Rev. and expanded ed. New York: Oxford University Press.

Gao, Hua. 2000. *Hong Taiyang Shi Zenyang Shengqi De: Yan'an Zhengfeng Yundong de Lailongqumai.* Hong Kong: Zhongwen daxue chubanshe.

Garver, John W. 1993. *Foreign Relations of the People's Republic of China.* Englewood Cliffs, N.J.: Prentice-Hall.

1988. *Chinese-Soviet Relations, 1937–1945: The Diplomacy of Chinese Nationalism.* New York: Oxford University Press.

Gellner, Ernest. 1983. *Nations and Nationalism, New Perspectives on the Past.* Ithaca, N.Y.: Cornell University Press.

George, Alexander L. 1979. Case Studies in Theory Development: The Method of Focused, Structured Comparisons. In *Diplomacy: New Approaches in History, Theory, and Policy*, edited by Paul Gordon Lauren. New York: Free Press.

Giddens, Anthony. 1981. The Class Structure of the Advanced Societies. 2nd ed. *Hutchinson University Library. Sociology*. London: Hutchinson.

Gillin, Donald G. 1967. *Warlord: Yen Hsi-Shan in Shansi Province, 1911–1949*. Princeton, N.J.: Princeton University Press.

Gilpin, Robert. 1981. *War and Change in World Politics*. Cambridge, U.K.; New York: Cambridge University Press.

Gleditsch, Nils Petter, Peter Wallensteen, Mikael Eriksson, Margareta Sollenberg, and Håvard Strand. 2002. Armed Conflict 1946–2001: A New Dataset. *Journal of Peace Research* 39(5): 23–23.

Goldstein, Judith, and Robert O. Keohane. 1993. *Ideas and Foreign Policy: Beliefs, Institutions, and Political Change, Cornell Studies in Political Economy*. Ithaca, N.Y.: Cornell University Press.

Goldstein, Stephen M. 1994. Nationalism and Internationalism: Sino-Soviet Relations. In *Chinese Foreign Policy: Theory and Practice*, edited by Thomas W. Robinson and David L. Shambaugh. Oxford: Clarendon Press; Oxford University Press.

Goncharenko, Sergei. 1998. Sino-Soviet Military Cooperation. In *Brothers in Arms: The Rise and Fall of the Sino-Soviet Alliance, 1945–1963*, edited by Odd Arne Westad, xxii, 404 p. Washington, D.C.; Stanford, Calif.: Woodrow Wilson Center Press; distributed by Stanford University Press.

Goodman, David S. G. 2000. Resistance and Revolution, Region, and Rebellion: The Sixth Trigram Movement in Licheng, 1939–1942. In *North China at War: The Social Ecology of Revolution, 1937–1945*, edited by Chongyi Feng and David S. G. Goodman. Lanham, Md.: Rowman & Littlefield Publishers.

Gorski, Philip. 2003. *The Disciplinary Revolution: Calvinism and the Rise of the State in Early Modern Europe* Chicago: University of Chicago Press.

Goto, Ken ichi. 1986. *ShoOwaki Nihon to Indoneshia: 1930-Nendai "Nanshin" No Ronri "Nihon-Kan" No Keifu*. Tokyo: Keiso Shobo.

Gouda, Frances, and Thijs Brocades Zaalberg. 2002. American Visions of the Netherlands East Indies/Indonesia: U.S. Foreign Policy and Indonesian Nationalism, 1920–1949. In *American Visions of the Netherlands East Indies/ Indonesia*, 382 p. Amsterdam: Amsterdam University Press.

Gourevitch, Peter. 1978. The Second Image Reversed: The International Sources of Domestic Politics. *International Organization* 32(4): 881–912.

Graebner, Norman A. 1973. Hoover, Roosevelt, and the Japanese. In *Pearl Harbor as History: Japanese-American Relations, 1931–1941*, edited by Dorothy Borg and Shumpei Okamoto. New York: Columbia University Press.

Great Britain. Board of Trade. *Board of Trade Journal*. v., 125–199 (1930–1970). London: H. M. Stationery Office.

Board of Trade Journal and Commercial Gazette v., 1101–1751 (1918–1930). London: H. M. Stationery Office.

Grenville, J. A. S. 1964. *Lord Salisbury and Foreign Policy: The Close of the Nineteenth Century, University of London Historical Studies*. London: University of London, Athlone Press.

Grieco, Joseph M. 1990. *Cooperation among Nations: Europe, America, and Non-Tariff Barriers to Trade, Cornell Studies in Political Economy*. Ithaca, N.Y.: Cornell University Press.

References

1988a. Anarchy and the Limits of Cooperation: A Realist Critique of the Newest Liberal Institutionalism. *International Organization* 42(3): 485–85.

1988b. Realist Theory and the Problem of International Cooperation: Analysis with an Amended Prisoner's Dilemma Model. *The Journal of Politics* 50(3): 600–24.

Guo, Jianlin, Tang Aimin, Su Quanyou, and Qi Qingchang. 2003. *Minchu Beiyang San Da Neizhan Jishi*. Tianjin: Nankai daxue chubanshe.

Guo, Tingyi. 1987. *Jindai Zhongguo di Bianju*. Chu ban. ed. Taipei: Lianjing chubanshiyegongsi.

Haggard, Stephen, David C. Kang, and Chung-In Moon. 1997. Japanese Colonialism and Korean Development: A Critique. *World Development* 25(6): 867–81.

Haigh, R. H., A. R. Peters, and D. S. Morris. 1999. *The Soviet Union: Interventionism and the Search for Peace 1918–1934*. Sheffield: Sheffield Hallam University.

Hall, John A. 1986. *Powers and Liberties: The Causes and Consequences of the Rise of the West*. 1st California ed. Berkeley: University of California Press.

Han, Yongli. 2003. *Zhanshi Meiguo Dazhanlüe yu Zhongguo Kang Ri Zhanchang, 1941–1945 Nian. Di 1 ban. ed.*, Wuhan Daxue Xueshu Congshu. Wuchang: Wuhan daxue chubanshe.

Hara, Teruyuki. 1995. Japan Moves North: The Japanese Occupation of Northern Sakhalin. In *Rediscovering Russia in Asia: Siberia and the Russian Far East*, edited by Stephen Kotkin, and David Wolff. Armonk, N.Y.: M.E. Sharpe.

Hargreaves, J. D. 1953. Entente Manquee; Anglo-French Relations, 1895–1896. *Cambridge Historical Journal* 11(1): 65–92.

Harkavy, Robert E. 2007. *Strategic Basing and the Great Powers, 1200–2000*. London; New York: Routledge.

Hartford, Kathleen. 1995. Fits and Starts: The Chinese Communist Party in Rural Hebei, 1921–1936. In *New Perspectives on the Chinese Communist Revolution*, edited by Tony Saich and Hans J. van de Ven. Armonk, N.Y.: M.E. Sharpe.

Harvey, Barbara S. 1985. South Sulawesi: Puppets and Patriots. In *Regional Dynamics of the Indonesian Revolution: Unity from Diversity*, edited by Audrey Kahin. Honolulu: University of Hawaii Press.

Haseman, John B. 2002. *The Thai Resistance Movement During World War II*. Thailand: Silkworm Books.

Hawes, Grace M. 1977. *The Marshall Plan for China: Economic Cooperation Administration 1948–1949*. Cambridge, Mass.: Schenkman Pub. Co.

He, Yongji. 1942. On National Power Politics. *Zhanguoce* 30: 1–8.

1940. Zhengzhi Guan: Waixiang Yu Neixiang. *Zhanguoce* 1: 37–42.

Hearing to Receive Testimony on the Situation in Afghanistan. 2010. In *United States Senate Armed Services Committee*. Washington, D.C.: United States Senate.

Heine-Geldern, Robert. 1956. *Conceptions of State and Kingship in Southeast Asia*. Ithaca, N.Y.: Southeast Asia Program Dept. of Far Eastern Studies, Cornell University.

Herbst, Jeffrey Ira. 2000. *States and Power in Africa: Comparative Lessons in Authority and Control, Princeton Studies in International History and Politics*. Princeton, N.J.: Princeton University Press.

Herman, Arthur. 2004. *To Rule the Waves: How the British Navy Shaped the Modern World*. 1st ed. New York, N.Y.: Harper Collins.

Hewison, Kevin. 1989. *Bankers and Bureaucrats, Capital and the Role of the State in Thailand*. New Haven, Conn.: Yale Center for International and Area Studies; distributed by Yale University Southeast Asia Studies.

Hikita, Yasuyuki. 1988. Japanese Capital Exportation During the Fifteen Years of War. In *Nihon Shokuminchi Kenkyu*, edited by Nihon Shokuminchi Kenkyukai. Tokyo: Ryukei Shosha.

Hobsbawm, E. J. 1996. *The Age of Revolution, 1789–1848*. 1st Vintage Books ed. New York: Vintage Books.

1994. *Age of Extremes: The Short Twentieth Century, 1914–1991*. London: Michael Joseph.

1989. *The Age of Empire, 1875–1914*. 1st Vintage Books ed. New York: Vintage.

1984. *The Age of Capital, 1848–1875*. New York: New American Library.

Holubnychy, Lydia. 1979. *Michael Borodin and the Chinese Revolution, 1923–1925*. Ann Arbor, Mich.: Published for East Asian Institute, Columbia University by University Microfilms International.

Hong, Siqi. 1941. Shi Da Zhengzhi. *Zhanguoce* 10: 1–5.

Horowitz, Richard. 2006. Politics, Power, and the Chinese Maritime Customs: The Qing Restoration and the Ascent of Robert Hart. *Modern Asian Studies* 40(3): 549–81.

Houben, V. J. H. 1994. Profit Versus Ethics: Government Enterprises in the Late Colonial State. In *The Late Colonial State in Indonesia: Political and Economic Foundations of the Netherlands Indies, 1880–1942*, edited by R. B. Cribb. Leiden: KITLV Press.

Howard, Christopher H. D. 1974. *Britain and the Casus Belli, 1822–1902; a Study of Britain's International Position from Canning to Salisbury*. London: Athlone Press.

1967. *Splendid Isolation: A Study of Ideas Concerning Britain's International Position and Foreign Policy During the Later Years of the Third Marquis of Salisbury*. London, Melbourne, etc.; New York: Macmillan; St. Martin's Press.

Howard, Michael. 1991. British Grand Strategy in World War I. In *Grand Strategies in War and Peace*, edited by Paul M. Kennedy. New Haven, Conn.: Yale University Press.

Hu, Lancheng. 1940. *Zhannan Heyi Buyi, Zhonghua Ribao Congshu*. Shanghai: Zhonghua ribao guan.

Hu, Lizhong, and An'gang Dai. 1998. Wan Qing Shi. Chu ban. ed. *Ershiwushi Xinbian, 15*. Hong Kong: Zhonghua shuju (Xianggang) youxiangongsi.

Hu, Sheng. 1991. *From the Opium War to the May Fourth Movement*. 1st ed. 2 vols. Beijing: Foreign Languages Press.

Hu, Shi. 2001a. Guo Taiqi Dian Wang Chonghui Zhuan Jiang Jieshi (Di Ba Si Hao), April 29, 1941. In *Hu Shi, Ye Gongchao Shi Mei Waijiao Wenjian Shougao*, edited by Gu Zhou, 171–73. Taipei Shi: Linking Books.

2001b. Hu Shi Dian Chen Bulei, January 10, 1941. In *Hu Shi, Ye Gongchao Shi Mei Waijiao Wenjian Shougao*, edited by Gu Zhou, 119–27. Taipei Shi: Linking Books.

2001c. Hu Shi Dian Chen Bulei Zhuan Jiang Jieshi, October 24, 1940. In *Hu Shi, Ye Gongchao Shi Mei Waijiao Wenjian Shougao*, edited by Gu Zhou, 100–02. Taipei Shi: Linking Books.

2001d. Hu Shi Dian Chen Bulei Zhuan Jiang Jieshi, September 13, 1940. In *Hu Shi, Ye Gongchao Shi Mei Waijiao Wenjian Shougao*, edited by Gu Zhou, 87–90. Taipei Shi: Linking Books.

2001e. Hu Shi Dian Guo Taiqi, August 4, 1939. In *Hu Shi, Ye Gongchao Shi Mei Waijiao Wenjian Shougao*, edited by Gu Zhou, 39–41. Taipei Shi: Linking Books.

2001f. Hu Shi Dian Guo Taiqi, June 25, 1940. In *Hu Shi, Ye Gongchao Shi Mei Waijiao Wenjian Shougao*, edited by Gu Zhou, 77–78. Taipei Shi: Linking Books.

2001g. Hu Shi Dian Jiang Jieshi, June 28, 1941. In *Hu Shi, Ye Gongchao Shi Mei Waijiao Wenjian Shougao*, edited by Gu Zhou, 184–85. Taipei Shi: Linking Books.

References

253

2001h. Hu Shi Dian Jiang Jieshi, December 1, 1940. In *Hu Shi, Ye Gongchao Shi Mei Waijiao Wenjian Shougao*, edited by Gu Zhou, 108–09. Taipei Shi: Linking Books.

2001i. Hu Shi Dian Jiang Jieshi, November 4, 1940. In *Hu Shi, Ye Gongchao Shi Mei Waijiao Wenjian Shougao*, edited by Gu Zhou, 103–07. Taipei Shi: Linking Books.

2001j. Hu Shi Dian Waijiaobu (Di Jiu Ba Ba Hao), August 29, 1939. In *Hu Shi, Ye Gongchao Shi Mei Waijiao Wenjian Shougao*, edited by Gu Zhou, 59–67. Taipei Shi: Linking Books.

2001k. Hu Shi Dian Waijiaobu (Di Jiu Ba Qi Hao), August 29, 1939. In *Hu Shi, Ye Gongchao Shi Mei Waijiao Wenjian Shougao*, edited by Gu Zhou, 57–58. Taipei Shi: Linking Books.

2001l. Hu Shi Dian Waijiaobu (Di Liu Liu Hao), June 26, 1941. In *Hu Shi, Ye Gongchao Shi Mei Waijiao Wenjian Shougao*, edited by Gu Zhou, 178–83. Taipei Shi: Linking Books.

Huang, Meizhen. 1984. *Wang Jingwei Guomin Zhengfu Chengli*. Di 1 ban. ed., *Wang Wei Zhengquan Ziliao Xuanbian*. Shanghai: Shanghai renmin chubanshe; Xinhua shudian Shanghai faxingsuo jingxiao.

Huang, Meizhen, and Hanqing Yang. 2001. Nationalist China's Negotiating Position During the Stalemate, 1938–1945. In *Chinese Collaboration with Japan, 1932–1945: The Limits of Accommodation*, edited by David P. Barrett and Lawrence N. Shyu. Stanford, Calif.: Stanford University Press.

Huang, Meizhen, and Yun Zhang. 1984. *Wang Jingwei Jituan Toudi: Wang Wei Zhengquan Ziliao Xuanbian*. S.l.: s.n.

1984. *Wang Jingwei Jituan Toudi: Wang Wei Zhengquan Ziliao Xuanbian*. S.l.: s.n.

Huang, Ray. 1998. *Xinshidai de Lishiguan: Xixue Wei Ti, Zhongxue Wei Yong*. Chu ban. ed. Taipei: Taiwan Shangwu yinshuguan.

1993. *Zhongguo Da Lishi*. Taibei: Lianjing chuban shiye gongsi.

Huang, Yuhe. 2005. *Zhongshan Xiansheng yu Yingguo, Zhongshan Xueshu Wenhua Jijinhui Jushu*. Taipei: Taiwan xuesheng chubanshe.

Hui, Victoria Tin-bor. 2005. *War and State Formation in Ancient China and Early Modern Europe*. Cambridge, U.K.; New York: Cambridge University Press.

2004. Toward a Dynamic Theory of International Politics: Insights from Comparing Ancient China and Early Modern Europe. *International Organization* 58(1): 175–205.

Hunt, Michael H. 1983. *The Making of a Special Relationship: The United States and China to 1914*. New York: Columbia University Press.

Huntington, Samuel P., and Harvard University. Center for International Affairs. 1968. *Political Order in Changing Societies*. New Haven, Conn.: Yale University Press.

Huth, Paul K. 1988. *Extended Deterrence and the Prevention of War*. New Haven, Conn.: Yale University Press.

Ibrahim, Syukri. 1985. *History of the Malay Kingdom of Patani, Monographs in International Studies. Southeast Asia Series*. Athens: Ohio University, Center for International Studies.

Ienaga, Saburo. 1978. The Pacific War: World War II and the Japanese, 1931–1945. 1st American ed. *The Pantheon Asia Library*. New York: Pantheon Books.

Ikenberry, G. John. 2001. *After Victory: Institutions, Strategic Restraint, and the Rebuilding of Order after Major Wars, Princeton Studies in International History and Politics*. Princeton, N.J.: Oxford: Princeton University Press.

Imlah, Albert H. 1952. British Balance of Payments and Export of Capital, 1816–1913. *The Economic History Review* 5(2): 208–39.

Imlah, Albert Henry. 1958. *Economic Elements in the Pax Britannica; Studies in British Foreign Trade in the Nineteenth Century*. Cambridge, Mass.: Harvard University Press.

Indonesia, and Netherlands Regeeringsvoorlichtingsdienst. 1942. *Ten Years of Japanese Burrowing in the Netherlands East Indies. Official Report of the Netherlands East Indies Government on Japanese Subversive Activities in the Archipelago During the Last Decade*. New York: Netherlands Information Bureau.

Industry, Macmillan Committee on Finance and. 1997. Report. In The Gold Standard in Theory and History, edited by Barry J. *Eichengreen and Marc Flandreau*. London: Routledge.

Iriye, Akira. 1997. *Japan and the Wider World: From the Mid-Nineteenth Century to the Present*. London; New York: Longman.

    1992. *China and Japan in the Global Setting*. Cambridge, Mass.: Harvard University Press.

    1987. *The Origins of the Second World War in Asia and the Pacific, Origins of Modern Wars*. London; New York: Longman.

    1977. Continuities in U.S.-Japanese Relations, 1941–1949. In *The Origins of the Cold War in Asia*, edited by Yonosuke Nagai and Akira Iriye. New York: Columbia University Press.

    1967. *Across the Pacific: An Inner History of American-East Asian Relations*. New York: Harcourt Brace & World.

    1965. *After Imperialism; the Search for a New Order in the Far East, 1921–1931, Harvard East Asian Series*, 22. Cambridge, Mass.: Harvard University Press.

Ishikawa, Yasushi. 1995. *Kaigun Kokubo Shisoshi*. Tokyo: Hara Shobo.

Ismail, Muhammad Gade. 1994. The Economic Position of the Uleëbalang in the Late Colonial State: Eastern Aceh, 1900–1942. In *The Late Colonial State in Indonesia: Political and Economic Foundations of the Netherlands Indies, 1880–1942*, edited by R. B. Cribb. Leiden: KITLV Press.

Iwatake, Teruhiko. 1989. *Nanpo Gunsei Ronshu*. Tokyo: Gannando Shoten.

Jackson, Robert H. 1993. The Weight of Ideas in Decolonisation: Normative Change in International Relations. In *Ideas and Foreign Policy: Beliefs, Institutions, and Political Change*, edited by Judith Goldstein and Robert O. Keohane. Ithaca, N.Y.: Cornell University Press.

    1990. *Quasi-States: Sovereignty, International Relations, and the Third World, Cambridge Studies in International Relations*; 12. Cambridge, U.K.; New York: Cambridge University Press.

Jansen, Marius B. 1954. *The Japanese and Sun Yat-Sen, Harvard Historical Monographs*, 27. Cambridge, Mass.: Harvard University Press.

Jervis, Robert. 1976. *Perception and Misperception in International Politics*. Princeton, N.J.: Princeton University Press.

Jespersen, T. Christopher. 1996. *American Images of China, 1931–1949*. Stanford, Calif.: Stanford University Press.

Jiang, Pei. 2006. *Ri Wei "Zhi'an Qianghua Yundong" Yanjiu (1941–1942)*. Di 1 ban. ed. Tianjin Shi: Nankai daxue chubanshe.

Jin, Shixuan, and Wenshu Xu. 1986. *Zhongguo Tielu Fazhan Shi, 1876–1949*. Di 1 ban. ed. Beijing: Zhongguo tiedao chubanshe: Xinhua shudian Beijing faxingsuo faxing.

Johnson, Chalmers A. 1969. Chinese Communist Leadership and Mass Response: The Yenan Period and the Socialist Education Campaign Period. In *China in Crisis*, edited by Ping-ti Ho and Tang Tsou. Chicago: University of Chicago Press.

References

1962. *Peasant Nationalism and Communist Power: The Emergence of Revolutionary China*. Stanford, Calif.: Stanford University Press.

Joseph, Philip. 1928. *Foreign Diplomacy in China, 1894–1900: A Study in Political and Economic Relations with China*. London: G. Allen & Unwin.

Ka, Chih-ming. 2003. *Mitang Xiangke: Riben Zhiminzhuyi Xia Taiwan De Fazhan Yu Congshu*. Di 1 ban. ed., *Taiwan Shehuixue Congshu, 1*. Taipei: Qunxue chuba youxiangongsi.

1995. *Japanese Colonialism in Taiwan: Land Tenure, Development, and Dependency, 1895–1945*. Boulder, Colo.: Westview Press.

Kahin, Audrey, and George McTurnan Kahin. 1995. *Subversion as Foreign Policy: The Secret Eisenhower and Dulles Debacle in Indonesia*. New York: New Press; distributed by W.W. Norton.

Kahin, George McT. 1953. Post-War Problems in the Southeast Asia Policy of the United States. In *Southeast Asia in the Coming World*, edited by Philip Warren Thayer. Baltimore: Johns Hopkins Press.

Kahin, George McTurnan. 2003. *Southeast Asia: A Testament, Critical Asian Scholarship*. London; New York: RoutledgeCurzon.

1977. The United States and the Anti-Colonial Revolutions in Southeast Asia. In *The Origins of the Cold War in Asia*, edited by Yonosuke Nagai and Akira Iriye, ix, 448. New York: Columbia University Press.

1952. *Nationalism and Revolution in Indonesia*. Ithaca, N.Y.: Cornell University Press.

Kang, David C. 2005a. Hierarchy in Asian International Relations: 1300 to 1900. *Asian Security* 1(1): 53–79.

2005b. Why China's Rise Will Be Peaceful: Hierarchy and Stability in the East Asian Region. *Perspectives on Politics* 3(3): 551–54.

2004. Hierarchy, Balancing, and Empirical Puzzles in Asian International Relations. *International Security* 28(3): 165–80.

2002. *Crony Capitalism: Corruption and Development in South Korea and the Philippines, Cambridge Studies in Comparative Politics*. Cambridge, U.K.; New York: Cambridge University Press.

Kaple, Deborah A. 1998. Soviet Advisors in China in the 1950s. In *Brothers in Arms: The Rise and Fall of the Sino-Soviet Alliance, 1945–1963*, edited by Odd Arne Westad. Washington, D.C.: Woodrow Wilson Center Press.

Karnow, Stanley. 1989. *In Our Image: America's Empire in the Philippines*. New York: Random House.

Kartodirdjo, Sartono. 1978. Political Transformation in the Nineteenth Century. In *Dynamics of Indonesian History*, edited by Haryati Soebadio-Noto Soebagio and Carinne A. du Marchie Sarvaas. Amsterdam; New York: North-Holland Pub. Co.; distributors for the U.S.A. and Canada Elsevier/North-Holland.

Kat Angelino, Arnold Dirk Adriaan de, and Gustaaf Johannes Renier. 1931. *Colonial Policy*. The Hague: M. Nijhoff.

Katsuro, Yamamura. 1973. The Role of the Finance Ministry. In *Pearl Harbor as History: Japanese-American Relations, 1931–1941*, edited by Dorothy Borg and Shumpei Okamoto. New York: Columbia University Press.

Katz, Paul R. 2005. *When Valleys Turned Blood Red: The Ta-Pa-Ni Incident in Colonial Taiwan*. Honolulu: University of Hawai'i Press.

Kayaoğlu, Turan. 2010. *Legal Imperialism: Sovereignty and Extraterritoriality in Japan, the Ottoman Empire, and China*. Cambridge, U.K.; New York: Cambridge University Press.

256   References

Ke, Siming. 2005. *Zaoqi Guo Gong Guanxi Xinlun – Cong E Lian, Liangong Dao San Da Zhengce de Bianzheng (Xiuding Ban)*. Taipei: Xuesheng Shuju.

Keating, Pauline. 2000. Getting Peasants Organised: Village Organisations and the Party-State in the Shaan-Gan-Ning Border Region. In *North China at War: The Social Ecology of Revolution, 1937–1945*, edited by Chongyi Feng and David S. G. Goodman. Lanham, Md.: Rowman & Littlefield Publishers.

Kediri, The Resident of. 1977. Communist Disturbances in Blitar, 1927. In *Indonesia: Selected Documents on Colonialism and Nationalism, 1830–1942*, edited by C. L. M. Penders. St. Lucia: University of Queensland Press.

Kennan, George F. 1993. The Kennan "Long Telegram", Moscow, February 22, 1946. In *Origins of the Cold War: The Novikov, Kennan, and Roberts "Long Telegrams" of 1946, with Three New Commentaries*, edited by Kenneth M. Jensen. Washington, D.C.: United States Institute of Peace Press.

Kennan, George F. 1984. *American Diplomacy*. Expanded ed. Chicago: University of Chicago Press.

Kennedy, Andrew B. 2012. *Remaking the World: National Efficacy Beliefs and the International Ambitions of Mao and Nehru*. Cambridge: Cambridge University Press.

Kennedy, Greg. 2002. *Anglo-American Strategic Relations and the Far East, 1933–1939: Imperial Crossroads, Cass Series – Strategy and History*. London; Portland, Ore.: Frank Cass.

Kennedy, Paul M. 1987. *The Rise and Fall of the Great Powers: Economic Change and Military Conflict from 1500 to 2000*. 1st ed. New York: Random House.

Kennedy-Pipe, Caroline. 1998. *Russia and the World, 1917–1991, International Relations and the Great Powers*. London; New York: Arnold.

Keohane, Robert O. 1984. *After Hegemony: Cooperation and Discord in the World Political Economy*. Princeton, N.J.: Princeton University Press.

Keohane, Robert O., and Joseph S. Nye. 1989. *Power and Interdependence*. 2nd ed., *Scott, Foresman/Little, Brown Series in Political Science*. Glenview, Ill.: Scott Foresman.

Khong, Yuen Foong. 1992. *Analogies at War: Korea, Munich, Dien Bien Phu, and the Vietnam Decisions of 1965*. Princeton, N.J.: Princeton University Press.

Kim, Hakjoon. 1994. The Soviet Role in the Korean War. In *Russia in the Far East and Pacific Region*, edited by Il Yung Chung and Eunsook Chung, xi, 410 p. Seoul, South Korea: Sejong Institute.

Kimball, Warren F. 1969. *The Most Unsordid Act: Lend-Lease, 1939–1941*. Baltimore: Johns Hopkins Press.

Kindermann, Gottfried Karl. 1959. *The Sino-Soviet Entente Policy of Sun Yat-Sen 1923–1925*. PhD thesis, University of Chicago.

Kinhide, Mushakoji. 1973. The Structure of Japanese-American Relations in the 1930s. In *Pearl Harbor as History: Japanese-American Relations, 1931–1941*, edited by Dorothy Borg and Shumpei Okamoto. New York: Columbia University Press.

Kinzer, Stephen. 2006. *Overthrow: America's Century of Regime Change from Hawaii to Iraq*. 1st ed. New York: Times Books.

Kirby, William C. 1997. The Internationalization of China: Foreign Relations at Home and Abroad in the Republican Era. *The China Quarterly* (150): 433–58.

    1984. *Germany and Republican China*. Stanford, Calif.: Stanford University Press.

Kiser, Edgar, and Yong Cai. 2003. War and Bureaucratisation in Qin China: Exploring the Anamolous Case. *American Sociological Review* 68(4): 511–39.

References

257

Kissinger, Henry. 1994. *Diplomacy*. New York: Simon & Schuster.

Kohli, Atul. 2004. *State-Directed Development: Political Power and Industrialization in the Global Periphery*. Cambridge, U.K.; New York: Cambridge University Press.

Koo, V. K. Wellington, and yanjiusuo Zhongguo shehuikexueyuan. Jindaishi. 1983. *Gu Weijun Huiyilu*. Di 1 ban. ed. Beijing: Zhonghua shuju: Xinhua shudian Beijing faxingsuo faxing.

Koyle, Frederick T. 1953. Export-Import Problems in Southeast Asia. In *Southeast Asia in the Coming World*, edited by Philip Warren Thayer. Baltimore: Johns Hopkins Press.

Krasner, Stephen D. 2001. *Problematic Sovereignty: Contested Rules and Political Possibilities*. New York: Columbia University Press.

1999. *Sovereignty: Organized Hypocrisy*. Princeton, N.J.: Princeton University Press.

1993. Westphalia and All That. In *Ideas and Foreign Policy: Beliefs, Institutions, and Political Change*, edited by Judith Goldstein and Robert O. Keohane. Ithaca, N.Y.: Cornell University Press.

Kratochwil, Friedrich. 1986. Of Systems, Boundaries, and Territoriality: An Inquiry into the Formation of the State System. *World Politics* 39(1): 27–27.

Kuhn, Philip A. 2002. *Origins of the Modern Chinese State*. English ed. Stanford, Calif.: Stanford University Press.

1980. *Rebellion and Its Enemies in Late Imperial China: Militarization and Social Structure, 1796–1864, Harvard East Asian Series*, 49. Cambridge, Mass.: Harvard University Press.

Kuhonta, Erik Martinez. 2003. *The Political Foundations of Equitable Development: State and Party Formation in Malaysia and Thailand*. Ph.D. thesis, Princeton University.

Kuo, Jung-Chao. 1967. *Meiguo Ya'erda Mi Yue Yu Zhongguo: Jiantao Yi Ya'erda Miyue Wei Zhongxin De Meiguo Dui Hua Zhengce*. Zai ban. ed. Taipei: Shuiniu chubanshe.

Kupchan, Charles. 1994. *The Vulnerability of Empire, Cornell Studies in Security Affairs*. Ithaca, N.Y.: Cornell University Press.

LaFeber, Walter. 1993. *America, Russia, and the Cold War, 1945–1992*. 7th ed. *America in Crisis*. New York: McGraw-Hill.

1977. American Policy-Makers, Public Opinion, and the Outbreak of the Cold War. In *The Origins of the Cold War in Asia*, edited by Yonosuke Nagai and Akira Iriye. New York: Columbia University Press.

Lamley, Harry J. 1999. Taiwan under Japanese Rule, 1895–1945: The Vicissitudes of Colonialism. In *Taiwan: A New History*, edited by Murray A. Rubinstein. Armonk, N.Y.: M.E. Sharpe.

Lane, Kevin. 1990. *Sovereignty and the Status Quo: The Historical Roots of China's Hong Kong Policy, Westview Special Studies on China and East Asia*. Boulder, Colo.: Westview Press.

Lary, Diana. 1974. *Region and Nation: The Kwangsi Clique in Chinese Politics, 1925–1937, Cambridge Studies in Chinese History, Literature, and Institutions*. London; New York: Cambridge University Press.

Lee, Chong-Sik. 1967. *Counterinsurgency in Manchuria: The Japanese Experience, 1931–1940*. Santa Monica, Calif.: Rand Corp.

Lee, En-han. 1977. *China's Quest for Railway Autonomy, 1904–1911: A Study of the Chinese Railway-Rights Recovery Movement*. Singapore: Singapore University Press.

Lee, Kam-keung, Lau Yee-chung, and Mak King-sang, eds. 1999. *Jindai Zhongguo Haifang – Junshi Yu Jingji*. Hong Kong: Xianggang Zhongguo jindaishi xuehui.

Leffler, Melvyn P. 1992. *A Preponderance of Power: National Security, the Truman Administration, and the Cold War, Stanford Nuclear Age Series*. Stanford, Calif.: Stanford University Press.

Legge, J. D. 1988. *Intellectuals and Nationalism in Indonesia: A Study of the Following Recruited by Sutan Sjahrir in Occupation Jakarta*. Ithaca, N.Y.: Cornell Modern Indonesia Project Publications.

Lei, Haizong. 1968. *Zhongguo Wenhua yu Zhongguo de Bing*. Hong Kong: Longmen shudian.

———. 1941. Zhong Wai de Chunqiu Shidai. *Zhanguoce* 15–16: 1–6.

———. 1934. *Zhongguo Tongshi Xuandu*. Chu ban ed. Peking: Guoli Qinghua daxue.

Leifer, Michael. 2000a. *Asian Nationalism*. New York: Routledge.

———. 2000b. The Changing Temper of Indonesian Nationalism. In *Asian Nationalism*, edited by Michael Leifer. New York: Routledge.

Levine, Steven I. 1987. *Anvil of Victory: The Communist Revolution in Manchuria, 1945–1948*. Based on the author's PhD thesis, Columbia University Press, Harvard University.

Li, Jianrong. 1988. Kangri Zhanzheng Shiqi Sulian Dui Hua Daikuan yu Junhuo Wuzi Yuanzhu. *Jindaishi yanjiu* 3.

Li, Jinghao. 1990. Taipingyang Huiyi Riji (Xia) [a Diary of the Pacific Conference (II)]. *Jindaishi ziliao* 76: 1–50.

———. 1989. Taipingyang Huiyi Riji (Shang) [a Diary of the Pacific Conference (I)]. *Jindaishi ziliao* 75: 1–73.

Li, Jitang, and Zhongguo renmin zhengzhi xieshanghuiyi. Heilongjiang Sheng weiyuan-hui. Wenshi ziliao yanjiu weiyuanhui. Bianjibu. 1989. *Zhong E Miyue he Zhongdong Tielu de Xiuzhu*. Di 1 ban. ed., *Zhongdong Tielu Lishi Congshu*. Ha'erbin: Heilongjiang renmin chubanshe.

Li, Qifang. 2000. *Zhong E Guanxishi*. Chu ban. ed. Taipei: Lianjing chubanshiyegongsi.

Li, Shide. 1999. *Yingguo yu Zhongguo De Waijiao Guanxi (1929–1937), Minguo Shixue Congshu; 10*. Taipei: Guoshiguan: Jingxiaoshang Sanmin shuju.

Li, Y. u-chen, M. L. Titarenko, Rossiiskii tsentr khraneniiya yi izucheniiya dokumentov noveishei istorii., Vsesoyiuznaiya kommunisticheskaiya partiiya (bolshevikov), Communist International., Institut Dalnego Vostoka (Rossiiskaiya akademiiya nauk), and Freie Universität Berlin. Ostasiatisches Seminar. 1997. Liangong, Gongchanguoji yu Zhongguo. Chu ban. ed., *Cang Hai Cong Kan*. Taipei: Dongda tushugongsi.

Li, Yushu. 1966. Zhong Ri Ershiyitiao Jiaoshe. Chu ban. ed., *Zhongyang Yanjiuyuan Jindaishi Yanjiusuo Zhuankan; 18*. Taipei: Zhongyang yanjiuyuan jindaishi yanjiusuo.

Li, Yushu, and Huapeng Wu. 1987. Qingmo Zhong E Hulunbei'er Jiangjie di Chongkan. Chu ban. ed., *Meng Zang Xueshu Yanjiu Luncong*. Taipei: Meng Zang weiyuanhui.

Li, Zhancai. 1994. *Zhongguo Tielu Shi, 1876–1949*. Di 1 ban. ed. Guangdong Sheng Shantou Shi: Shantou daxue chubanshe.

Lian, Xinhao. 2004. *Zhongguo Haiguan yu Duiwaimaoyi*. Changsha: Yuelu shushe.

Liang, Jingchun. 1978. *1945 Nian Zhong-Su Youhao Tongmeng Tiaoyue zhi Qianding Yuqi Neimu Zhenxiang*, edited by Paul K.T. Sih. Taipei: Taiwan shangwu yinshuguan.

Liang, Qichao, and Qichao Liang. 1990. *Bianfa Tongyi: Fu Kaiming Zhuanzhi Lun*. Di 1 ban. ed. Yangzhou Shi: Jiangsu Guangling guji keyinshe.

References

Liddle R. William. 1970. *Ethnicity, Party, and National Integration: An Indonesian Case Study, Yale Southeast Asia Studies*. New Haven, Conn.: Yale University Press.

Lin, Shiming. 1980. *Yihetuan Shibian Qijian Dongnan Hubao Yundong zhi Yanjiu*. Taipei: Taiwan shangwu yinshuguan.

Lin, Tongji. 1940. Zhanguo Shidai de Chongyan. *Zhanguoce* 1: 1–8.

Lin, Tongji, and Haizong Lei. 1971. *Zhongguo zhi Weiji*. Hong Kong: Huanghe chubanshe.

Lissak, Moshe. 1976. *Military Roles in Modernization: Civil-Military Relations in Thailand and Burma*. Beverly Hills, Calif.: Sage Publications.

Liu, Jingzhong, and Bofu Tian. 2004. *Guominjun Shigang*. Beijing: Remin chubanshe.

Liu, Weisen. 1999. *Sun Zhongshan yu Meijia Huaqiao*. Chu ban. ed. Taipei: Jindai Zhongguo chubanshe.

Liu, Ximing. 2002. *Wei Jun: Qiangquan Jingzhu Xia de Zuzi, 1937–1949*. Revision of the author's PhD thesis, Daoxiang chubanshe, Guoli Taiwan shifan daxue.

Liu, Xinli. 1994. Chongqing Guomin Zhengfu yu Yingguo Zhengfu Guanyu Xianggang Wenti De Jiaobu. *Jindaishi yanjiu (Research on Modern History)* (4): 191–200.

Liu, Yan, and Fangchen Li. 1962. *Zhongguo Waijiao Shi*. Taipei: Sanmin shuju.

Liu, Zenghe. 2005. *Yapian Shuishou yu Qingmo Xinzheng*. Edited by He Zhang, *Jindai Zhongguo de Zhishi yu Zhidu Zhuanxing Congshu*. Beijing: Sanlian shudian.

Lo, Jiu-jung. 2001. Survival as Justification for Collaboration, 1937–1945. In *Chinese Collaboration with Japan, 1932–1945: The Limits of Accommodation*, edited by David P. Barrett and Lawrence N. Shyu. Stanford, Calif.: Stanford University Press.

Lowe, Peter. 1997. *Containing the Cold War in East Asia: British Policies Towards Japan, China, and Korea, 1948–53*. Manchester; New York: Manchester University Press; distributed in the U.S.A. by St. Martin's Press.

———. 1981. *Britain in the Far East: A Survey from 1819 to the Present*. London; New York: Longman.

Lu, An. 2001. *Qingdao Jinxiandai Shi*. Di 1 ban. ed. Qingdao Shi: Qingdao chubanshe: Xinhua shudian Beijing faxingsuo faxing.

Lukes, Steven. 2004. *Power: A Radical View*. 2nd expanded ed. Houndmills, Basingstoke, Hampshire; New York: Palgrave Macmillan.

———. 1986. *Power, Readings in Social and Political Theory*. New York: New York University Press.

Luo, Ergang. 1997. *Wan Qing Bingzhi*. Di 1 ban. ed. Beijing: Zhonghua shuju.

M, H. 1927. British Memorandum on China. *Journal of the Royal Institute of International Affairs* 6(1): 62–68.

Ma, Shuli. 1957. *Yinni Duli Yundong Shi*. Chu ban. ed. Hong Kong: Xinwen tiandi she.

Ma, Yinchu. 1932. *Ma Yinchu Yanjiang Ji, Zhongguo Jingji Xueshe Congshu*. Shanghai: Shangwu yinshuguan.

Ma, Zhendu, and Rugao Qi. 1998. *Jiang Jieshi yu Xitele: Minguo Shiqi de Zhong De Guanxi*. Chu ban. ed. Taipei: Dongda tushugongsi.

MacKinnon, Stephen R. 1980. *Power and Politics in Late Imperial China: Yuan Shi-Kai in Beijing and Tianjin, 1901–1908*. Berkeley: University of California Press.

Maddison, Angus. 1990. Dutch Colonialism in Indonesia: A Comparative Perspective. In *Indonesian Economic History in the Dutch Colonial Era*, edited by Anne Booth, W. J. O'Malley and Anna Weidemann. New Haven, Conn.: Yale University Southeast Asia Studies.

Maddison, Angus, and Organisation for Economic Co-operation and Development. Development Centre. 2003. *The World Economy: Historical Statistics*,

Development Centre Studies. Paris, France: Development Centre of the Organisation for Economic Co-operation and Development.

2001. *The World Economy: A Millennial Perspective, Development Centre Studies*. Paris, France Development Centre of the Organisation for Economic Co-operation and Development.

Maekawa, Kaori. 2005. The Heiho During the Japanese Occupation of Indonesia. In *Asian Labor in the Wartime Japanese Empire: Unknown Histories*, edited by Paul H. Kratoska. Armonk, N.Y.: Sharpe.

Mahan, A. T. 1957. *The Influence of Sea Power Upon History, 1660–1783*. New York: Sagamore Press.

1918. *The Influence of Sea Power Upon the French Revolution and Empire, 1793–1812*. 14th ed. 2 vols. Boston: Little, Brown.

1905. *Sea Power in Its Relations to the War of 1812*. Boston: Little, Brown.

Mahan, Alfred Thayer. 1999. *Mahan on Naval Warfare*. Edited by Allan Wescott. Mineola, N.Y.: Dover Publications, Inc.

Mangoenkoesoemo, Tjipto. 1977. Power or Fear, 1913. In *Indonesia: Selected Documents on Colonialism and Nationalism, 1830–1942*, edited by C. L. M. Penders. St. Lucia: University of Queensland Press.

Mann, Michael. 1988. *States, War, and Capitalism: Studies in Political Sociology*. Oxford Oxfordshire; New York: Basil Blackwell.

1986. *The Sources of Social Power*. Cambridge, U.K.; New York: Cambridge University Press.

Mao, Tsetung. 1979a. The People's Democratic Dictatorship. In *The People's Republic of China: A Documentary History of Revolutionary Change*, edited by Mark Selden. New York: Monthly Review Press.

1979b. The Present Situation and Our Tasks. In *The People's Republic of China: A Documentary History of Revolutionary Change*, edited by Mark Selden and Patti Eggleston. New York: Monthly Review Press.

Mao, Xixue, and Dezhang Li. 1995. *Kang Ri Genjudi Caijing Shigao*. Di 1 ban. ed. Zhengzhou: Henan renmin chubanshe.

Mao, Zedong. 1954. *The Chinese Revolution and the Chinese Communist Party*. 1st ed. Peking: Foreign Languages Press.

1952a. *Xin Minzhuzhuyi de Xianzheng*. Beijing: Renmin chubanshe.

1952b. *Xin Minzhuzhuyi Lun*. Beijing di 2 ban. ed. Beijing: Renmin chubanshe: faxing Xinhua shudian.

1951. *Mao Zedong Xuanji*. Beijing di 1 ban. ed. Beijing: Renmin chubanshe.

1948a. *Zhongguo Geming yu Zhongguo Gongchandang*. Chu ban. ed. Hong Kong: Zhengbao she.

1948b. *Zhongguo Geming Zhanzheng de Zhanlüe Wenti, Mao Zedong Xuanji Zhongguo Geming Zhanzheng Zhidao Lilun*. Hong Kong: Xinminzhu chubanshe.

Marix Evans, Martin. 2000. *Encyclopedia of the Boer War, 1899–1902*. Santa Barbara, Calif.: ABC-CLIO.

Marx, Karl. 1978a. Contribution to the Critique of Hegel's Philosophy of Right: Part I. In *The Marx-Engels Reader*, edited by Karl Marx, Friedrich Engels, and Robert C. Tucker. New York: Norton.

1978b. The German Ideology: Part I. In *The Marx-Engels Reader*, edited by Karl Marx, Friedrich Engels, and Robert C. Tucker. New York: Norton.

McCord, Edward Allen. 1993. *The Power of the Gun: The Emergence of Modern Chinese Warlordism*. Berkeley, Calif.: University of California Press.

References

McLean, D. 1973. Chinese Railways and the Townley Agreement of 1903. *Modern Asian Studies* 7(2): 145–64.

McMahon, Robert J. 2006. The Point of No Return: The Eisenhower Administration and Indonesia, 1953–1960. In *The Eisenhower Administration, the Third World, and the Globalization of the Cold War*, edited by Kathryn C. Statler and Andrew L. Johns. Lanham, Md.: Rowman & Littlefield.

McMillan, Richard. 2005. *The British Occupation of Indonesia 1945–1946: Britain, the Netherlands and the Indonesian Revolution, Royal Asiatic Society Books*. London; New York: Routledge.

McVey, Ruth Thomas. 1965. *The Rise of Indonesian Communism*. Ithaca, N.Y.: Cornell University Press.

Mead, Kullada Kesboonchoo. 2004. *The Rise and Decline of Thai Absolutism*. 1st ed. *Routledgecurzon Studies in the Modern History of Asia*. London; New York: RoutledgeCurzon.

Memorandum on United States Investments in Japan. 1933. *Memorandum (Institute of Pacific Relations, American Council)*, 2(13).

Meyer, John W. 1980. The World Polity and the Authority of the Nation-State. In *Studies of the Modern World-System*, edited by Albert Bergesen. New York: Academic Press.

Meyer, John W., John Boli, George M. Thomas, and Francisco O. Ramirez. 1997. World Society and the Nation-State. *The American Journal of Sociology* 103(1): 144–44.

Mi, Rucheng. 2002. *Zhonghua Minguo Tielushi Ziliao, 1912–1949*. Di 1 ban. ed. Beijing: Shehuikexue wenxian chubanshe.

Michael, Franz. 1964. Regionalism in Nineteenth-Century China. Introduction. In *Li Hung-Chang and the Huai Army: A Study in Nineteenth Century Chinese Regionalism*, edited by Stanley Spector. Seattle: University of Washington Press.

Migdal, Joel S. 2001. *State in Society: Studying How States and Societies Transform and Constitute One Another, Cambridge Studies in Comparative Politics*. Cambridge: Cambridge University Press.

————. 1994. *Introduction: Developing a State-in-Society Perspective*, 1–34. Cambridge, U.K.; New York: Cambridge University Press.

————. 1988. *Strong Societies and Weak States: State-Society Relations and State Capabilities in the Third World*. Princeton: Princeton University Press.

Miller, Benjamin. 2007. *States, Nations, and the Great Powers: The Sources of Regional War and Peace, Cambridge Studies in International Relations*. Cambridge, U.K.; New York: Cambridge University Press.

Milner, Helen. 1988. Trading Places: Industries for Free Trade. *World Politics* 40(3): 350–76.

Min, Tu-gi, Philip A. Kuhn, and Timothy Brook. 1989. *National Polity and Local Power: The Transformation of Late Imperial China, Harvard-Yenching Institute Monograph Series*, 27. Cambridge, Mass.: Council on East Asian Studies Harvard University: Harvard-Yenching Institute; distributed by Harvard University Press.

Ministry of Foreign Affairs, ROC. 1999. Waijiaobu Minguo 24 Nian 11 Yue Gongzuo Baogao. In *Guomin Zhengfu Shiqi Waijiaobu Gongzuo Baogao (Minguo 22 Nian Zhi 26 Nian)*, edited by Xiuhuan Zhou. Taipei: Guoshiguan.

Mitchell, B. R. 1962. *Abstract of British Historical Statistics*. Cambridge: Cambridge University Press.

Mitter, Rana. 2000. *The Manchurian Myth: Nationalism, Resistance, and Collaboration in Modern China*. Berkeley, Calif.; London: University of California Press.

Mizuno, Akira, and Liangsheng Zheng. 1998. *Dongbei Junfa Zhengquan Yanjiu: Zhang Zuolin · Zhang Xueliang zhi Kangwai yu Xiezhu Tongyi Guonei De Guiji*. Chu ban. ed., *Shijie Xueshuyizhu*. Taipei: Guoli bianyiguan.

Mokrapong, Thawatt. 1976. The Causes of the Revolution. In *Modern Thai Politics: From Village to Nation*, edited by Clark D. Neher. Cambridge, Mass.: Schenkman Pub. Co.

Morant, Robert Laurie, Pritsadang, and Nigel J. Brailey. 1989. *Two Views of Siam on the Eve of the Chakri Reformation*. Whiting Bay, Arran, Scotland: Kiscadale.

Moravcsik, Andrew. 1998. *The Choice for Europe: Social Purpose and State Power from Messina to Maastricht, Cornell Studies in Political Economy*. Ithaca, N.Y.: Cornell University Press.

Mrázek, Rudolf. 2002. *Engineers of Happy Land: Technology and Nationalism in a Colony, Princeton Studies in Culture/Power/History*. Princeton, N.J.; Oxford: Princeton University Press.

⸻ 1978. *The United States and the Indonesian Military, 1945–1965: A Study of an Intervention, Dissertationes Orientales*. Prague: Oriental Institute in Academia, Pub. House of the Czechoslavak Academy of Sciences.

Munholland, J. Kim. 1972. The French Connection That Failed: France and Sun Yat-Sen, 1900–1908. *The Journal of Asian Studies* 32(1): 77–95.

Muscat, Robert J. 1990. *Thailand and the United States: Development, Security, and Foreign Aid*. New York: Columbia University Press.

Mutsu, Munemitsu. 2005. *Jiawu Zhanzheng Waijiao Milu*. Translated by Pengren Chen. Taipei: Haixia xueshu chubanshe.

Nagai, Yonosuke. 1977. The Roots of Cold War Doctrine: The Esoteric and the Exoteric. In *The Origins of the Cold War in Asia*, edited by Yonosuke Nagai and Akira Iriye. New York: Columbia University Press.

Nagazumi, Akira. 1972. *The Dawn of Indonesian Nationalism: The Early Years of the Budi Utomo, 1908–1918*. Tokyo: Institute of Developing Economies.

Nakami, Tatsuo. 1995. Russian Diplomats and Mongol Independence. In *Rediscovering Russia in Asia: Siberia and the Russian Far East*, edited by Stephen Kotkin and David Wolff. Armonk, N.Y.: M.E. Sharpe.

Nankai daxue. Lishi xueyuan. 2005. *Lei Haizong yu Er Shi Shiji Zhongguo Shixue: Lei Haizong Xiansheng Bai Nian Danchen Jinian Wenji*. Di 1 ban. ed. Beijing Shi: Zhonghua shuju.

Naquin, Susan. 1981. *Shantung Rebellion: The Wang Lun Uprising of 1774*. New Haven, Conn.: Yale University Press.

⸻ 1976. *Millenarian Rebellion in China: The Eight Trigrams Uprising of 1813, Yale Historical Publications: Miscellany 108*. New Haven, Conn.: Yale University Press.

Nathan, Andrew J. 1976. *Peking Politics, 1918–1923: Factionalism and the Failure of Constitutionalism, Michigan Studies on China*. Berkeley: University of California Press.

Nathan, Andrew J., and Robert S. Ross. 1997. *The Great Wall and the Empty Fortress: China's Search for Security*. 1st ed. New York; London: W.W. Norton.

Neher, Clark D. 1976. Constitutionalism and Elections in Thailand. In *Modern Thai Politics: From Village to Nation*, edited by Clark D. Neher. Cambridge, Mass.: Schenkman Pub. Co.

Nexon, Daniel H. 2009. *The Struggle for Power in Early Modern Europe: Religious Conflict, Dynastic Empires, and International Change, Princeton Studies in International History and Politics*. Princeton: Princeton University Press.

References

2004. *Sovereignty, Religion, and the Fate of Empires in Early Modern Europe.* Dissertation, Columbia University.

Niu, Jun. 1998. The Origins of the Sino-Soviet Alliance. In *Brothers in Arms: The Rise and Fall of the Sino-Soviet Alliance, 1945–1963,* edited by Odd Arne Westad, xxii, 404 p. Washington, D.C.; Stanford, Calif.: Woodrow Wilson Center Press; distributed by Stanford University Press.

North, Douglass Cecil. 1990. *Institutions, Institutional Change, and Economic Performance, The Political Economy of Institutions and Decisions.* Cambridge, U.K.; New York: Cambridge University Press.

1981. *Structure and Change in Economic History.* 1st ed. New York: Norton.

Novikov, Nikolai. 1993. The Novikov Telegram, Washington, September 27, 1946. In *Origins of the Cold War: The Novikov, Kennan, and Roberts "Long Telegrams" of 1946, with Three New Commentaries,* edited by Kenneth M. Jensen. Washington, D.C.: United States Institute of Peace Press.

Nurkse, Ragnar. 1997. The Gold Exchange Standard. In *The Gold Standard in Theory and History,* edited by Barry J. Eichengreen and Marc Flandreau. London: Routledge.

Oemarjati, Boen. 1978. Development of Modern Indonesian Literature. In *Dynamics of Indonesian History,* edited by Haryati Soebadio-Noto Soebagio and Carinne A. du Marchie Sarvaas. Amsterdam; New York: North-Holland Pub. Co.; distributors for the U.S.A. and Canada Elsevier/North-Holland.

Ong, Hok Ham. 1978. The Inscrutable and the Paranoid: An Investigation into the Sources of the Brotodiningrat Affair. In *Southeast Asian Transitions: Approaches through Social History,* edited by Ruth Thomas McVey, Adrienne Suddard, and Harry Jindrich Benda. New Haven, Conn.: Yale University Press.

Owen, Norman G. 2005. *The Emergence of Modern Southeast Asia: A New History.* Honolulu: University of Hawaii Press.

Peleggi, Maurizio. 2007. *Thailand: The Worldly Kingdom.* London: Reaktion.

Pepper, Suzanne. 1999. *Civil War in China: The Political Struggle, 1945–1949.* Lanham, Md.; Oxford: Rowman & Littlefield.

1991. The KMT-CCP Conflict, 1945–1949. In *The Nationalist Era in China, 1927–1949,* edited by Lloyd E. Eastman, x, 406 p. Cambridge, U.K.; New York: Cambridge University Press.

Perkins, Dwight H. 1967. Government as an Obstacle to Industrialization: The Case of Nineteenth-Century China. *The Journal of Economic History* 27(4): 478.

Perry, Elizabeth J. 1980. *Rebels and Revolutionaries in North China, 1845–1945.* Stanford, Calif.: Stanford University Press.

Phillips, Steven. 1999. Between Assimilation and Independence: Taiwanese Political Aspirations under Nationalist Chinese Rule. In *Taiwan: A New History,* edited by Murray A. Rubinstein. Armonk, N.Y.: M.E. Sharpe.

Philpott, Daniel. 2001. *Revolutions in Sovereignty: How Ideas Shaped Modern International Relations, Princeton Studies in International History and Politics.* Princeton: Princeton University Press.

Phongpaichit, Pasuk, and Christopher John Baker. 2002. *Thailand, Economy and Politics.* 2nd ed. Oxford: Oxford University Press.

Platt, D. C. M. 1968. *Finance, Trade, and Politics in British Foreign Policy 1815–1914.* Oxford, London: Clarendon Press.

Poeze, Harry A. 2005. The Road to Hell: The Construction of a Railway Line in West Java During the Japanese Occupation. In *Asian Labor in the Wartime Japanese Empire: Unknown Histories,* edited by Paul H. Kratoska. Armonk, N.Y.: Sharpe.

1994. Political Intelligence in the Netherlands Indies. In *The Late Colonial State in Indonesia: Political and Economic Foundations of the Netherlands Indies, 1880–1942*, edited by R. B. Cribb, vi, 295 p., [5] p. of plates. Leiden: KITLV Press.

Poggi, Gianfranco. 1990. *The State: Its Nature, Development, and Prospects.* Cambridge, U.K.: Polity Press.

———. 1978. *The Development of the Modern State: A Sociological Introduction.* Stanford, Calif.: Stanford University Press.

Pomerantz-Zhang, Linda. 1992. *Wu Tingfang (1842–1922): Reform and Modernization in Modern Chinese History.* Hong Kong: Hong Kong University Press.

Powell, Robert. 1991. Absolute and Relative Gains in International Relations Theory. *The American Political Science Review* 85(4): 1303–03.

Prados, John. 2006. The Central Intelligence Agency and the Face of Decolonisation under the Eisenhower Administration. In *The Eisenhower Administration, the Third World, and the Globalization of the Cold War*, edited by Kathryn C. Statler and Andrew L. Johns. Lanham, Md.: Rowman & Littlefield.

Preger, W. 1944. *Dutch Administration in the Netherlands Indies.* Melbourne: F. W. Cheshire pty. ltd.

Programme, Uppsala Conflict Data, and International Peace Research Institute. 2008. Armed Conflicts Version 4–2007. Available. (Accessed August 13, 2010).

Provisional Verbatim Minutes. 1951. Tokyo: Ministry of Foreign Affairs.

Putnam, Robert D. 1988. Diplomacy and Domestic Politics: The Logic of Two-Level Games. *International Organization* 42(3): 427–27.

Pye, Lucian W. 1971. *Warlord Politics: Conflict and Coalition in the Modernization of Republican China, Praeger Library of Chinese Affairs.* New York: Praeger.

Qi Bangyuan (Chi Pang-yuan). 2009. *Juliuhe.* Taipei: Tainxia yuanjian chuban.

Qian, Gang. 2004. *Da Qing Haijun Yu Li Hongzhang: The Qing Dynasty's Navy and Li Hung-Chang.* Chu ban. ed. Hong Kong: Zhonghua shuju.

Qingdao shi bowuguan, Zhongguo di 1 lishi dang'anguan, and Qingdao shi shehuikexue yanjiusuo. 1987. *Deguo Qinzhan Jiaozhouwan Shiliaoxuanbian, 1897–1898.* Di 1 ban. ed. Jinan: Shandong renmin chubanshe: Shandong sheng xinhua shudian faxing.

Raben, Remco. 2005. Indonesian Romusha and Coolies under Naval Administration: The Eastern Archipelago, 1942–1945. In *Asian Labor in the Wartime Japanese Empire: Unknown Histories*, edited by Paul H. Kratoska. Armonk, N.Y.: Sharpe.

Rankin, Mary Backus. 1997. State and Society in Early Republican Politics, 1912–18. *The China Quarterly* (150): 260–81.

Rawski, Thomas G. 1989. *Economic Growth in Prewar China.* Berkeley: University of California Press.

———. 1980. *China's Transition to Industrialism: Producer Goods and Economic Development in the Twentieth Century, Michigan Studies on China.* Ann Arbor: University of Michigan Press.

Record of Proceedings: Supplement. 1952. Washington, D.C.: U.S. Govt. Print. Off.

Record of Proceedings. 1951. Washington, D.C.: U.S. Govt. Print. Off.

Reid, Anthony. 2006. Colonial Transformation: A Bitter Legacy. In *Verandah of Violence*, edited by Anthony Reid, 96–108. Singapore: NUS Press.

———. 2005. *An Indonesian Frontier: Acehnese and Other Histories of Sumatra.* Singapore: Singapore University Press.

———. 1974. *The Indonesian National Revolution, 1945–1950.* Hawthorn, Vic.: Longman.

References

1969. *The Contest for North Sumatra: Atjeh, the Netherlands, and Britain, 1858–1898*. Kuala Lumpur, New York: University of Malaya Press; Oxford University Press.

Remick, Elizabeth J. 2004. *Building Local States: China During the Republican and Post-Mao Eras, Harvard East Asian Monographs; 233*. Cambridge, Mass.: Harvard University Asia Center; distributed by Harvard University Press.

Report of the Meeting of the Partij Sarekat Islam Held on 26 January 1928, to Commemorate Its Fifteen Years of Existence. 1977. In *Indonesia: Selected Documents on Colonialism and Nationalism, 1830–1942*, edited by C. L. M. Penders. St. Lucia: University of Queensland Press.

Reynolds, E. Bruce. 2005. *Thailand's Secret War: The Free Thai, OSS, and SOE During World War II, Cambridge Military Histories*. Cambridge, U.K.; New York: Cambridge University Press.

Richardson, Philip. 1999. *Economic Change in China, c.1800–1950, New Studies in Economic and Social History*. New York: Cambridge University Press.

Richmond, Herbert W. 1934. *Sea Power in the Modern World*. London: G. Bell & Sons Ltd.

1946. *Statesmen and Sea Power*. Oxford: The Clarendon Press.

Ricklefs, M. C. 1993. *A History of Modern Indonesia since c. 1300*. 2nd ed. Houndmills, Basingstoke, Hampshire: Macmillan.

Riggs, Fred. 1976. The Bureaucratic Polity as a Working System. In *Modern Thai Politics: From Village to Nation*, edited by Clark D. Neher. Cambridge, Mass.: Schenkman Pub. Co.

Riggs, Fred Warren. 1966. *Thailand: The Modernization of a Bureaucratic Polity*. Honolulu: East-West Center Press.

Risse, Thomas. 2000. Let's Argue! Communicative Action in World Politics. *International Organization* 54(1): 1–39.

Roadnight, Andrew. 2002. *United States Policy Towards Indonesia in the Truman and Eisenhower Years*. New York: Palgrave Macmillan.

Roberts, Frank K. 1993. The Roberts Cables, Moscow, March 14–18, 1946. In *Origins of the Cold War: The Novikov, Kennan, and Roberts "Long Telegrams" of 1946, with Three New Commentaries*, edited by Kenneth M. Jensen. Washington, D.C.: United States Institute of Peace Press.

Robertson, J. B., and J. Spruyt. 1967. *A History of Indonesia*. Melbourne, London, etc.; New York: Macmillan; St. Martin's Press.

Rosenau, James N. 1970. *The Adaptation of National Societies: A Theory of Political System Behaviour and Transformation*. New York, N.Y.: McCaleb-Seiler Publishing Company.

Rothwell, V. H. 1975. The Mission of Sir Frederick Leith-Ross to the Far East, 1935–1936. *The Historical Journal* 18(1): 147–69.

Roy, Denny. 2003. *Taiwan: A Political History*. Ithaca, NY; London: Cornell University Press.

Ruggie, John Gerard. 1993. Territoriality and Beyond: Problematizing Modernity in International Relations. *International Organization* 47(1): 139–39.

1989. International Structure and International Transformation: Space, Time, and Method. In *Global Changes and Theoretical Challenges: Approaches to World Politics for the 1990s*, edited by Ernst Otto Czempiel and James N. Rosenau. Lexington, Mass.: Lexington Books.

1986. Continuity and Transformation in the World Polity. In *Neorealism and Its Critics*, edited by Robert O. Keohane. New York: Columbia University Press.

1982. International Regimes, Transactions, and Change: Embedded Liberalism in the Postwar Economic Order. *International Organization* 36(2): 379–415.

Sadao, Asada. 1973. The Japanese Navy and the United States. In *Pearl Harbor as History: Japanese-American Relations, 1931–1941*, edited by Dorothy Borg and Shumpei Okamoto. New York: Columbia University Press.

SarDesai, D. R. 1997. *Southeast Asia, Past & Present*. 4th ed. Boulder, Colo.: Westview Press.

Sarkees, Meredith Reid. 2000. The Correlates of War Data on War: An Update to 1997. *Conflict Management and Peace Science* 18(1): 22–22.

Sartori, Anne E. 2005. *Deterrence by Diplomacy*. Princeton, N.J.: Princeton University Press.

Sato, Shigeru. 2005. Economic Soldiers in Java: Indonesian Labourers Mobilised for Agricultural Projects. In *Asian Labor in the Wartime Japanese Empire: Unknown Histories*, edited by Paul H. Kratoska. Armonk, N.Y.: M.E. Sharpe.

1994. *War, Nationalism and Peasants: Java under the Japanese Occupation, 1942–1945*. Armonk, N.Y.: M.E. Sharpe.

Satow, Ernest Mason, and George Alexander Lensen. 1966. *Korea and Manchuria between Russia and Japan, 1895–1904: The Observations of Sir Ernest Satow, British Minister Plenipotentiary to Japan (1895–1900) and China (1900–1906)*. Tallahassee: Diplomatic Press.

Scalapino, Robert A., and George T. Yu. 1985. *Modern China and Its Revolutionary Process: Recurrent Challenges to the Traditional Order, 1850–1920*. Berkeley: University of California Press.

Schaller, Michael. 1979. *The United States and China in the Twentieth Century*. New York: Oxford University Press.

Scheiber, Harry N. 1969. World War I as Entrepreneurial Opportunity: Willard Straight and the American International Corporation. *Political Science Quarterly* 84(3): 486–511.

Schelling, Thomas C. 1966. *Arms and Influence*. New Haven, Conn.: Yale University Press.

Schimmelpenninck van der Oye, David. 2001. *Toward the Rising Sun: Russian Ideologies of Empire and the Path to War with Japan*. DeKalb, Ill.: Northern Illinois University Press.

Schneider, Adam. 1998. The Taiwan Government-General and Pre-War Japanese Economic Expansion in South China and Southeast Asia, 1900–1936. In *The Japanese Empire in East Asia and Its Postwar Legacy*, edited by Harald Fuess. München: Iudicium.

Schoonover, Thomas David. 2003. *Uncle Sam's War of 1898 and the Origins of Globalization*. Lexington: University Press of Kentucky.

Schoppa, R. Keith. 2001. Patterns and Dynamics of Elite Collaboration in Occupied Shaoxing County. In *Chinese Collaboration with Japan, 1932–1945: The Limits of Accommodation*, edited by David P. Barrett and Lawrence N. Shyu. Stanford, Calif.: Stanford University Press.

Schultz, Kenneth A. 2001. *Democracy and Coercive Diplomacy, Cambridge Studies in International Relations, 76*. Cambridge, U.K.; New York: Cambridge University Press.

References

Scott, James C. 1998. *Seeing Like a State: How Certain Schemes to Improve the Human Condition Have Failed, Yale Agrarian Studies*. New Haven, Conn.: Yale University Press.

——— 1985. *Weapons of the Weak: Everyday Forms of Peasant Resistance*. New Haven, Conn.: Yale University Press.

——— 1976. Corruption in Thailand. In *Modern Thai Politics: From Village to Nation*, edited by Clark D. Neher. Cambridge, Mass.: Schenkman Pub. Co.

Scott, James C., and Benedict J. Kerkvliet. 1986. *Everyday Forms of Peasant Resistance on South-East Asia*. London; Totowa, N.J.: Frank Cass.

Selden, Mark. 1995. *China in Revolution: The Yenan Way Revisited, Socialism and Social Movements*. Armonk, N.Y.: M.E. Sharpe.

——— 1971. *The Yenan Way in Revolutionary China, Harvard East Asian Series, 62*. Cambridge, Mass.: Harvard University Press.

Seybolt, Peter J. 2001. The War within a War: A Case Study of a County on the North China Plain. In *Chinese Collaboration with Japan, 1932–1945: The Limits of Accommodation*, edited by David P. Barrett and Lawrence N. Shyu. Stanford, Calif.: Stanford University Press.

Sha, Jiansun. 2005. *Zhongguo Gongchandang he Ziben Zhuyi, Zichan Jieji*. 2 vols. Vol. 1. Jinan: Shandong Renmin Chubanshe.

Shao, Zonghai. 1995. *Meiguo Jieru Guo Gong Hetan zhi Jiaose*. Chu ban. ed., *Nianyi Shiji Da Zhonghua Congshu*. Taipei: Wunan tushuchubangongsi.

Shen, Yu. 2005. *Riben Dalu Zhengceshi (1868–1945)*. Di 1 ban. ed., *Zhongguo Shehui Kexueyuan Zhong Ri Lishi Yanjiu Zhongxin Wenku*. Beijing Shi: Shehuikexue wenxian chubanshe.

Shen, Yunlong. 1963. *Li Yuanhong Pingzhuan, Zhongyang Yanjiuyuan Jindaishi Yanjiusuo Zhuankan*. Taipei: Zhongyang yanjiuyuan jindaishi yanjiusuo.

Sheridan, James E. 1975. *China in Disintegration: The Republican Era in Chinese History, 1912–1949, The Transformation of Modern China Series*. New York: Free Press.

——— 1966. *Chinese Warlord: The Career of Feng Yü-Hsiang*. Stanford, Calif.: Stanford University Press.

Shi, Jiashun. 1992. *Liang Guang Shibian zhi Yanjiu*. Chu ban. ed. Gaoxiong Shi: Fuwen tushu chubanshe.

Shi, Yuanhua. 1994. *Zhonghua Minguo Waijiao Shi*. Di 1 ban. ed. Shanghai: Shanghai renmin chubanshe.

Shippee, Lester Burrell. 1936. German-American Relations, 1890–1914. *The Journal of Modern History* 8(4): 479–79.

Shiraishi, Takashi. 1990. *An Age in Motion: Popular Radicalism in Java, 1912–1926, Asia East by South*. Ithaca, N.Y.: Cornell University Press.

Siffin, William J. 1976. The Essential Character of the Contemporary Bureaucracy. In *Modern Thai Politics: From Village to Nation*, edited by Clark D. Neher. Cambridge, Mass.: Schenkman Pub. Co.

——— 1966. *The Thai Bureaucracy: Institutional Change and Development*. Honolulu: East-West Center Press.

Simon, Herbert A. 1982. *Models of Bounded Rationality*. Cambridge, Mass.: MIT Press.

Singer, J. David, and Melvin Small. 1994. Correlates of War Data: International and Civil War Data, 1816–1992. *(ICPSR 9905, 1994)*.

Skocpol, Theda. 1979. *States and Social Revolutions: A Comparative Analysis of France, Russia, and China*. Cambridge, U.K.; New York: Cambridge University Press.

268   *References*

Small, Melvin, J. David Singer, and J. David Singer. 1982. *Resort to Arms: International and Civil Wars, 1816–1980*. 2nd ed. Beverly Hills, Calif.: Sage Publications.

Smith, Anthony D. 1983. *Theories of Nationalism*. 2nd ed. New York, N.Y.: Holmes & Meier.

Snow, Edgar. 1937. *Red Star over China*. Left Book Club ed. London: V. Gollancz.

Snow, Edgar, and Zedong Mao. 1979. *Mao Zedong Yi Jiu San Liu Nian tong Sinuo de Tanhua: Guanyu Ziji de Geming Jingli he Hongjun Changzheng Deng Wenti*. Di 1 ban. ed. Beijing: Renmin chubanshe: Xinhua shudian faxing.

Snyder, Jack L. 2000. *From Voting to Violence: Democratization and Nationalist Conflict*. 1st ed. New York; London: W.W. Norton.

    1991. *Myths of Empire: Domestic Politics and International Ambition, Cornell Studies in Security Affairs*. Ithaca, N.Y.: Cornell University Press.

    1984. *The Ideology of the Offensive: Military Decision Making and the Disasters of 1914, Cornell Studies in Security Affairs*. Ithaca, NY: Cornell University Press.

Soerjaningrat, R. M. Soewardi. 1977. If Only I Were a Netherlander, 1913. In *Indonesia: Selected Documents on Colonialism and Nationalism, 1830–1942*, edited by C. L. M. Penders. St. Lucia: University of Queensland Press.

Soong, T. V., and Shi Hu. 2001. Song Ziwen Hu Shi dian Jiang Jieshi, October 26, 1940. In *Hu Shi, Ye Gongchao Shi Mei Waijiao Wenjian Shougao*, edited by Gu Zhou, 116–18. Taipei Shi: Linking Books.

Spector, Ronald H. 2007. *In the Ruins of Empire: The Japanese Surrender and the Battle for Postwar Asia*. 1st ed. New York: Random House.

Spector, Stanley. 1964. *Li Hung-Chang and the Huai Army: A Study in Nineteenth-Century Chinese Regionalism, University of Washington Publications on Asia*. Seattle: University of Washington Press.

Spence, Jonathan D. 1999. *The Search for Modern China*. Vol. 2. New York: W.W. Norton.

    1969. *To Change China: Western Advisers in China, 1620–1960*. 1st ed. Boston: Little, Brown.

Spruyt, Hendrik. 2005. *Ending Empire: Contested Sovereignty and Territorial Partition, Cornell Studies in Political Economy*. Ithaca, N.Y.: Cornell University Press.

    1994. *The Sovereign State and Its Competitors: An Analysis of Systems Change, Princeton Studies in International History and Politics*. Princeton, N.J.: Princeton University Press.

Steinberg, David Joel. 1985. *In Search of Southeast Asia: A Modern History*. Honolulu: University of Hawaii Press.

Stowe, Judith A. 1991. *Siam Becomes Thailand: A Story of Intrigue*. London: Hurst.

Strauss, Julia C. 1997. The Evolution of Republican Government. *The China Quarterly* (150): 329–51.

Strayer, Joseph Reese. 1970. *On the Medieval Origins of the Modern State*. Princeton, N.J.: Princeton University Press.

Suehiro, Akira. 1989. *Capital Accumulation in Thailand, 1855–1985*. Tokyo, Japan: Centre for East Asian Cultural Studies.

Sun, E. tu Zen. 1954. *Chinese Railways and British Interests, 1898–1911*. New York: King's Crown Press, Columbia University.

Sun, Ke. 1945. *Sanmin Zhuyi Xin Zhongguo*. Chongqing: Shangwu yinshuguan.

Sun, Yat-sen. 1954. *Jianguo Fanglüe; Jianguo Dagang, Zhengzhong Wenku. Di 2 Ji; 2*. Taipei: Zhengzhong shuju.

    1927. *Sanmin Zhuyi*. [n.p.]: Xinshidai jiaoyushe.

References

1926. *Jianguo Fanglüe*. Shanghai: Minzhi shuju.

Sun, You-Li. 1993. *China and the Origins of the Pacific War, 1931–1941*. New York: St. Martin's Press.

Sunaga, Noritake. 1988. Japanese Loans to China During the First World War. In *Nihon Shokuminchi Kenkyu*, edited by Nihon Shokuminchi Kenkyukai. Tokyo: Ryukei Shosha.

Surjomihardjo, Abdurrachman 1978. National Education in a Colonial Society. In *Dynamics of Indonesian History*, edited by Haryati Soebadio-Noto Soebagio and Carinne A. du Marchie Sarvaas. Amsterdam; New York: North-Holland Pub. Co.; distributors for the U.S.A. and Canada Elsevier/North-Holland.

Swift, Ann. 1989. *The Road to Madiun: The Indonesian Communist Uprising of 1948*. Ithaca, N.Y.: Cornell Modern Indonesia Project, Southeast Asia Program, Cornell University.

Tadashi, Aruga. 1977. The United States and the Cold War: The Cold War Era in American History. In *The Origins of the Cold War in Asia*, edited by Yonosuke Nagai and Akira Iriye. New York: Columbia University Press.

Tagliacozzo, Eric. 2005. *Secret Trades, Porous Borders: Smuggling and States Along a Southeast Asian Frontier, 1865–1915*. New Haven, Conn.: Yale University Press.

Tahara, Tennan. 1928. Occupation and Relations Amongst the Great Powers (1913). In *Foreign Diplomacy in China, 1894–1900: A Study in Political and Economic Relations with China*, edited by Philip Joseph. London: G. Allen & Unwin.

Taliaferro, Jeffrey W. 2004. *Balancing Risks: Great Power Intervention in the Periphery, Cornell Studies in Security Affairs*. Ithaca, N.Y.; London: Cornell University Press.

Tang, Degang (Tong Te-kong). 2004. *Yuan Shi Dangguo*. Xianzai Zhongguo dalu diqu faxing ed. Guilin: Guangxi Shifan Daxue chubanshe.

Tang, Lixing. 1993. *Shangren yu Zhongguo Jinshi Shehui*. Di 1 ban. ed., *Zhongguo Shehuishi Congshu*. Hangzhou: Zhejiang renmin chubanshe: Zhejiang sheng xinhua shudian faxing.

Tang, Qihua. 1998. *Beijing Zhengfu yu Guoji Lianmeng*, edited by Yufa Zhang, *Zhongguo Xiandaishi Jvshu*. Taipei: Dongda tushu gufen youxiangongsi.

Tanigawa, Yoshihiko. 1977. The Coninform and Southeast Asia. In *The Origins of the Cold War in Asia*, edited by Yonosuke Nagai and Akira Iriye. New York: Columbia University Press.

Tarling, Nicholas. 2005. *Britain, Southeast Asia and the Impact of the Korean War*. Singapore: Singapore University Press.

2004. *Nationalism in Southeast Asia: If the People Are with Us, Routledgecurzon Studies in the Modern History of Asia*. London; New York: RoutledgeCurzon.

2001a. *Southeast Asia: A Modern History*. South Melbourne, Vic; Oxford: Oxford University Press.

2001b. *A Sudden Rampage: The Japanese Occupation of Southeast Asia, 1941–1945*. London: Hurst.

1998. *Britain, Southeast Asia and the Onset of the Cold War, 1945–1950*. Cambridge, U.K.; New York: Cambridge University Press.

1993. *The Fall of Imperial Britain in South-East Asia, South-East Asian Historical Monographs*. Singapore; New York: Oxford University Press.

1975. *Imperial Britain in South-East Asia*. Kuala Lumpur; New York: Oxford University Press.

Taylor, Brian D., and Roxana Botea. 2008. Tilly Tally: War-Making and State-Making in the Contemporary Third World. *International Studies Review* 10(1): 30–30.

Taylor, Jean Gelman. 2003. *Indonesia: Peoples and Histories*. New Haven, Conn.; London: Yale University Press.

Teng, S. Y. 1969. Comments by S. Y. Teng. In *China in Crisis*, edited by Ping-ti Ho and Tang Tsou. Chicago: University of Chicago Press.

Terwiel, B. J. 2005. *Thailand's Political History: From the Fall of Ayutthaya in 1767 to Recent Times*. Bangkok London: River; distributed by Thames & Hudson.

Thayer, Philip Warren. 1953. *Southeast Asia in the Coming World*. Baltimore: Johns Hopkins Press.

Thongchai, Winichakul. 1996. Maps and the Formation of the Geo-Body of Siam. In *Asian Forms of the Nation*, edited by Stein Tønnesson and Hans Antlöv. Richmond, Surrey: Curzon.

　1994. *Siam Mapped: A History of the Geo-Body of a Nation*. Honolulu: University of Hawaii Press.

Tian, Youru. 2000. Social and Political Change in the Villages of the Taihang Anti-Japanese Base Area. In *North China at War: The Social Ecology of Revolution, 1937–1945*, edited by Chongyi Feng and David S. G. Goodman. Lanham, Md.: Rowman & Littlefield Publishers.

Tilly, Charles. 1990. *Coercion, Capital, and European States, AD 990–1990*. Cambridge, Mass.: B. Blackwell.

　1984. *Big Structures, Large Processes, Huge Comparisons, 75th Anniversary Series*. Vol. 2. New York: Russell Sage Foundation.

Tjokroaminoto. 1977. Speech at the Sarekat Islam Congress, 1916. In *Indonesia: Selected Documents on Colonialism and Nationalism, 1830–1942*, edited by C. L. M. Penders. St. Lucia: University of Queensland Press.

To Receive Testimony on the Situation in Iraq and Progress Made by the Government of Iraq in Meeting Benchmarks and Achieving Reconciliation. 2008. In United States Senate Committee on Armed Services, 74. Washington, D.C.: United States Senate.

Tompkins, Pauline. 1949. *American-Russian Relations in the Far East*. New York: Macmillan.

Tong, Dong, Zhendu Ma, Yueqin Zhao, Zhongyang dang'anguan (China), Zhongguo di 2 lishi dang'anguan, and Jilin Sheng shehuikexueyuan. 2004. *Wang Wei Zhengquan. Di 1 ban. ed., Riben Diguozhuyi Qin Hua Dang'an Ziliao Xuanbian*. Beijing Shi: Zhonghua shu ju.

Tønnesson, Stein, and Hans Antlöv. 1996. *Asian Forms of the Nation*. Richmond, Surrey: Curzon.

Toru, Yano. 1977. Who Set the Stage for the Cold War in Southeast Asia? In *The Origins of the Cold War in Asia*, edited by Yonosuke Nagai and Akira Iriye, ix, 448. New York: Columbia University Press.

Tsou, Tang. 1963. *America's Failure in China, 1941–50*. Chicago: University of Chicago Press.

Tucker, Nancy Bernkopf. 1994. *Taiwan, Hong Kong, and the United States, 1945–1992: Uncertain Friendships, Twayne's International History Series; No. 14*. New York Toronto New York: Twayne Publishers; Maxwell Macmillian Canada; Maxwell Macmillan International.

　1983. *Patterns in the Dust: Chinese-American Relations and the Recognition Controversy, 1949–1950, Contemporary American History Series*. New York: Columbia University Press.

Tucker, Nancy Bernkopf, and Association for Diplomatic Studies and Training. 2001. *China Confidential: American Diplomats and Sino-American Relations,*

References

1945–1996, Adst-Dacor Diplomats and Diplomacy Series. New York: Columbia University Press.

Tucker, Spencer, and Jinwung Kim. 2000. *Encyclopedia of the Korean War: A Political, Social, and Military History*. Santa Barbara, Calif.: ABC-CLIO.

Twitchett, Denis Crispin, and John King Fairbank. 1978. *The Cambridge History of China*. Cambridge, U.K.; New York: Cambridge University Press.

Uldricks, Teddy J. 1979. *Diplomacy and Ideology: The Origins of Soviet Foreign Relations, 1917–1930*. London; Beverly Hills: Sage Publications.

United States. Bureau of the Census. 1975. Historical Statistics of the United States Colonial Times to 1970. Available from http://purl.access.gpo.gov/GPO/LPS55561 http://digitalarchive.oclc.org/request?id%3Doclcnum%3A56992924 http://purl.access.gpo.gov/GPO/LPS55811 (Accessed December 1, 2004.)

United States. Dept. of State. Foreign Relations of the United States. In Department of State publication, *v*. Washington, D.C.: U.S. Govt. Print. Off.

United States. Dept. of State., and United States. Dept. of State. Bureau of Public Affairs. 1966. Far Eastern Series. In *Dept. of State publication*. Washington, D.C.: The Department [for sale by the Supt. of Docs., U.S. Govt. Print. Off.].

United States. Dept. of the Treasury. Division of Bookkeeping and Warrants. 1900. *Statement of Balances, Appropriations and Expenditures of the Government for the Fiscal Year. v*. Washington, D.C.: U.S. Govt. Print. Off.

Uppsala Conflict Data Program (UCDP), and Peace Research Institute Oslo (PRIO). 2007. Armed Conflicts Version 4–2007. In *UCDP/PRIO Armed Conflict Dataset*: Centre for the Study of Civil War, the International Peace Research Institute, Uppsala Data Conflict Program, Department of Peace and Conflict Research, Uppsala University.

Usui, Katsumi, and Pengren Chen. 1994. *Zhang Xueliang Yu Riben*. Chu ban. ed. Taipei: Lianjing chubanshiyegongsi.

———. 1990. *Zhong Ri Guanxishi*. Chu ban. ed. Taipei: Shuiniu chubanshe.

van Asbeck, F. M. 1940. Foreign Relations of the Netherland Indies. In *Problems of the Pacific, 1939: Proceedings of the Study Meeting of the Institute of Pacific Relations, Virginia Beach, Virginia, November 18—December 2, L939*, edited by Kate Louise Mitchell, and W. L. Holland. New York: Institute of Pacific Relations.

van Creveld, Martin L. 1999. *The Rise and Decline of the State*. Cambridge, U.K.; New York: Cambridge University Press.

van de Ven, Hans. 1997. The Military in the Republic. *The China Quarterly* (150): 352–74.

van de Ven, Hans J. 2003. *War and Nationalism in China, 1925–1945, Routledgecurzon Studies in the Modern History of Asia*. London: RoutledgeCurzon.

———. 1996. Public Finance and the Rise of Warlordism. *Modern Asian Studies* 30(4): 829–68.

van den Bosch, J. 1977. Report on His (Van Den Bosch's) Activities in the East Indies. In *Indonesia: Selected Documents on Colonialism and Nationalism, 1830–1942*, edited by C. L. M. Penders. St. Lucia: University of Queensland Press.

van den Doel, H. W. 1994. Military Rule in the Netherlands Indies. In *The Late Colonial State in Indonesia: Political and Economic Foundations of the Netherlands Indies, 1880–1942*, edited by R. B. Cribb. Leiden: KITLV Press.

Van der Veur, Paul W. 2006. *The Lion and the Gadfly: Dutch Colonialism and the Spirit of E.F.E. Douwes Dekker, Verhandelingen Van Het Koninklijk Instituut Voor Taal-, Land- En Volkenkunde*. Leiden: KITLV Press.

van Dijk, Kees. 1994. The Threefold Suppression of the Javanese: The Fight against Capitalism, the Colonial State, and the Traditional Rulers. In *The Late Colonial State in Indonesia: Political and Economic Foundations of the Netherlands Indies, 1880–1942*, edited by R. B. Cribb. Leiden: KITLV Press.

Van Evera, Stephen. 1999. *Causes of War: Power and the Roots of Conflict*. Ithaca, N.Y.: Cornell University Press.

van Niel, Robert. 1990. The Legacy of the Cultivation System for Subsequent Economic Development. In *Indonesian Economic History in the Dutch Colonial Era*, edited by Anne Booth, W. J. O'Malley, and Anna Weidemann. New Haven, Conn.: Yale University Southeast Asia Studies.

van Slyke, P. Lyman. 1991. The Chinese Communist Movement During the Sino-Japanese War, 1937–1945. In *The Nationalist Era in China, 1927–1949*, edited by Lloyd E. Eastman. Cambridge: Cambridge University Press.

Vandenbosch, Amry. 1941. *The Dutch East Indies, Its Government, Problems and Politics*. Berkeley, Los Angeles: University of California Press.

Vickers, Adrian. 2005. *A History of Modern Indonesia*. Cambridge, U.K.; New York: Cambridge University Press.

Vlekke, Bernard H. M. 1945. *The Story of the Dutch East Indies*. Cambridge, Mass.: Harvard University Press.

    1943. *Nusantara: A History of the East Indian Archipelago*. Cambridge, Mass.: Harvard University Press.

Vogler, Carolyn M. 1985. *The Nation State: The Neglected Dimension of Class*. Aldershot, Hants, England; Brookfield, Vt.: Gower Pub. Co.

Vu, Tuong. 2010. *Paths to Development in Asia: South Korea, Vietnam, China, and Indonesia*. New York: Cambridge University Press.

    2010. Studying the State through State Formation. *World Politics* 62(1): 148–75.

Vu, Tuong, and Wasana Wongsurawat. 2009. *Dynamics of the Cold War in Asia: Ideology, Identity, and Culture*. 1st ed. New York: Palgrave Macmillan.

Wakeman, Frederic E. 1975. *The Fall of Imperial China, The Transformation of Modern China Series*. New York: Free Press.

Waldron, Arthur. 1995. *From War to Nationalism: China's Turning Point, 1924–1925, Cambridge Studies in Chinese History, Literature, and Institutions*. Cambridge, U.K.; New York: Cambridge University Press.

    1991. The Warlord: Twentieth-Century Chinese Understandings of Violence, Militarism, and Imperialism. *The American Historical Review* 96(4): 1073–100.

Walker, R. B. J. 1992. *Inside/Outside: International Relations as Political Theory, Cambridge Studies in International Relations, 24*. Cambridge, U.K.; New York: Cambridge University Press.

Walt, Stephen M. 1996. *Revolution and War, Cornell Studies in Security Affairs*. Ithaca, N.Y.: Cornell University Press.

Waltz, Kenneth Neal. 1979. *Theory of International Politics, Addison-Wesley Series in Political Science*. Reading, Mass.: Addison-Wesley Pub. Co.

Wang, Jia-tang. 1989. 1900 Nian 5 Yue 21 Ri Wang Jiatang Zhi Liu Kunyi Hangao Shu Hou [Letter from Wang Jiatang to Liu Kunyi, May 21, 1900]. *Jindaishi ziliao* 74: 168–76.

Wang, Kewen. 2001. *Wang Jingwei, Guomindang, Nanjing Zhengquan, Minguo Shixue Congshu*. Chu ban. ed., *Minguo Shixue Congshu, 14*. Taipei: Guoshiguan.

Wang, Liangxing. 1997. *Jindai Zhongguo Duiwaimaoyishi Lunji*. Vol. 7, *Mingshan Cang*. Taipei: Zhishu shufang chubanshe.

References

Wang, Peter Chen-mian. 1999. A Bastion Created, a Regime Reformed, an Economy Reengineered, 1949–1970. In *Taiwan: A New History*, edited by Murray A. Rubinstein. Armonk, N.Y.: M.E. Sharpe.

Wang, Tieya. 1957. *Zhongwai Jiuyuezhang Huibian*. Di 1 ban. ed., 3 vols. Beijing: Shenghuo, dushu Xinhua shudian faxing.

Wang, Yijia, Ming Zhen, and Guoquan Sun. 2002. *Zhongguo Haiguan Gailun*. Xiu ding ban, Di 1 ban. ed., *Xiandai Tongguan Shiwu Congshu*. Beijing: Zhongguo haiguan chubanshe.

Wang, Yongxiang. 2003. *Ya'erda Miyue yu Zhong Su Ri Su Guanxi*. Chu ban. ed. Taipei: Dongda tushu gongsi.

Wang, Yuyan, and Ming He. 2005. *Sulian Chubing Dongbei Shimo*. Di 1 ban. ed. Beijing: Renmin chubanshe.

Wang, Zengcai. 1979. *Zhong Ying Waijiao Shi Lunji*. Chu ban. ed. Taipei: Lianjing chuban shiye gongsi.

———. 1967. *Yingguo Dui Hua Waijiao yu Menhukaifang Zhengce*. Taipei: Zhongguo xueshuzhuzuo jiangzhu weiyuanhui; Taiwan shangwu yinshuguan zongjingxiao.

Wang, Zhen. 2003. *Kang Ri Zhanzheng yu Zhongguo de Guoji Diwei*. Di 1 ban. ed., *Zhongguo Shehuikexueyuan Zhong Ri Lishi Yanjiu Zhongxin Wenku*. Beijing Shi: Shehuikexue wenxian chubanshe.

Watson, Adam. 1992. *The Evolution of International Society: A Comparative Historical Analysis*. London; New York: Routledge.

Watt, D. C. 1977. Britain and the Cold War in the Far East, 1945–1958. In *The Origins of the Cold War in Asia*, edited by Yonosuke Nagai and Akira Iriye. New York: Columbia University Press.

Weathersby, Kathryn. 1998. Stalin, Mao, and the End of the Korean War. In *Brothers in Arms: The Rise and Fall of the Sino-Soviet Alliance, 1945–1963*, edited by Odd Arne Westad, xxii, 404 p. Washington, D.C., Stanford, Calif.: Woodrow Wilson Center Press; distributed by Stanford University Press.

Weber, Max. 1994a. The Nation State and Economic Policy. In *Weber: Political Writings*, edited by Max Weber, 1–28. Cambridge, U.K.: Cambridge University Press.

———. 1994b. The Profession and Vocation of Politics. In *Weber: Political Writings*, edited by Max Weber, 309–69. Cambridge, U.K.: Cambridge University Press.

Wei, Henry. 1956. *China and Soviet Russia*. Princeton, N.J.: Van Nostrand.

Wei, Hongyun. 2000. Social Reform and Value Change in the Jin-Cha-Ji Anti-Japanese Border Region. In *North China at War: The Social Ecology Revolution, 1937–1945*, edited by Chongyi Feng and David S. G. Goodman. Lanham, Md.: Rowman & Littlefield Publishers.

Weigley, Russell F. 1973. The Role of the War Department and the Army. In *Pearl Harbor as History: Japanese-American Relations, 1931–1941*, edited by Dorothy Borg and Shumpei Okamoto. New York: Columbia University Press.

Wendt, Alexander. 1999. *Social Theory of International Politics, Cambridge Studies in International Relations, 67*. Cambridge, U.K.; New York: Cambridge University Press.

Weng, Tonghe, and Wango H. C. Weng. 2003. *Jiawu Zhanzheng*. Chu ban. ed., *Weng Tonghe Wenxian Congbian, 5*. Taipei: Yiwen yinshuguan.

Westad, Odd Arne. 2003. *Decisive Encounters: The Chinese Civil War, 1946–1950*. Stanford, Calif.: Stanford University Press.

White, Lynn T. 1998. *Unstately Power*. Armonk, N.Y.: M.E. Sharpe.

Whiting, Allen S. 1951. The Soviet Offer to China of 1919. *The Far Eastern Quarterly* 10(4): 355–64.

Whiting, Allen Suess. 1954a. *Soviet Policies in China, 1917–1924.* New York: Columbia University Press.

1954b. *Soviet Policies in China, 1917–1924.* New York: Columbia University Press.

Whiting, Allen Suess, and Shih-ts ai Sheng. 1958. *Sinkiang: Pawn or Pivot?* East Lansing: Michigan State University Press.

Wiarda, Howard J. 2007. *The Dutch Diaspora: Growing up Dutch in New Worlds and the Old: The Netherlands and Its Settlements in Africa, Asia, and the Americas.* Lanham, Md.: Lexington Books.

Wilbur, C. Martin. 1969. Military Separatism and the Process of Reunification under the Nationalist Regime. In *China in Crisis*, edited by Ping-ti Ho and Tang Tsou, 2 v. in 3. Chicago: University of Chicago Press.

Wilkins, Mira. 1982. American-Japanese Direct Foreign Investment Relationships, 1930–1952. *The Business History Review* 56(4): 497–518.

1973. The Role of U.S. Business. In *Pearl Harbor as History: Japanese-American Relations, 1931–1941*, edited by Dorothy Borg and Shumpei Okamoto. New York: Columbia University Press.

Williams, Lea E. 1976. *Southeast Asia: A History.* New York: Oxford University Press.

Wilson, David A. 1976. Political Tradition and Political Change in Thailand. In *Modern Thai Politics: From Village to Nation*, edited by Clark D. Neher. Cambridge, Mass.: Schenkman Pub. Co.

1962. *Politics in Thailand.* Ithaca, N.Y.: Cornell University Press.

Wohlforth, William C. 1999. The Stability of a Unipolar World. *International Security* 24(1): 5–5.

1987. The Perception of Power: Russia in the Pre-1914 Balance. *World Politics* 39(3): 353–81.

Wohlforth, William Curti. 1993. *The Elusive Balance: Power and Perceptions During the Cold War, Cornell Studies in Security Affairs.* Ithaca, N.Y.: Cornell University Press.

Wolf, David C. 1983. "To Secure a Convenience": Britain Recognizes China –1950. *Journal of Contemporary History* 18(2): 299–326.

Wolff, David. 1995. Russia Finds Its Limits: Crossing Borders into Manchuria. In *Rediscovering Russia in Asia: Siberia and the Russian Far East*, edited by Stephen Kotkin and David Wolff. Armonk: M.E. Sharpe.

Wolters, Willemm. 1994. From Corvée to Contract Labour: Institutional Innovation in a Central Javanese Village around the Turn of the Century. In *The Late Colonial State in Indonesia: Political and Economic Foundations of the Netherlands Indies, 1880–1942*, edited by R. B. Cribb. Leiden: KITLV Press.

Wong, Roy Bin. 1997. *China Transformed: Historical Change and the Limits of European Experience.* Ithaca, N.Y.: Cornell University Press.

Wright, Stanley Fowler. 1950. *Hart and the Chinese Customs.* Belfast: Published for the Queen's University by W. Mullan.

1939. *The Origin and Development of the Chinese Customs Service, 1843–1911. An Historical Outline.* Shanghai: s.n.

1927. *The Collection and Disposal of the Maritime and Native Customs Revenue since the Revolution of 1911, with an Account of the Loan Services Administered by the Inspector General of Customs.* 2nd ed. Shanghai: Statistical Department of the Inspectorate General of Customs.

References

Wright, Tim. 1980. Sino-Japanese Business in China: The Luda Company, 1921–1937. *The Journal of Asian Studies* 39(4): 711–27.

Wu, Ai-ch en. 1950. *China and the Soviet Union; a Study of Sino-Soviet Relations.* New York: J. Day Co.

Wu, Yu-lin. 1995. *Memories of Dr. Wu Lien-Teh, Plague Fighter.* Singapore; New Jersey: World Scientific.

Wu, Yuexing. 1999. *Zhongguo Xiandaishi Dituji, 1919–1949.* Beijing Shi: Zhongguo ditu chubanshe.

    1995. *Zhongguo Kang Ri Zhanzheng Shi Dituji, 1931–1945.* Di 1 ban. ed., *Zhongguo Kang Ri Zhanzheng Shi Congshu.* Beijing: Zhongguo ditu chubanshe.

Wu, Yuexing zhu bian. 1999. *Zhongguo Xiandaishi Dituji.* Beijing: Ditu chubanshe.

Wyatt, David K. 1984. *Thailand: A Short History.* New Haven, Conn.: Yale University Press.

    1969. *The Politics of Reform in Thailand: Education in the Reign of King Chulalongkorn, Yale Southeast Asia Studies.* New Haven, Conn.: Yale University Press.

Xu, Dixin, and Chengming Wu. 1993. *Xin Minzhuzhuyi Gemingshiqi di Zhongguo Zibenzhuyi.* Di 1 ban. ed., *Zhongguo Zibenzhuyi Fazhanshi; Di 3 Juan.* Beijing: Renmin chubanshe.

    1990. *Jiu Minzhuzhuyi Gemingshiqi di Zhongguo Zibenzhuyi.* Di 1 ban. ed., *Zhongguo Ziben Zhuyi Fazhan Shi; Di 2 Juan.* Beijing: Renmin chubanshe: Xinhua shudian jingxiao.

Xu, Guangqiu. 2001. American-British Aircraft Competition in South China, 1926–1936. *Modern Asian Studies* 35(1): 36–36.

Xu, Yisheng. 1962. *Zhongguo Jindai Waizhaishi Tongjiziliao: 1853–1927.* Di 1 ban. ed., *Zhongguo Jindai Jingjishi Cankao Ziliao Congkan; Di 6 Zhong.* Beijing: Zhonghua shuju.

Xu, Yuming. 1999. *Wang Zhaoming yu Guomin Zhengfu: 1931 Zhi 1936 Nian Dui Ri Wenti Xia de Zhengzhi Biandong.* Chu ban. ed., *Minguo Renwu Zhuanji Congshu.* Taipei: Guoshiguan.

Xue, Yi. 2005. *Guomin Zhengfu Ziyuan Weiyuanhui Yanjiu [a Study on the Resource Committee of National Government].* Di 1 ban. ed., *Zhongguo Shehuikexueyuan Zhong Ri Lishi Yanjiu Zhongxin Wenku.* Beijing Shi: Shehuikexue wenxian chubanshe.

Yahuda, Michael B. 1996. *The International Politics of the Asia-Pacific, 1945–1995.* London; New York: Routledge.

Yamamoto, Mitsuru. 1977. The Cold War and U.S.-Japan Economic Cooperation. In *The Origins of the Cold War in Asia*, edited by Yonosuke Nagai and Akira Iriye. New York: Columbia University Press.

Yang, Kuisong. 2005. Jiang Jieshi, Zhang Xueliang Yu Zhongdong Lu Shijian Zhi Jiaoshe [Chiang Kai-Shek, Zhang Xueliang, and the Negotiations Surrounding the Chinese Eastern (Rail)Road Incident]. In *Yijiuerling Niandai de Zhongguo*, edited by jindaishi yanjiusuo Minguoshi yanjiushi Zhongguo shehuikexueyuan, Sichuan shi-fan daxue, lishi wenxueyuan bian. Beijing: Shehui kexue wenxian chubanshe.

    1997. *Zhonggong yu Mosike de Guanxi, 1920–1960.* Chu ban. ed. Taipei: Dongda tushugongsi.

Yi, Laoyi. 1978. Difang Zhengzhi he Zhongyang Zhengfu: Yunnan yu Chongqing. In *Ba Nian Dui Ri Kangzhan Zhong zhi Guomin Zhengfu: 1937 Nian Zhi 1945 Nian*, edited by Paul K. T. Sih, 354–82. Taipei: Taiwan Shangwu yinshuguan.

Young, Arthur N. 1971. *China's Nation-Building Effort, 1927–1937; the Financial and Economic Record*. Stanford, Calif.: Hoover Institution Press.

1963. *China and the Helping Hand, 1937–1945, Harvard East Asian Series*. Cambridge, Mass.: Harvard University Press.

Young, Crawford. 1994. *The African Colonial State in Comparative Perspective*. New Haven, Conn.: Yale University Press.

Yu, Heping. 1993. *Shanghui yu Zhongguo Zaoqi Xiandaihua*. Edited by Yufa Zhang. Vol. 3, *Zhongguo Xiandaishi Jushu*. Taipei: Dongda tushu gufen youxiangongsi.

Yu, Maochun. 2006. *The Dragon's War: Allied Operations and the Fate of China, 1937–1947*. Annapolis, Md.: Naval Institute Press.

Yu, Zidao, Qikui Liu, and Zhenwei Cao. 1985. *Wang Jingwei Guomin Zhengfu "Qingxiang" Yundong: Wang Wei Zhengquan Ziliao Xuanbian*. Hong Kong: s.n.

Yung, Wing, and Joseph Hopkins Twichell. 1909. *My Life in China and America*. New York: H. Holt and Company.

Zhang, Gaoyuan, and Peirong Liu. 1933. *Jiao Ao Zujie Shimo Diancun, Guoxue Wenku; Di 5 Bian*. Beiping: Wendiange shuzhuang.

Zhang, Haipeng. 1984. *Zhongguo Jindaishigao Dituji*. Peking Shanghai: Ditu chubanshe; Xinhua shudian Shanghai faxingsuo faxing.

Zhang, Huanzhong. 1996. *Shanghai Zongshanghui Yanjiu (1902–1929)*. Chu ban. ed., *Ming Shan Cang, 5*. Taipei: Zhishufang chubanshe: zongjingxiao shupin wenhua shiyeyouxiangongsi.

Zhang, Ruide. 1989. *Zhongguo Jindai Tielu Shiye Guanli Di Zhengzhi Cengmian Fenxi (1876–1936)*. Taipei: s.n.

Zhang, Shu Guang. 1998. Sino-Soviet Economic Cooperation. In *Brothers in Arms: The Rise and Fall of the Sino-Soviet Alliance, 1945–1963*, edited by Odd Arne Westad. Washington, D.C.: Woodrow Wilson Center Press.

Zhang, Xizhe, and Sanjing Chen. 1997. *Huaqiao yu Sun Zhongshan Xiansheng Lingdao de Guomin Geming Xueshu Yantaohui Lunwenji*. Chu ban. ed. Taipei: Guoshiguan.

Zhang, Yongjin. 1991. *China in the International System, 1918–20: The Middle Kingdom at the Periphery, St Anthony's/Macmillan Series*. Basingstoke: Macmillan in association with St. Anthony's College, Oxford.

Zhang, Yucai. 1997. *Zhongguo Tiedao Jianshe Shilue (1876–1949)*. Di 1 ban. ed. Beijing: Zhongguo tiedao chubanshe.

Zhang, Zhongzheng. 2004a. *Sun Yixian Boshi yu Meiguo, 1894–1925*. Di 1 ban. ed., *Antoushu Wenku, 27*. Taipei: Guangda wenhua shiye youxiangongsi.

2004b. *Sun Yixian Boshi yu Meiguo, 1894–1925*. Di 1 ban. ed., *Antoushu Wenku, 27*. Taipei: Guangda wenhua shiye youxiangongsi.

Zheng, Liangsheng. 2001. *Zhong Ri Guanxi Shi*. Chu ban. ed. Taipei: Wunan tushuchubangongsi.

2001. *Zhong-Ri Guanxishi*. Chu ban. ed. Taipei: Wunan tushuchubangongsi.

Zheng, Yongnian. 1999. *Discovering Chinese Nationalism in China: Modernization, Identity, and International Relations, Cambridge Asia-Pacific Studies*. Cambridge, U.K.; New York: Cambridge University Press.

Zhongguo ditu, chubanshe, and jinianguan Xinhai geming Wuchang qiyi. 1991. *Xinhai Gemingshi Dituji*. Di 1 ban. ed. Beijing: Zhongguo ditu chubanshe: Xinhua shudian Beijing faxingsuo faxing.

Zhongguo shehuikexueyuan, jindaishi yanjiusuo Minguoshi yanjiushi, Sichuan shifan daxue, lishi wenxueyuan bian. 2005. *Yijiuerling Niandai de Zhongguo, Zhongguo*

References 277

Shehuikexueyuan Zhongdian Xueke Jianshe Gongcheng Congshu Zhonghua Minguoshi Xueke. Beijing: Shehui kexue wenxian chubanshe.

Zhongguo tielushi bianji yanjiu zhongxin. 1996. *Zhongguo Tielu Dashiji (1876–1995)*. Di 1 ban. ed. Beijing: Zhongguo tiedao chubanshe.

Zhongyang dang'anguan (China). 2000. *Wei Manzhouguo de Tongzhi yu Neimu: Wei Man Guanyuan Gongshu*. Di 1 ban. ed. Beijing: Zhonghua shuju.

Zhongyang yanjiuyuan. Jindaishi yanjiusuo. "Koushulishi" bianji, weiyuanhui. 1996. *Junxi yu Minguo Zhengju, Koushu Lishi*. Taipei: Zhongyang yanjiuyuan jindaishi yanjiusuo.

Zhou, Fohai, and Dejin Cai. 2003. *Zhou Fohai Riji Quanbian*. Di 1 ban. ed. Beijing: Zhongguo wenlian chubanshe: Jingxiao quanguo Xinhua shudian.

Zhou, Gu. 1997. *Sun Zhongshan Yu Disan Guoji*. Chu ban. ed., *Wanjuan Wenku*. Taipei: Dadi chubanshe.

ed. 2001. *Hu Shi, Ye Gongchao Shi Mei Waijiao Wenjian Shougao*. Chu ban. ed. Taipei Shi: Linking Books.

Zhou, Xiuhuan. 1999. *Guomin Zhengfu Shiqi Waijiaobu Gongzuo Baogao (Minguo 22 Nian Zhi 26 Nian), Minguo Shiliao Congshu*. Taipei: Guoshiguan.

Zhu, Hongyuan. 1995. *Cong Bianluan Dao Junsheng: Guangxi de Chuqi Xiandaihua, 1860–1937, Zhongyang Yanjiuyuan Jindaishi Yanjiusuo Zhuankan, 76*. Taipei: Zhongyang yanjiuyuan jindaishi yanjiusuo.

Zuo, Shuangwen. 2005. Zailun 1929 Nian Zhongdong Lu Shijian De Fadong [Re-Discussing the Initiation of the 1929 Chinese Eastern (Rail)Road Incident]. In *Yijiuerling Niandai De Zhongguo*, edited by jindaishi yanjiusuo Minguoshi yanjiushi Zhongguo shehuikexueyuan, Sichuan shifan daxue, lishi wenxueyuan bian. Beijing: Shehui kexue wenxian chubanshe.

Index

A.E.G., 146n217
Abe Nobuyuki, 115n18
Abkhazia, 229
Aceh, 9, 176, 179, 181–182, 192,
    194, 195
Acemoglu, Daron, 228n2
Acheson, Dean, 130
Adams, Brooks, 83n52
Afghanistan
    British actions in, 97
    foreign intervention in, 1, 4, 26, 224, 225,
        229, 231
    Obama administration and, 229–230
Africa
    Britain and, 202n5
    decolonisation, 5
    France and, 104, 149, 178, 202n5, 204
    Germany and, 178
    precolonial state forms, 6
    Scramble for, 35
    sovereign state creation in, 37
African Union, 229
Aisin Gioro Puyi, 50
Aisin Gioro Zaifeng, 49
Alexeyev, Evgenii, 97, 99
Amau (Amo) Declaration, 117n30, 117, 126,
    132n122
Amau Eiji, 117n30
Ambalat, 7
Ambon, 176n12, 195
American Asiatic Society, 84
American Group, 87
Amoy (Xiamen), 96
Ananda Mahidol, King of Thailand, 218n84,
    218
Anderson, Benedict R. O'G., 38, 232
Anderson, Perry, 40
Anfu Clique
    Britain and, 81
    commercial interests and, 62
    defeat in Zhili-Anfu War, 51
    efforts toward a unified China, 56, 57
    Japan and, 58, 69, 108, 227
Anglo-Chinese Company, 78n19

Anglo-Dutch Treaties (1824, 1871), 177,
    181n39, 181
Anglo-French Agreement (1896), 104
Anglo-French Alliance, 202
Anglo-Siamese Treaty (1855), 208
Anglo-Siamese Treaty (1909), 202n6, 202
Anglo-Soviet Trade Agreement (1919),
    137n153
Anti-Yuan Campaign (1916), 50, 57, 60
Arab Spring (2011), 26, 225
Araki Sadao, 115n17
Ashmead-Bartlett, Ellis, 77n15
Asquith, H. H., 76, 80
Athens, 12
Attlee, Clement Richard, 123, 189, 212
Australia, 12, 122n58, 134, 177
Austria-Hungary, 99, 105

Bahasa Indonesia, 197n116, 197
Bai Chongxi (Pai Chung-hsi) See Guangxi
    Clique
Baikal, Lake, 98
Baldwin, Stanley Baldwin, Earl, 81, 120n45,
    120n49, 120, 121
Balfour, Arthur James Balfour, Earl of, 77n15,
    78–79, 82
Bali, 179
Balkans, 26
Bangkok-Singapore Railway, 202
Bank of Communications, 61
Barnhart, Michael, 113
Battambang, 205n24
Beach, Michael Hicks, 77n15
Beijing-Hankou-Guangdong Railroad, 68
Beijing Tariff Conference (1926), 124, 131
Beiyang (Peiyang) Army and Navy, 65, 68, 69
Beiyang (Peiyang) governments, 52n35, 52, 56,
    61, 74, 95
Belgium, 105
bellicist theories of state formation, 41–43,
    63–65, 169–171, 233
Beresford, Charles, 77n15
Berlin Blockade, 187n71–188n71
Bezobrazov, A. M., 97, 99

279

Board of Trade Journal, 122n58
Boer War, 31–32, 76n5, 76, 201
Boli, John, 37
Bolshevik Revolution, 91–92, 102
Borneo, 9, 179
Borneo Oil Company, 177
Borom Maha Si Suriyawong, Somdet
    Chaophraya, 208
Bowles, Thomas Gibson, 77n15
Bowring Treaty (1855), 202
Boxer episode, 48–49n11, 49n11–49, 83, 85, 96
Boxer Indemnity, 83, 87, 124
Boxer Protocol, 89
Britain
    access privileges in Siam, 202n6–202,
        202–202n6
    Chinese external autonomy and, 73
    Chinese infrastructure projects and, 68
    colony in India, 5, 76, 78, 97, 129
    control of Lower Yangzi, 52n34, 52, 77–78,
        82, 103
    December Memorandum, 124n70
    Duan Qirui cabinet and, 66
    East Indies and, 9, 189n80, 193–194
    economic interests in China, 77n15–78n19,
        77–77n15, 78n19–78, 78n20, 120,
        122n58, 122, 154
    economy, 76–77, 121–122
    France and, 82, 104, 109, 177, 202n5, 202,
        203n14
    General Strike of 1926, 121
    Germany and, 103n192
    Japan and, 82, 109, 122, 123, 126–127
    loans to Chinese entities, 67, 68, 81
    lobby for suppression of Nationalists, 121
    Maritime Customs Service and, 52, 80
    neglect of military, 122
    Netherlands and, 177, 181n39, 181
    New Armies and, 68–69
    perceived costs of intervention in China,
        75–76, 79, 106, 120–123, 154, 157
    perceived costs of intervention in East Indies,
        177–178, 179, 188–189, 190, 198
    perceived costs of intervention in Siam, 18,
        201–203, 206, 211, 216, 228n2
    Russian Civil War and, 137, 138
    Russo-Japanese War and, 92n119
    strategic concerns, 76, 78–79, 177
    support for central Chinese government, 46,
        79–83, 106–107, 123, 124, 156
    support for centralised Thai state, 203, 209,
        220
    support for Indonesian republic, 189, 197,
        198
    Triple Entente, 99
    United States and, 82, 88, 122n58, 134
    Wang Zhanyuan and, 59
    during World War I, 76, 77, 201
    Yuan Shikai and, 80n35–80, 80–80n35

British and Chinese Corporation, 78n19,
    121n50
British Chamber of Commerce, 121n50
British Residents' Association, 121n50
Brook, Timothy, 119
Bryan, William Jennings, 83
Budi Utomo, 180
Bugis, 176n12
Bukharin, Nikolai Ivanovich, 136, 137
Bull, Hedley, 10n28
bupati, 176
Burma
    British control of, 104, 177, 201, 203n14,
        203, 204
    communist insurrection in, 187n71–188n71
    decolonisation, 5
    Japanese wartime designs on, 213
    limits on domestic oversight in, 15
    prevalence of malaria inShans in, 208, 213,
        228n2
    wartime annexation by Siam, 212
Burma Road, 127
Burundi, 26
Butterfield, Swire, and Company, 121n50

Cadogan, Alexander, 121n51
Cai E (Tsai Ao), 50
California Texas Oil Corporation (Caltex), 177,
    195n111
Cambodia
    France and, 203n14, 204, 205n24, 205, 212
    as Siamese vassal state, 1, 9, 203n14, 204,
        205n24, 212n56
    United Nations state-building effort, 26, 229
    wartime annexation by Siam, 213
Campbell-Bannerman, Henry, 82
Canada, 12, 122n58
Canton (Guangzhou), 62, 103
Cao Rulin (Tsao Ju-lin), 61
Caribbean, 84, 85
Central Asia, 5, 77
Central Europe, 5
Central Plains War (1930), 158n31, 158
Chahar, 59, 95, 116, 126n82, 158
Chamberlain, Austen, Sir, 120
Chamberlain, Joseph, 76, 77n15, 78
Chamberlain, Neville, 120n45, 120n49, 121,
    127n86, 127
Champassak, 205n24
Chan, Anthony, 69
Chang Chih-tung (Zhang Zhidong), 49n11, 65
Changgufeng (Changkufeng), 115n18
Changjiang (Yangzi River), 52, 125
Chang Tso-lin *See* Zhang Zuolin (Chang Tso-
    lin)
Chanthaburi, 205n24
Chartered Bank of India, Australia, and China,
    121n50
chartered trading companies, 6

Index

Chechnya, 229
Chen Duxiu (Ch'en Tu-hsiu), 61, 144
Chen Jiongming (Chen Chiung-ming), 51, 57–58, 61
Chiang Kai-shek (Jiang Jieshi), 118n37, 122, 140, 145
Chiang Mai, 207n27, 221
Ch'i Hsi-sheng, 54, 64–65
Chin (Qin)-Doihara Agreement (1935), 126n82
China
  arms embargo on, 81, 88n93, 88
  bellicist perspectives on, 63–65, 169–171
  external autonomy, 52–53, 73–74, 160, 163–164
  as a feudalised state, 47–53
  institutional commitment perspectives on, 59–63, 168–169
  modern notions of sovereignty and, 8
  nationalist movements, 5, 56–59, 61, 62–63, 165–168, 231
  1911 Revolution, 49
  1913 Second Revolution, 50, 57, 60, 80
  opportunity costs of intervention in, 20–21, 22–23, 106, 157, 228
  political centralisation, 66–70, 157–159, 161–162
  Spring and Autumn period, 54
  standard historical narratives of, 17, 44, 47, 151
  territorial exclusivity, 51–52, 70–73, 159–160, 162
  Warring States period, 6, 54
  war with Japan, 19, 89, 90, 92
  See also Chinese Communist Party (CCP), Nationalists, Qing Dynasty
China Aid Act (1948), 135n138
China Association, 121n50
China Bondholders' Committee, 121n51
China Committee, 121n50
China Eastern Railway, 101, 141
China Merchants' Steam Navigation Company, 68
China Relief Expedition, 85
China-Studien-Gesellschaft, 146n217
Chinchow-Aigun (Jinzhou-Aihun) Railroad, 88
Chinese Central Railways, 78n19
Chinese Civil War, 161
Chinese Communist Party (CCP)
  base in Manchuria, 142, 154, 162
  capacity for capitalised coercion, 170–171
  Chen Duxiu and, 61, 144
  Korean War and, 32, 154, 232
  nationalism and, 167
  Nationalists and, 135, 140, 141, 144–145
  peasant class and, 168–169
  Soviet aid for, 140–141, 144n208–145, 144–144n208, 161–162
  willingness to cede Northeast China to Soviets, 227

Chinese Nationalist Party *See* Nationalists
Chinese Revolutionary Alliance (Tongmenghui), 166
Choibalsan, Khorloogiin, 141, 153
Chongqing (Chungking), 127, 133
Chuang Bunnag (Si Suriyawong), 208
Chulalongkorn, King of Siam, 19, 206, 207n27
Chun, Prince, 49
Churchill, Winston, 76, 78, 120n49, 121, 123, 125, 156
city leagues, 6, 13
city-states, 12–13
Cixi (Tz'u Hsi), Empress Dowager, 49
Cohen, Warren, 134
Cold War
  China and, 129–130, 152
  Indonesia/East Indies and, 187, 188, 197
  intervention cost expectations and, 129–130, 152, 232
  self-determination movements and, 1, 230–231
  Soviet Union and, 137
  Thailand/Siam and, 214, 217
  United States and, 129–130, 187, 197, 214, 217
Colijn, Hendrikus, 185n58
colonial states, 4, 5, 12, 25, 38
Comintern, 144, 145
Communications Clique, 61
Coolidge, Calvin, 131
Correlates of War Project (COW), 233n13, 233
Cranborne, Viscoun *See* Salisbury; James Edward Hubert Gascoyne-Cecil, Marquess of (1861–1947)
Cuba, 85n65
Curzon of Kedleston, George Nathaniel Curzon, Marquess, 77n15
Czechoslovakia, 187n71–188n71

Daimler-Benz, 146n217
Dai Viet, 12
Dalian, 98
Damrong Rajanubhan, Prince of Siam, 207n27
Dawes Plan (1923), 137
Deutsche-Asiatische Bank, 146n217
Devawongse Varoprakar, Prince of Siam, 209
Deventer, Conrad Théodoor van, 175
Dewantara, Hadjar, 192
Diaoyutai Islands, 7
Dilke, Charles, 77n15
Ding Wenjiang, 61
Diponegoro, 5
Djibouti, 28
Dokdo Island, 7
Dominican Republic, 85n65
Dongnan hubao yundong, 49n11, 49
Dorniern, 146n217
Duan Qirui (Tuan Ch'i-jui)
  Britain and, 66, 81

Index

Dorniern (cont.)
  commercial interests and, 62
  efforts to create sovereign state, 56, 66, 107–108
  Japan and, 69, 95, 107–108, 227
  Nationalists and, 57
  professional background, 61
  United States and, 66, 86
  Yuan Shikai and, 50
Durkheim, Emile, 41n43

Eastern Europe, 5
East Indies
  army, 176n12, 176, 185n57
  cash crop production, 174, 177
  colonial economy, 181
  colonial governance structure, 9, 175–176n15, 176n15–177, 179–181
  colonial statehood, 228
  cultuurstelsel cultivation system, 174n1, 174
  decolonisation, 5
  economic importance to metropole, 174–175, 182–183, 184–185
  Ethical Policy, 19, 175–176, 180, 185n58
  ethnic Chinese in, 176n15, 176
  external autonomy, 181–182, 191, 192–193
  Japan and, 9, 17–18, 183, 185n61, 192n91, 213
  oil industry, 174, 177
  opportunity costs of intervention in, 20–21, 22–23
  political centralisation, 179–181, 190–191, 192, 193–196
  size and population, 175, 183–184
  territorial exclusivity, 181, 191, 192–193
  See also Indonesia
East Sumatra, 192, 194, 195
East Timor, 26, 224, 229
Eden, Anthony, 120n49
Egypt, 1, 26, 225
empires, 4, 6, 12n35–12, 12–12n35
Entente Cordiale, 104, 202
Europe
  British strategic concerns in, 122, 123
  French, German, and Russian strategic concerns in, 178
  sovereign state ideal and, 6
  Soviet Union and, 137–138
  U.S. economic interests in, 84
  U.S. military action in, 85n65
  U.S. strategic commitment to, 129–130, 135, 178

Federation of British Industries, 121n50
Feng Guozhang (Feng Kuo-chang), 61, 62
Fengtian Clique
  American and British abandonment of, 156
  capacity for capitalised coercion, 65
  efforts toward a unified China, 56, 57
  Feng Yuxiang and, 51

  government, 131, 144, 158
  Japan and, 58, 69, 93, 108, 124, 153, 227
Fengtian-Zhili Wars (1920, 1924), 57
Feng Yuxiang (Feng Yü-hsiang)
  defection, 51
  dubious revolutionary credentials, 153
  political base, 62
  Soviet support for, 59, 69, 124, 145, 153
Ferguson, Niall, 121
feudalised states, 4, 12, 38
First United Front, 144
Fisher, John Arbuthnot, 78
France
  administration of Salt Gabelle, 52
  Britain and, 82, 104, 109, 177, 202n5, 202, 203n14
  Chinese infrastructure projects and, 68
  colonies in Africa, 104, 149, 178, 202n5, 204
  colonies in Indochina, 104, 149, 204
  control of south and southwest China, 73, 103–104, 178, 202n5
  exclusive privileges in China, 52, 160
  feudalised state forms in, 12, 55
  Germany's rise and, 203–204
  loans to Chinese entities, 67, 68
  local Chinese actors and, 69
  Maritime Customs Service and, 72
  Nationalists and, 58–59, 149
  perceived costs of intervention in China, 103–104, 106, 148, 157
  perceived costs of intervention in East Indies, 178
  perceived costs of intervention in Siam, 18, 201, 203–205, 206, 211, 216, 228n2
  Russian Civil War and, 137
  support for centralised Thai state, 205, 209, 220
  Triple Entente, 99
  Triple Intervention, 92, 98, 100
  Vichy government, 148, 149, 185n61
  during World War I, 203–204
  during World War II, 148–149, 211
Franco-Siamese treaties, 204
Free Thai, 212, 215
Fujian (Fukien), 85, 92, 93, 109, 152, 178
Fujian Clique, 51
Fujian Mutiny (1933–1934), 158
Funk, Walter, 146n217
Fushimi Hiroyasu, 115n17
Fuzhou (Foochow) Shipyard, 64

Gansu, 95
Gellner, Ernest, 38
Gerindo, 192
Germany
  Communist Uprising (1921), 137
  control of Shandong, 52, 73, 90, 91, 102–103n192, 103n192–103, 107
  economic difficulties, 146

Index

283

economic interests in China,
145n215–146n215, 146n217, 147n223
interest in Chinese tungsten, 146, 147, 155
Japan and, 146, 147–148
loans to Chinese entities, 46, 67, 68
Nationalists and, 146–147, 156
New Armies and, 68–69
perceived costs of intervention in China,
102–103, 106, 145–146, 154,
155–156, 157
perceived costs of intervention in
East Indies, 178
powers of veto in, 15
rising power, 75, 99, 129, 146
Soviet Union and, 137, 138
surrender at end of World War II, 18n55
surrender of privileges in China, 145
Triple Intervention, 92, 98, 100
Gilpin, Robert, 27, 36, 44n53
Gobi Desert, 98
Goebbels, Josef, 215n69
Goryeo Dynasty, 12
Goto Shimpei, 91, 92
Graeff, Andries C.D. de, 185n58
Great Depression
Britain and, 121
East Indies and, 185, 191
France and, 148
Germany and, 146, 147n223
Netherlands and, 183, 184
Soviet Union and, 138
United States and, 128, 132, 214
Greater East Asia Co-Prosperity Sphere, 117,
167, 193
Great Patriotic War, 138
Greece, 135n138
Grey of Fallodon, Edward Grey, Viscount,
77n15, 80
Grieco, Joseph, 2n4, 32n21, 32
Guam, 85
Guandong (Kwantung) Army, 113n3, 115n19,
116, 118, 126
Guangdong (Kwangtung)
Britain and, 104
Chen Duxiu and, 61
French-built railways in, 104
Japan and, 95, 149, 227
Nationalist control of, 62, 81, 227
as transit area for Allied war supplies, 149
Guangdong-Guangxi Incident (1936), 158
Guangxi (Kwangsi), 58, 69, 103, 104, 149
Guangxi Clique, 51
Guangzhou (Canton), 62, 103
Guangzhou Bay, 149
Guangzhou Incident (1926), 145
Guangzhou National Government
Chen Jiongming and, 51
external aid for, 58–59, 81
external autonomy, 52

participation at peace conferences, 53n36, 74
reluctance to divide China, 57
tensions with northern governments, 57
United States and, 87
See also Nanjing National Government,
Nationalists
Gu Hongming (Ku Hung-ming), 6n15, 63
Guided Democracy, 232
Guomindang (GMD) See Nationalists
Guominjun (Kuominchun) Clique, 69, 124,
145, 153
Gu Weijun (Wellington V.K. Koo), 61, 74

Haiti, 85n65
Halifax, Edward Frederick Lindley Wood, Earl
of, 120n49
Hamaguchi Osachi, 113n2, 113n7,
114n13, 114
Handelsgesellschaft für Industrielle Produkt
(HAPRO), 146n217
Hanseatic League, 13
Hanyang, 69
Hanyeping Company, 63–64, 66–67
Hara Takashi (Kei), 90, 91, 92, 96
Harcourt, William, 77n15
Harding, Warren G., 83, 86, 127, 131, 155
Harriman, Edward Henry, 84
Hatta, Mohammad, 191n84, 192, 193n100,
193, 194n107, 197
Hawaii, 85, 91
Hay, John, 82, 84, 88n89
Hayashi Senjuro, 115n17
Hebei, 116, 126n82
Heiho, 192
Herbst, Jeffrey, 37
Hiroshima, 167
Hitler, Adolf, 138, 147
Ho (He)-Umezu Accord (1935), 126n82
Hoare, Samuel, 120n49
Hobsbawm, Eric, 41
Holy Roman Empire, 12, 55
Hong Kong
Britain and, 78, 91, 125, 163
Chinese acceptance of separation from, 168
institutional commitment perspective
on, 169
strategic importance, 28
supply of arms to Nationalists through, 127
Hong Kong and Shanghai Banking
Corporation, 78n19, 121n50
Hong Kong and Whampoa Docks, 78n19
Hoover, Herbert, 128
Hsinkiang See Xinjiang (Hsinkiang)
Hsu Shih-chang (Xu Shichang), 53n36, 53, 57,
73, 74, 86
Huabei Regime, 118n37
Huang Xing (Huang Hsing), 61
Hubei (Hupei), 59, 61
Hughes, Charles Evans, 84n53

284 *Index*

Hu-Guang Railroad, 87
Hulunbei'er, 97, 102
Hunan, 58
Hunan Clique, 51
Hutchinson International, 78n19

I.G. Farben, 146n217
Idenburg, Alexander W.F., 176n9
India
  British defence of, 76, 78, 129
  British-Russian relations and, 76, 97
  British trade with, 122n58
  decolonisation, 5
  movement of supplies to Chongqing through,
    127, 133
  proximity to East Indies, 177
Indië weerbaar, 176
Indische Partij, 180
Indochina
  Anglo-French relations and, 104, 204
  French access regulation over, 104, 204
  French lack of interest in East Indies and, 178
  Japanese occupation, 149, 185n61
  postwar French efforts to recolonise, 149
  prevalence of malaria in, 228n2
  proximity to southwest China, 149
  Siam's wartime annexation of, 214, 217
  state forms in, 9 *see also under individual
    countries*
Indonesia
  bellicist perspectives on, 198
  declaration of independence of, 193n100, 193
  Guided Democracy and *Konfrontasi*, 232
  institutional commitment perspectives
    on, 198
  Madiun Rebellion, 188
  nationalist movements in, 5, 173, 192, 194,
    197–198, 231
  negotiations in the creation of, 195n110–195,
    195–195n110
  standard historical narratives of, 8–9, 17, 44
  See also East Indies
Inner Mongolia
  Japan and, 91, 93
  Japanese-sponsored regimes in, 118n37, 118,
    158
  Russia and, 97, 99, 100
  secret Russo-Japanese pacts and, 101, 109
  Soviet Union and, 152
Inner Mongolia Autonomous Government,
  158
institutional commitment theories of state form,
  39–41, 60–63, 168–169
International Crisis Behaviour Project
  (ICB), 233
International Peace Research Institute, 233
Inukai Tsuyoshi, 91
Iran, 97
Iraq

foreign intervention in, 1, 4, 26, 224, 225,
  229, 231
Sunni Awakening, 33, 229
United States' progress in, 229
Ishiwara Kanji, 115n17
isomorphism, 37–38
Israel, 229
Itagaki Seishiro, 115n17
Italy, 69, 105, 181–182
Ito Hirobumi, 92, 93

Jackson, Robert, 37
Japan
  access denial efforts in China, 115–119
  access regulation in Manchuria, 93, 111,
    152, 178
  access regulation in Shandong, 93, 111,
    152, 178
  Aceh and, 181–182
  Army-Navy coalition, 114–115n17,
    115n17–115
  attack on Shanghai (1932), 126n82, 126, 132
  Britain and, 82, 92n119, 109, 123, 126–127
  Chinese external autonomy and, 73
  domestic lobby for annexation of
    Shandong, 91
  East Indies and, 9, 17–18, 183, 185n61,
    192n91
  Germany and, 146, 147–148
  incursions into Outer Mongolia, 141
  invasion of Manchuria, 117, 126n82,
    126, 132
  loans to Chinese entities, 67, 68, 94–95
  local Chinese actors and, 58, 69, 93–94, 95,
    116–117, 118–119
  local Indonesian actors and, 191–192
  London Naval Conference and, 114n10, 114
  Nationalists and, 58–59, 117, 118, 135n137,
    135, 153
  New Armies and, 68–69
  Open Door principle and, 106–107
  Paris and Washington conferences and, 53,
    81, 88, 96
  perceived costs of intervention in China,
    89–90, 92–93, 106, 112–114, 115,
    151–154, 157, 167
  perceived costs of intervention in East Indies,
    178, 179, 186–187, 190
  perceived costs of intervention in Siam, 206,
    211, 213, 216
  postwar U.S. reconstruction, 129–130
  role in formation of Indonesian republic, 193,
    197, 198
  Russia and, 96, 98, 101, 109, 111
  Russian Civil War and, 138
  Siberia and, 92, 96
  Soviet Union and, 113, 114, 118, 138,
    143, 153
  sponsored collaborationist regimes, 158–159

Index

285

state form in, 9
strategic concerns, 90, 91–92, 114–115
takeover of Shandong during WWI,
90, 107
trade with United States, 128
Triple Intervention and, 100
U.S. defeat and occupation, 113, 115,
167, 186
Wang Zhanyuan and, 59
war with China, 19, 89, 90, 92
during World War II, 28, 129, 149
Yuan Shikai and, 90–91
Zhang Zuolin and, 116, 124
See also Japanese Imperial Army
Japanese Imperial Army
avoidance of clashes, 96, 113n3, 114
coalition with Navy, 114–115n17,
115n17–115
East Indies auxiliary force, 192
Manchuria and, 90, 91
military support for local actors, 93, 95
withdrawal from Siberia, 92
Jardine, Matheson, and Company, 78n19,
121n50
Java, 174, 176, 179, 194, 195–194, 195
Java War, 5
Jawa Hokokai, 192
Jehol (Rehe), 116
Jiang-Gui War (1929), 158n31, 158
Jiang Jieshi (Chiang Kai-shek), 118n37, 122,
140, 145
Jiangnan (Kiangnan), 61
Jiangnan Arsenal, 64, 68
Jiangnan Shipyard, 64, 68
Jiangxi (Kiangsi), 147
Jiangxi Clique, 51
Jiaozhou (Kiaochow) Bay, 90, 91, 102, 116
Jinzhou-Aihun (Chinchow-Aigun) Railroad, 88
Jogjakarta, 194
Johnson, Simon, 228n2
John Swire and Sons, 78n19
Jonge, Bonifacius C. de, 185n58
Jordan, John Newell, Sir, 80

Kaiserliche Marine, 76, 103
Kalimantan, 179
Kangde Emperor of Manchukuo (Puyi), 50
Kang Youwei, 6n15
Kantogun (Kwantung Army), 113n3, 115n19,
116, 118, 126
Karakhan Manifestos (1919, 1920), 142
Kato Kanji, 115n17
Kato Takaaki, 90, 113n2, 113n7, 113, 114
Kato Tomosaburo (Admiral), 92, 96, 113n2
Katsura Taro, 93, 96
Kedah, 202
Keibodan, 192n95
Kelantan, 202
Kennan, George, 130

Kenseikai, 113n2
Keohane, Robert, 27
Kiangnan (Jiangnan), 61
Kiangsi (Jiangxi), 147
Kiaochow (Jiaozhou) Bay, 90, 91, 102, 116
Kimberley, John Wodehouse, Earl of, 77n15
Knatchbull-Hugessen, Hughe, 121n51
Knox, Philander C., 83, 88
Koiso Kuniaki, 115n18
Komité Nasional Indonesia Pusat (KNIP),
193n100
Konfrontasi, 232
Koninklijk Nederlands Indisch Leger (KNIL),
176n12
Konoe Fumimaro, 115n18
Koo, Wellington V.K., 61, 74
Korea, 9, 12, 90, 97, 98, 113, 178
Korean War
Chinese involvement in, 32, 154, 232
intervention cost expectations and, 130,
136, 214
Soviet-Chinese relations and, 141,
154, 161
U.S. oversight of Taiwan and, 163
Kosovo, 229
Kowloon, 82
Krasner, Stephen, 16–17, 37, 22 1n102
Krupp, 146n217
Ku Hung-ming (Gu Hongming), 6n15, 63
Kui Jun, 49n11
Kuominchun (Guominjun) Clique, 69, 124,
145, 153
Kuomintang (KMT) *See* Nationalists
Kuril Islands, 167
Kuropatkin, Alexey, 97, 99
Kwangsi (Guangxi), 58, 69, 103, 104, 149
Kwangtung *See* Guangdong (Kwangtung).
Kwantung (Guandong) Army, 113n3, 115n19,
116, 118, 126

Labouchere, Henry, 77n15
Lampson, Miles, 121n51
Lampson Policy, 124n70
Lansing, Robert, 83
Laos
Anglo-French relations and, 204
as former Siamese vassal, 9, 203n14, 204
France and, 205n24, 205, 212
wartime annexation by Siam, 212n56, 213
Latin America, 84
Law, Andrew Bonar, 120n45
League of Nations
British appeasement of Japan and, 126–127,
127n86
China's membership in, 53
France and, 148
Japanese withdrawal from, 117
price of Japanese support for, 89, 91
Soviet Union's membership in, 137n153

Index

Lebanon, 229
Lei Haizong, 54
Leith-Ross, Frederick, 121n51
Leith-Ross Economic Mission (1936–1937), 125, 126
Lenin, Vladimir Il'ich, 136, 137, 144
Liangguang Incident (1936), 158
Liangjiang, 65
Liaodong (Liaotung) Peninsula, 90, 92, 98, 141
Libya, 1, 26, 225
Li Hongzhang (Li Hung-chang), 49n11
Li Houji, 93, 116
lijin transit tax, 64n88–64n89, 64n89–64, 64–64n88, 71n123
Li Liejun, 50
Linggajati Agreement (1946), 189n80, 194n106
Liu Kunyi, 49n11
Li Yuanhong, 57, 61, 62
Li Zongren (Li Tsung-jen) *See* Guangxi Clique.
Liang Qichao (Liang Ch'i-ch'ao), 6n15
Liu Xun, 51
Lloyd George, David, 76, 120n45, 121
Locarno Treaty (1925), 137
Lodge, Henry Cabot, 84
Lombok, 179
London Naval Conference, 114n10, 114
London Treaty (1824), 181n39
Lower Yangzi (Yangtze), 52, 77–78, 82, 103
Lowther, James, 77n15
Luang Prabang, 1, 205n24
Lu Rongting, 69, 104
Lushunkou (Port Arthur), 98, 101
Lu Zhengxiang (Lou Tseng-tsiang), 74
Lytton Mission, 117, 126

Macau, 168
MacDonald, James Ramsay, 120n45, 120n49
MacMurray, J.V.A., 84n53
Madiun Rebellion, 188
Madura, 176n12, 194
Mahan, Alfred Thayer, 83n52
Majlis Syuro Muslimin Indonesia (Masyumi), 192
Malacca Straits, 9
malaria, 228n2
Malaya
    Anglo-Dutch treaties and, 181n39
    British control of, 177, 189, 203n14, 203, 204
    British trade with, 122n58
    communist insurrection, 187n71–188n71, 189n79
    decolonisation, 5
    foreign intervention and state form in, 1
    former Siamese vassals in, 202, 213
    Japanese wartime designs on, 213
    prevalence of malaria, 228n2
    as source of raw materials, 202n9
    wartime annexation by Siam, 212n54, 212
Malayan Communist Party, 212n57

Malayan Emergency, 214
Malay language, 197n116, 197
Malay Peninsula, 1, 9
Malaysia, 5
Manchukuo (Manzhouguo), 141, 143, 148, 153, 158, 160, 162
Manchuria
    Anfu Club and Fengtian Clique and, 58
    Chinese acceptance of Soviet extraterritoriality in, 168
    Communist base in, 142, 154, 162
    domestic Japanese politics and, 90, 91
    institutional commitment perspective on, 169
    Japanese access regulation over, 93, 111, 152, 178
    Japanese invasion in 1931, 117, 126n82, 126, 132
    Japanese use of local actors in, 116
    lack of central government rule, 167
    proximity to Siberia, 152
    Russia and, 72, 97, 99, 100, 101n180, 101, 178
    secret Russo-Japanese pact on, 101n183–101, 101–101n183, 109
    Soviet attempts to regulate access to, 141, 142
    Soviet invasion of, 167
    Soviet relinquishment of rights in, 139
    Triple Intervention and, 100
    U.S. interest in, 83, 101n183
    Washington Conference and, 96
    Yalta Conference and, 143
    Zhang Zuolin and, 62
Mansur, Mas, 192
Mao Zedong (Mao Tse-tung), 140, 171
March 20th Incident (1926), 145
Maritime Customs Service
    Britain and, 52, 80
    foreign administration of, 70, 72, 159
    National Government takeover of, 125, 162
    United States and, 89, 131
Marshall Mission (1945–1947), 135
Marshall Plan, 135n138, 135, 155n21, 155, 183n48
Marxian perspectives, 39–41n43, 41n43–41
Masampo, 98
May Fourth Movement, 56
Ma Yinchu, 64n89
McCord, Edward, 60
McKinley, William, 32, 83, 84, 85, 86
Mekong River, 204
Mengjiang (Mongolian Autonomous State), 118n37, 153, 158, 160
Mexican silver currency, 64n91
Mexico, 85n65
Meyer, John, 37
Middle East, 77, 202n5, 204
Midleton, William St. John Fremantle Brodrick, Earl of, 77n15
Mikoyan, Anastas, 171

Index

287

Minangkabau, 176, 192
Min Bian (Fujian Mutiny) (1933–1934), 158
Minseito, 113n2
Molotov-Ribbentrop Pact, 138
Mongol Empire, 12
Mongolian Autonomous State (Mengjiang),
  118n37, 153, 158, 160
Mongolian People's Republic, 141, 143
Mongolian Region Autonomous Political
  Affairs Committee, 158
Mook, Hubertus J. van, 185n58, 194n106, 194
Morgenthau, Henry, 132–133
Mukden (Shenyang), 69

Nagasaki, 167
Namibia, 26, 229
Nanjing (Nanking) Incident (1927),
  125–126, 132
Nanjing National Government
  as collaborationist regime, 118, 153, 160
  France and, 149
  Germany and, 147, 148
  internal divisions and wars, 158
  vs. mainstream Nationalists, 118n37
  See also Guangzhou National Government,
    Nationalists
Nanjing Provisional Government, 52
Napoleonic Wars, 183
Nathan, Andrew, 64n91
nationalist movements
  vs. collaboration, 25
  in China, 5, 56–59, 61, 62–63, 165–168, 231
  in East Indies, 5, 173, 192, 194, 197–198, 231
  in Siam, 5, 9, 219, 221–222, 231, 232
  in the Philippines, 5, 32
  sovereign statehood and, 4–6, 10, 18–19,
    37–39, 231–233
Nationalists
  attempt to seize salt taxes and customs, 81
  British appeasement of Japan and, 122, 123,
    126–127
  British support for, 123, 124–125, 127
  Chen Jiongming and, 51, 57–58
  commercial interests and, 62
  Communists and, 135, 140, 142–143,
    144–145
  conflict with Britain in Nanjing Incident,
    125–126
  enticements for foreign aid, 58–59
  France and, 58–59, 149
  Germany and, 146–147
  Japan and, 58–59, 117, 118, 135n137,
    135, 153
  militarist cliques and, 51
  Northern Expedition, 124, 125–126, 158
  principle of self-determination and, 167
  reduced capacity for capitalised coercion,
    169–170
  reluctance to divide China, 57

Sheng Shicai's defection to, 143
Soviet aid for, 69, 124, 127, 140, 145, 153
Soviet moves to undermine, 142
Soviet recognition of government of, 143
surrendered Japanese forces and, 129,
  134–135n137, 135n137–136
tensions with the north, 57
U.S. aid to, 132n122, 133, 134–136,
  155n21–155, 155–155n21, 161–162
U.S. extraterritorial rights and, 132
See also Guangzhou National Government,
  Nanjing National Government
Natuna Islands, 9
Netherlands
  Britain and, 177, 181n39, 181
  efforts to recolonise East Indies,
    194n107–195, 194–194n107, 194,
    197–198
  German occupation, 183, 184
  Japan and, 185n61–186, 185–185n61, 191
  Java War, 5
  perceived costs of intervention in East Indies,
    17–18, 174, 175, 179, 190
  suppression of indigenous political groups,
    180, 184, 185n57, 191n84–191,
    191–191n84
  system of colonial governance, 9
  United States and, 183n48, 183, 184–185,
    188, 198
  use of local actors, 176–177, 184, 191,
    227
New Armies, 61, 65, 68–69
New Communications Clique, 61
New Consortium Loan, 87, 88
New Guinea, 177
New Territories, 169n70
Ng Choy (Wu Tingfang), 63
Nicholas II, Emperor of Russia, 28, 97
Nine Power Treaty (1922), 88, 113, 127n86,
  128
Nishihara Loan, 95
Nomonhan, 115n18
North Borneo, 177
North China Political Affairs Commission, 153,
  159
Northern Shanxi Autonomous Government,
  158
North-South Armistice (1912), 66, 80
North-South War (1917), 57, 60

Obama, Barack, 229–230
October Revolution (1917), 137, 139, 152
Okuma Shigenobu, 90, 92, 93
Old Consortium Loans, 87, 88
Old Guangxi (Kwangsi) Clique, 104
Open Door Notes, 82, 86, 88n89, 88
Open Door principle, 82, 98, 102, 103,
  106–107, 120
Opium Wars, 44, 79

288   *Index*

opportunity costs of intervention
  calculating, 32n21–33n21
  expectations of, 2–3, 28–33, 34,
    35, 36
  high, 2, 18, 30–31, 32, 35, 226
  low to moderate, 17–18, 24, 35, 226
Ott, Eugen, 147
Ottoman Empire, 35, 99, 204, 228
Otto Wolff, 146n217
Outer Mongolia
  Chinese acceptance of separation, 168
  Chinese claims on, 19
  failure to achieve sovereignty, 167
  institutional commitment perspective on, 169
  secret Russo-Japanese pact and, 109
  Soviet-sponsored regimes in, 159
  Soviet Union and, 141, 152, 163, 178
  Tsarist Russia and, 97, 99, 101–102, 139, 178
  Yalta Conference and, 143
overseas Chinese, 62–63n80, 63n80–63,
  176n15, 176, 207, 217, 219n94, 219

Pakistan, 229–230
Palestinian Liberation Organisation, 229
Panama, 28, 85n65
Paris Peace Conference (1919), 53, 74, 81, 145,
  209–210
Partai Komunis Indonesia (PKI), 180, 191
Partai Nasional Indonesia (PNI), 191
Partai Sarekat Islam Indonesia, 191
Partai Sosialis, 191
Partindo, 191
Pattani, 9, 208, 221
Pauling and Company, 78n19
Peiyang (Beiyang) governments, 52n35, 52, 56,
  61, 74, 95
Peking (Beijing) Tariff Conference (1926),
  124, 131
Pekin Syndicate, 78n19
Pembela Tanah Air (PETA), 192
Pendidikan Nasional Indonesia, 191
penghulus, 176, 192
Perlis, 202
Pescadores, 97
Pétain, Philippe, 148
Phibun Songkhram, 212n57, 212, 213, 215n68,
  215n69, 215, 217, 219
Philippines
  communist insurrection,
    187n71–188n71
  decolonisation, 5
  Japan and, 85
  nationalist movements in, 5
  Siam-purchased aircraft and, 215n68
  state forms, 9
  United States and, 32, 85n65, 85, 91, 178,
    215n68
Poland, 137
Port Arthur (Lushunkou), 98, 101

Powell, Robert, 2n4, 32
Prajadhipok, King of Siam, 218
Preah Vihear, 7
priyayi, 176n15, 176, 192
Provisional Government of Republic of
  China, 158
Pusat Tenaga Rakyat (Putera), 192
Puyi, 50

Qingdao, 103
Qin Shuren, 143
Qing Dynasty
  Boxer episode and, 48–49, 53, 83
  Britain and, 52n34
  collapse and overthrow, 5, 49–50
  decentralisation during, 16, 48, 59–60
  efforts to shore up authority, 48n7
  external autonomy, 53, 73
  France and, 103
  Germany and, 102–103
  Japan and, 90
  nationalist movements *vs.*, 6n15
  Opium Wars, 79
  overseas Chinese support for, 63
  restoration attempt, 57, 66
  Russia and, 97, 98, 99, 100–101, 101n184
  Self-Strengthening Movement, 8, 63
  Triple Intervention and, 100
  Yuan Shikai and, 56

Rapallo Treaty (1922), 137n153
Reformed Government of the Republic of
  China, 158
Rehe (Jehol), 116
Reichsverband der deutschen Industrie,
  146n217
Reichswehr, 146n217
Reinsch, Paul S., 83n52
Renville Agreement (1948), 187n69, 194n106
Re-Organisation Loan (1913), 80, 87, 88, 94, 95
Rheinmetall, 146n217
Robinson, James, 228n2
Rockhill, William W., 83n52, 83–84
Rong Hong (Wing Yung), 63
Roosevelt, Franklin D.
  colonisation of Philippines and, 32
  Nationalists and, 132, 133n127, 133, 155
  perception of cost of intervening in China,
    128, 129
  preoccupation with Great Depression, 128
  Stalin and, 134
Roosevelt, Theodore, 84, 85, 86
Root, Elihu, 84
Rosebery, Archibald Primrose, Earl of, 77n15
Royal Dutch Shell, 177, 195n111
Royal Navy, 76, 91
Ruggie, John Gerard, 41n43
Russia
  control of Manchuria, 72

Index

eastward expansion, 76, 90, 97–98
exclusive privileges in China, 52
loans to Chinese entities, 67
local actors and, 46, 101–102
opposition to state creation in
 Chechnya, 229
perceived costs of intervention in China,
 97, 106
strategic concerns, 97–100
support for Chinese autonomy, 73
Triple Entente, 99
Triple Intervention, 92, 98
See also Russo-Japanese War, Soviet Union
Russian Civil War, 102, 137, 139
Russo-Japanese War
 Japanese conclusion of, 96
 Japanese financing of, 92n119, 92
 Japanese naval superiority after, 85
 Russian defeat, 28, 99, 101
 Russian eastward expansion and, 98
 Russian forces in Manchuria during,
  101n180
Rwanda, 26
Ryukyu Islands, 9

Saionji Kinmochi, 93, 94, 114n13
Sakhalin, 96, 167
Salim, Agus, 194n107
Salisbury, James Edward Hubert Gascoyne-
 Cecil, Marquess of (1861–1947), 77n15
Salisbury, Robert Cecil, Marquess of (1830–
 1903), 77n15, 82
Salisbury-Courcel Agreement (1894), 104,
 202n5, 202
Salt Gabelle, 52, 64n88, 65, 70
San Francisco Treaty, 18n55, 18, 134, 167
Sansha (Samsah) Bay, 85
Sarekat Islam, 180n32, 180
Sayre, Francis B., 214n67
Schacht, Hjalmar, 146n217
Schurman, Jacob Gould, 84n53
Scramble for Concessions, 102, 108
second-image reversed approach, 3n6, 3, 45,
 230, 235
Second United Front, 140
seeckt, Hans von (Colonel-General), 146n217
Seiyukai, 90, 113n2
self-determination, principle of, 5, 38
Self-Strengthening Movement, 8, 63
Seni Pramoj, 215n69
Senkaku Islands, 7
Sha'anxi (Shensi), 59
Shandong
 German control of, 52, 178
 Japanese access regulation over, 93, 111,
  152, 178
 Japanese lobby for formal annexation of, 91
 Japanese takeover during WWI,
  90, 107

Japanese use of local actors in, 116
at the Paris and Washington conferences, 53,
 81, 88, 96
Triple Intervention and, 100
Shanghai, 91, 95, 126
Shanghai Ceasefire Agreement (1933), 126n82
Shanghai Peace Conference (1919), 66, 87
Shans, 208
Shan states, 212n54, 213
Shanxi (Shansi), 58, 62, 95, 116, 158
Sheng Shicai (Sheng Shi-ts'ai), 143, 153
Sheng Xuanhuai (Sheng Hsuan-huai), 49n11
Shensi (Sha'anxi), 59
Shenyang, 69
Shidehara Kijuro, 113n7, 114n13
Shimonoseki, Treaty of, 97
Shi Zhaoji (Alfred Sze Sao-ke), 61, 74
Siam
 bellicist perspectives on, 220–221
 Britain and, 202n6, 203, 212n54–212,
  212n55, 212n57, 212–212n54, 218
 Buddhism in, 207n27
 centralisation of governance in, 16
 Chakri monarchy as local actor, 227
 change of name to Thailand, 200n1, 219
 changes in state form, 200, 210
 ethnic Chinese in, 207, 217, 219n94, 219
 ethnic Malays in, 219
 external autonomy, 209–210, 216–217
 former vassal states, 202, 212n54, 212n56
 France and, 18, 201, 203–205, 205n24, 205,
  212, 217
 institutional commitment perspective on, 221
 Japan and, 210, 212n54–212, 212–212n54,
  213, 215n69
 modernising reforms, 19, 206–207
 nationalist movements, 5, 9, 219, 221–222,
  231, 232
 opportunity costs of intervention in, 18,
  20–21, 22–23, 206, 216, 228
 political centralisation, 206–208, 218–219
 standard historical narratives of, 17, 44, 200
 suzerain status, 1, 9, 210
 territorial exclusivity, 208–209, 217–218
 United States and, 210n48, 215n68, 215n69,
  217
Siamese Expedition Force, 209
Si'an (Xi'an) Incident (1936), 140, 158
Siberia, 92, 96, 97, 139, 142, 152, 178
Sichuan (Szechwan), 58, 103, 104
Sichuan Clique, 51
Sichuan-Yunnan-Guangxi Railroads, 68
Siemens, 146n217
Siem Reap, 205n24
Sierra Leone, 229
Silver Purchase Act (1934), 133n126, 133
Simon, John, 120n49
Singapore, 5, 12, 28, 78, 189n79
Sino-British Trade Council, 121n50

Sino-Japanese War, 19, 47, 89, 90, 92, 97
Sino-Soviet Treaty (1924), 141, 142
Sino-Soviet Treaty of Friendship, Alliance, and Mutual Assistance (1950), 141, 154, 161
Sino-Soviet Treaty of Friendship and Alliance (1945), 141, 142, 154, 161
Sisophon, 205n24
Si Suriyawong *See* Borom Maha Si Suriyawong, Somdet Chaophraya.
Sjahrir, Sutan, 191n84, 194n106, 194n107, 197
Sjarifuddin, Amir, 191n84
Smith, Samuel, 77n15
Somalia, 26, 35, 229
Somaliland, 229
South China Sea, 7
Southeast Asia, 129
South-East Asia Command, 193
Southeast Mutual Protection Movement, 49
Southern Chahar Autonomous Government, 158
Southern Military Government *See* Guangzhou National Government
Southern Sudan, 229
South Manchurian Railway, 52, 101, 141
South Ossetia, 229
South Sudan, 229
South Sulawesi, 195
sovereign statehood
    characteristics, 4, 11, 12
    cultural identity and, 6, 38
    history, 4–6, 7, 230–231
    opportunity costs of intervention and, 2
    scholarly approaches to, 14–16, 25, 36–43
Soviet Communist Party, 137, 138
Soviet-Japanese Neutrality Pact (1941), 138, 143
Soviet Red Army, 115n18, 118, 142, 148
Soviet Union
    aid to Nationalists, 69, 124, 127, 140, 145, 153
    Communist-Nationalist cooperation and, 140–141
    entente with the West, 137n153
    Japan and, 113, 114, 118, 138, 143, 153, 167
    limits on domestic oversight, 15
    moves to undermine central Chinese government, 143–144, 153
    moves to undermine Nationalists, 142, 143
    perceived costs of intervention in China, 136–137, 139–140, 151–154, 157
    perceived costs of intervention in East Indies, 189, 190
    polities emerging from, 229
    recognition of Nationalist government, 162
    role in CCP victory, 142–143, 144n208–145, 144–144n208, 154, 161–162, 170–171
    strategic concerns, 137–139, 152
    support for formation of Indonesian republic, 197, 198
    total wartime aid to China, 140n174
    United States and, 129–130, 142–143
    use of local actors, 59, 69, 139, 143–144, 145, 159
    See also Russia
Spain, 5
Spruyt, Hendrik, 12n35, 14, 43
St. John Brodrick, William, 77n15
Stahlunion, 146n217
Stalin, Joseph
    access regulation to central and northeast Asia, 138, 152
    Chinese Communists and, 143
    consolidation of power, 137
    entente with the West, 137
    Nationalists and, 140, 142
    scaling back of regulation efforts, 153
    strategic concerns, 136
    support for sovereign China, 153–154
    Yalta Conference and, 134, 143
Standard Vacuum Oil Company, 177, 195n111
Starkenborgh Stachouwer, Alidius W.L. Tjarda van, 185n58
state, defined, 11
state form
    access denial and, 27–28, 227–228, 230
    bellicist theories of, 41–43
    classification criteria, 11, 13
    defined, 10
    equation showing effect of intervention on, 34n23
    ideational theories of, 37–39
    indigenous approaches, 7
    in East Asia, 7, 9–10, 16
    institutional commitment and, 39–41
    institutional governance and, 16, 230
    local actors and, 3, 30, 33, 35, 37–40, 226–227
    perceived opportunity costs and, 34, 35, 36
    systems change and, 44–45
    varieties of, 11, 25
Stimson, Henry A., 128, 132
Stolypin, Pyotr, 98
Straight, Willard, 84
Stresemann, Gustav, 146
Sudan, 26
Suetsugu Nobumasa, 115n17
Suiyuan, 59, 95, 116, 158
Sukarno, 191n84, 192, 193n100, 193, 194n107, 197, 232
Sulawesi, 194, 195
Sumatra, 192, 194
Sumatra, Treaty of (1871), 181n39
Sun Chuanfang, 61
Sundanese, 176n12
Sunda Straits, 9
Sunni Awakening, 33, 229
Sun Yat-sen (Sun Yixian, Sun Zhongshan)
    anti-Yuan efforts, 50
    Britain and, 81

Index

Chen Jiongming and, 51, 57–58
concessions to foreign powers, 58–59
efforts to create sovereign state, 56
First United Front with Communists, 144
professional background, 61
United States and, 130
Surabaya, 189n80, 194
suzerain states, 4, 8
Suzuki Kuntaro, 115n18
Sze, Alfred (Sze Sao-ke), 61, 74
Szechwan (Sichuan), 58, 103, 104

Taft, Robert, 131
Taft, William Howard, 32, 83, 86,
88, 101n183
Taiwan
archives in, 17
Chinese acceptance of separation, 168
failure to achieve full sovereignty, 167, 229
institutional commitment perspective on, 169
Japan and, 91, 96, 97, 113, 152, 178
Nationalist retreat to, 136
political status, 7, 8, 19
Soviet Union and, 141
Taiwan Strait crises, 232
United States and, 130, 136, 163
Taiyuan, 69
Takeshima Island, 7
Taliban, 229–230
Tamils, 6
Tanaka Gi'ichi, 113n2, 113n7, 114
Tanggu (Tangkoo) Ceasefire Agreement (1933),
126n82
Tang Jiyao, 69, 104
Tatars, 6
Terwiel, B.J., 215n69
Thailand See Siam
Thai language, 207n27, 207–207n27, 207,
217, 219
Thyssen, 146n217
Tibet, 97, 167, 169
Tilly, Charles, 11, 14, 37n25, 42n47, 42, 70
Timorese, 176n12
Timor Leste, 26, 224, 229
Ting Wen-chiang (Ding Wenjiang), 61
Togo Heihachiro, 115n17
Tojo Hideki, 115n17, 115n18, 117
Tongmenghui (Chinese Revolutionary
Alliance), 166
Trans-Siberian Railroad, 90, 97, 98
Trat, 205n24
Trautmann, Oskar, 147
Trengganu, 202
Triple Alliance, 202
Triple Entente, 99
Triple Intervention, 92, 98, 100
Trotsky, Leon, 136
Truman, Harry S.
acceptance of Communist government, 155

Dutch recolonisation efforts and, 187,
195n110
focus on Europe and Japan, 188
Marshall Plan and, 135, 155
perception of cost of intervening in China,
130, 155
prioritisation of Europe over China, 127, 129,
135n138, 135
Tsai Ao (Cai E), 50
Tsao Ju-lin (Cao Rulin), 61
Tuan Ch'i-jui See Duan Qirui (Tuan Ch'i-jui).
Turkey, 97, 99, 135n138
Tuva
absorption into Soviet Union, 163
Chinese acceptance of separation of, 168
failure to achieve sovereignty, 167
institutional commitment perspective
on, 169
Russia and, 97, 102
secret Russo-Japanese pacts and, 109
Soviet access regulation over, 141, 152
Soviet-sponsored regimes in, 159
Twenty-One Demands, 89, 90–91, 96, 114
Tz'u-Hsi (Cixi), Empress Dowager, 49

U.S. Navy, 85, 132
Uchida Yasuya
ulamas, 192
uleëbalangs, 176, 192
United China Relief (UCR), 132n125
United Mongolian Autonomous Government,
118n37, 153, 158
United Nations
China's admission to, 141, 163
formalisation, 167
Indonesian decolonisation process and,
187n69, 194n106, 197
statebuilding efforts, 229
Thailand's admission to, 212, 215
United States
Aceh and, 181–182
aid to Nationalists, 132n122, 133, 134–136,
155n21–155, 155–155n21, 161–162
appeasement of Japan, 89, 132n122–132,
132–132n122
Britain and, 82, 88, 122n58, 134
Chiang Kai-shek and, 130–131
Chinese economy and, 83, 84n55–84,
84–84n55, 128n93–128, 128–128n93
Chinese external autonomy and, 73
domestic powers of veto, 15
Duan Qirui cabinet and, 66
funding of Russo-Japanese War, 92n119
interventions in Caribbean and elsewhere,
85n65, 85
isolationist elements, 106, 128, 131, 135,
187, 214
Korean War, 32
Lend-Lease aid, 134, 155

United States (cont.)
loans to Chinese entities, 68, 87
Maritime Customs Service and, 72, 89, 131
Netherlands and, 183n48, 183, 184–185, 187, 188, 195
perceived costs of intervention in China, 83, 85–86, 106, 127–131, 155, 157
perceived costs of intervention in East Indies, 178, 179, 187–188, 190
perceived costs of intervention in Siam, 206, 211, 214–216
Philippines colonisation, 5, 32, 85, 91, 178
plan for Japanese forces to arm Nationalists, 129, 134–135n137, 135n137–136
refusal to recognize Communist government, 163
role of expertise in modernisation projects, 68
Soviet Union and, 129–130, 142–143
support for central Chinese government, 83–84, 86–87, 106–107, 131, 156
support for centralised Thai state, 215–216, 220
support for formation of Indonesian republic, 188, 195n110, 197–198
support for Nanjing Government, 132
support for Palestinian Liberation Organisation, 229
Taiwan and, 130, 136, 163
trade with Japan, 128
during World War II, 28, 129, 133–134
Yuan Shikai and, 89
Uppsala Conflict Data Project, 233

Vajiravudh, King of Siam, 207, 218
vassal states, 4, 8, 12
Venice, 12
Versailles Conference
Britain and, 81
China and, 53n36, 53, 74, 81, 86, 89, 110
Germany and, 146
Japan and, 81, 89, 91
principle of self-determination and, 5
Siam and, 214
United States and, 86, 89, 214
Vickers, Adrian, 194n107
Vientiane, 1
Viet Minh, 149
Vietnam, 104
Vladivostok, 97
Volksraad, 176n15, 176, 184, 190

Wachirayan, Prince of Siam, 207n27
Wakatsuki Reijiro, 113n2, 114n13
Walton, Joseph, 77n15
Wan Clique See Anfu Clique
Wang Chonghui (Wang Chung-hui), 61
Wang Jingwei (Wang Ching-wei), 118n37, 118, 148, 149, 153, 159
Wang Zhanyuan, 59, 62

Wang Zhaoming (Wang Chao-ming), 118n37, 118, 148, 149, 153, 159
Wang Zhengting (Wang Cheng-ting), 74
War on Terror, 1
War Preparation Loan, 95
Washington Conference
China and, 47, 81, 86, 89, 110
conclusion of World War I, 18n55, 18
Japan and, 53, 81, 88, 89, 91, 92
United States and, 86, 89
Washington Naval Treaty (1922), 113, 128
Weihaiwei (Weihai), 78, 82, 91, 103n192
Wendt, Alexander, 10n28
West Java, 195
West Kalimantan, 195
West New Guinea, 185, 188n75, 195, 196
Williams, E.T., 84n53
Wilson, Woodrow, 83, 86–87, 88, 89, 214n67
Wing Yung (Rong Hong), 63
Witte, Sergius, 97, 98
World War I
Britain and, 76, 77, 201
China and, 53, 86
France and, 203–204
Japan and, 90, 107, 113
Netherlands and, 175, 181
peace process, 18n55, 18
Russia and, 99
Siam and, 209
United States and, 85, 178
World War II
China and, 133, 149
France and, 148–149, 211
peace process, 18n55, 18
self-determination movements of, 1, 230–231
Siam and, 210, 211, 212n54, 214–215, 215n69, 217
Soviet Union and, 137
United States and, 133
Wuchang Uprising, 49
Wu Lien-teh (Wu Liende), 63
Wu Peifu (Wu P'ei-fu), 61, 62, 81
Wu Tingfang (Ng Choy), 63
Wuxu Reformers, 166

Xhosa, 6
Xiamen (Amoy), 96
Xi'an (Si'an) Incident (1936), 140, 158
Xinjiang (Hsinkiang)
Russian control of, 97, 98, 99, 141
secret Russo-Japanese pacts on, 109
Sheng Shicai and, 143, 153
Soviet Union and, 143, 152
Xuantong Emperor (Puyi), 50
Xu Shichang (Hsu Shih-chang), 53n36, 53, 57, 73, 74, 86
Xu Shuzheng, 93
Xu Yingji, 49n11

Index

293

Yalta Conference (1945), 134, 143, 161
Yamagata Aritomo, 93, 96
Yamamoto Gonnohyoe, 93, 113n2
Yan'an (Yen'an), 144, 158
Yangzi (Yangtze) River, 52, 125
Yan Xishan (Yen Hsi-shan), 58, 62
Yerburgh, Robert Armstrong, 77n15
Yogyakarta, 194
Yonai Mitsumasa, 115n18
Yoshizawa Kenkichi, 185n61
Yuan Shikai (Yuan Shih-kai)
  attempt to become emperor, 50, 66,
    80n35, 80
  Britain and, 80n35–80, 80–80n35
  campaign against, 50, 57, 60
  Dongnan hubao movement, 49n11
  efforts to create sovereign state, 56
  forced retirement, 49, 56
  Japan and, 90–91
  Nationalists and, 57
  New Army, 65
  presidency, 50, 52, 66
  Qing overthrow and, 49
  supporters among gentry class, 62

  United States and, 86, 89
Yunnan, 58, 69, 95, 103, 104, 149
Yunnan Clique, 51, 104
Yuwachon ("Angry Youth") movement, 218

Zai Feng, Prince Regent, 49
Zhang Xun, 6n15, 57, 66
Zhang Zhidong (Chang Chih-tung),
  49n11, 65
Zhang Zongchang, 116
Zhang Zuolin (Chang Tso-lin)
  assassination, 116
  effort to create sovereign state, 56
  Japan and, 93, 95, 116, 124,
    153, 227
  political base, 62
Zhejiang, 105
Zhili, 65
Zhili-Anfu War (1920), 51, 57, 60, 62
Zhili Clique, 51, 56, 57, 62, 81,
  107, 144
Zhili-Fengtian Wars, 51, 60
Zhongshan Warship Incident (1926), 145
Zhukov, Gregorii, 141

For EU product safety concerns, contact us at Calle de José Abascal, 56–1°,
28003 Madrid, Spain or eugpsr@cambridge.org.

 www.ingramcontent.com/pod-product-compliance
Ingram Content Group UK Ltd.
Pitfield, Milton Keynes, MK11 3LW, UK
UKHW011949090825
461507UK00005B/120